An Extraordinary Ordinary Woman

An Extraordinary Ordinary Woman

The Journal of Phebe Orvis, 1820–1830

Susan M. Ouellette

excelsior editions
AN IMPRINT OF STATE UNIVERSITY OF NEW YORK PRESS

The watercolor on the cover is a representation of the figure of Phebe Orvis walking on the way to her new home in New York. Courtesy of the artist Ginny Joyner.

Published by State University of New York Press, Albany

Printed in the United States of America

Excelsior Editions is an imprint of State University of New York Press

For information, contact State University of New York Press, Albany, NY
www.sunypress.edu

Production, Ryan Morris
Marketing, Kate R. Seburyamo

Library of Congress Cataloging-in-Publication Data

Names: Ouellette, Susan M., 1954–
Title: An extraordinary ordinary woman : the journal of Phebe Orvis, 1820–1830 / by Susan M. Ouellette.
Description: Albany, NY : State University of New York Press, [2017] | Series: Excelsior editions | Includes bibliographical references and index.
Identifiers: LCCN 2016031419 (print) | LCCN 2017001941 (ebook) | ISBN 9781438464961 (pbk. : alk. paper) | ISBN 9781438464978 (ebook)
Subjects: LCSH: Orvis, Phebe, 1801– | Women—Vermont—History—19th century. | Women—New York (State)—History—19th century. | Women—Vermont—Social conditions—19th century. | Women—New York (State)—Social conditions—19th century. | Quakers—United States—History—19th century. | Vermont—Social life and customs—History—19th century. | New York (State)—Social life and customs—History—19th century.
Classification: LCC HQ1438.V47 O98 2017 (print) | LCC HQ1438.V47 (ebook) | DDC 305.40974309/034—dc23
LC record available at https://lccn.loc.gov/2016031419

10 9 8 7 6 5 4 3 2 1

Contents

Introduction

When Phebe Orvis began her journal in July of 1820, she was nineteen, and living with her maternal grandparents on their farmstead in the hill town of Bristol, Vermont. She was lively yet introspective; popular yet at times shy. At the start of her journal, Orvis was unmarried, but close to the age where her family expected she soon would be. She was literate and loved learning; she was educated beyond common school standards, with a keen interests in books, literature, and life beyond the New Haven Valley. She may have had dreams of something more, but her family expected her to marry, become her husband's helpmeet, and raise children. In short, she was an ordinary woman of her time, with all the inconsistencies and similitude inherent in any human being. What sets Orvis apart—even now in the twenty-first century—is her diary. The manuscript she left behind is a lens into the intimate details of Orvis's life, but also into another age. Although the diary is sometimes formulaic with obscure and even cryptic passages at times, it is also a charming and honest account of her days. It is not literature; rather, it is typical of the type of daybook kept by many individuals—men and women—of Orvis's time.[1] Most of her entries begin with a short—sometimes one-word—description of the weather. This observation is often followed by a list of her daily work, social events, and other details that captured her notice that day. It is not organized in a true narrative form, except that it is chronological. For most of the diary the text moves along in fits and starts and is riddled with unfinished, coded language that made sense to the writer, but not necessarily to a casual reader. So, to follow Orvis's story, a reader must use imagination and make certain leaps of faith to tease out the details.

On the other hand, the sum of her prose tells Orvis's story. And, her feelings—secret and acknowledged—peep coyly from underneath the somewhat terse wording. On occasion Orvis did elaborate more descriptively on her deeper feelings—a rhythm shared by many diarists of her day. For instance, in the daybook of Martha Ballard, a midwife who lived on the frontier of Maine settlements from 1785 to 1812, just such a pattern emerges. Mundane references to the weather and lists of chores are interspersed with bouts of introspection that are more revealing.[2] Similarly, Orvis's journal is first a daily record of weather and work, but is also a storehouse of observations that become the seeds of stories, rather than being stories in and of themselves. As one historian has suggested, "someone else has to identify the people, places, and allusions," as well as "explain actions and events" not explicitly detailed by a diarist. This is true for Orvis's journal.[3] Yet, the stories are there, often just under the surface, and have to be coaxed to the surface through a careful reading and a little additional research.

It is through those stories that Orvis's journal provides a glimpse into the period during which she lived—even as it provides a lens into one woman's experience. Moreover, this peek into Orvis's experiences reveal fascinating details into particular stages of life, such as her launch into adulthood. In this way, Orvis's journal extends the world evoked by Martha Ballard's journal; Ballad was a mature woman with mostly grown daughters. Orvis's story explores the broader narrative of ordinary women who were contemporaries of Ballard's daughters. One can imagine the discussion if these young women met for tea, at a frolic, or exchanged correspondences.

In other ways, Orvis's journal bridges the ledger-style journals of Ballard's contemporaries and the more emotive, even garrulous, diaries of women whose sensibilities were heightened and trained to see their world through a more distinctly romantic lens. This difference seems to surface in tandem with the emerging class distinctions of the early Republic. Such works were penned by women of more privileged families—or women who were exposed to more affluent relatives. Their authors lived primarily in the more urbane settings of long-settled New England coastal communities.[4] Orvis was, in comparison to most of these women, less privileged and more ordinary—and lived in a frontier setting. In many ways, these differences make her words more precious.

Like Ballard and other early-nineteenth-century diarists, everything in Orvis's life could become grist for her writing. Orvis was a keen observer of her surroundings, and during the period she was actively writing she made entries every day. She was both a participant in and a witness to the affairs of her family, neighbors, and community. And while Orvis rarely wrote more than fifty words in a single entry, the sum of her words frame the details of her life at that time. She was so attuned to the idea of the narrative flow of life, in general, that she likened her own life story to the lyrics of a song or the text of a novel.

Despite her philosophical approach to the narrative of her life, the journal is not a tidy story with a beginning, middle, and end. The entries made at the beginning in July 1820 actually place the reader in the middle of one of Orvis's stories: the never-consummated love affair with Adolphus Taylor. This episode captures her life as an unmarried girl with a desire for an education, and a romantic view of married love. It ends with her final capitulation to her family's desire to marry someone else. The rest of her journal captures the stories of her marriage to Samuel Eastman—her family's choice for her—and the first years of her life as a wife and mother. Toward the end of the journal, Orvis's entries become less regular and more fragmented; her work and family responsibilities clearly occupied all her waking hours. This shift may also be related to the loss of her sense of broadening possibilities as her life took on the same trajectory of all the women she knew.[5] Taken together, the entries made from July of 1820 until October 1830, outline the compelling story of her ambitions, triumphs, sorrows, and failures.

On the other hand, Orvis's observations clearly transmit an embedded, and gendered, commentary on her world. For instance, in a period when abolitionism is moving to the forefront of middle-class sensibilities, especially in the Northeast, Orvis invokes a cultural stereotype, the slave in bondage, to portray her own overworked situation. There is little ambiguity in this pointed entry:

[Tues July 3rd, 1821]

Cool. trimmed the Bar Room in high style. made the colour for the flagg for the Liberty pole. Baked pies. swept the door yard. waited upon twenty four Gentlemen and Ladies at supper in as good a style as possible. tore my white frock. sadly. several requests from guests to join them. Mr. Hawkins, Mr. Lee called. went to Mr. E's to get rid of the noise. spent the eve with R.E. if ever I was a slave for nothing it has been today. retired at three.

Orvis understood the injustice of the unwaged labor of slaves because she was also conscious of her role as unpaid labor in the household of her family. This is a deliberate observation; Orvis was familiar with the abolition debate. She knew the Robinsons, a Quaker family in Ferrisburgh who belonged to her meeting, whose farm was a destination for the escaped slaves on the Underground Railroad. Closer to home, her half-brother John Orvis became an active abolitionist lecturer.[6] Here is an unsolicited commentary on the undervalued and largely unnoticed (by modern and nineteenth-century men alike) female labor of her community. In the context of her life, herein is the central irony of Orvis's (and many others like her) social and economic position: while their labor was a fundamental necessity in these new raw communities, they seldom were recognized for their efforts. At the same time, aspiring middle-class women, Orvis included, were asked to adhere to high ideals of moral and material standards. How much harder would that be in a rude cabin whose log walls shed dirt and harbored insects?

At the same time, Orvis's diary is simply a narrative of the time written by one observer. The journal depicts the lives of family members, neighbors, and strangers as she tells their stories, too. Throughout the diary, Orvis is both a spectator and an actor in the dramas that unfold. At times her style is matter of fact and at others quite dramatic. For instance, near the end of the journal, Orvis ponders whether "perhaps this is the last day of my life. God only knows."[7] She was not particularly prescient that day, but her entry acknowledges the fact that the delivery of her fourth child, James, was imminent. She knew this could mean her death or the death of her child. Such was the fate of many women of her day with multiple pregnancies, miscarriages, stillborns, and, if the child and mother survived, years of worry and care. Despite the risks and deprivations of her pioneer life, Orvis successfully raised ten children to adulthood over two decades beginning in 1824, with the arrival of her first child, Henry Clinton. Sharing the experience of most early-nineteenth-century married women, Orvis was pregnant nearly every other year until her last child, Joseph, was born in 1843. The survival of her children is as much a testament to her determined care as to their healthy constitutions. Indeed, the only child lost in infancy was the first Joseph, born in 1840. Young Joseph was a casualty, along with two of his Eastman cousins, of a scarlet fever epidemic that swept through Saint Lawrence County in February of 1842.[8] James Sawyer was born less than six weeks after her fearful confession.

[Fryd 2nd July, 1830]

Very warm & pleasant. Arose at one o'clock morn. Oh my God wilt thou assist me to bear with patience what thou hast appointed. Obliged to ask the assistance of our neighbours.

> *Pleasant indeed between the hours of one and two P.M. was blessed with a fine son weighing eight lbs. six oz. My God what a day of distress has this been and how wonderfully hast thou carried me through the trials of this world.*

By October of 1830, the regular entries just stop. Further research into her life reveals that this was the predictable result of overwhelming family demands that swallowed all Orvis's time. From 1830 onward, she was pregnant and gave birth at least eight more times. Between the first and last child born, Orvis survived at least thirteen pregnancies, bore eleven live children, and lived to see ten of them achieve adulthood. Minor notations and random comments in the final pages of the journal, a letter, and two tiny travelogues add details to her later life, but the pages left empty are perhaps more eloquent of the realities of her life. The double burden of household production and family reproduction ended her habit of journal writing.

The diary itself is physically unassuming; small with cardboard covers and closely written pages, it was deemed valueless by the book collector who unearthed it in the yard sale in Plattsburgh, New York.[9] Indeed, the commonplace nature of Orvis's entries have convinced some that the journal had limited importance. In a film interview regarding Martha Ballard's journal, historian Laurel Ulrich observed a similar response by historians who dismissed Ballard's work as "ordinary."[10] Despite the indifferent attitude toward women's writings by some, the life described in Orvis's journal is no less complicated, serious, or fraught with circumstance than that of any individual of her time—male or female. So, in this context, the journal is a legacy and a road map for navigating everyday life in the American Republic two hundred years in the past.[11] In this way, Orvis's journal becomes an extraordinary and rare resource not only because it is a voice from the past, but also because Orvis *was* ordinary; she was not a member of the elite classes with the leisure to write.

Despite her social difference from women who were more likely to keep journals, Orvis's writing habit is not totally surprising. Her deeply held Quaker faith encouraged her to self-reflection and undoubtedly prompted her to write about it. She was born into a community that prized deep introspection. This was likely something she became aware of very early; she was added as an enrolled member of the Ferrisburgh Meeting when she was five years old.[12] Throughout her journal, many entries evidence a profound level of self-analysis. Herein is one of the more interesting stories to emerge from the journal. After her marriage, she struggled to reconcile her own beliefs with her husband's adoption of an evangelical Baptist doctrine. In the throes of the Second Great Awakening, Samuel Eastman is "saved" and expected his wife to be as well. While Orvis clearly desired her husband to adopt greater piety, she was not prepared for the ferocity of his evangelization once he was saved. She suddenly found herself, and her Quaker faith, under a formidable assault. Evidence elsewhere tells us that she eventually lost the struggle to resist baptism and her husband's ministry, although she did not describe the details of her final capitulation in her journal.

The second powerful influence that surely compelled Orvis to write were her educational achievements. At the time Orvis began this particular journal, she was a young woman with multifaceted intellectual pursuits; to further those interests, she financed her own education at the

Middlebury Female Seminary with wages earned from her textile work. At Emma Hart Willard's groundbreaking institution, Orvis joined the first generation of ordinary women seeking an expanded, classical education—an ambition not possible in early-Republic period common school scope and curriculum. Her educational experiences may have led her to even more ambitious plans for travel and fulfillment. Although the evidence is tenuous, and yet tantalizing,Orvis may have developed a secret desire to be a foreign missionary. Her keen interest in travel literature established by the numerous references to various books and pamphlets written by missionaries, both ancient and contemporary, imply an awareness beyond intellectual inquiry. Moreover, a careful transcription of Mandarin Chinese in the back pages of her journal is a startling anomaly. Did she hope to learn the Chinese language? What would be the utility of learning such a language if not for missionary work? China was certainly the new missionary frontier in the early nineteenth century and Quakers, especially Quaker women, had a long history of traveling ministries. It is possible that in the throes of her educational experience she daydreamed about such possibilities even as she suppressed her true desires.[13]

Other stories that abound in the journal chronicle the trials and triumphs of daily life, both lived and observed. An almost endless cast of characters move in and out of the narrative in an intricate quotidian dance of life. Just as in our own experience, Orvis shared her days with many different people—sometimes familiar while at other times complete strangers. Here again, the value of the journal is evident even if sometimes difficult to follow. Orvis's observations describe the shift from the social and cultural trappings of colonial society in the Revolutionary period to the new American, class-dominated, market-oriented life of the early Republic. So, while many of Orvis's entries demonstrate that the Brooks/Orvis/Eastman family was comprised of concerned neighbors connected to the fabric of their neighborhood very much reminiscent of colonial era sensibilities, Orvis worked for wages, read newspapers, borrowed books from the Sabbath school library, and shopped for factory-produced goods at local merchants. In other words, Orvis came of age on the Vermont frontier as it shifted from howling wilderness to settled countryside. Her account of those changes tells us how that experience touched ordinary folks.

In the period after her marriage, Orvis was a frontier wife, not unlike Martha Ballard in Maine. She traveled west out of the Lake Champlain Valley to the Saint Lawrence region of north central New York. Her husband's homestead was located along the "old" Military Turnpike, which only a few years before had been a main thoroughfare for American and British forces during the War of 1812. In the period of Samuel Eastman's settlement, this area was on the fringes of white settlement. In her new role as the wife of one of the original proprietors, Orvis helped to maintain a common school for the children of her new neighborhood, and witnessed the birth of the expansion of American society in the postwar era. There in Saint Lawrence County, Orvis shared the homesickness of emigrants for people and places left behind; she kept touch with family in the East through constant correspondence and the much-looked-for occasional visitors. As her children began to arrive, she also struggled to create a civilized home for them.

In her forty plus years of marriage, although she mainly lived on the periphery of the more thickly settled New York territory, Orvis was not immune to the social, political, and economic upheaval of her day. She personally experienced, or vicariously experienced through her friends and family, some of the most tumultuous events and social trends of the nineteenth century, including the Second Great Awakening, the temperance movement, Abolition, the Civil War, the early women's rights movement, and the postwar migration to the frontier.

The totality of Orvis's life is not available to us through her writing. The journal spans only a decade, and two short travel narratives written toward the end of her life are all that now exists of her writings. The gaps left between have been filled—though incompletely—by town, county, and state records; newspapers, church documents, and the New York State and federal censuses. Despite these additional resources, large gaps persist and none of these official sources record her thoughts. All part and chapter titles are drawn directly from Orvis's own words. Part One, "The sweet, single life,"[14] spans the period before her marriage to Samuel Eastman Jr. The chapters that explore the first part of the journal stories are meant to contextualize the significant events, various people, and expand the stories found there. In particular, the first chapter, "A delightful prospect of my Nativity,"[15] examines Vermont, Addison County in particular, and traces the social and cultural world that Orvis inhabited. The second chapter, "I conclude there are some strange intentions,"[16] explores the larger historical trends of a more liberal (and romantic) post-Revolution society and its influence on parental authority, especially on the marital choices made by their children. The third chapter, "rendered . . . more ignorant than others,"[17] considers the educational opportunity afforded Orvis by her proximity to one of the first institutions of higher learning for women established by Willard in Middlebury.[18]

In part two, "New Modes of Living among Strangers,"[19] the chapters explore Orvis's marriage, childbirth, and motherhood, as well as the influence of the cultural changes affecting the Saint Lawrence region. The fourth chapter, "perhaps the partner of his joys,"[20] probes Orvis's experience with the religious revivals of the Second Great Awakening as these events inspire her husband and intrude on her family's life.[21] In their case, the middle-class mandate for women to bring their families to a life of Christian piety is turned on its head in the Eastman/Orvis household. The fifth chapter, "retired, much fatigued,"[22] looks at the volume, type, and breadth of Orvis's labors as a housewife. Orvis was both a producer of manufactured goods and a purveyor of middle-class sensibilities to the children she bore. The sixth chapter, "he cumbers the ground no more,"[23] explores the themes of illness and mortality that are found throughout the journal. The romanticism of this era cannot entirely mask the stark realities of life in rural towns. This chapter also recounts a portion of Orvis's story that is not represented in the journal. A final closing chapter, "beneath the spreading Oak and Hickory,"[24] brings the interpretive portion of the text to a close. This is followed by the complete text of the journal.

For the purposes of accessibility, I have annotated the journal entries with full names and relationships (where possible) of the myriad of individuals who appear in the narrative; I have also defined some of the more obscure references to housework, textiles, and medicinals that may not be immediately recognizable to the twenty-first-century reader. I have left the text with the original misspellings and random punctuation intact as Orvis wrote them; any mistakes, misinterpretations, or oversights are my own.

Part One

“The sweet, single life”

Chapter One

"A delightful prospect of my Nativity"

In February 1822, twenty-one-year-old Phebe Orvis journeyed back to Vermont after spending nearly a year away from home with maternal relatives, the Durfeys. The interlude with her aunt and uncle at their tavern in Saint Lawrence County, New York, had not been of her own choice. Instead, Orvis was more or less coerced into the trip and then held there by the conventions of obedience to parental authority. The evening after traveling down from the Lake Champlain Islands to Burlington and onward toward home she wrote, "I have not thought much about returning to my native place but [in the view] from Burlington and Williston I could discover the Mountains rising with majestic grandeur, their snowy tops mingling with the clouds spread a delightful prospect of my Nativity."[1] Despite her disclaimer that she had "not thought much about" her return, earlier entries in her journal imply otherwise. During her stay in New York State, Orvis often longed for her Vermont home and felt exiled for most of her time away. The small villages of her "native place" and the foothills of the Green Mountains that cradled and defined them were important to her, and she returned to them with no small measure of joy.

Orvis clearly clung to an overly romantic vision of her childhood home in Vermont. She considered the small triangle of territory that encompassed the villages of Bristol, Vergennes, and Middlebury the epitome of refined, civilized beauty and order; yet, in reality all three villages that made up the bulk of her "home place" were hardly that. Despite mid-eighteenth-century town charters that established their legal existence—Bristol was chartered in 1762—the bulk of Vermont, especially northern Addison County towns, were "paper towns" that did not see actual settlement until the period following the Revolution. Most of the work wrestling order from the chaos of the wilderness was done by her father's generation, who were part of the generation of families whose migration to the frontier represented an attempt to establish a new kind of independence.[2] The delay in settling the region was largely due to two major impediments: land grant disputes between colonial New York and Massachusetts over the actual placement of the New Hampshire Grants territorial boundary; and decades of military clashes between the French who claimed the Champlain Valley by right of exploration, the British in the Revolution, and Native Americans who continued to live in their traditional communities. Despite limited attempts—mainly by New Englanders—to colonize the area in the years between the end of the French and Indian War and the Revolution, there were very few permanent settlements able to hang on in such a marginal territory. One of the issues was its isolation. The Champlain Valley is ringed by the Adirondacks on the west, the Green Mountains on the East, and the rising escarpments of the Catskills to the south. Roads from the south and east were merely rough footpaths that followed ancient native trails and were impractical for the habitual movement of goods and livestock. There were few white settlements in the Adirondack region, except for the scattered logging camps seasonally occupied by French Canadians. By far the largest population on the western side of Lake Champlain were the Iroquois villages—mainly Mohawk. The only viable economic connection with an established series of travel routes into the valley was from the north. The outlet of Lake Champlain is the Richelieu River, which flows north to the Saint Lawrence. Even this connection was tenuous in various seasons. Frozen winter ice could be traversed, sometimes quite easily, but spring freshets swelled the shallow rapids and shoals along the Richelieu's course and made even established portages difficult and dangerous. So, the first major wave of Americans determined to stay began to filter into the Addison County area with great difficulty in the last years of the Revolution. These indomitable settlers were most likely lured by the recollections of the militia who served with the Continental Army in its attempts to capture Quebec, and then to hold the valley against British invasion. Many of these men saw promise in the thick forests and rich river bottomland in the Champlain Valley and brought their families north and west from New England.

As members of the first surge of post-Revolution settlement in the area, Orvis's father, Loren, and his brother, Philander, purchased several hundred acres of land bordering the east side of Bristol township and straddling the nearby townships of Starksboro and Lincoln in 1790.[3] The land they acquired was undeveloped dense woodland bisected by the fall of Baldwin Creek and situated on the west side of a ridge that runs north to south along the east side of Lewis Creek; here was where they were determined to create homes for themselves and their future families. The "hill farms" the Orvis brothers envisioned seemed to hold promise; there were plenty of trees to fell—the gold of new settlers. These massive old-growth trees provided the building materials for their homes, animal sheds, and barns, while the detritus of the logging provided for the manufacture of potash and pearl ash for sale in the Montreal market. Moreover, the newly cleared land was very productive. At first that fertility yielded crops that fed families, their livestock and held promise for commercial pursuits. However, that initial flush of enthusiasm was dampened when in less than a decade of continuous cultivation, the thin, mainly acidic soils quickly declined in fertility. Consequently, most of these farms were not destined to develop into lush centers of agricultural bounty; instead, as the soil eroded and failed, they tended to produce more rocks to build the stone walls that surrounded the fields than needful crops in the "improved" postglacial soil. Yet for the Orvis brothers, the potential of their farms drove them to tremendous efforts. They felled trees, wrenched out stumps, used the logs to build their cabins and cowsheds, plowed the cleared land, and attempted to wrest a living from the newly opened fields. Often, the byproducts of their land clearing—lumber, potash, and pearl ash—was the most valuable marketable produce.

At the time of the Orvis brothers' arrival, the land they purchased was reputedly so wild that family traditions attest that the first night Loren Orvis spent on his land he slept in a tree to avoid being attacked by wolves.[4] Other accounts indicate that Orvis was not alone; perhaps he and

Philander sheltered in the tree limbs together that first night. Whatever their initial experiences, the two men set about the work of creating their new home that first season. Once the first log house was completed and enough ground for a potential kitchen garden plot was cleared, Loren Orvis took the next step in establishing his independence: he married. Philander, five years Loren's junior, remained in his brother's household and worked alongside him for eight more years until 1799, when he also married and set up separate housekeeping arrangements.

The original land purchase of 1790 was eventually subdivided by 1798, perhaps in anticipation of Philander's independence, into two separate farms facing each other across Baldwin Creek. These homesteads became the core of a small settlement along what became known as the Quaker Road. Indeed, an early map of the area indicates that the Orvis farm was the first to be created in that area. Other families, the Delongs, Purringtons, Heddings, and Varneys, located along the new road over the next few years. Finally, in 1798, there were enough people living in the Lincoln township to call it a settlement and the first annual meeting was held in March of that year. By then, six families were officially listed as resident in the town with a total population of about fifty individuals. This was the kernel from which the Orvis family's new society would grow.

At this first annual town meeting in 1798, Loren Orvis's status as a "freeman" and local leader was established. He was elected selectman, lister, sealer of weights and measures, fence viewer, and tithingman. Clearly, he was now a town worthy. Yet, his multiple offices likely had more to do with the small settlement size than his actual status. There were few fences to view, only a handful of properties to value, and limited commercial activity to measure. So, the various municipal responsibilities did not hinder him as he continued to develop his farm and expanded the family fortunes. As for most early pioneers, the bounty of trees yielded important profits for the Orvis brothers. As they developed their homesteads, they also took advantage of the considerable timber resources and constructed a saw mill on the steep fall of Baldwin Creek. This new business venture gave them the ability to convert the ash, cedar, beech, maple, chestnut, and oak trees they harvested from their farms into lumber, timber beams, and shingles as well as barrel staves, furniture, and other household items to supply the new settlements of Lincoln, Starksboro, and Bristol.

Eventually Philander Orvis took the helm of the lumber business and Loren Orvis used his share of the profits to acquire more farmland, some better situated than his original holdings, and expanded his livestock holdings of cattle and kine, including the purchase of a team of oxen. The team allowed him to clear and plow more land and, as a consequence, reap greater benefit from his newly opened fields. In addition, he rented the oxen to neighbors. This surge of activity quickly expanded the farms, fields, and families who lived along Quaker Road and beyond.

In December of 1791, when Loren Orvis brought his new bride, Elizabeth Brooks, home to the rough hill farm, he hadn't traveled far to find her. Brooks was the daughter of another early proprietor, Samuel Brooks, who settled in nearby Bristol.[5] Together, the couple worked to build their family, improve their homestead and the outlying farmland, and create an established community. When Philander Orvis married in 1799, he chose Phebe Chase, a young Starksboro woman from another Quaker family settled in the neighborhood. By 1800, the Orvis clan was well established on farms that faced each other across Baldwin Creek.

Both couples proved fruitful. According to the federal census and town records, their combined households included nine children by early 1801.[6] As the ninth child born into the extended family, Phebe Orvis joined a rapidly expanding circle of kinfolk with marriage connections that tied them to the growing neighborhood along Quaker Road. These expanded connections also created important ties that linked the communities of Starksboro, Lincoln, and Bristol. There were also extended family relationships in the nearby settlements of Monkton, Vergennes, and Middlebury. At the same time that the attenuated network of Orvis family relationships helped to populate Addison County, the physical hallmarks of civilization had begun to transform its rough appearance. Roads, bridges, homesteads, schoolhouses, churches, and commercial ventures reshaped the landscape into the conventional, orderly setting Orvis came to cherish.

The expansion and development of her beloved "native place," romanticized by Phebe Orvis at nineteen, was so new it had not developed a true patina; in fact, it was still very much the New England frontier. Even Middlebury, by far the most cultured of the village centers in Orvis's estimation—and in the consciousness of its citizens—was barely settled, with most residents arriving in the previous two decades.[7] Indeed, it is generally held that the decision of the Vermont Legislature to meet in Middlebury for their fall session in 1800 offered them an opportunity to "arrive." The impending legislative session sparked a vigorous effort on the part of Middlebury citizens to make their community worthy of being chosen for such an honor. Houses were painted, fences repaired, the official courthouse structure was finished, and the main thoroughfare graded. Pride of place, its role as a shire town, and a not-so-secret hope it might be the state capital, likely kept Middlebury's citizens vigilant about their care of the community's appearance. Consequently, the admiration that Orvis held for Middlebury as the epitome of order and beauty was somewhat misplaced.

Although not quite as cultured as Middlebury—they lacked the college and the female seminary—the villages of Bristol and Vergennes had also achieved veneers of respectability that Orvis esteemed. In reality, all of these communities were only a short generation more venerable than the Saint Lawrence County settlement that Orvis found so primitive. The paint applied to the rough boards over hewn logs was barely dry.[8]

In the opening pages of her journal, Orvis describes a well-traveled triangle of territory that encompassed the three main town centers of Bristol, Middlebury, and the new city of Vergennes. She visited friends and relatives widely and freely, attended regular worship at area Friends' meetings, borrowed books from the Sabbath School library, drove her Grandmother Brooks (referred to in her journal as "Grandma'am") all over that immediate area for regular shopping trips, and contracted outwork mainly in textiles for a number of merchants and neighbors. The northern quadrant of Addison County and southern edge of Chittenden County, including the townships of Hinesburg, Ferrisburgh, Monkton, New Haven, Bristol, and Middlebury, comprised the outward boundaries of her world. That is not to say she never traveled beyond them, but rather it was within these bounds that she most comfortably and easily moved, frequently alone or in the company of her friends. For her, these villages and their surrounding woodlots, fields, and farms became the standard she compared all others against, often unfavorably. It was also the place she deeply mourned when Samuel Eastman took her to his farmstead in the crude wilderness of north central New York State.

Some of her disdain for the Saint Lawrence County region was the result of the circumstances of her birth and childhood. Although Orvis was born on the hill farm along Baldwin Creek, she did not grow up there. In early 1802, Orvis, a tiny infant, was transferred to her maternal grandparents' home when her mother suddenly died, likely from puerperal fever. The Brooks' home was located in the area of Bristol Township locally known as the "Flats." While her father and older siblings remained on the farm along Baldwin Creek, the child named for her Aunt Phebe Chase Orvis was folded into the life of her grandparents, Ruth Sawyer and Samuel Brooks. From that spring onward, the Brooks' Bristol Flats farm became the childhood place she most treasured. Too young to have memories of the Orvis homestead, she identified with the older, better established farm of her grandparents. When she traveled to her father's farm in September 1822, she wrote in her journal that this was when she met her uncle Philander's family, whom she had not "seen before."[9] From her perspective, the Orvis homestead was a strange place populated by unfamiliar people; her return to her grandparents' place in Bristol at the end of this visit was a "return home." Her adoption by the Brooks couple brought her into a world that was better established, less frontier and more respectable. It also made them her guiding lights and the primary authorities in her life until she married.

So, Orvis's sense of the superiority of Bristol and its environs was related to her life in the Brooks household. Her grandfather Samuel Brooks was one of the original settlers of Bristol Township in the mid-1780s. A member of the group who purchased proprietor shares in what was originally called the Pocock Settlement, Brooks chose to settle on the level, fertile land west and south of Bristol village along the banks of the New Haven River. This area was likely open meadowland (or only lightly forested) at the time Brooks made his purchase, as it was in these same meadows that the Abenaki grew their maize, beans, and squash gardens. These alluvial soil deposits along the New Haven river were favorite settlement areas for the native Vermonters before successive seventeenth- and eighteenth-century wars and waves of disease brought by soldiers and settlers disrupted their lives.[10] According to Samuel Swift, who published an early history of Addison County, stone arrowheads, knives, and axes were ubiquitous in the area soils and farmers collected baskets of them in their fields after every plowing. In his *Early History of Bristol, Vermont*, antiquarian Harvey Munsill wrote, "In many places when the first settlement commenced in Bristol in 1786 there was to be found many places having the appearance of having been cleared and afterwards grown up and covered with a second growth of timber."[11] Although the nineteenth-century histories of the area all claim that Native people were gone by the time that American colonists arrived, Abenaki families persisted. Indeed, Samuel Brooks's eldest son married an Abenaki woman named Betsey Rorapaugh.[12] The Rorapaughs lived somewhere near the Brooks's place along the "Flats," contradicting the supposed native "absence" from the land.

Similar to the Orvis brothers' settlement on Baldwin Creek, the Brooks homestead was a raw frontier homestead in the 1780s. When Nathan Perkins, a young Connecticut missionary, visited the area in 1789, he was not impressed. Perkins later wrote that in his opinion, Vermont, in the vicinity of Monkton, Bristol, and New Haven towns, had "a bad appearance." In New Haven he slept in "an open log house, where it rained on me, in the night. . . ." He rode on to Monkton and Bristol where he found "mud belly deep to my horse" and people who "dressed coarse, & mean, & nasty, & ragged." As he made his way across the state, he "thought I should have perished; felt warm gratitude to heaven that my life was spared."[13]

Perkins was not far off the mark; the early community had rude cabins, bad roads, and was certainly unhealthy. In the first decades of settlement, smallpox, influenza, scarlet fever, typhus, and an unspecified illness locally referred to as "spotted fever" flashed through the town in succession. Smallpox made two documented visits in the period (both times imported from urban centers outside the state), first in 1798 and again in 1820. During the 1798 epidemic, the Brooks farm hosted the "pest house," which was constructed on a corner of the farm property. By this period, although smallpox was greatly feared, many attempted to immunize themselves by infecting themselves with the disease. In the case of the 1798 visitation, neighbors who wanted to be inoculated shared space with Cyprian Eastman, who had contracted the disease "in the natural way" and died from his illness.[14] The arrival of this dreaded disease prompted the community to quickly organize, ask for help from a Middlebury physician, and isolate those who were ill or exposed. The immediate response, isolation of the sick, and careful monitoring of people's movements in the town averted a major outbreak of the disease and limited the mortality connected to it. This successful outcome was in part due to the history of smallpox outbreaks in New England generally. Most towns had strict laws governing their citizens' behavior in the face of such a crisis. Now here in Vermont, the citizens of Bristol reacted in a time-honored, established method to contain the contagion and protect its citizens.

Other epidemic disease events were more deadly. In the first years of the nineteenth century there were epidemics of scarlet fever, measles, whooping cough, and influenza. As one antiquarian observed, "[these diseases] prove[d] to be very destructive of human life, especially among children."[15] The regular wave of epidemics coupled with the seasonal illnesses that afflicted frontier settlements took a toll on the inhabitants, especially infants and the elderly, of northern Addison County and the Orvis/Brooks family.

Despite the unwholesome conditions of the early days, the growth and expansion of the early settler families as well as the arrival of new settlers over the next two decades created the more polished, mature community of Phebe Orvis's teenage years. It was an admittedly thin veneer of civilization; yet, the adjacent communities grew, expanded, and became more solidly established. Between 1790 and 1820, the population of Bristol township grew from 211 people to more than 1,200 families. In a little more than three decades, the community transcended its rough origins and assumed the civility of a seasoned, well-ordered, if modest, New England village.

Located on a plateau of land lying above the New Haven River and nestled against the foothills of the Green Mountains, Bristol village spread out in a grid pattern around four principle streets laid out in compass directions. According to the observations of travelers in the 1820s, Bristol had a respectable, even well-appointed, appearance. The center of the village contained a grass commons enclosed by a rail fence. The town common was surrounded by stone, brick, and frame buildings with commercial establishment sharing frontage with fine residential homes.

By 1820, Bristol possessed a significant commercial manufacturing economy founded on lumber, potash, grain, wool, leather, and a small iron forge. Shoemakers, harness makers, coopers, cloth dressers, and shopkeepers of all kinds set up business in the expanding village.

When Orvis strolled along the common with her friends (Orra Copeland or Harriet Charter, for instance), she could shop in establishments such as the dry goods store owned by Sidney Dunton. There, a customer could purchase anything available in a moderately sized town along the New England coast.[16] Orvis could take tea (and no doubt did) at Robert Hawley's public house known as the Bristol Hotel.[17] She could also purchase medicinal items at the drug store, as well as a pair of shoes from the local cobbler. Dry goods, machine-made fabrics or thread, and millinery supplies were also available. The produce of the Industrial Revolution was readily available in the shops and businesses of Bristol village.

As we have seen, Orvis's grandfather purchased land in the Bristol township and his principal farm—and the homestead—was conveniently located adjacent to the commercial center of the town. Perhaps more propitious, the Brooks's farm was situated on the principle road connecting Bristol and the expanding industrial center at New Haven Mills. This was also the route that linked Bristol with Middlebury. There, along one of the first improved roads in the county, the Brooks farm was an ideal location for both business and farming ventures, including the expansion into sheep husbandry that began to dominate Vermont farms by the 1820s.[18]

Aside from livestock, Brooks alternately engaged in raising various grain crops, including wheat and Indian corn, and vegetables, including potatoes. In addition to the farm produce, Brooks also sold lumber cut from his woodlot as well as manufactured potash for the Montreal market. His economic prosperity and social success is reflected in the deference accorded to him by fellow town citizens. Between 1786, when Bristol organized its municipal government, and his death in 1831, Brooks served as selectman, constable, fence viewer, road viewer, and various other political roles multiple times.[19]

Thus, Orvis's childhood home was not just a center of domestic production, but was also a place connected in significant ways to the economic, social, and political life of Bristol village and the surrounding communities of Middlebury, Vergennes, Monkton, New Haven, and New Haven Mills. This connectedness and the ambiance of social success probably helped to nurture Orvis's mental image of her Vermont home as cultured civilization personified.

Within the Brooks household, Orvis was clearly a cherished daughter. Though never indulged immoderately, she was certainly encouraged to pursue her own interests. As her journal demonstrates, she did constant and important work to sustain the household and, as her grandmother aged, probably took on a great many of the domestic demands. While she also shared these duties with her uncle John Brook's wife, Lovina, it is clear she remained essential to the labors of the household. When she proposed to relocate to her cousin Benjamin Clapp's home in Monkton to spin wool, her grandmother forbid this plan.[20] It is unlikely that her grandmother's objection was over the suitability of such a plan; many young women moved in and out of neighbor's homes to do this kind of labor. Indeed this was a well-established process of sharing important female skills that harks back to seventeenth century and the coastal settlements of New England.[21] Therefore, it seems reasonable to assume that Orvis's labor was too important to lose; she contributed a significant part of the housework necessary to the comfort and operation of her grandmother's household. Yet, despite the demands on her time for various tasks, Orvis also found time to read, and kept up a wide ranging correspondence with family and friends away from Bristol. Moreover, she found time to perform paid textile work—sewing, spinning or weaving—for neighbors and local merchants.[22] All this outwork eventually made it possible for Orvis to attend Willard's female seminary in Middlebury in the fall of 1820.[23]

This freedom of movement seems to have been accepted behavior for adolescents such as Orvis; in many ways, her life was surprisingly mobile, almost modern in its fluidity. Rather than being tied to the "door yard" of the Brooks farm, she traveled widely in the immediate area. Often, Orvis hitched up the horse and wagon and went off to nearby communities for work, visiting, and parties. For instance, in August 1820, she recounted such a day:

> *I took horse and wagon in company with Miss Copeland. Drove to the Borough in Middlebury. called at Mrs. Gowdy's shop. Mr. Stewarts Store, Mr. McDonald, Mr. Hough Mr. Hegers, Mr. Woods, Mr. Gison, Mr. Hooker and Brewsters, bought a thimble. Mr. McDonough purchased a comb and Lemay. Mrs. Kilburns Shop, Orra bought a bonnet. had to wait for it to be trimmed. Went to Mr. S. bought white crape made it for ruff. had two crimped. Saw a gentleman from Georgia. called at Miss Olmstead saw Mr. Calvin Cook. called at Mr. Tars to see Miss Alpha and Almeda Olmstead. Drove through the river and spent the afternoon at Mr. Nashes saw Mr and Mrs Munsill. invited to visit them, hard shower, called at the carding machine. came home heard we had fourteen visitors . . .*[24]

As a young woman from a respected household, Orvis easily navigated the landscape of her community in social, economic, and geographical terms.

Another of the revealing aspects of her journal is the frequency and duration of the social activities held by and for Orvis and her unmarried friends, male and female. The young people of Bristol enjoyed a lively social life that included group parties and individual courting, both experimental and permanent, a host of weddings, and a surprising freedom to associate away from the scrutiny of adults. On the surface, it would seem that the rhetoric of the Revolutionary generation had permeated their approach to and philosophy of child rearing. This more liberal attitude explains the wide-ranging, even freewheeling, travels around the neighboring towns for shopping or social events.

One of Orvis's frequent destinations was the nearby city of Vergennes. If Bristol was the ideal New England village center, Vergennes was an exciting new incarnation of the commercial capitalism evident in the New Republic.[25] Located on the lower falls of Otter Creek, the mechanical water power potential of the falls attracted entrepreneurs who harnessed it for a variety of lumber, sash, textile, and other types of commercial manufactures. The falls also marked the farthest extent to which the Otter Creek could be navigated by larger lake vessels. Indeed, it was at the Vergennes fall-line of Otter Creek that Thomas Macdonough built the American fleet destined to trounce the British in Plattsburgh Bay in 1814. The height of the falls and the breadth of Otter Creek inspired many to take advantage of the site and numerous entrepreneurs vied for space along the banks and especially at the falls. As the commercial center began to expand outward, the mercantile interests at the falls became concerned that their general well-being may not harmonize with those of the farmers in the broader townships of Ferrisburgh and New Haven. The merchants, entrepreneurs, and mechanics of the "Falls" commercial district became convinced that the demands of the majority of the townspeople, mainly farmers, might overshadow their needs; this prompted business leaders to petition for a city charter in 1788. When the legislature granted their request, Vergennes became the first city in the state to be created by charter and only the third in New England.[26]

Vergennes quickly developed into an early nineteenth-century manufacturing powerhouse fueled by Otter Creek. Along the river frontages, a densely packed assemblage of mills ground grains, tanned leather, cut lumber, fulled cloth, as well as a host of other water-powered manufactories developed. As we have seen, the city also became a center of shipbuilding for eastern Lake Champlain. Along with warships built for the American Navy during the War of 1812, shipwrights also manufactured ferries, lake schooners, steam-powered vessels, and, eventually, specialized craft designed for the transport of goods and people on the Champlain Canal.[27]

Economic success in the era of the Republic made Vergennes a patriotic city and the city often hosted Fourth of July parades and celebrations. It was also the hub where the region's militia engaged in training exercises. In the first years recorded in the journal, Orvis visited Vergennes frequently to take part in the festivities, admire the uniformed officers, and patronize the shops. Indeed, as an important lake port and trans-shipping point, Vergennes served the entire Brooks/Orvis family. Her uncle John Brooks, her father, and her grandfather regularly brought produce, lumber, and other goods to be shipped to markets around the lake or more often into Canada via the Richelieu River. When the Champlain Canal opened in 1832, they also shipped produce down the Hudson River into New York.

Vergennes was not the only industrial center close to the Brooks's farm. New Haven Mills was only a short walk to the south. The "Mills," as it was locally known in Orvis's day, provided her access to the newest of factory-made products of her time: machine-spun cotton warps for her loom. She also took advantage of the carding mill to prepare her wool for spinning at home, the fulling mill to "finish" her woven cloth, and purchased factory-woven cloth. New Haven Mills was also the home of Noble and Ira Stewart's general store. There, Orvis could choose from local manufactures, imported goods from the larger New England towns, as well as internationally imported wares, such as China silk, French brandy, or Indian cotton.[28]

Farther south and west of New Haven Mills, was the village center of Middlebury. This was the cultural and intellectual heart of Orvis's world. The home of Middlebury College, a school for young men established in 1800, it became a center of liberal education in the early nineteenth century. Indeed, Middlebury prided itself as a progressive community invested in its self-image as a seat of learning. The College not only trained young men, it also provided teachers and tutors to common schools and grammar institutes for girls and boys throughout the region. The educational aspirations of Middlebury businessmen also extended to their daughters; it was this first girls' school that brought Emma Hart Willard to Middlebury as a young teacher in 1807, and later inspired her to establish her own version of female higher education in the Middlebury

Female Seminary. Consequently, Middlebury was the place where Orvis was able to embark on a more fully realized intellectual life.

Similar to Vergennes and Bristol, Middlebury was an important commercial center, especially in the antebellum period. The Page cotton mill, as well as a number of other commercial mills and businesses took advantage of the upper falls of the Otter Creek. Just as in Vergennes, the town center developed around this natural source of economic power. The rapid growth of Middlebury in the first decades of its settlement was measured by the number of constructed buildings by a local resident, Jabez Rogers. He observed that in 1793 the settlement contained a total of sixty-two buildings "of all kinds." By 1813, the inhabitants of Middlebury had expanded that number to more than three hundred, many of which were commercial. As one town historian observed, "the period from 1810 to 1820 was one of particularly rapid growth in the village in all its material interests, while at the same time farmers of the town were transforming their homes [and fields]."[29] It was this confluence of rapidly paced expansion and economic prosperity in Middlebury that informed Orvis's estimation of the village and its environs' gentility. Eventually, Middlebury was bypassed by the heavier industrial development of the latter half of the nineteenth century since it lacked good transportation and did not have a navigable connection to Lake Champlain, but in Orvis's time the village was a vital economic, political, and social center.[30]

While many settlers were drawn to make their permanent homes in the Champlain Valley region of central Vermont, some paused only briefly before they moved on. Of these peripatetic families, a number were drawn farther west into the territory of northern New York. Many of these families relocated as a result of their menfolks'military service on the Niagara frontier during the Revolution and later in War of 1812. Vermonters who served in the New England militias saw action between 1812 and 1815 in the Saint Lawrence Valley under the leadership of Alexander Macomb. Under the immediate command of General Ezekiel Dunton, Addison County militiamen, many of whom were recently settled in the county, fought at the Battle of Plattsburgh with Macomb and his regular army forces.

As Bristol militia recruits, the Eastman and Durfey menfolk were among those who served in actions taking them into what would become Franklin and Saint Lawrence Counties in New York State. For those men who struggled to make productive farms on the stony, thin soil of the Vermont hill towns, the wide, level, and fertile plain of the Saint Lawrence River Valley proved to be a revelation. At the end of the war, many of these former soldiers helped to found new towns on the New York frontier, including Parishville and Hopkinton.[31] Among others, Samuel Eastman Sr. and his sons joined the rush to take up the newly opened western lands; indeed, Eastman drew on his militia contacts, including General Alexander Macomb, the son of one of the original land patentees in that region,[32] to make their claims to the new frontier.[33] Of particular importance to the Orvis saga, Samuel Eastman Sr. purchased a large tract that he eventually divided between his six sons (Samuel Jr., Stephen, Lee, Roswell, David, and William), giving the three eldest each a one hundred acre farm and dividing other lands as the three youngest came of age. Together, the family worked to build cabins as well as to clear and improve their land. Just as in the first days of Vermont settlement, the combination of land clearing, potash manufacturing, and general purpose farming occupied the first generation of farmers in the region. Economic conditions in the new settlements of the Saint Lawrence Valley were such that according to a town historian, potash stocks became a local currency. Farmers traded their potash to merchants and traders for seed, equipment, and a little cash. The merchants then consolidated the potash, and more valuable pearl ash, to ship to Fort Covington for trans-shipment up the Saint Lawrence to the Montreal market. In exchange, Montreal merchants sent manufactured goods back down the river for payment.[34] Engaged in this regional market as well as participating in the rounds of work bees and barn/house raisings in their neighborhood, the Eastman sons collectively developed their individual farms and prepared for adulthood. By 1819, two of the Eastman sons, Lee and Samuel Jr., were ready for the next phase of their lives and actively looked for brides among a sparse set of frontier homesteads much like their own, but eligible young women were scarce.

Despite the postwar land rush on the New York frontier, there were few families within the circle of the Eastmans' settlement with suitable daughters. This shortage of single young women on the New York frontier propelled many of the former Vermonters, including the Eastman brothers, back east to Vermont and Addison County to find wives. This is precisely how Orvis eventually came to live along the road between Hopkinton and Parishville as a married woman.

Despite the timelessness that Orvis invested in the notion of her genteel "native place" in Vermont, the region was actually in a state of almost constant flux during the years she lived on her grandparents' farm. Bristol and the surrounding communities of northern Addison County found themselves caught up in the dynamic shift from the older, more static culture of general purpose farms dominated by the mentalité of subsistence living to the recent market-oriented consumerism of the New Republic. For many Vermonters this was not a reluctant shift as much as it was an enthusiastic plunge into this newfangled socioeconomic milieu drawn by the vibrancy and allure of the new republic's chattering factories and the goods they produced. In many ways, Orvis was herself a human reflection of that dynamic conflict between old and new, rustication and sophistication, self-sustaining and entrepreneurial.

Chapter Two

"I conclude there are some strange intentions"

From 1820 to 1823, Phebe Orvis was single, eligible, and engaged in the social whorl of young people's leisure pursuits. Therefore, Orvis's observations of the courtship rituals she and her close friends experienced in the years before they married reveal valuable insights into the youth culture of early Vermont and, by extension, the new American Republic more generally. Indeed, her writings convey in some detail the almost modern social freedoms enjoyed by the young people of her neighborhood as well as beyond. Courted by no less than five hopeful young men over that period, Orvis eventually married her family's choice, but not before she survived a dizzying round of parties, heartbreak over a failed love affair, the machinations of friends and family, and some very determined suitors.

At the time Orvis commenced her journal, she was barely nineteen and already immersed in the rounds of visiting and parties that were the prelude to the pairing up of couples. The tenor and style of Orvis's entries on her social milieu demonstrates that northern Addison County society was deeply enmeshed in the more liberal social climate of the post-Revolutionary era.[1] Generally American parents, especially those aspiring to middle-class status, considered the variety of public and private social activities such as "walking out," riding, and "frolics," as well as dances, work bees, and parties suitable for their young people's custom in this period.[2] Orvis's journal entries reveal that this social landscape was open to her and her contemporaries as they congregated freely for work and to play. While their parents or married older siblings may have indirectly supervised these activities, there is no overt evidence of any effort to control the range of pastimes indulged by their offspring. As the journal demonstrates, Orvis's contemporaries frequently chaperoned each other, and adults did not always accompany them in their forays about town and countryside.

Although the entries begin almost "midstream" in this period of her life, Orvis's observations reveal the typical activities of her social calendar. She frequented the singing school, went to local dances, and attended holiday parties and celebrations. In addition, she engaged almost daily in a round of visiting (both going to friends' residences and receiving guests at home), walks, shopping trips, and carriage rides. The distance over which she traveled to these events varied widely; she could walk next door to a neighbor or take a wagon fifteen miles away to Middlebury or Vergennes. Commencement ceremonies at Middlebury College, Fourth of July or Freeman's Day public holiday celebrations, private balls, and parties at public houses in the area—all were grist for Addison County's youth, including Orvis. She walked, rode horseback, drove a wagon, or hitched a ride with friends. Certain events, such as the annual commencement festivities at Middlebury College, sometimes required overnight stays; Orvis often spent the night with friends or relatives. Just as often, she hosted them at her own home and overnight visitors at the Brooks's farm were the norm. At other times, she would return home from an event in the wee hours of the morning. A series of entries from July 1820 indicates some of the range of possibilities:

> *Drove to Ferrisburgh in company with Mrs. Clapp. Went about six miles round. arrived at Cousin Frederick VanVliets and took dinner. Very warm forenoon. A high wind and rain ensued for about an hour. Visited at Cousin Sarah [Brooks] Rogers. Returned to F.V.V. [Frederick VanVliets] and made a bonnet. Staid overnight. The air became cool after the shower. Retired much fatigued.*[3]
>
> *[Next day]*
>
> *Called at Cousin S[arah] R[ogers] and Cousin Enoch Brooks. Arrived Father's [Loren Orvis] found them in good health and spirits. Visited at Mr. Stephen Fishes. Had a pleasant visit with Miss Lydia Fish. came to my brother's Tarr'd [tarried] all night.*[4]

A visit to Ferrisburgh from Bristol began with a drive in the company of her maternal aunt, Mrs. Samuel Clapp, from Bristol to Monkton. Orvis dined at her Van Vliet cousins' home, made a stop at the Rogers's home along the road between Monkton and Ferrisburgh. She returned to the Van Vliets and spent the night. The next morning, Phebe continued on her own to her father's new home on Middlebrook Road in Ferrisburgh (about five miles or so).[5] The afternoon included a visit with the Fish family and then a final stop at brother Silas's home, where she spent the night. The next day, Phebe continued from Silas's home on the Monkton Road back through Monkton Village, where she made several visits with cousins and friends, and then finally returned to her grandparents' home in Bristol on the third evening.

The peripatetic movements described in her journal imply that Orvis was relatively free to pursue an active social life; yet, she did not belong to a promiscuous community. As a young, unmarried woman, Orvis faced certain social proscriptions her male acquaintances did not. Despite the rhetoric of the new, freethinking Republic where young people were expected to choose their future spouses without restrictions and discussion of "companionate marriage" abounded, women operated with a somewhat less freewheeling posture than their male counterparts. The liberality of the early Republic barely dented patriarchy, and the underlying male prerogatives of American society certainly placed men in a far more autonomous position than the women with whom they socialized. So, although Orvis could "walk out" with a group of young people that included men and women, she couldn't necessarily be too obvious about whom she wanted to walk with. She had to wait for a particular young man to come to her and begin the process of courtship rather than initiate the process herself.

Orvis's journal demonstrates this lopsided social reality. While she could freely "visit" her female friends and ask for the company of other women, she had to wait for young men to seek her out. Of course, Orvis could show pleasure in the company of certain young men, but she had little, if any choice, as to which of them might take a fancy to formally "call on her." For example, Independence Day in 1820 was celebrated with a round of parties and visiting in nearby Vergennes. Orvis and her close friend, Orra Copeland, attended. They were escorted by their young Hinesburg acquaintance, Adolphus Taylor, in the company of a large group of young, single people. In the late afternoon, they gathered at the home of the prominent Bristol businessman and celebrated war hero, General Ezekiel Dunton. One of the young women in the group was actually engaged to Dunton's son, although her fiancé was away from home on business at the time. The festivities went on until late in the evening and, consequently, Orvis did not return home until long after midnight. Despite the riotous celebrations, she indicated in her journal entry that she returned home with "the fruit of disappointment."[6] Her disappointment centered on the fact that Adolphus Taylor seemed more interested in lavishing his attention on Orra Copeland than herself.

Despite Taylor's disinterest, Orvis was obviously fascinated by him. When she noted his presence at any gathering in her journal (which was nearly every day in that period), she seldom used his initials to designate him, as was her common practice with many others. Instead she frequently wrote out his name, "Mr. A. Taylor," or his whole name "Mr. Adolphus Taylor," and in a few instances simply as the familiar "Adolphus." While she dwelled on him—perhaps obsessively—in her journal, her public behavior could not, by convention, betray her interest.

In the weeks after the 1820 Fourth of July holiday, Orvis met Taylor frequently at other social events, but he did not call on her for a private visit. His social calls to the Brooks home were always in the company of other men and women, especially as an escort to Orra Copeland. In the etiquette of the time, this was a bad sign. Orvis knew that when a young man of her neighborhood began to call exclusively on one young woman, their mutual interest was certain and courtship was under way. Courtship activities could include direct personal exchanges of letters, far more intimate (not physical intimacy necessarily) contact, public appearances as a couple, and some unsupervised time—acknowledged by parents—spent together. All of this was done with the permission of the woman's parents. The ritual of asking permission could be direct, or could take place between the couple; in the case of a mutually agreed affection, the woman informed her parents of her courtship. The key event would be the young man asking for permission to "visit" more particularly from either the object of his affection or her parents. From Orvis's perspective, her hopes were just that; Taylor did not make any of the social gestures that would have indicated his special interest toward her.

Orvis's disappointment was rooted in the distinction between particular visits and neighborly interaction. In this period there was a definite distinction between "courting," which was behavioral and "courtship," which was more contractual. Courting was an informal social activity and recreational behavior that young men and women engaged in without a firm commitment. They could attend parties and "walk out" together in a group, but no further obligation was understood. This type of informal social pairing was merely a prelude to courtship. Couples "practiced" courting with less social pressure than a more formal relationship would entail, very often with the explicit approval of both sets of parents.

An example of this kind of informal courting occurred at the end of July 1820. That day, Orvis and some friends rowed boats out on Bristol Pond for an afternoon interlude. Later that day the group traveled together to the Carpenter home where they celebrated the return of their mutual friend, Thaddeus Dunton, from a business trip to Virginia.[7] At least four women and several men were in the initial party, but only one couple was formally engaged: Thaddeus Dunton and Harriet Charter. The rest of the group was not.[8] The relationship of Dunton and Charter had proceeded from courting to a formal courtship by the time of the summer rowing party. Herein lay the difference in practical terms; courtship was an altogether more solemn commitment, where marriage was intended and understood by all parties. It often included the exchange of gifts; these could be personal items including, but not limited to jewelry. This kind of formal courtship also included direct personal communications, sometimes intimate, through letters. The neighborhood all knew of Dunton and Charter's particular relationship and expected a "publishing of the banns" to establish the date of their marriage. This kind of serious commitment carried responsibilities for the couple and could result in a legal tangle if the relationship dissolved before marriage. To end an engagement of this sort could trigger a "breach of contract" litigation, especially if a young woman's character was at risk.

Her infatuation with Taylor probably caused Orvis to daydream of that kind of long-term, more serious commitment to her, but in reality she could not force the issue or even engage in a candid discussion with Taylor of her interest. According to convention, she simply could not voice her desires. In her case, she did not even confidentially acknowledge her desires in her private journal. Numerous entries note their social interactions at private gatherings and public places, but the tone of those entries express a deepening, if always vague, disappointment.

Adolphus Taylor's behavior may not have been entirely due to disinterest or slow male wits. Instead his failure to make more explicit overtures—to Phebe or to Orra—may have been because he believed himself unready to engage in a serious courtship. His current profession made him an itinerant; he was a teacher. His higher aspiration to be a minister would have brought him only a little better employment possibility. While this romantic image of the possibility of being a country minister's wife played well in Jane Austen's novels, the reality was much more difficult, especially in the American backcountry. Taylor's education at the Hinesburg Academy had prepared him for either of these two possible professions, teaching or ministering. Both were respectable and worthy pursuits—and would become more so closer to the Civil War era. However, in 1820s Vermont, the nature of these career choices did not guarantee a lucrative living. His future was dependent on the whims of the communities—or parishes—who would hire him to teach—or preach—as the case may be. Nothing was assured.

In addition, he had no other financial reserve to rely on in the event he was not successful in securing a living as a minister or in finding employment as a teacher. This was one very serious impediment to marriage; he did not own land to farm or a house in which to set up housekeeping—and was not in a position to inherit either. In this way, Taylor's lack of a solid foundation for future security was a serious blemish on his eligibility as a good marriage prospect in this period. Among the farming families of Vermont and, even in Middlebury where education was respected, his lack of land ownership—or prospects—was critical.[9] His chosen professions were too uncertain. As a teacher or tutor, his tenure persisted from one teaching quarter to the next. To make matters worse, teachers' wages were variable and could be quite meager.

In 1821, the town of Parishville, New York paid its teaching staff $9.92 plus board for three months' salary. Teaching at a nearby school in Madrid later that year, Taylor could not have been paid much more. Even with bed and board provided, there was little financial opportunity for savings, which would allow someone like Taylor to marry and start a family.[10] Under this system and with no other prospects, he was doomed to poor earnings, no savings for self-improvement, and consequently little upward mobility. This last, the possibility for upward mobility was increasingly important among Americans in the early Republic.

Taylor's ministerial ambitions could result in a more respected position, but in the aftermath of the Revolutionary generation's embrace of New Light churches, ministers were disconnected from town tax support. Thus, the older patterns of town subsidized provisions for resident ministers were considerably diminished. Even with a bona fide ministry there was no guarantee that Taylor could adequately support a family or presume long-term stability, despite the respect his position as a minister commanded.

Although American society developed a greater appreciation for professional careers in the antebellum period, ambivalence toward men without the tangible evidence of prosperity in the form of actual real property and livestock remained. Moreover, particularly in the Middlebury area there was a renewed distrust of professional men in these years due to a terrific bank scandal. A robbery of the National Bank of Middlebury's deposits deemed an "inside job" ruined a number of professional men in the town and left locals with a healthy distrust of their kind.[11]

If Taylor's professional credentials did not deter him, competition from other young men may well have. In particular, a neighbor from New Haven, Alva Sprague, actively pursued Orvis in 1820. In the months just before she began her journal in July, Sprague had apparently visited Orvis regularly. In the opening pages, she noted his visits, but not with any particular enthusiasm or emphasis. It seems clear that although Alva Sprague was interested in her, Orvis did not reciprocate his attentions. Instead, she seems to have continued to wait hopefully, if in vain, for Taylor.

His reluctance to engage in formal courtship could have been related to the culture of the time rather than a rejection of Orvis. A young man's decision to engage a woman seriously was one of the fundamental, transformative experiences of a his life as he transitioned from adolescence into mature adulthood. Married men were the head of their households with the awesome responsibility of providing for and governing the family. In short, marriage was the final step into adulthood and one that established them (or ruined them, as the case may be) in their community. A wrong choice could be a grave error. Added to the uncertainty of choice was the fear that even if they found the right woman, she may not respond positively. Worse, the desired one may want to embarrass or humiliate the potential suitor.

Young women such as Orvis may have lacked the freedom and broad initiative of male suitors, but they still controlled the final outcome. Many could and did reject unlikely suitors. Caught up in the social uncertainty of their suits, young men feared that women "used their attractiveness and their power to say no as a way to make fools of men and to gratify their own vanity."[12] Imagine, then, the reluctance of someone like Taylor who might have feared that his future success was less assured and was not prepared to openly compete with a young man with better prospects. In this, Sprague had a great advantage.

In the Brooks/Orvis neighborhood, Alva Sprague was an attractive catch. The son of a substantial farmer established in New Haven, Sprague was a landowner in his own right. He was also a determined suitor. Orvis's journal entries reveal that Sprague visited her frequently over the course of the summer. His intentions seem clearly understood; she coupled herself with him explicitly in her journal in the weeks between July 1st and September 10th. One entry described a visit where they attended Sabbath worship as a couple and then "walked out" with two other couples, at least one of the other pairs explicitly engaged.[13] Despite his efforts, Sprague's pursuit was not successful. Orvis ended their informal courtship when, on a Sunday evening in September, she "gave him his dismission."[14] Whatever her reason, Orvis exercised her right to refuse an unwanted suitor.

Her refusal to accept Sprague's courtship did not mean she was finished with the possibilities of a romance. The same week she "dismissed" Alva Sprague, she crafted a truly sentimental love-token: a ring woven with a lock of her own hair. Given the circumstances, this trinket was clearly not meant for poor Mr. Sprague. Instead, Orvis looked hopefully toward Taylor. She continued to note his presence at gatherings and frequently tried to engage him in conversation, but still he did not respond in kind.

Instead, yet another prospective suitor, "Mr. John Seymour," a young man also from the New Haven area known as Lanesboro requested permission to visit her. Without any explanation in her journal, she accepted. This may have been a ploy to demonstrate her own desirability to Taylor or a way in which to continue to participate in group expeditions where she may come into contact with him. Whatever the motivation, over the next several months Orvis accompanied Seymour on walks and rides, went to public social gatherings, and entertained him at her family's home. However, by the end of November, "John Seymour" stopped visiting, no doubt "dismissed" and became "J.S." in the journal entries once more. Then, the dreaded Samuel Dolbear came on the scene.

In the middle of October, Orvis's grandfather hired Dolbear, the son of yet another New Haven Mills family, to work on the family farm. Perhaps Dolbear thought that as the Brooks's indulged granddaughter she would have some financial claim on the Brooks's estate. He may have simply though that Orvis was attractive and available. Whatever his intentions and beliefs, Dolbear began an aggressive campaign to win her affections. But Orvis plainly felt assaulted. In the middle of November she wrote: "Mr. Dolbear tarried overnight. Why is it I dislike him? why can I not feel towards him as he does towards me? . . . tried to appear familiar in vain."[15] Orvis was never explicit in her reasons for disliking Dolbear, perhaps he was an inept suitor or simply an unattractive oaf. In the end, she escaped him when she left the farm and went to board at Dr. Stearns's Middlebury home. This move was made in order to realize her intellectual aspirations. That month, Orvis began a term in the "Ladies Quarterly School" at the Middlebury Female Seminary.

Orvis's move to Middlebury accomplished more than just putting distance between her and the erstwhile suitor Dolbear, it finally precipitated a courtship move from Taylor. He was among the first of her "acquaintances" from Bristol to visit her at school in Middlebury.[16] Within days of this first visit, he returned to escort her to Orra Copeland's home to study. Over the early winter months Taylor continued to visit her while she was at school. Perhaps Middlebury offered a "neutral ground" where they could meet and share their mutual respect for intellectual pursuits. Middlebury was also far away from the measuring glances of Orvis's grandparents and family. By the end of January, Orvis felt confident enough to make a visit to the school where Taylor taught; this was clearly a prelude to a more particular relationship.

The text of Orvis's journal reveals that her romantic dreams were made real in her Middlebury interlude. Now "Adolphus" came for her and *they* picked up Orra Copeland rather than the other way around. One entry at the end of January describes this shift in their relationship: "Took a ride to Bristol with Mr. Taylor. *Took Orra with me* [my emphasis].Visited General Dunton. Fine visit."[17]

Once Taylor began to seriously court her, Orvis expected that her family would approve. Certainly, she felt a strong attraction to his scholarly manner and pious nature. Yet, there seems to have been an internal family discussion brewing over the appropriateness of Taylor. Despite the language of companionate marriage—choosing a spouse based on romantic notions of companionship—the family seems to have fixed on more pragmatic concerns. How was Taylor going to provide for her future economic and social stability? Certainly, these apprehensions were not entirely lost on Orvis. Such themes seem to have dominated the exchanges between Orvis and her female friends as they kept up a running correspondence and engaged in lively debates on what she often formally referred to as "the State of Matrimony." One friend in particular, Harriet Charter, argued at length with Orvis about the true nature of marriage. While we will never know the exact narrative of their exchanges, it is clear that these conversations provided the young women a forum for exploring the shift in attitude toward marriage in this period. The notion of companionate marriage and the role that genuine affection played in spousal choice were key topics. Perhaps their individual choices reflect their particular sides in this debate. Charter chose to marry a very wealthy, notable man more than ten years her senior who was also a widower with small children. This decision indicates that Charter likely chose a more pragmatic approach to marriage. Moreover, as an aspiring middle-class woman, social position may have been of higher value than romantic love in Charter's estimation.

Orvis, on the other hand, seemed guided by her romantic attraction to Taylor in her selection of her "life companion." Taylor was certainly very different from Charter's suitor; he was Orvis's contemporary, seemed to hold her intellectual and emotional life in high esteem, and shared her Christian leanings, if not her Quaker faith. These qualities were obviously important to Orvis and reflect the more broadly defined romantic notions of "companionate marriage." At this point, without their actual correspondence we can only speculate on the tenor and content of the two women's discussions on their respective philosophies, but developments revealed in the journal's narrative indicate that they were not the only people engaged in a heated debate over the suitability of Orvis's and Taylor's presumed courtship.

In fact, despite their outwardly tolerant behavior, Orvis's family—especially her grandparents—seem not to have approved of her choice of suitor. It is likely that they were fixated on the practical considerations of their granddaughter's future. Taylor was landless and did not possess the means for long-term economic stability and security that property represented. Moreover, his prospective professions, although respectable, were unreliable by nature. While his intellect, demonstrative piety, and education were attractive to Orvis, these virtues seem not to have swayed her family's opinions.

Here is where Orvis's narrative becomes more difficult to interpret. Her journal entries do not reflect a clear understanding of the family's subsequent actions, and Orvis seems to have been wholly (perhaps willfully?) ignorant of their motives. Yet, even without entirely acknowledging their actions, Orvis described quiet maneuverings on her behalf that she did not question. Taken together, the evidence suggests that her family conspired to separate her and Taylor permanently—and to have pushed Orvis toward a more "suitable" partner that the family held in greater esteem.

In mid-January, Orvis received a letter from her uncle, Phineas Durfey, requesting that she come west to his home in Saint Lawrence County, New York.[18] Orvis must have discussed this request among her friends because Jerusha Sprague made an offer to accompany her on the visit to her relatives.[19] Then, a little more than a week later, Orvis's maternal aunt, Mrs. Ruth Durfey, and her husband arrived in Bristol. Considering the distance and the difficulty of making such a journey over poor roads in the middle of winter, the appearance of the Durfeys was not the result of a casual or unplanned event for them or for the Brooks. More importantly, her aunt and uncle landed with the expectation that Orvis was to return with them to Parishville. The Durfeys' homestead was a tavern along the "old military road" in Saint Lawrence County, situated in a rather new, raw settlement area. Orvis's journal seems not to reflect an understanding that her aunt and uncle's arrival was related to her. Yet, it seems unlikely that a middle-aged couple would travel a two-hundred-mile round trip on sleighs and over the spring ice of Lake Champlain on a mere whim. Clandestine family machinations were more likely the cause. Again, Orvis's lack of awareness is reflected in the journal. Orvis wrote little on the plan to travel to Parishville until after the arrival of her relatives. Once they appeared, Orvis more directly confronted her family's proposal to send her to Parishville. Her reluctance is palpable. Despite the letters she had from her uncle Phineas Durfey indicating his wish for her to visit him, she seemed to ignore the family's determination for her to go and the fact that she had little choice in the matter.[20] Other evidence suggests the trip was prearranged. For instance, the local school trustees in Parishville had already been alerted of Orvis's arrival and waited for her to take up a teaching post in their common school located near the tavern. The Durfeys, in collusion with the Brooks, must have made these arrangements in advance. It seems likely that Orvis's removal to Parishville was intended to terminate her association with Taylor and to soothe her disappointed feelings, the family found her attractive employment. Even more likely, given the scarcity of young single women in the Durfey's neighborhood and the eligibility of certain Bristol-born men, the plan likely included Orvis's introduction to other, more suitable, bachelors. By committing her to teach at least one term in the school, her family knew that it would be months, perhaps even a year before she could easily return home. The distance—more than a hundred miles over rough roads and across Lake Champlain—would guarantee that she could not just decide to return home on her own without the cooperation of her Durfey relatives. It was a well-executed maneuver.

Yet, Orvis did not acknowledge the implications of everything that developed during her aunt's visit in her journal. When she and Taylor said good-bye, she described a "visit" to the Durfey home implying a brief respite. Then, most significantly, before her trip west commenced, she and Taylor traded monogrammed handkerchiefs. This was a significant exchange of personal items. From Orvis's perspective it was a promise of a more intimate relationship as well as a public declaration in the future. That evening she wrote in her diary that she was "absorbed in grief" at their separation.[21] At the same time, Orvis must also have been happy in their move toward a formal engagement. So, although it was hampered by her removal to New York State, Orvis was finally joined in a courtship with the man of her choice.

The trip out to Parishville was not a happy adventure; instead the journal description reads like a passage into exile. Orvis described her feelings graphically:

> *Took leave of my home that has sheltered me nineteen years to see a new country. Left them in tears. As we rode slowly in a waggon in the winter season everyone at their window of my acquaintance it appears as if I were following some friend to the tomb.*[22]

Despite her promise, Jerusha Sprague did not accompany Orvis and now she was a captive in a strange place with no familiar faces, except for the Durfeys. And they had a mission to detach her from Taylor and find her a new beau.

In Parishville, Orvis found herself in the midst of a busy whirl of activity. As the successful proprietor of a tavern and inn that was an important stop on the road out to the Niagara frontier, Phineas Durfey was a busy and important man. Situated on a tract of open land about three miles west of the small village of Hopkinton, the homestead was more than the sandstone building completed in 1818 that housed the tavern and family living quarters. In fact, it was a collection of buildings, including three log cabins, various cowsheds, a chicken house and the kitchen garden. Beyond the immediate area around the tavern, there were also cultivated fields that supported the tavern inhabitants and patrons as well as contributed to the economic power of the family. Durfey was ambitious, active in local politics, and considered a prominent citizen in the town. The tavern hummed with constant social activity. As another set of capable hands, Orvis was quickly folded into the Durfeys' busy lives. Initially, she helped to cook, serve, and clean in her uncle's tavern. When the spring school quarter began, she took up the promised teaching position in the local common school, but, in the tradition of unmarried women's roles, continued to work at home as well.

In 1821, Parishville, New York was a raw frontier settlement. Unlike Bristol, the hamlet had no town center and was more a collected group of homesteads populated by people Orvis found coarse and ill bred. Reminiscent of Nathan Perkins's indictment of early Vermonters, Orvis found Parishville residents to be "coarse, & mean, & nasty, & ragged." She pined for Vermont, her friends, grandparents, and Taylor. During this period she wrote and received many letters from him, her friends, and family in Vermont, as well as walked many a solitary mile trying to come to terms with her feelings of exile. Yet she was not a timid soul. She argued forthrightly with the master of the schools regarding her desire to take children for nature walks where they could learn botany and natural science.[23] But she could not refuse her aunt and uncle's request for her labors.

Orvis disliked working in the tavern and often described the work as exhausting and demeaning. On the evening of the Fourth of July celebration for 1821, she wrote in her diary that "if ever I was a slave for nothing it has been today."[24] The school term was also disappointing; the children seemed to have no manners and no discipline. Despite the best efforts of the Durfeys to introduce her to new friends and include her in their lives, she remained resolutely unhappy and homesick. In one entry she writes, "What would I give to spend one hour in the land of my nativity."[25]

Throughout the spring, Orvis's aunt and uncle diligently kept to what was undoubtedly the family plan: they introduced her to eligible men. And they also encouraged her to cultivate female friends. Since making friends and settling in would bind her more fully to her new "home," this effort was likely in response to Brooks's desire that Orvis's interests be directed away from Taylor. Despite the activity surrounding the tavern, this required some ingenuity. The neighborhood around the Durfeys' place along the connecting road to Postdam was primarily made up of sixty- to one-hundred-acre farms. The homes were spread thinly across this expanse of fields and forests, which had only recently been occupied. In fact, Joseph Durfey, the eldest child of her aunt and uncle, was reputedly the first white child born in the town after it organized. The Durfeys were confident in the success of the town and their business; the tavern was a regular stop along the road for travelers whose appearance had become more frequent. And, perhaps as important, the tavern was the political center of the town. It was the gathering point for the local militia on training day, and Phineas Durfey was captain of the local militia (1820 to 1824). So, although the geography of Parishville was not the familiar New England landscape of her Vermont home, the life of the tavern must have been reminiscent of her grandfather's busy farm.

Eventually, Orvis's loneliness won out over her reticence and she made friends with Betsey Eastman, a near neighbor and younger sister of the two most eligible bachelors in the neighborhood, Lee and Samuel (Jr.) Eastman. The Eastman family, as already noted, was part of a general migration of Addison County people to the Saint Lawrence Valley after 1800. Samuel Eastman Sr. seems to have purchased land during the period of the War of 1812, although he waited to take possession until after 1814 and the decisive Battle of Plattsburgh. By 1821, when Orvis came to live at the Durfey place, Samuel Eastman Sr. had a large family of ten children—six sons and four daughters—from two marriages. The eldest son, Stephen Eastman, was married and settled, while the three youngest sons were adolescents. This meant that Samuel Jr. and Lee were the eligible bachelors that the Durfeys hoped would attract Orvis's attention and interest.

Much to their disappointment, despite the Eastman brothers' efforts to socialize with Orvis, she remained indifferent. She maintained—at least in her journal—that her stay in Parishville was a short exile and she did not intend to build permanent ties there. She taught at the common school, walked to Hopkinton Village for the meager shopping available there and wrote piles of letters to her friends and family members at home in Vermont.

In May 1821, everything changed. Adolphus Taylor arrived unexpectedly to take up a teaching post in nearby Madrid. He was now close at hand and Orvis was delighted at his arrival. She wrote, "[unexpectedly came] home to see Mr. Taylor my very good friend from Vermont."[26] Taylor settled into his new teaching job for the summer term and they picked up the threads of their relationship. As the summer progressed, the couple spent considerable time together, deepened their commitment, and exchanged significant new love-gifts. Orvis presented him with the hair ring she'd quietly preserved for almost a year, and Taylor left his precious pocket watch in her safekeeping.[27]

Yet, the Orvis/Taylor relationship thus renewed did not entirely ward off other interested men. No doubt armed with the knowledge that the family preferred their suit, the Eastman brothers both vied for her attention. Lee Eastman asked her to a dance held on "training day," perhaps to dazzle her with his militia uniform as well as his dancing; she was not impressed. She later described the dance and the attendants as uncultured and wrote that she did not enjoy herself.

> *Pleasant. [Militia] Training. Received invitation to a dance by Mr. L[ee]. Eastman. Walked to Mr. E.('s) at noon. Very rude to appearance but it left an inward sting behind. Dressed in white. the party broke up at three. How disagreeable to my feelings but they know it not.*[28]

Samuel Eastman (Jr.) also called at the tavern often and seems to have taken advantage of his younger sister's friendship with Orvis. Betsey Eastman may have been enlisted in the conspiracy with the family, but she also appeared genuine in her friendship for Orvis. A number of times Eastman invited Orvis to come and stay at her parent's home where she could not help but be in the company of one or both of her brothers. Orvis did not feel entirely comfortable with the arrangement, but did stay with Eastman several times. Once she convinced Orvis to engage in a "Clandestine walk to the West Parishville to take a view of her Brother's farm."[29] The farm Orvis viewed was actually a large tract divided between the two brothers. On paper, Samuel and Lee Eastman owned upward of a hundred acres each, but the actual parcels were contiguous and farmed collectively by the family. As the elder of the two, Samuel Eastman had a more developed home place at this point. A cabin and livestock sheds were already constructed, but the topographical openness of the area would have made viewing the collective holdings far more impressive. Perhaps Eastman thought that she could persuade Orvis of her brothers' merits over Taylor with a view of their potential wealth and relative comfort.

Although Orvis never wrote explicit journal entries regarding the discussion of her unmarried state—or her relationship with Taylor—she did make references to the fact that she was constantly lectured by her aunt: the "tatting tongue lies not dormant." Often, she felt "dejected spirits as a result."[30] The "tatting tongue" of her Aunt Durfey did not practice discretion with regard to Orvis. She wrote that her aunt was a "torment to tranquility" and that she held a "slavish fear of my aunt under which I labor rendered [her visit] unpleasant indeed."[31] A third entry described an "insulting lecture, she cried, talked and acted like a mad fool all night."[32]

What is more evident is the family campaign to replace Taylor with one of the Eastmans, preferably Samuel Jr., the elder of the two. Some very heavy-handed machinations occurred. Her uncle Phineas Durfey insisted she attend the Independence Ball and then escorted her there only to leave her with Eastman. The Eastman brothers came often to the tavern to visit at Durfeys' invitation, then to be served by Orvis. Yet, she remained firm in her commitment. Under terrific pressure to reject Taylor and accept one of the Eastman brothers, she took walks and often stayed late at the schoolhouse to "indulge my tears alone." One heartfelt entry described her attempts at cheerfulness in the face of overwhelming strain:

> *I endeavored to hide my gloominess, but my feelings are indescribable. Oh, if I were in some desert I think I could be happy . . . very melancholy. It is noticed. Melancholy reigns within my breast no friend to unbosom my feelings to. No one to advise me or protect me from insults . . . my mind greatly agitated with the tricks of others and for want of counsel and Consolation, a Mother, a friend to place trust.*[33]

Finally, Samuel Jr., who was enthusiastic for the parental plans, could contain himself no longer and revealed all to her when he escorted her home from a church meeting.

> *. . . walked home with Mr. Samuel Eastman, [he] spent the evening. Surprising that he should request my heart and hand at the first visit. What can all this mean? If this is the method he takes to gain my esteem he will meet many obstructions. I conclude there are some strange intentions.*[34]

This was certainly not their first meeting, so her choice of words implies that she finally acknowledged Samuel's intention to call on her formally. It may be that she agreed to allow him to "call" to deflect some of the family strong-arm tactics. Whatever the reason, this walk home from church was understood as a more formal courtship visit and Eastman immediately proposed marriage. She was shocked and dismayed, although whether her feelings were directed at her family's betrayal of her desires or Eastman's abrupt proposal is not clear. It is obvious, though, that she did not want to marry him.

At the same time that Orvis attempted to fend off the Eastman proposal, Taylor must also have been under a great deal of pressure to withdraw his attentions from her. Possibly the power and influence of the Durfeys in Saint Lawrence County threatened his further employment or perhaps Taylor simply lacked the personal fortitude to stay the course. The reality of the situation was that if they defied parental wishes and married, they faced serious censure despite the liberal atmosphere of the times.

Whatever his reasons, Taylor was convinced. He visited Orvis at the tavern in the end of August 1821 and ended their formal relationship. He returned her ring, she returned his watch, and then they took a "friendly leave of each other."[35] Although Orvis's entries through the period after Taylor's departure are tinged with sadness, she did not write bitterly, nor does she seem to have blamed Taylor for the end of their courtship. Perhaps she understood his retreat, especially as the Durfeys and their allies stepped up the campaign for the Eastman proposal.

All through the fall and early winter of 1821, Eastman pressed his suit with Orvis; he took her to dances, on walks and for rides. Yet, she refused to accept him. In her journal Orvis began to wrestle over the question of whether marriage was appropriate for her at all. The prospect of spinsterhood in the context of the society she lived was daunting. Women were expected to become wives and mothers as part of the divine plan. Yet, Orvis knew women who were single and whose lives were not as marginalized as the stereotype suggested. These women cultivated their educational opportunities and pursued vocational work that gave them some independence.[36] In her confusion and under assault, she sought enlightenment. In one entry she wrote,

> *I have this evening the most trying scene of the kind that I have ever experienced. Hard case. I must either relinquish my resolutions of matrimony or make one miserable leave his friends forever or else my heart melts at the thought.*[37]

For Orvis, the central question was whether she could give up everything she wanted—her home in Vermont, books and writing, an intellectual life—to live on a raw frontier farm with a man who shared none of her interests, but would command and control the rest of her life. In this, she would have been right. In the period of the early Republic, male authority was certainly supreme, and the emerging ideology of "true womanhood" too new to give Orvis any greater authority in the private space of her own home. The slight measure of personal autonomy offered by singlehood was small indeed.

In October, still undecided, she took a second, intentional clandestine walk to view Eastman's farm. She wrote, "walked alone to the west, saw perhaps the place of my future abode, but God grant that it may never be my lot."[38] Clearly marriage to Eastman and life on his smallholding did not appeal to her in the same way that her romantic attachment to Taylor had. By the end of the year, with her dilemma still troubling her, she finally was able to escape.

In January, her grandmother and maternal uncle, John Brooks, arrived in Parishville to take her home. A flurry of packing and farewells was followed by the arduous winter journey back to Vermont. Despite the failure of her romance with Taylor and her struggle to deflect Eastman's insistence that they marry, her spirits rebounded. She wrote profoundly of how she loved her home in Vermont. Her first sight of the Green Mountains was joyful, "from Burlington and Williston I could discover the mountains rising with majestic grandeur, their snowy tops mingled with clouds spread a delightful prospect of Nativity."[39]

Back again in Bristol, Orvis attempted to resume her life on the Brooks's farm as if she never left. She took up textile outwork with enthusiasm, visited with family and friends, and happily resumed her attendance at Quaker meetings. Before long, she also encountered Taylor who had returned to Vermont earlier that fall. Now, he courted her dearest friend, Orra Copeland. This might have been why her family consented to her return to Vermont—she was no longer in danger from Taylor's suit since he was now publicly engaged to Copeland. When their banns were read at meeting, Orvis wrote, "indulged my tears plentifully."

Yet, despite her regret over Taylor, Orvis was herself being courted—although long distance. Eastman had not given up his pursuit. Letters frequently arrived from him and his sister, Betsey. In the meantime, Orvis seems to have delayed accepting his proposal and instead settled back to her "single life" in Vermont. One entry describes her social rounds:

> *Mrs. Pratt went with me to Mr. Lee's and staid all day. We were all very rude indeed. Mr. Gales Frisby left his school expressed himself as unfortunate in love without acquaintance. Requested an introduction. We had a great deal of sport about it. Mr. Stephen Blackman carried me home to the poor creature's mortification I find my health everyday regaining.*[40]

Every day she found herself regaining what she'd lost in the pressurized atmosphere of the Durfey tavern. Yet, the specter of an unresolved marriage proposal still haunted her, and each report of a new married couple among her friends elicited a worried entry up on her own situation. At one wedding announcement, she wrote: "Thanks to my God I am not in their situation."[41] Moreover, her journal musings at times took on morbid images of death and unresolved conflict. One long self-reflective passage ended with:

> *[Man] thinks his cup is full his burthen is greater than he can bear. Thus he is afflicted, he strives to regain his former security of pleasure but the stream of time swiftly carried him down unless some kind of assistance comes to his relief.*[42]

In a strange way, Orvis seemed to be praying for a fate worse than marriage. At the least, she equated marriage to a certain kind of death. In this, she was correct. Under the law, what little autonomy she had as a single woman disappeared with marriage. As a wife, she would be completely subject to the will of her husband. Marriage also meant children and the possibility of death in the throes of childbirth. In reality, Orvis's capitulation would result in the end of her life as she knew it and the real possibility of following her mother's fate.

In June, Eastman arrived in Bristol, determined to resume his courtship of Orvis in earnest. He remained in Bristol for three months until Orvis finally capitulated. It seems significant that although she wrote at length of her reluctance regarding marriage, she never explicitly recorded her final acquiescence to Eastman's proposal. Orvis never wrote explicitly of the decision at all. The evidence of her acceptance is there in the journal, but in obscure references and embedded in her activities. From September 1822 onward, she became astonishingly productive of what were undoubtedly "going to housekeeping" goods. She spun, wove, and sewed a vast assortment of household fabric goods, clothing, and bedding, as well as bartered and purchased kitchen implements. So, although Orvis did not expressly write of the impending wedding, she diligently prepared for it. One such shopping trip is illustrative:

> *Cloudy. Drove to Middlebury. accompanied by Lovina and Sally D. Bought at the Looking Glass Factory a plain gilt for one dollar fifty in cash. Traded four dollars seventeen cents by order at Hough's Store. visited the Cotton Factory. purchased one tea kettle, one small Pot and Spider of Philip Heart by cash. one spelling book by cash at Hagar's Book Store. one Bible, Box of wafers by credit. Tired of shopping without cash. Took tea at third store with Mrs. Crane. returned home by Curby Street. dark getting home.*[43]

Perhaps because the date of her wedding loomed large in her mind, Orvis finally began to record her fears in January:

I dread to see it snow. How can I leave friends? Twenty-one years agoe my mother leaft me. Oh that I were ready to follow.[44]

A little more than a week later she wrote:

The coldest day that has passed this winter. wove all day for almost nothing. almost sick with cold. Ironed Ah whither am I going to leave Celibacy soon. Oh, awful the thought. why have I been so weak as to engage for life in so dangerous an engagement. Oh my God support me through this most trying scene. How incapable am I of filling the place of a companion.[45]

And then the next day:

Cold snow some. received a visit this P.M. from Mr. Harry Java. Stormy P.M. George Dayfoot published to Miss Laura Munson. Alas, I soon experience the same ceremony. soon leave my relatives and new modes of living among strangers. how singular to leave all for one of the other sex. Attended singing school at the village. an agreeable letter from Miss Betsey Eastman. received a pair of shoes.[46]

Finally on her wedding day, she wrote:

Pleasant. What a dreadful day is this. Miss [Electa] Prime waited upon me today and this eve and Mr. Henry Byington [was] Mr. Eastman's waiter to the ceremony performed by Esq. Pier. Farewell to a sweet single life, I can no more enjoy you. Packed my goods and ready to depart. What a change to relinquish parents and friends all for one of the other sex. Surprising and unpleasant.[47]

The day after her wedding, Orvis left her cherished home in Vermont and accompanied her new husband back to the wilds of the New York frontier. While it is difficult to know if she was fearful or resigned or simply chose the path of least resistance for the sake of peace in her family, it is clear that her spousal choice had been largely dictated by her family's desires. Orvis's story plainly demonstrates that not all Americans embraced the liberal leanings of the new century. Orvis's experiences were clearly influenced by the provincial world in which she lived, the social class of her family, and her own aspirations for a romantic relationship were directly affected. Her family, although they allowed her some latitude, curtailed her freedom to choose. To that end, they came together, enlisted the aid of a vast network of relatives and friends, and worked diligently to ensure that Orvis married the appropriate suitor, in spite of her own desires. Revolutionary rhetoric aside, reality undermined the romantic notions Orvis and her friends venerated; her entry into married life accentuated those limitations.

Chapter Three

"rendered . . . more ignorant than others"

While we may mourn with Orvis's lost love and sympathize with her less-than-romantic marriage, there were other successful moments in her single life. Before her "visit" to Parishville and the final capitulation to Samuel Eastman's proposal, Orvis was able to pursue her dreams of continuing her education. Her journal entries ardently express how deeply Orvis valued an intellectual life. Her love of books and learning undoubtedly began with a common school education and was nourished further through her access to reading materials housed in the local Sabbath school library. It is also likely that her occasional employment as a teacher in the common school near where she lived whetted her appetite for better and more expanded opportunities for knowledge. Wherever the impulse came from, the accident of her proximity to Middlebury provided Orvis with an almost unprecedented opportunity: formal enrollment in one of the vanguard efforts at providing women with a classical education designed by Emma Hart Willard.

Her first day at school was a revelation and a source of anxiety as well:

> *Attended the Ladies Quarterly School taught by Miss Lucy Burnap. Enjoyed very disagreeable feelings from various courses. First on account of my being an entire stranger to most of the Ladies and they to me. Second being entirely unacquainted with the manner and customs of the school. Third [I] have not attended any kind of school for some years which of course rendered me more ignorant than others of the school. (These reflections I conclude [are the] effects of injured pride) . . .*[1]

This passage reflects a surprisingly modern sensibility. Orvis's concerns—that she arrived at school unknown to the rest of her fellow students, unsure of her dress and demeanor, and her fears of being not prepared or intelligent enough to fit in—all have been echoed by incoming freshmen college women many times since that day in 1820. And continue to resonate to this day. Seen in this light, we can imagine Orvis as being typical of the many young women who have gone off to school in every generation for almost two hundred years. Yet, we must also recognize that despite the modernity inherent in her words, Orvis represents one of the first generation of American women to seek higher education. The very concept of female higher education was brand new—and radical—in her day. Orvis's experience, though certainly not unique, surely helped to break new ground for American women.

In the early nineteenth century, the evolving ideology of "republican motherhood" led many Americans to believe that a good education for women was imperative for the well-being of the new nation. Yet, this general agreement over the prudential effect of educated middle-class women did not translate into a universal understanding of the nature and scope of a revised female education program, especially with regard to the dimensions of more advanced instruction. The broad debate extended across ideological territories that included those who desired education of girls and women for its value in an emerging capitalist economy, those who saw the political potential in an educated female citizenry, and those who believed that women were the primary, if not most important, source of civic education for American children.[2] As a result, despite the heightened general interest in promoting female higher education, there was no fundamental agreement on what shape those opportunities might take and consequently educational prospects for women remained inconsistent.

Contemporary historians who have studied the evolution of female higher education in this period have chiefly been concerned with its institutional development. Interest has focused on the way in which schools were founded, the educators who created them, how specific curriculum developed, or how institutions conformed (or did not) to the social expectations of middle-class female behavior.[3] To date, few historians have studied the individual experiences of students as they pursued higher education or what the results of that quest might have been.

Orvis's writings provide important insights into how women of her generation acquired and experienced higher education. Of equal importance, it offers significant clues as to how these women were able to balance the demands of family (what Jane Addams later in the century called the "family claim") and manage the cost of their education. Finally, Orvis's experiences clearly demonstrate the limitations faced by many women of her time, both in the attainment as well as use of their education. In this, her journal is an unrefined, forthright source of her thoughts and observations and a chronicle of her experiences at the Middlebury Female Seminary.

As earlier noted, Orvis began her education in the common school of her community as well as enjoyed the educational benefits of the Sabbath school and its library. She was obviously a good student; her journal is well written and even erudite in places. Her educational accomplishments at the point she commenced her journal were sufficient to qualify her to teach several terms at the nearby Monkton town common school. Yet, she was determined to further her intellectual development at the Middlebury Female Seminary. Her other, more domestic, skills undoubtedly learned from her grandmother, Ruth (Sawyer) Brooks, and aunt, Lovina (Hawkins) Brooks, enabled her to pursue that goal since she needed to earn the money to finance her education. Therefore, Orvis drew on her traditional female skills as a spinner, weaver, and seamstress, to achieve her more unconventional aspirations. In this, she was not alone. Most of her school friends worked either to help pay for their school fees or boarding costs or both.

To achieve her intellectual ambitions, Orvis needed sufficient funds to buy books and other materials, pay board and tuition, and to possess an adequate wardrobe to decently present herself. An advertisement in Middlebury's newspaper, *National Record*, laid out those expenses for the prospective seminary student: tuition was calculated as \$3.50 per quarter with an additional \$5.50 per quarter to add painting and art; board was estimated at \$2.25 per week throughout the quarter.[4] In sum, for an individual to attend the school for a quarter would cost approximately $40.00. To earn that money, Orvis devoted months of labor. In the opening pages of the journal, her work regimen was meant to commence when her cousin, Benjamin Clapp, "engaged [her] to spin two or three weeks."[5] Her grandmother objected to her being out of the house for that long and informed her that "if I left home and went out to work, I would be deprived of a home here."[6] Orvis returned to Bristol and opted to pursue paid labors that she could incorporate into her home duties.

Over the course of the next four months through to the end of November, Orvis spun, wove, and sewed a veritable mountain of textile goods. At times, she alternated between the loom and spinning wheel as she worked along. In total, she recorded finishing more than 300 yards of various fabrics. Over and above the production of cloth, she also wove four complete bed coverlets (approximately another 24–30 yards), eight blankets (48 yards) and an unspecified length of fabric patterned in Diamond Key, which she then made up into bed curtains.

Certain of the yarns spun by Orvis went into the woven fabrics, including twenty-one knots of linen yarn that she spun and prepared for the loom. In addition, she purchased cotton yarns, used mainly for warps and almost certainly spun at the newly established Warren Cotton Mill in nearby Middlebury.[7] Furthermore, she was provided yarns, both handspun and factory produced, from the merchants or neighbors who engaged her to weave finished cloth for their purposes.

Aside from her spinning and weaving, Orvis also knitted and sewed for herself, her family members, and for the local merchants. She frequently sewed men's shirts for Mr. Thayre, a Middlebury merchant who also provided her with manufactured warp yarns for woven fabric. She knitted at other times, producing stockings, mittens, shawls, and scarves. Although her writing does not specifically identify this flurry of production as a means to support her education, when Orvis recorded how she spent the proceeds, her intentions become clear.

In mid-October of 1820, she began to purchase books, a trunk, new shoes, and silk fabric for a gown and pelisse.[8] These were the goods and clothes she would take with her to Middlebury. Sometimes these transactions for particular items were the result of "reckoning her accounts" with the local merchants, but Orvis also took currency payments. This hard cash undoubtedly paid for her tuition and board bills.

As we have seen, her family did not actively oppose her intellectual aspirations, but they were not enthusiastic enough to provide the means for her to do so. The breadth of the domestic work reported in her journal entries clearly indicate that she was not excused from any of the regular household labor to engage in her extramural textile manufactures. A close read of the journal reveals that Orvis frequently sandwiched her paid outwork between her regular household chores. A typical entry went as follows:

> *Did the housework. washed all the floors, from top to bottom. Wove three yards and half. Our people came home brought Cousin Lucinda Nicholson with them . . .*[9]

In addition to her textile production and housework, Orvis frequently helped out with sick and/or pregnant neighbors' work. She sat up with Mrs. Copeland, a neighbor and a close friend's mother, during a serious illness. She also applied several heroic medicinal remedies, including shaving Mrs. Copeland's head and the application of blister poultices. It is not clear whether Phebe was always compensated for this work, but it clearly added to her daily labors.

Over and above the endless household tasks and outwork, Orvis continued to pursue her intellectual growth. She read widely, including travel narratives and novels as well as history, philosophy, and religious tracts. Closer to home, she perused the work of Middlebury scholars, including the "inaugural Oration delivered by Mr. Joshua Bates professor of Middlebury College, 26 pages."[10] Many entries indicate that Orvis read anywhere from seventy to a hundred pages in an evening.[11]

Other than her reading and household manufactures, Orvis also worked constantly at a veritable mountain of personal correspondence. She was a prodigious letter-writer, exchanging letters with friends locally, family members from neighboring towns as well as family living in New York, Ohio, and Ontario, Canada. She may have been the link for the Brooks household to other family households across the region. Often she worked long into the evening with her correspondence.

By November of 1820, Orvis was ready to begin the winter term at the Middlebury Female Seminary. This move represented another development in antebellum New England's history: a kind of "semi-independence" for certain unmarried women even if it was short-lived. While Orvis and her fellow students at the Seminary boarded with families away from home and attended school, others went to work in the new factories in places like Lowell, Massachusetts and Winooski, Vermont.[12]

Mill girls represented a shift in the traditional labor force that began in this period. While young women like Orvis had long done piecework and stints of labor in neighboring households for cash and kind, the first wave of mill girls who left home to work in places like Lowell or Winooski earned cash wages. Although the wages legally belonged to the fathers of these young women, many of them were still able to command the spending of the money they earned. The route they took to the factory was often as varied as the woman who traveled it; some girls were sent by their cash-strapped fathers to help with family debt, while others went to the manufacturing centers to have access to education, wages, and a broader experience beyond the farms. For most, the experience was a short interlude between adolescence and marriage, but it was a formative experience all the same. Harriet Robinson, a Lowell Mills employee, observed:

> *We can hardly realize what a change the cotton factory made in the status of the working women. Hitherto woman had always been a money-saving rather than a money earning, member of the community.*[13]

While Orvis had undoubtedly had some advantage over the women who were sent to Lowell or Winooski by their parents, she was very much a kindred spirit of those who chose to go on their own to find a more satisfying life. The fact that Orvis was able to choose school was certainly related to her family's social status, but the limits to the range of her choices were entirely connected to her gender.

Young women such as Orvis could only choose school or the factory as a short-term deviation from their most important vocation: marriage. While not employed in a factory, Orvis did finance her education with the proceeds from textile labors. Her participation in outwork provided by local merchants made it possible for her to earn wages without having to leave home for the factory towns. In this way, Orvis is an example of the transitional workforce that spanned the years between the time when all manufacturing was cottage production and the new model of factory labor. In Bristol, Orvis had a foot in both worlds as she did piecework for wages and traded her work directly for particular articles she needed.

Whatever the payment type, Orvis took up the work provided by three merchants located in New Haven, New Haven Mills, and Bristol. Periodically, she brought her finished work to the merchants and exchanged it for more unfinished pieces. Once at school, she continued to work at her sewing before and after lessons to be able to pay for board and other necessities. In the end she was able to finance the entire school term through her sewing, knitting, and spinning skills.

Despite her misgivings on the first day of school, she quickly made friends and became immersed in her lessons. She described a typical school day as thus:

> *The school commences by reading two verses of a piece of Scripture. Miss B. [Miss Lucy Burnap, the preceptress] makes an introductory prayer[.] next attend to writing Hebromon (?), a lesson in Cummings' Geography, parsing English grammar in the afternoon. Rhetoric, Logic, Philosophy, other studies. Have singing instead of reading before prayer in the evening . . .*[14]

The subjects Orvis listed reflect the newly emerging philosophies of educators generally. President Jeremiah Day, in describing the curriculum at Yale in a report published in 1828, observed that mathematics, physical sciences, classical literature, English reading, logic, rhetoric, oratory, and composition were important knowledge that college-educated people (in his case he meant men) must get from higher education. Reasoning, deductive skills, critical thinking, eloquence in speech and writing, as well as an elevated sense of taste would be the product of those subjects.

> *If the student exercises his reasoning powers only, he will be deficient in imagination and taste, in fervid and impressive eloquence. . . . If he relies principally on his memory, his powers of invention will be impaired by disuse . . . [a student] must maintain such a proportion between the different branches of literature and science, as to form in the student a proper balance of character.*[15]

The Middlebury Female Seminary under Emma Hart Willard's influence clearly embraced this approach; the school's curriculum included a broad range of subjects and emphasized an extensive set of skills, including physical science and the humanities.

This curricular scheme was adopted by Willard who, just a few years earlier, had been the pivotal figure in creating the girls' program in Middlebury. Indeed, Willard wrote her *Plan for Improving Female Education* in Middlebury the previous year.[16] Willard's desire to transition female education from decorative arts and "soft learning" to the more masculine curriculum of places like

Middlebury College was born of her own intellectual aspirations. She'd come to Middlebury to take over the position of teacher at the girls' academy to have the ability to teach with her own philosophical edge. Unfortunately, she found that the Middlebury businessmen were reluctant to see their academy change. She married a local businessman, withdrew from teaching, and lived in quiet envy across the village green from Middlebury College. She boarded students, including her husband's nephews, and vicariously experienced their educations by reading their books and previewing their exams. Eventually, the opportunity to launch a school that embraced her educational vision came with the same bank robbery that convinced Middlebury citizens that professional men could be slippery. As her husband's fortunes declined in the aftermath of the robbery—he was one of the trustees of the bank—Willard stepped forward to create the Middlebury Female Seminary with her version of female intellectual rigor in mind.

Beyond Middlebury, female seminaries and academies in the forefront of the new educational initiatives for women adopted similar curricula. For instance, the Litchfield Female Academy and Morris Academy (also located in Litchfield, Connecticut), followed identical models; rigorous academic studies and less emphasis on the decorative arts characterized these schools.[17] Willard did not stay in Middlebury, she relocated her school to Waterford, New York, and then on to Troy, New York, where it took permanent root and still flourishes today. There, Willard was able to expand on her vision and influenced multiple generations of young women who created schools and academies of their own across the country. In Middlebury, that legacy continued under the direction of enthusiastic local businessmen and one of Willard's star pupils, Lucy Burnap.

At the Middlebury Female Seminary, Burnap continued to follow the curriculum established by Willard. A Middlebury newspaper announcement for the commencement of the 1820 spring term, demonstrates Willard's influence on Burnap's program:

"Ladies School"

The subscribers would hereby inform the public that they propose to continue [my emphasis] the Ladies' School in this village, through the ensuing season, and in addition to the common branches of literature, will instruct in Geography, ancient and modern, History, Rhetoric, Moral Philosophy, Logic, Natural Theology, and an abridged system of Natural Philosophy and Astronomy. Also, if requested, in Drawing, Painting, and in various kinds of elegant Needlework. Tuition for literary branches, 3 dollars per quarter. For the polite branches, from 4 to 7 dollars per quarter. Ladies from abroad can be accommodated with convenient boarding houses on reasonable terms. It will be the object of the instructors to correct the taste, improve the mind, and inculcate such sentiments and habits, as may render their pupils respectable, useful, and happy through life, and be the means of preparing them for a future state of existence. The second quarter will commence on Monday the 28th inst.

Uzziah C. Burnap
Lucy Burnap
Middlebury February 20, 1820.[18]

Under the Burnap administration, there was an unmistakable emphasis on intellectual rigor. In short, hard work was the order of the day with multiple reading and writing assignments. In one entry, Orvis describes that rigor:

> *For the first time wrote a composition on Composition. [Did] two lessons in geography, one [in] grammar. Miss Mills exchanged boarding awhile[.] went to Mrs. Phelps to study with Miss Jerusha Hoyt.*[19]

In her first month at school, Orvis wrote lessons and compositions in all of the various subjects, including philosophy, history, geography, and logic. Often she recited those lessons in public forums as well as turned in her written work for evaluation. Orvis "parsed grammar" and wrote many essays on "self-knowledge." Halfway through the quarter, a collection of oral recitations seems to represent a kind of midterm examination period. For example, a December entry: "Commenced a review of Geography. Finished writing Astronomical Geography. Passed in Pope's essay. [and] lesson map." The next day: "Took a review of Alexander's grammar. Went through this forenoon. Commenced Rhetoric. recited four lessons today. Very tired."[20]

In addition to written lessons and preparations of recitations, Orvis also drew and painted a variety of maps. She frequently read accompanying texts to these drawing assignments. In one Geography assignment, she read the *Prince of Abyssinia* while she worked on drawing and painting a map of the Middle East. By the end of the winter term, she created an entire globe deemed worthy of framing by Lucy Burnap.[21] Her interest in foreign lands may have been piqued by the geography assignments; at some point she began to record a Chinese language glossary gleaned from a travel memoir, perhaps in anticipation of learning a foreign language, although for what purpose is not clear.[22]

Aside from a concentration on the humanities and classics, the Middlebury Female Seminary also emphasized science in its curriculum. Again this is reflective of the national trend in college curricula. Orvis and her fellow students studied astronomy and botany as well as engaged in "scientific experiments," although she was never explicit about what those experiments might have been. The lessons in botany included field trips where students observed the natural world as well as created watercolor paintings of local flora. Later, as a teacher, Orvis tried to incorporate these studies into her own curriculum by taking her students on "nature walks" where they made firsthand observations in the area surrounding the schoolhouse.

Beyond her course work, Orvis also negotiated a broadened social world and a new territory of living arrangements. While at first she expressed fears with regard to her ability to make new friends, she was quickly absorbed into the Middlebury social scene. She met a variety of new female as well as male friends and participated in the constant rounds of visiting, studying, and exchange of boarding situations, which to some degree seem very modern. In the week between December 13th and 21st, Orvis's study and leisure schedule was packed solid:

> *13th: Wrote a composition on Modesty. Heard thirty recitations and a Dialogue written by scholars. Recited once through the Atlas. . . . Went in to store to purchase a handkerchief,*

half a quire of paper. One hair comb. Wrote a letter to Miss Copeland. Broke my large hair comb. P. [Prudence Hills] and myself rude couple.

14th: . . . Miss Patty Hoyt called. Strong invitation to visit her. Wrote letters until twelve o'clock at night. Read a number of letters . . .

21st: (Thanksgiving Day) . . . Heard a discourse by Rev. Josiah Hopkins. Invited to Esq. James Sexton's to supper. Disappointed of going to Bristol. Saw Miss Lucretia Gowdy[,] Miss Marsha Ann Satterlee from Middlebury. Ladies of this street took a ride to Town Hill . . .[23]

While at school, Orvis boarded at two different homes in Middlebury. Her first place was with the family of a local physician, Dr. Stearns. Stearns charged her $3.33 for the first month's room and board. This was less than was generally advertised, but the difference was predicated on the expectation that she "help out" with the household chores. So, although Orvis was a full-time student, she continued to do double, and sometimes triple, duty with housework and other chores.[24]

In mid-December, Orvis moved to a new boarding situation. The Sexton home, a place she visited many times as a guest, and which was undoubtedly a more accommodating place for students. Several of her friends lodged there and since the pace of her schoolwork accelerated, the fact that the Sextons were less demanding of her time for domestic work was welcome. Clearly, Orvis was better able to cope with the rigors of schoolwork, but also could partake of the rounds of parties and visiting as well.

Much to her disappointment, Orvis was not to continue in the next academic session. On the 10th of January, she received a letter from her family. She needed to prepare for what she referred to as a "western journey."[25] She was able to complete the current term, but would not be able to remain for the spring quarter. With regret, Orvis acknowledged in her journal that her time at school was painfully short. At the end of the term, she returned to the family home in Bristol, but managed to revisit Middlebury twice. On these subsequent trips she attended several of her friends' lesson recitations and turned in her finished maps to be approved by Lucy Burnap.

Despite her scholarly ambitions and the constant work to support them, Orvis was not able to ignore her family's expectation that she leave school. She simply could not refuse their demand that she accompany her aunt and uncle Durfey home to Parishville. While her family did not oppose her educational aspirations, they did have clear expectations of what her future should entail. As we have seen, they expected her to marry and take up the role of wife and mother, they had clear preferences for her prospective husband, and a respectable life. Her education might be attractive to someone like Eastman, but her family was not about to allow her to choose education over the prospects of finding a proper husband.

In Middlebury, Orvis enjoyed an active social life and was pursued by a number of prospective beaux. She expressed interest in many of the young men of her acquaintance, but was more concerned with going to friends' weddings than participation in one of her own. Indeed, many entries display a clear reluctance for marriage, and more than one entry demonstrated her understanding that a wedding would mean the end of her ability to study, write, and read.[26]

For those months while at school, Orvis's recorded thoughts make it clear that her most absorbing interests were intellectual. She minutely described her course work, reading and writing assignments, as well as her attendance at other scholarly functions in Middlebury, including Middlebury College commencements, which were events of great interest to her. Even after leaving Middlebury, Orvis continued to pursue a life of the mind; she read widely, wrote in her journal, and continued her vast correspondence. Despite several short stints as a common schoolteacher, though, she was not destined to resume her intellectual aspirations after the end of the fall term at Middlebury. Instead, as we know, she married, became a housewife, and was soon afterward the mother of a growing brood of children.

While we might consider her later life as a housewife a waste of her intellect and education, Orvis did fulfill some of the expectations of education proponents. She taught at the Parishville common school until her first child was born, bringing her educational experience to the frontier community. After the birth of her children, she actively participated in their education, providing them with the civic education so important to the ideologues of the early Republic. Finally, she functioned as the chief record keeper of the family, kept the farm accounts, the family vital statistics, and maintained the family connections through her continued correspondence with Vermont, New York, and Ohio relatives.

Orvis may not have transcended the traditional female roles of her time, but given the expectations of her society, this is no surprise. The less tangible effect of her education was her ability to cope with life in a backwater community with little opportunity for intellectual pursuits. Her pleasure in writing and reading continued throughout her life, if limited by the demands of her housework and family, and seemed to offer comfort in many instances. Where she was able, she borrowed and read a number of historical works, travel memoirs, and Shakespeare plays. Moreover, she frequently transcribed favorite passages or wrote commentaries:

> *[R]ead several tracts and the Indian Captive. Zadock Steele. He was taken by the Indians under refugees and Tories from Randolph, Vt., On the 17th day of October 1780 to Canada through a wilderness of three hundred miles in seven days, where underwent almost everything but death. They made their escape from Prison Island by digging under the Pickets with a Jack knife. Twenty feet underground, twenty two and half in length in two years. After enduring famine and distress, they arrived at home at Ellington, Connecticut . . .*[27]

In this case, perhaps Orvis felt a kinship with Steele and his captivity, although clearly her experience on the frontier was not a true parallel. Another literary reference in her journal reveals Orvis's consumption of novels as an escape from the trials of everyday life:

> *Read the History of Zoa, who released Rodomond from a pit in her Father's garden, the Banyan in disguise. They fled from the Malays, this beautiful female Indian afterwards became*

> *his wife. Read also Lisette and Login who were deeply in love. Login a nobleman, Lisette a peasant daughter, the only child of her widowed Mother[.] at length [length] Lisette by the purest love yielded her innocence to her lover. He then left her under the pretence of the army. instead of which he married a rich widow. Poor Lisette drowned herself in consequence of her lost lover and the mother her daughter.*[28]

One can imagine that the fictional heroines, tragic or blissful, must have provided a welcome respite from a life filled with the dirt, worry, work, and children in a log cottage on the New York frontier.

Part Two

"New modes of living among strangers"

Chapter Four

"perhaps the partner of his joys"

A few weeks before her wedding day, Phebe Orvis asked herself, "to what am I hastening?"[1] This soul searching was both a reflection of her prewedding anxiety while also the expression of unspoken fears regarding her fate as a married woman. Certainly she had a fair idea of her future in "the married state" already. Heretofore, Orvis witnessed more than a dozen family members as well as many of her friends and neighbors joined in marriage. Moreover, she had observed them as they lived together afterward. As a young child in her grandparent's home, she not only witnessed a good share of the thirty-year married relationship of the Brookses, but also the more recent marriage of her Uncle John and Aunt Lovina who shared the elder Brooks's homestead. These lessons in adult life do not seem to have been overly frightening or to have encouraged Orvis to shun marriage altogether, but she still seems to have been a reluctant bride. Her prewedding jitters may also have been a reflection of her worry that marriage would be an end, literally and figuratively, to her life. On the one hand, she must have been anxious that her love of intellectual pursuits would be severely limited, if not curtailed altogether. Built into the role of wife was an enormous commitment of unremitting toil, with little time for leisure pursuits such as reading, writing letters, or quiet, solitary contemplation. On the other hand, she was acutely aware that marriage meant children, and multiple pregnancies had the potential to rob her of her natural health and vigor. A loss of health could mean that she would be ripe for the same fate as her mother: a premature death due to childbed fever. Orvis surely understood the overwhelming burden of physical, social, and spiritual work that her marriage to Eastman entailed.

Despite all of her initial misgivings, once she married Samuel Eastman, Orvis seems not to have overly mourned her former life. If they were not two people with the ideal of romantic love, who met, fell in love, and married, neither were they complete strangers forced to cohabitate in a kind of long-range endurance test. Instead, the Eastmans seem to have developed a mutual affection—even if it was punctuated by discord at times. We only know about their relationship from Orvis's words, and she did not write descriptively of her feelings for Eastman often or at length except when she was exercised over his bad habits or diverged from her expectations or assumptions. Even less discernible is the relationship from Eastman's perspective. We can only speculate what Eastman may have thought or felt about his wife. He must have thought her a worthy bride; he pursued her for more than a year and followed her back to Bristol, after all. And Orvis did agree to accept him even if it was a "dreadful decision."

Whatever her internal reservations, Orvis tackled her new status as Eastman's wife with the same vigor that she applied to her education and then her prenuptial textile labors. The day that she moved into Eastman's log cottage she wrote, "Moved home *for so I must call it.* [My emphasis]"[2] She was prepared to make the best of her situation.

Embarked on her new role as a wife, Orvis's understanding of how to proceed as a married woman was shaped by influences from within and without. Schooled from childhood by her "Grandma'am," Orvis understood the importance of adopting appropriate behaviors and refining the skills necessary for being a good wife and a righteous woman. Other women of her family also provided models for proper behavior at each stage of life from blushing bride to dowdy matron. And, there was no question that Orvis/Brooks women were to be wives and mothers; all of Orvis's female siblings and cousins who lived to maturity married. They were a prolific clan and most raised families of seven to ten children. The large families were due in part to the relatively early ages of Orvis/Brooks brides: the extended Brooks/Orvis clan married, on average, before age twenty-one. The young men of the family married also, but usually between twenty-five and twenty-five. Following deep-seated New England traditions, the pattern was for fathers to divide land off the original holdings and make their sons' transition to independent adult households possible. Loren Orvis accomplished this for at least six of his nine sons. Again according to custom, Orvis daughters were never given real estate; instead they were presented with livestock and movable property in the form of household goods and textiles. Perhaps because it was less taxing on the family capital to provide a few cows and some "go to housekeeping" implements, Orvis/Brooks women tended to marry five to seven years earlier than their brothers. Born into this milieu, it is no surprise that Orvis finally accepted the inevitability of her marriage.

Beyond the obvious influence of custom and tradition in her life, as a literate and aspiring middle-class woman, Orvis consumed the popular literature romanticizing marriage, motherhood, and children. Novels, poetry, and instructional literature reinforced the cultural expectations rooted in the female stereotype of middle-class American society. In short, Orvis was expected to get married and "go to housekeeping," armed with domestic skills to care for the physical well-being of her husband and future children. She was also expected to possess spiritual skills to minister to their souls. In other words, a woman of Orvis's time would have understood that it was a good wife's proper duty to see that her household was orderly, clean, and nourished—in both the physical and spiritual realms.

In reality, as a committed wife Orvis found both duties difficult in the first decade of her marriage. The rough-hewn log cabin she shared with her new husband on the New York frontier was difficult to keep clean and orderly. The log walls shed dirt and harbored insects and the unglazed windows let in more. Her new abode did not compare well with her grandfather's fine Vermont home. At the same time, her new husband was unruly if not down-right recalcitrant toward the disciplined spiritual life she envisioned for them both. He disdained Sabbath prayer and often refused to participate in religious services, opting to fish and hunt with his brother Lee instead. It was Eastman's impious nature that troubled Orvis the most. Even before their children came, she worried that her husband's irreligious approach to life was dangerous and had the potential to rob both of them of their spiritual potential. One journal entry asked for divine guidance in this spiritual struggle:

Ah God wilt thou warm the heart of my companion with thy love?[3]

Another mourned the lost fellowship of home and the lack of interest in creating their own home-grown services:

Pleasant. no meeting to attend. no religious exercise at home. Oh Lord suffer us not to remain thus stupid but may we set out anew to serve thee. Oh give us more love to thee and less to the world, a broken heart, a praying spirit, a contented mind.[4]

As the daughter of Quakers, Orvis was committed to a well-ordered, contemplative, and devout way of life. Moreover, she was intimately aware of the uncertain nature of existence. She experienced the brevity of life initially through her own mother's early demise, but also witnessed others' mortality in her short life. These losses taught her caution and emphasized the need to be spiritually prepared for death at any moment. Orvis may even have felt a certain responsibility for her mother's passing in the feverish aftermath of her own birth. Certainly, Orvis noted her mother's death every year she kept her journal, sometimes expressing an extraordinary sense of loss.

Twenty years this morn since my mother left this world. Ah! Where is she? Is not her spirit hovering o'er my head entreating her infant daughter to reclaim her wandering steps? yet little does she [her daughter] realize it.[5]

In other ways, Orvis's self-analysis is not surprising. Her membership in the Monkton/Starksboro/Ferrisburgh Meeting from such an early age brought her into contact with a fellowship steeped in the culture of self-reflection. Such self-knowledge was valued by members of the Friends as the first step toward sensing the light of faith. By the time she began to keep her journal, she was a regular participant at the monthly meetings near her grandparents' home.[6] Orvis did not lack for inspiration from other Quakers, since there were ample opportunities to attend Friends' meetings (both informal and organized) in her grandparents' neighborhood. In fact, the majority of settlers who arrived in Addison County at the end of the eighteenth century were Quakers; in the opinion of one early historian of the area: "Those who did not belong with them were the exceptions."[7] In the first decade of settlement in Bristol township, meetings were informally organized and held in various members' homes. By 1801, four years before Orvis became a full member, the Friends were formally organized in their local Society and had applied to the Quarterly Meeting at Easton, New York, which became their "mother" meeting. Although no money for building a meetinghouse was immediately forthcoming from their "mother" meeting, the local Friends constructed a log structure for their use in Bristol. The informal nature of the early years of the Society of Friends in that region meant that meetings and Sabbath schools were held in various locations, including Bristol, New Haven Mills, Ferrisburgh, Starksboro, and Lincoln, on any given Sunday. Orvis appears to have attended most Sundays, even when there were "few scholars" at the Sabbath school or the weather was inclement.[8]

Despite some speculation that regular meeting attendance had more to do with social interaction than religious obligation, Orvis paid serious attention to the texts and the testimony given at the meetings. She often recorded the text, sometimes copying it out in her journal, frequently with her own commentary attached. Moreover, her writing reveals a level of self-analysis that would have been worthy of a Puritan zealot. Often, her self-analysis led to self-censure: "Why am I discontented?" she would write in her journal. Then, in answer to herself, she would write: "Wickedness."[9] Self-examination revealed what she believed was her shameful lack of piety; her soul was not as spiritually pure as she wished. Often these observations were in part an acknowledgment of the fragility of life: "So slides time away faster than we prepare for death and Eternity."[10] Usually, her observations were brief and to the point, but she could write at length and eloquently. The image of life passing quickly and the chances for salvation being even more ephemeral connected in her mind to the fast-flowing and sometimes dangerous, if beautiful, river near her home:

> *[T]ook an agreeable walk to the river. . . . Oh how changed many of the places where I have read and sang hours, my voice reaching with the rolling waves are now no more, they have plunged the stream while I view the place of past scenes. I think the comparison may be applied to mankind. sometimes the current moves easy and beautiful but soon it rushes with impetuosity, renders the Sublimity strikingly majestic, trees torn from their native soil, are tossed to and fro, rising and plunging with the furious torrent. So is man. Sometimes his circumstances are flattering, his mind is easy, he slides sweetly along the stream of life. But alas! soon some sudden and unseen affliction hovers around him and tosses him upon the billows of despair unless his hope is rested upon the rock of salvation where he is safe [from] all harm. but if his afflictions are placed upon the fading of this world. perhaps a little property, perhaps a dear friend or relative, perhaps the partner of his joys, the companion of his bosom is torn from him. then he thinks his cup is full his burthen is greater than he can bear. thus he is afflicted, he strives to regain his former security of pleasure but the stream of time swiftly carries him down unless some kind assistance comes to his relief.*[11]

Her need to remain focused on the Divine Truth and avoid worldly concerns of wealth, personal vanity, and even of earthly love sprinkle the passages of her journal. Marriage to such an irreverent man as Eastman complicated this philosophy.

In other ways, Orvis's marriage drastically changed her life. First, she lived in a rude log cabin on the raw frontier of New York State. Second, she was wife to a man she barely knew and with whom she was expected to build an intimate life. Finally, Eastman had not been her first choice and her husband was aware of this fact. Although Eastman had pursued her diligently, his coarse ways and irreligious manner confused and sometimes frightened her. Eventually she relented, accepted his proposal, and, once married "for better or worse," Orvis seemed determined to make the best of her situation.

In the first few weeks after moving into the cabin, she expended enormous effort bringing order to her uncultivated and crude new home. Her journal reflects both her hopes and her frustrations in that time; entries contain numerous references to being disgusted with herself and mourning Vermont from what she clearly thought was an isolated, backwater condition. Then, her guilty conscience would attack. She wrote:

> *Oh what a wicked creature I am, neglect my maker as I do. Lord forbid that I should continue to live in sloth, may I not renounce the things of an earthly nature, and seek superior bliss? God grant that we may live no longer in such a stupid Backslidden condition but may we both run the race that is set before us with alacrity, till we arrive on Canaan's happy shore.*[12]

From this point on, Orvis's writing regains her self-reflective style, but her worry over Eastman's lack of piety and her own occasional lapses of devotion continued. She anguished over the lack of regular Friends' meetings. It is not clear whether there were no Quaker meetings in the area or she could not convince her husband to attend and felt unable to attend alone. She was certainly frustrated with his impious attitude and observed the passing of the Sabbaths with a mixture of self-criticism and annoyance with Eastman's irreverence.

Ironically, Orvis's first love, Adolphus Taylor, became an example of the piety and devotion she desired in her husband. When Taylor married her girlhood friend, Orra Copeland, he took his new bride back out to Saint Lawrence County to his current teaching post. This meant that when Eastman and Orvis married and "went to housekeeping" on the farm in Parishville in the early spring of 1823, the Taylors were already settled in the nearby town of Stockholm. It must have been a bittersweet revelation to Orvis given the distressing turns of her emotional investment in Taylor, their near engagement, and then his marriage to her girlhood friend. Yet, the two couples appear to have developed a close friendship. Within a month of her marriage to Eastman and arrival in Parishville, the Taylors visited the Eastmans in their new home.[13] At this point, Copeland was heavily pregnant and on April 4th she gave birth to her first child. In July, the Eastmans visited the Taylors in Stockholm and attended a religious service there during their visit. Their brief stay in the Taylor home underscored the difference in the two couples' lifestyle. While Eastman remained an unrepentant gadabout, Adolphus Taylor was a more serious-minded individual. Orvis observed:

> *we took uncle's horses, rode to Stockholm. visited my good friends Mr [and Mrs.] Taylor. walked one mile. hear Elder Road [Rhodes] "Who then can be saved" These people live in the enjoyment of religion. Oh that we might follow their example. very tired.*[14]

Her feeling that the Taylors lived "in the enjoyment of religion" was surely difficult to accept. Not only did Copeland marry the man that Orvis originally fancied, she benefited from his pious approach to their life. Eastman, on the other hand, continued to be obstinate, irreligious, and downright unruly when it came to regular observances of prayer, and especially in his approach to Sabbath activities.

Although there may have been an earlier miscarriage, Orvis gave birth to her first child in May 1824. His arrival coincided with a renewed evangelical impulse:

> *Rainy. Oh my god what a day is this and how hast though [sic] supported me through it. At half past ten A.M. didst thou make me the Mother of a lovely son weighing seven pounds four oz. thanks to my God it will never be a mother. since it has been thy will to restore me to my bosom friend with this little pledge of love instead of taking me from him, wilt thou grant us wisdom to bring it up in thy fear, teach him to remember his Creator in the days of his youth.*[15]

And:

> *Oh God wilt thou not save him [Henry Eastman] from the errors of his Parents. Ah teach him to love thee with his whole heart, soul, might, mind & strength.*[16]

From this point on, Orvis reengaged in a battle with her husband over the welfare of his soul and the piety of their household. Since Eastman was not inclined to religious devotion, his Sundays were spent fishing, hunting, or, as Orvis described, passed the day "dull and stupid." Her tactics seem straightforward: she refused to participate in his wanton ways, even when it was difficult. More than once Orvis refused to cook whatever he brought home from a Sunday's hunt or fishing campaign, despite her husband's protests. Yet her campaign to end the dull and stupid Sundays did not yield much fruit. Eastman continued to participate in Sabbath hunting and fishing forays with his brothers, as well as using the day to recover from the more than occasional Saturday drinking (also with his brothers) under the guise of militia training. Horrified, she wrote:

> *I can do nothing as long as this man of sense is drowned in Liquor. Oh Lord wilt thou not put an end to his love of ardent spirits and quicken him with thine holy fire?*[17]

As their young son began to grow, Orvis worried that he would adopt Eastman's impious and disrespectful bearing.

In April of 1825, an informal Quaker meeting commenced at the schoolhouse in Parishville near Orvis's home. These meetings were dependent on a gathering of the few Quakers in the area and often coincided with the presence of traveling ministers; in this case a missionary from England named Wilkinson. The meetings occurred intermittently through the summer, but by fall, Wilkinson had moved on and Orvis was sorely disappointed by his departure.

> *Stormy A.M. Pleasant P.M. one poor traveler called. I had the pleasure of giving him a meal which is highly gratifying to my feelings, to impart a trifle to the poor but still there is an aching void that lies continually in my breast. His parents are careless about the things that be his and bring their everlasting peace. no example worthy [of] his imitation and, can I bear to see the little innocent thus live? Oh God forbid. wilt thou give us a praying spirit, family religion, a pious heart and may it ere long be our meat and our drink to do the will of our Father.*[18]

Her frustration with an unrepentant husband continued to mount over the next year. The birth of her second child, a daughter, born somewhat prematurely (she referred to the birth as untimely, but was not specific), seems to have deepened her frustration, anxiety, and her resolve. An epidemic of influenza that appears to have been accompanied by a severe bronchial infection, which swept through the community at the end of 1826, proved to be the catalyst for her husband's salvation, but not the one that Orvis imagined.

When he first became ill, neither she nor Eastman were overly concerned. On the third and fourth days of his illness he insisted that she keep to her plan of attending a quilting bee at a neighbor's home. Over the next few days, his health declined further and finally after more than a week of illness, the doctor was called in. Apparently the infection was far more serious than the Eastmans initially understood. After his examination of Samuel, the doctor was not optimistic. This truly frightened both Eastmans, but especially Orvis. She knew the plight of widows with children and no head of the house to steer the family ship firsthand from among families of her own acquaintance. In the aftermath of the doctor's revelation to them, they must have discussed those fears, although Orvis did not recount the discussion explicitly in her journal. However, it is clear that Eastman made a promise (presumably to both his wife and his God) to mend his irreligious ways if he recovered.

When his deathbed prayer was answered and Eastman recovered, he acted quickly to fulfill his sickbed promise. As soon as he was physically able, Eastman and Orvis attended the nearest Christian meeting, the Parishville Baptists, nearby. Eastman's choice of church meeting given his wife's professed faith might seem surprising, so to understand we must look to Eastman's parents. Just a generation before the Samuel Eastman Sr. and his wife had been professed Quakers in New England. However, once in Parishville, Samuel Sr. became a founding member of the new Baptist Church. The reason for this shift in religious affiliation is not clear, but it is likely that this familial association with the Baptists is what led the son there. That, and the sheer proximity of the church to their home.

Whatever the impetus, in the weeks following his recovery Eastman turned over a new leaf, much to his wife's relief.

> *. . . Mr E attended conference this eve. I hope the Lord has seen fit to awaken his mind in some measure. He for the first time attempted family prayer. Oh Lord may he Persevere and never omit it again in life. I thank my God that he has heard the prayer of my heart and thus far answered it. Oh that I was more engaged in his cause.*[19]

Eastman's newfound religious enthusiasm delighted his wife, but presented a problem for her as well. Inadvertently, Eastman had chosen to attend the Baptist meeting at the moment when it became enmeshed in the religious upheaval known as the Second Great Awakening. This was a social and religious phenomenon of such epic proportions that the geographic areas where it was most concentrated came to be known as "burned over" by the flame of passionate revivalists.

Eastman was typical of many American men who heeded the revivalists' message. A farmer with a hundred-acre plot of good land along a well-traveled military post road, Eastman was a member of the growing middle class on the New York frontier.[20] An officer in the local militia troop, he had status among his peers. And with a young wife and two young children, he was concerned with the future financial as well as social success of his family. Church membership was increasingly associated with middle-class gentility and the awakening fervor accentuated the growing membership of mainline churches. This would not have been entirely lost on Eastman.

Even before her husband's conversion, Orvis was not unaware of the religious enthusiasm of her day. Although western New York State has been generally understood as one of the more notable "burned over" districts, the flames of religious revivals flared up over much of the northeastern United States. Urban and rural areas alike were affected. Vermont was not immune, as historian Jeffrey Potash has pointed out that awakeners helped to "visibly alter the religious landscape."[21]As a young unmarried woman in Addison County, Vermont, Orvis attended many events in Bristol and Middlebury that featured religious speakers and topics. In September of 1820, she noted that her Uncle John Brooks attended a "camp meeting" that was organized in nearby Charlotte.[22] Moreover, members of Orvis's family would variously experiment with most of the major religious enthusiasms of the day. While her elder brother Loren remained resolutely Quaker and eventually committed to the escape and resettlement of former slaves in his community in Ontario, another brother became a devoted Mormon. Orvis's younger half-brother, John Orvis, became a Transcendentalist and participated in the establishment of Brook Farm with his wife Marianna Dwight. Therefore, the arrival of an awakening spirit in Parishville was neither surprising nor explicitly unwelcome to Orvis, even if it was not in the exact nature of her own religious leanings.

In many ways, Orvis was also typical of most American women who heeded the call of awakeners to ignite the revivalist fires. Historians generally agree that women outnumbered male converts during those years.[23] Attracted to the more emotional message of the revivalist ministers, they internalized a more sympathetic view of themselves as saved individuals rather than as tainted daughters of Eve. Historians of the era describe American women, inspired by the religious renewal of the revival experience, proselytizing their husbands and children. Many of these women believed this effort was an important part of their duties as wives and mothers.[24] Certainly as the ideology of domesticity became more widespread among American, Protestant middle-class families, wives and mothers became the moral centers of the household. In this context, Orvis was clearly part of the mainstream cultural narrative of her day.

Yet, at the same time Orvis could not avoid being personally divided over her husband's new enthusiasm. She was devoted to the customs and traditions of Quakerism. Historians of Quaker philosophy have pointed out that the wave of "domesticity" and its ideal of female moral superiority originated among the Quaker households of the Mid-Atlantic States.[25] Quaker women were respected as spiritual leaders in their households; Orvis would have internalized this validated role early in her life. On the other hand, the awakening enthusiasm in Parishville was centered in the Baptist church. And, the expectations of that sect ran counter to the Quaker spiritual ideals.

Where Second Great Awakening ideology joined with Quaker domesticity, Orvis was assured in her beliefs. She clearly prized her faith and held fast to it even when Friends' meetings were not easily accessible. Indeed, her faith was the central truth within which all other obligations, expectations, and values were rooted. But this was not to be the case when her husband accepted the call to his salvation.

In the aftermath of his new status as a believer, Eastman reversed the roles he and his wife played in household spiritual enlightenment. Eastman's evangelical attraction to the Baptist meeting and his acceptance of this new religious doctrine set the family on a different course, away from his wife's Quaker spiritual foundations. Indeed, it set the stage for a serious marital dispute: this time over Eastman's enthusiasm for baptism as the vehicle for salvation and formal membership in the Parishville Baptist Church. As a Quaker, Orvis rejected the notion of baptism as a necessary component of spiritual salvation; she particularly did not wish her children to be "sprinkled." The couple squarely disagreed.

In the face of Orvis's refusal to accept his lead, Eastman called on the Baptist membership for help. The minister made several visits to their home. In addition, Eastman enlisted his extended family members, who had succumbed to the awakening at the Parishville church, to participate in the process. Throughout the winter and spring after his awakening, Eastman doggedly proselytized Orvis. The greatest friction between the couple arose over the question of baptism for the Eastman children. In the midst of this turmoil, Orvis found herself in a terrible quandary. She had deliberately stepped away from the role of dutiful wife, lost the mantle of spiritual light in her household, and found herself roundly chastised for her recalcitrance. She wrote about it at length:

> *Very wet and muddy indeed. Mr E & myself walked and carried my Babe to the other district, attended meeting. Heard eleven give their relations to the Church, viz; Mrs. Huldah Chase, Parker & Daniel Rose, Mrs. Elizabeth Capil [Capel], Henry Capil [Capel], Lorenzo Hoyt, Lucinda Brownell, Betsey Newton, Josepher Brownell, Patience Simonds, Martha Welch. Returned home after sunset. Went to Mr. Lee's and brought home my little boy. I was by this time very tired indeed with a violent headache. It seemed as though I could not sit up when Mrs. Lee came and insisted on my spending the evening at their house with Mr & Mrs Flower [the Baptist minister and his wife]. I told her I felt as though I could not go; however, I did. My visit was not agreeable, for it was all twitting and ridiculing the Church to which I belonged. I was accused of having a Baptist heart and a Congregational head by my husband. Another says "Samuel will bring her over to be a Baptist." Another says "what are you going to do with your children? They have not been sprinkled, etc." In the frame of mind I was then in and not being able to sit up, disappointed of an agreeable religious visit, (it being Rainy, tarried late), it seemed as if my heart would burst. I waited for my Babe to awaken as long as I could and left her for her Pa'a to bring home when the rain ceased. As soon as I came into the road I burst into tears and prayers until I reached home, that if I was in an error respecting doctrine, that God would direct me in the right way. When I went from home I felt in my mind if I was alone as to sentiment of that Church and all the object of my visiting this evening was thinking possibly sooner or later I might be united with my husband in a peace. possibly some light might be thrown in my darkened mind. But alas I am much farther from it than ever. I feel as if I had not a friend in the*

> *world, my nearest friend against me. But, oh, my God, may I not judge but may God forgive them for they know not what they do. I do not think they meant to injure my feelings but to make me dislike every order but theirs. But their lack of charity drove me from it more than my Bible.*[26]

Eastman was now immersed both literally and figuratively in the affairs of the Baptist church. The church at the "corners" was obviously experiencing a full-on revival; week after week large numbers (sometimes as many as two dozen) were baptized. Interested Baptist members waited expectantly for Orvis to step forward, but she failed to do so. One week her sister-in-law visited and insisted on escorting her to the meeting. Once at the church, Orvis found that Eastman and his supporters had conspired to persuade (or coerce) her to be "immersed" that week. She flatly refused. Instead, she prayed for her and her husband to come to some kind of compromise. Her journal reveals the sadness she felt in going her own way. Yet Orvis could not bring herself to give in to Eastman's demand that she follow him into the Baptist Church fellowship.

> *Sister Betsey [Eastman] came this way alone to meeting and insisted upon my going with her. I knew not why. I have since learned that Elder Culver told her that I was going forward in Baptism. Strange report. She & sister Sophrona were immersed and twenty one others. Oh, God, wilt thou keep them in the strait and narrow path until they should arrive at the Bar. Attended conference this eve but the expressions I heard on the way deprived my mind of that enjoyment I could wish.*[27]

Over the next three years, their struggles continued as evidenced in Orvis's journal entries. She remained adamant, but Eastman wavered between devout observance of the Baptist meetings and going back to his earlier "mis-use" of the Sabbath. When he was enthusiastic, Eastman tried to draw his wife along with him and he was not alone. Orvis's closest female in-laws, Betsey and Sophronia Eastman, immersed members of the church in 1826, tried to use their powers of persuasion on her as well. The pressure brought to bear on Orvis by her husband, the male authority in her life, and her sisters-in-law, the female influence, must have been terrific. And yet for the years covered in the journal, Orvis resisted the pressure to join the Baptists and tried to find a way to continue on her own religious path.

In 1829, several families of Friends (Delong and Harkness) moved to the Parishville area and they, in turn, were visited by Quakers from the Friends' meeting established at Peru, New York. Orvis happily joined in their informal meetings and borrowed religious tracts to read at home. Yet, she remained emotionally torn between her beloved faith traditions and her desire for a tranquil religious communion with her husband. She worried over her disloyalty to her spouse and her family, but could not reconcile with her dislike of the Baptist doctrine—especially the concept of original sin and the need for baptism.

Throughout the period, her husband continued to attend the church "at the corners" for regular and special speakers, sometimes with more enthusiasm than others. Orvis avoided many of these meetings and her internal conflict spilled over into her journal:

> *Alone with my children. while my family and others are gone to hear I fear an imposter. God be with them. I feel a wish to visit my Friends in Vermont but God's will be done if I never see them again until the judgement. I am favored with more earthly blessings than I deserve. I want to live more to the glory of God and see all those around me laying up their treasures in Heaven instead of earth and then our little ones will learn the way. The preacher Mr E. heard today denies the Trinity.*[28]

By the end of 1830 when her journal entries end, the story of religious division in the Orvis/Eastman household remained unresolved. Orvis's literary silence after 1830 leaves only the official records to finish the tale. Despite her misgivings and for reasons kept only to herself, Orvis finally capitulated to her husband's desires. A brief notation indicates that she was baptized into church membership by Elder Brand on October 24, 1838, nearly a dozen years after her husband's first eager attempt to baptize her by stealth. Her final resting place next to her husband in the Parishville Baptist Church cemetery underscores her membership in that church.

Against the backdrop of the "burned over district," the Orvis/Eastman marital strife over the question of which spiritual tradition the family would practice offers an alternative view of the Second Great Awakening and the evangelical work of middle-class American women in their homes. Not everyone (nor every woman) was attracted to the evangelical revivals, and the Great Awakening of the antebellum period may have divided as many homes and families as it united. In the Orvis/Eastman home, the conflict raged for more than a decade and ended with her capitulation. In the absence of her words, we can only speculate as to what circumstances finally facilitated Orvis's conversion.

Chapter Five

"Retired, much fatigued"

On the anniversary of the first year that Orvis took up residence in her new home, perhaps inspired by the appearance of a recently hibernating animal out of his burrow for the first time in early spring, she took stock of her household:

> *Cold, frozen hard. The snow fled. The Chipping Squirrel [Chipmunk] makes his appearance. Washed large wash of linen. One year this day since we took possession of our cottage. Ah what have I done[?] Ah nothing for my maker and but little for my partner. Spun only 73 runs wove seventy yds, one coverlet, knit three pair of socks etc. I hope more for both this year.*[1]

Taken on face value, the tone of this entry ("I hope more for both this year") implies that Orvis believed her exertions as a housewife fell short. Yet, the sum of her labors dutifully recorded in her journal that year paints a very different picture. The small mountain of spun yarn, woven fabric, a bed coverlet, and various knitted items inventoried by Orvis were just the leading edge of a veritable avalanche of manufactured items and food provisions. In addition, the totality of finished goods did not adequately reflect the almost endless array of services Orvis performed for her husband, extended family, and community. Truly, the few items Orvis identified on that early spring day represented only a small fraction of her overall labors that first year.

So, given her daily exertions it is not surprising that Orvis often wrote the phrase, "retired, much fatigued" (or some variation of it) in her journal, and, it was definitely not an affectation. Instead, Orvis's fatigue was the tangible result of the endless and unremitting tasks that fell as a matter of course to a farmwife of her time. In this effort, Orvis was quite typical among her contemporaries. As a woman, wife, and then mother, Orvis carried out a broad range of labors that were often subsumed (and just as often dismissed) under the somewhat innocuous general heading of "housekeeping." Indeed, many women's journals have been disdained by historians because the bulk of their contents focused on "menial housewifery" and not "important" themes and subject matter. A close examination of Orvis's journal reveals how shortsighted that understanding really is; the bland title of housewife veils the considerable labors required to successfully fulfill the average homemaker's duties. A typical woman processed, prepared, and preserved foodstuffs; created textiles, both utilitarian and fancy; constructed clothing items and finished textile goods; manufactured cleaning compounds and soap; compounded and prepared basic medicinal herbals; manufactured various household items such as candles; washed, ironed, and repaired laundry; nursed sick family members and neighbors; nurtured and cared for children and elderly household members as well as neighbors; and, finally, reproduced the family through multiple pregnancies. In short, every day women fed, clothed, and sustained their families' health while they also expanded the family's material wealth through their labors. Orvis's words speak to all of these various occupations, and the story that emerges from her writings is one of unending, if dutiful, toil that demands a deeper understanding of those labors, both for the individuals who accomplished this work and those who benefited from it despite its unwaged status.

At the outset of her marriage, Orvis experienced some anxiety that she was unprepared to carry out her duties. On the day the newly married couple arrived in Parishville, Orvis wrote that she felt "ignorant of labour" and "incapable of filling my station."[2] This seems to have been mainly a nervous reaction to finding herself in the new, strange world of marriage. Evidence drawn from her journal demonstrates that her doubts were groundless. Orvis spent her youth perfecting the necessary householding skills under the tutelage of her "grandma'am" and aunts. In the last few years before her marriage, she performed much of the daily domestic labor in the Brooks's home. So despite her initial angst, she was fundamentally equipped for this new role, even if she felt emotionally unprepared to accept the responsibilities of housewife.

Within a day of her arrival in Parishville, Orvis seems to have shed most of her doubts and immediately set about her work. Within a week, Orvis had already established a routine of housekeeping, food preparation, and domestic manufacture. Indeed, she began to put her energy into the long-term household items needed with the production of twelve dozen candles.[3] Orvis also set about making her new home welcome to guests by unpacking her "going to housekeeping" goods and initiating a round of food preparation that included baking bread, pies, and preparing refreshments to offer visitors.

Almost immediately the couple began to receive the inevitable visitors. No doubt excited to welcome Orvis as a new, permanent member of the neighborhood, the Durfey and Eastman families made multiple calls to the home of the newlyweds. In addition, most of the younger unmarried women in the neighborhood who'd been part of Orvis's original social circle in 1821 made visits to congratulate the couple and renew their friendships. The circle of family and neighbors that socialized with the Eastmans was small by Orvis's standards, but represented the new social world she inhabited. Within a month of their arrival, the newlyweds entertained nearly all of the neighborhood as well as a number of visitors from much farther afield. Orvis served meals and refreshments to all comers as a matter of course; "country hospitality" dictated that this must be so. Moreover, this round sociability was an important part of the melding of the new couple into the community and cementing relationships in the neighborhood, town, and perhaps beyond.[4] How the Eastman/Orvis household fared in these interludes, both in social as well as material terms, helped to establish their status.

Most of the refreshments for these gatherings were brought from Vermont among their "going to housekeeping" supplies. Others were garnered from neighbors or family members or purchased outright. Few of the meal fixings served to guests were procured from the farm since without a wife to engage her skills the previous summer, Samuel Eastman's larder was probably dependent on his mother and sisters who had households of their own to provision. No doubt his skills as a hunter and fisherman were the main source of sustenance until Orvis was installed as his wife. This shortfall would never be repeated; just as soon as the ground thawed and spring arrived, Orvis began the work of preparing her kitchen garden and gathering her own resources to fill the pantry, attic, and larder.

In April Orvis worked up her garden soil, "begged" seeds and other items for the garden from her aunt and uncle Durfey. She also planted seeds she brought from Ferrisburgh, harvested from gardens in Bristol and Ferrisburgh earlier in fall of 1822.[5] By mid-July, her garden began to produce vegetables that she divided between immediate consumption and processing for later use. The size of her garden is not explicit in her journal, but as the summer unfolded, the harvest she described provides a glimpse of the vegetables that she grew. First, green beans and cucumbers began to appear; by mid-August corn and melons were also part of her harvesting work. Although the journal was not precise on this topic, other staple vegetables such as potatoes, leeks, green peas, carrots, pumpkins, and various varieties of squash were undoubtedly harvested. Some of this bounty was served, but much more of it was processed, dried, and stored. It was Orvis's responsibility to put as much of the summer's bounty away as they would need to feed themselves over the coming winter and spring, or the couple would not eat.

Yet, not all of the victuals that were served on the Eastman table were the results of husbandry or horticulture; many dishes offered to guests were decidedly not "domesticated." Throughout the summer months, Eastman and Orvis appeared to have supplemented the family's diet with wild food. Eastman hunted and Orvis gathered beyond his plowed fields or her turned garden beds. Squirrels, pigeons, deer, and fish all found their way onto the family table from hunting and fishing forays. Orvis participated in this use of wild comestibles when she processed what Eastman brought home from hunting, but also processed what she collected. She boiled maple sap into syrup and sugar; picked wild strawberries, blueberries, blackberries, and raspberries as they appeared in season; and fished from the nearby creek herself. She dried berries, salted venison and fish, and made preserves. Although from a modern perspective, these food-gathering and pantry-stocking duties may seem time-consuming and even overwhelming, they were hardly the only tasks that consumed Orvis. Rather, they were only a part of her regular round of tasks and were performed in tandem with many other duties.

Orvis's food gathering and preparation was not simply for human consumption on the Eastman place, because they were not the only mouths to feed on the farm. At the same time that Orvis cooked and provided meals for her husband, family, and guests, she also tended the family livestock that lived in immediate proximity to the farmhouse, including their milch cow, pigs, sheep, and chickens. These animals' welfare was vital since they provided the household with meat, skins, feathers, tallow, eggs, milk, butter, and cheese. Therefore, the care and feeding of these nonhuman members of the farmyard was essential. In addition, Orvis had a vested interest in them as they represented some of the assets she brought to her marriage.

Immediately after their wedding, Orvis's father presented them with two cows from his dairy herd.[6] The trip out from Ferrisburgh had been slow in part because of the need to drive the cows along with the loaded wagon brimming with their collective "going to housekeeping" goods. The cows represented a portion of her future inheritance. Indeed, when Loren Orvis divided his estate in a later will, he referred to the goods and items he'd already lavished on married children, including Orvis. She seems to have held a proprietary attitude toward the cows:

> *More moderate. cannot get along with weaving. my web is very tender. Killed the last cow I had. Good Beef, sold half.*[7]

In practical terms, the minute that Orvis married, Eastman became the rightful owner of anything she possessed and any potential wages she might earn. So, these animals were an important contribution to the future well-being of the family whether Orvis saw them as her husband's, her own, or her future children's property. And she accepted the daily responsibility for them. As the journal demonstrates, it was Orvis who often went to retrieve the "ramblers" when they wandered too far from the farm. It was also Orvis who milked and then churned butter or made cheese from the liquid milk. And, it was Orvis who rendered their bodies into tallow; cooked, dried, and salted their meat; and sewed their hides into various items, including leather mittens.[8]

The benefits from the bovine livestock were supplemented by the other barnyard-dwelling animals, including the sheep. While Orvis rarely mentions them, there was a small flock on the Eastman farm. The utility of sheep as a dual-purpose animal that provided textile fibers and meat was not lost on an astute Yankee farmer such as Eastman. The utility of their yearly production of wool was not lost on a capable farm wife either. Orvis noted when the sheep were sheared or washed as well as when she processed the wool. And, having the experience from the Brooks's farmholding, she was familiar with their care. A few months before her marriage, she copied a remedy for a pernicious sheep parasite from a popular agricultural journal. This was surely in preparation for the care of her own flock.[9]

In addition to the cows and sheep, the Eastman farm produced and sold a large quantity of pork. Each fall, Orvis noted the butchering, rendering, and weight of the pigs they slaughtered. Between 1825 and 1827, Orvis recorded more than twenty-seven pigs butchered; the total weight of these animals is difficult to estimate, but by Orvis's own tally there was at least four and a half tons of meat produced. Orvis fed at least some of these pigs herself:

> *I have as much as I can do to wait upon him, the children and* keep potatoes boiled for the Hogs. (My emphasis)[10]

Whether or not she fed all the pigs on the farm herself, Orvis did participate in the processing of their carcasses. The result for this harvest was a combination of hams, bacon, sausages, mince pies, animal fat tallow, and the income from the marketed surplus.[11]

Perhaps most important to Orvis's everyday larder and household concerns, were her poultry flock, likely a wedding present given to her by "Uncle Brooks."[12] When the hens were laying, the eggs Orvis collected would have been an important staple in her cooking. Chickens past laying—or superfluous roosters—would have become part of her meat pies, stews, and so on. In addition to the culinary use of the chickens, Orvis saved and sorted the plucked feathers, used them in the manufacture of bedding and other household items. Over all, the poultry would have been kept close as they would have been in the most danger from local predators. And because they lived in the "dooryard" of the farmhouse, the responsibilities for the care, feeding and culling the flock would have fallen to Orvis.

As she folded herself into the daily workings of the farm, Orvis assumed more than just her responsibilities as a housewife, she also became a full partner in the ongoing collective labor of farm life as it was lived in Parishville. At harvest time, she worked by her husband's side in the field. At other times she supported the work from her kitchen.

For instance, in order to accomplish the heavy fieldwork on his farm, Eastman participated in a round of collective work gangs that went from farm to farm to break new ground, plow fields, plant crops, bring in the hay, pick the corn crop, and harvest the field grains. This pattern of farmers sharing their labor and plow animals across property lines was an ancient practice that made as much sense on the New York frontier in the 1820s as it did in earlier times elsewhere. In addition, the nature of their family-owned acreage meant that Eastman had already forged a pattern of shared labors with his father and brothers before his marriage. Extending that outward to new neighbors, related or not, cemented important economic and social ties in the community. When the work bees moved to the Eastman farmland, feeding the workmen fell to Orvis, who prepared and sometimes delivered their meals into the fields where they worked. At times she also provided sleeping arrangements for those who lived too far to travel home in the evenings. Consider these brief entries:

[Mond 18 August, 1823]

Washed. prepared dinner for ten men. took cold. the first corn.

[Tues 19 August 1823]

Pleasant. ten men again. unable to sit up much today.

Wedn 20 August 1823]

Pleasant. seven men. Picked pigeons. visited at Mr. Rockwell's.

Thus, the demands of casual country hospitality and the support of her husband's work customs kept Orvis busy. Throughout the growing and harvest seasons, Orvis expected to feed an additional eight to ten working men at times when Eastman's fields were the focus of production. And, these duties came in addition to her own round of harvesting and preservation that put food on the Eastman table in the depths of the winter.

While the physical landscape of Saint Lawrence County attested to the labors of the men who carved farm fields and pastures from the wilderness, the material comfort of the homesteads dotting the landscape was in the hands of industrious farmwives. As such, Orvis did not just "do housework" in the Eastman home, she manufactured in whole or part most of the items that made life more comfortable. For instance, Orvis's efforts to keep her "cottage" tidy meant that she not only had to sweep or mop, but she also had to formulate the ingredients for a clean home. To that end, Orvis made her own soap from wood ashes, lye, and animal tallow. She washed her floors, linen, babies, and dishes with variations of this same cleansing agent. Her first solo foray into the manufacture of soap occurred within a month of her arrival at the farm:

> *A pedlar of Essence dined with us. commenced making soap for the first time in my life. Bought half oz. Camphor.*[13]

Perhaps the camphor she purchased became part of her soap production, although she was not often specific about ingredients unless she recorded a recipe.

Another cleaning product Orvis manufactured began with the collection of pine boughs. After gathering the branches complete with their needles intact, she boiled them down and skimmed the essential oils that floated to the surface. These oils became the foundation for the pine cleaner she used on the floors and woodwork of her home. The residual "tea" left behind after the oil was skimmed could also be used as an astringent solution to wash wounds, treat diaper rash, or soothe insect bites.

Aside from cleaning agents, Orvis also constructed her own cleaning tools. She wove utilitarian cloths for toweling, diapers, feminine napkins, and dish rags from yarns spun on her wheel and perhaps from flax grown in her own fields. In addition, Orvis created the specialized yarn she used to fit up her household mop, as she noted in her journal: "spun doubled twisted yarn for a mop."[14]

Finally, to achieve a clean, presentable home, Orvis crushed lime and chalk, blended the crushed minerals with milk or water, and created a utilitarian whitewash paint. Used as a sealer on the log walls of her home, this homemade paint was probably the makeshift measure that made living in a log home without plastered walls more palatable. While whitewashing the interior walls would have limited the dirt and dust shedding off the rough-hewn logs, and may have discouraged insects from taking up permanent residence, the act of painting the dark walls would also have brightened an otherwise drab (and primitive) interior. As she noted wryly, "A log house is a dirty thing."[15]

Within those whitewashed walls, many of the creature comforts enjoyed by the Eastmans were also due largely to Orvis's manufacturing efforts. The piles of feathers plucked from the Eastman poultry, as well as the wild geese and pigeons taken in hunting forays, filled pillow biers, softened seat chairs, and fluffed bed ticks and bedding. The candles that illuminated their winter evenings were manufactured from tallow rendered from animal fat and wicks spun from her own tow fibers. Indeed, she produced more than thirty-dozen candles in that first year of housekeeping. Surprisingly, she did not include this in the year-end memorial tally. Perhaps this was because candles, like foodstuffs, constantly disappeared. Furthermore, candles were in many ways a byproduct of her food processing (tallow rendering) and her prodigious textile labors (flax spinning); perhaps she grouped them into a category of everyday items, which she ignored in her "inventory" because of their commonplace nature. Conceivably the primary reason her inventory focused on her textiles was simply because they were the more tangible and durable evidence of her home manufacturing. This would explain why she recounted the yarns and yard goods in greater detail over almost everything else in her first anniversary compilation. Finally, she may have taken great pleasure and pride in the creative nature of this work; textiles were not only the most obvious and durable fruit of her labors, they may also have been the most visually appealing. More than 6,000 yards of yarn and 70 yards of cloth, not to mention the other cloth items, is a prodigious output for one woman working without supplemental help and with the burdens of all the additional work of the household.

The textiles manufactured in the Eastman home were as varied in substance and style as the available technology and fibers allowed, although Orvis chiefly produced utilitarian linen and woolen cloth. For both of these fabric types, there was a great deal of preparation to make fibers into finished articles. For flax, the process began in the farm field. While it is not clear if Orvis grew her own flax or procured it from a neighbor, she did process the flax plants into viable fibers, yarn, and linen cloth. Orvis wrote of these activities; she hatcheled flax fibers, combed them in preparation for spinning, sorted the various fibers for different outcomes, and spun them into assorted types of linen thread.[16] Herein lay the frugal nature of frontier huswifery which led Orvis to "waste not, want not" as she processed the flax for spinning; the finer flax filaments were separated from the more coarse fibers. The various grades of fibers were set aside for specific uses. The "roughest" fibers were spun into the tow yarn that Orvis used for candle wicks as well as a practical twine that would have had a broad range of uses in her household and farmyard. The finer combed flax was spun into yarns bound for her loom. These would have been woven into a variety of fabrics, including shirting, sheeting, toweling, underclothes, baby diapers, aprons, and cheese cloth. Linen could also be bleached white as well as dyed to produce colorful fabrics for home goods and clothing.

Aside from her prodigious linen production, Orvis also manufactured woolen yarns and fabrics. Wool processing was somewhat less onerous than that of linen. Sheared fleeces were washed, picked clean of debris, carded and then spun into a variety of yarn weights, depending on what the finished article might be. The yarns could also be plied together to increase the weight and density of the intended end product. Yarns, single strands or worsted, were knitted into a variety of goods, including stockings, mittens, hats, and scarves. Orvis also wove woolen yarns into a variety of fabric types, plain and more fancy, for bed covers, bed curtains, blankets, and heavier outer clothing of all sorts. Given the harsh conditions of a frontier cabin and the long North Country winters, all of this industry guaranteed that Orvis's family members would be warm, dry, and protected from the weather. Her husband wore the stockings she knitted for his comfort; her babies were swaddled in the warm blankets she wove.[17]

In the first year of her marriage, unencumbered by children, Orvis also produced yarns, fabric, and sewn goods on consignment to her neighbors to supplement the Eastman household economy. Her work sometimes took her into neighbor's homes as she produced fabrics on the Durfey's loom (which she later borrowed for her own use), spun yarn for the Squire family, and sewed various clothing items for other neighbors. Of course, this flurry of outwork was accomplished between and alongside of her own "choring." For Orvis, this was business as usual, since she had always performed her household duties at the Brooks's home alongside her independent work to earn money for school tuition and board. After her marriage, the enticement of school was not there to motivate her, but, in her new circumstances, she remained vigorous in her efforts. Clearly, Orvis supplemented the household income and brought many valuable goods and comforts to the Eastman home. All of these efforts were directed at creating the civilized haven she imagined for her family. Finally, the sheer volume of Orvis's labors, the litany of chores, and list of manufactures for just that first year of marriage endures as an astonishing chronicle of one woman's tireless dedication to her family. Equally amazing is the fact that for nearly five months of that year, Orvis toiled away in spite of the debilitating effects of her first successful pregnancy.

At first, the daily entries in her journal do not reveal her condition; she wrote of being "unwell" or experiencing lameness or rheumatism. As her pregnancy progressed through the winter, Orvis began to write indirectly of her coming confinement. Most revealing was her shift from textile outwork to linen and woolen items for the "one who was unknown."[18] Between January and April, her spinning, weaving, and sewing efforts included articles she referred to as "shirtees," "small nightgowns," and small blankets. In other words, the work on her first layette had quietly commenced. Throughout the early spring, Orvis stockpiled clothes and other needful items for the coming baby. On the 5th of May, she wrote that she had completed the "fiftieth garment for my unborn." The next day she ventured out for a long walk accompanied by several of the women who eventually assisted with her birthing; perhaps this walk was intended to bring along the cramps she felt from the 5th onward to a full-blown labor. If that was the intention, the walk was successful, as the hard birth pains began almost immediately when she returned home that afternoon. Early the next morning, Orvis sent her husband to "procure assistance" for her. Finally, later that day on May 7th, the first of her eleven children, Henry, was born.

Orvis's entry into motherhood may have fulfilled her feminine destiny, but it also launched her into a new phase of her life with expanded demands on her labor and her health. In most ways, Orvis's first pregnancy and childbirth experiences were fairly typical of her time. With the fertility of youth and no birth control, such pregnancies were inevitable. While she may have had an early pregnancy that ended with a spontaneous miscarriage, Orvis became pregnant again about six months after her marriage, and three months after her first anniversary her son was born. Throughout her pregnancy, Orvis continued with the same rhythm of household and manufacturing work. Her pace only seems to slow in the final weeks of her third trimester. When she ultimately went into labor, Orvis did not face the birth alone. Instead, her labors were assisted by three women of her neighborhood: Ruth Brooks (her aunt), Mrs. Rockwell, and Mrs. Flower. All of these women were experienced mothers and had a working knowledge of the mechanics of childbirth; and, undoubtedly due to their collective experience as well as Orvis's youth and health, her labor and her first son's birth seems to have passed with no major difficulties. Mother and child thrived; the immediate threat from her travail was averted.

In the initial week afterward, her attendants as well as other neighborhood women, including her favorite sister-in-law Betsey Eastman, came in to help the new mother transition from childbed back to full health. By the end of that time, despite some unspecified difficulties with breastfeeding, Orvis was on the mend. However, she remained anxious over the health of her newborn. She wrote that the "babe was worrisome, but tolerable well."[19] Nine days after Henry's birth, Orvis dismissed her nurse and reassumed her household responsibilities. But, all was not well. Subsequent entries in her journal demonstrate that Orvis struggled to regain her momentum under the double burden of a fractious newborn and uncertain health. She caught a cold and then displayed symptoms of a fever. Almost as soon as she began to emerge from her own postpartum illness, the baby, now named Henry, became ill and showed signs of developing a disturbing bout of fever and diarrhea. This was serious because Orvis's child was born in the late spring just before the season of "summer complaints" that often carried infants and weakened postpartum women off. Orvis worried that she was not coming back to health as quickly as she hoped and Henry was not thriving as he should.

No doubt some of this worry was the result of "first-time mother" phantom apprehensions, but Orvis had genuine concerns for a sick baby. After all, she knew from experience that babies were vulnerable to many illnesses, including all the epidemic diseases, measles, scarlet fever, and whooping cough, as well as more insidious illnesses. The "summer complaint" could dangerously dehydrate an infant and carry them off without warning.

The sudden death of the Wright infant is a case in point. In August of 1823, this child simply died in the night with little warning.[20] His death could have been an accident (many children smothered in their parents' bed) or due to a fast-moving infection undetected until too late. Certainly, there was a spate of severe illnesses and deaths in that month among the neighbors surrounding the Wright child's demise. On the 7th of July, Orvis visited Nathan Rockwell a neighbor living north of Caleb Wright's home. She found him "very ill." In the intervening month, there was sickness and death in the Sampson, Brand, Thomas, and Wright homes. Orvis's fears for her own son were validated by her own experience nursing the sick in her immediate community.

Orvis's anxieties were also for herself. While they were rooted in her family's history and her mother's premature death from puerperal fever, the fear of death from the rigors of childbirth was widespread and often expressed in nineteenth-century America.[21] Most women accepted that with each pregnancy they faced the possibility of their own death. Indeed, given the influence of Christian teachings, many American women were taught that the pain, suffering, and possible death were Eve's legacy to them. As a professed Quaker, Orvis may not have entirely internalized this negative inheritance of original sin, but she did lose her mother mainly as a result of her own birth. It is no surprise that she believed this pregnancy—or any of the ones that followed—could be lethal. Indeed, with no effective contraception available, women of Orvis's time faced this fearful reality many times as they experienced multiple pregnancies. According to the available statistics in nineteenth century America, the risk of death became greater with each passing pregnancy.[22] Since this regular cycle of pregnancy and childbirth characterized the greatest proportion of their adult lives, Orvis and her contemporaries lived constantly with the specter of premature death just over their shoulders.

In this respect, Orvis was very much an average American woman—perhaps even above average in her reproductive efforts. The statistics available on this period establish that most American women bore more than seven live children during their fertile years. Orvis outpaced this by birthing eleven live children, ten of whom lived beyond infancy. Between 1823 when she married and 1843 when her last child was born, Orvis spent almost half that period, the equivalent of nine years' time, pregnant; the other half of those years she spent nursing her infants. As more children arrived with each passing year, her duties expanded to include the care and early education of toddlers and small children. One presumes that the phrase "retired, much fatigued" could describe most of Orvis's nights in those twenty-plus years.

Another source of anxiety for Orvis was in the debilitating effects of pregnancy. As a young farmwife, Orvis was expected to shoulder a great proportion of the household labor as well as the care of the children. Until her daughters, Mary and Lucinda, were old enough to provide some help to their mother, Orvis toiled on mostly alone with only periodic help from neighbors. Each new pregnancy surely took its toll on her health and vigor and no doubt made it more difficult to carry out her responsibilities. Indeed not all of Orvis's pregnancies terminated in a live birth. Aside from the possibility of a miscarriage in 1823, Orvis clearly suffered a miscarriage in July 1829; this was her fourth pregnancy. In the days approaching, her regular workload was complicated by warm weather, the care of three young children, and neighborhood commissions for textile work. The toll of her burdens resulted in what she called a spontaneous abortion.

> *In great distress, abortion followed, in great distress through the day. Mother E [Eastman] spent a part of the day with me. Aunt Brooks the night, as comfortable as I could expect. very weak.*[23]

While this miscarriage did not disrupt the alternating birth years of her children, it did mean that she actually sustained more than one pregnancy in the months between March 1828 and July 1830. Later, between the birth of her last two children, Sarah and the second son named Joseph, she likely experienced a third miscarriage. While historians have been unable to calculate the number and effects of miscarriage on American women accurately, Orvis's experiences provide us with a window on these episodes in her life, especially the 1829 occurrence.[24] After this miscarriage, Orvis stayed in bed for more than a week and was unable to attempt even the lightest of duties. A neighborhood girl lived in and several of her neighbors, including her mother-in-law and her Aunt Brooks, came by to help with the nursing. More than a month passed before Orvis was able to leave her bed for more than a few moments, and it was two months before she resumed her normal routine. Yet, by the middle of October, only three months after the miscarriage, Orvis was already pregnant with James. These miscarriages plus the live births of her eleven children mean that Orvis sustained at least thirteen and likely fourteen pregnancies over her fertile years,+ and the physical strain to her body compounded her vulnerability to injury and illness associated with childbearing.

While we do not know the specific effects on Orvis's vitality in the long term, historians of women's health have described a series of common physical disabilities that affected women as a direct result of pregnancy. For instance, the violence of birth could and did cause tears in the perineal tissues, postpartum infections, and holes in the bladder or rectum, The most debilitating and painful of these were the vaginal tract "fistula," or holes in the bladder or rectum walls that caused leaking through the vaginal opening. In the absence of any surgical relief, these kinds of conditions condemned women to suffer for the rest of their lives.[25] Another common gynecological complaint was prolapsed uteri—or "fallen womb"—for which there was little effective treatment available in Orvis's time.

If Orvis escaped the pain and indignity of the various postpartum problems rampant among women in this period, she still faced the single most serious problem: multiple recurring pregnancies. And, in a twist of fate, the survival of ten of the children born to her made this burden more arduous. Although on the face of this statistic, it would seem that Orvis was particularly adept (and lucky) at keeping her children healthy and seeing them into adulthood, this also meant she was increasingly burdened with the work of feeding, clothing, caring for, and teaching her large brood with the successful birthing of each new infant.

Perhaps the greatest casualty of Orvis's fertile years is the demise of most of her leisure pursuits such as reading, letter writing, and her daily journaling. As more children were born, her regular writing habit certainly suffered. Gaps begin to appear and her last entries were sparse and intermittent. This is the condition of the journal the year of James's birth; he was her fourth child and fifth pregnancy and seems to have tipped the balance. After that, Orvis seems to have lost the time to write. Between July and October of 1830 (when she made her very last regular entry), the daily inscriptions are short and more erratic. At long last, the multiple burdens of good neighbor, housewife, and mother forced her to give up her journal, and her oft-written refrain—"Retired, much fatigued"—was lived rather than inscribed.

Chapter Six

"He cumbers the ground no more"

Throughout her married life, Orvis struggled to maintain a balance between the work and cares in her husband's log house along the road from Hopkinton and her responsibilities as a neighbor and Parishville community member.[1] At times, her neighbors' cares superseded her own. This was especially true when disease threatened the community. In July of 1828, the weather was extremely hot and humid; consequently the dreaded summer season illnesses ran rampant in Parishville that year. In the space of a month, four young women of Orvis's neighborhood died. In the custom of a good neighbor, she visited the sick households and offered her help to the families. In the end, she also helped to prepare the body of one of the young women, Mary Rockwell, the sixteen-year-old daughter of a neighboring family. Orvis must have felt great sorrow as she participated in the death ritual of the little girl who had surely been well known and loved by the Eastmans. To be sure, this was certainly not the first death that Orvis had witnessed, but it was the first time she had been called upon to "put a body in a coffin" for burial.[2] So, it was an emotional tie to the Rockwells as well as her responsibility as a neighbor that compelled Orvis to lay the girl in her final repose.

Although this experience of placing a body in the coffin was a new one for Orvis, the regularity of death was dreadfully familiar. Before and after her marriage, Orvis helped to care for the dying and no doubt witnessed the final passing of many family members and neighbors from the time she was old enough to help with nursing duties. Moreover, she was well aware that death could be sudden and capricious in its visitation on unsuspecting families. Long before she arrived in Parishville, Orvis participated in the rituals of sitting with the dying, attending the funerals of old and young, men and women, babies and children; these experiences had instilled in her a sense of the brevity of life at the same time they informed her Christian piety.

The common pervasive illness that seems to have taken Mary Rockwell that summer was also something of which Orvis had knowledge and experience; she referred to it as "Cholera morbus" in her journal. Known generally today as gastroenteritis—or dysentery—this disease is primarily an inflammation of the small intestine accompanied by vomiting, diarrhea, and severe dehydration.[3] Throughout the nineteenth century, epidemics of this kind occurred most frequently in the summer and early fall, most likely because of the heat, humidity, and likelihood of bacterial contamination in food and drinking water. The combination of seasonal occurrence and diarrhea earned the disease yet another designation: "summer bowel complaint." As we have seen, *Cholera morbus*, sometimes also called *Cholera infantus*, was extremely dangerous for infants and the elderly, whose immune responses and general ability to recover from the extreme dehydration that accompanied the illness was not as good as relatively healthy adolescents and adults. Others who had weakened constitutions, women with advanced pregnancies, or anyone with a compromised immune system were also susceptible. Orvis's own experiences taught her that no one was immune; she experienced the disease nearly every summer she kept her journal, and it is in its pages that she recorded the hopeful recipe for its cure:

> *Cure for the Choleras Morbus "Put one spoonful of hot ashes into a tumbler of old Cider. give the patient three table spoonfuls of it. the cure will be affected in half of an hour."*[4]

As Orvis's "cure" demonstrates, nineteenth-century people, physicians and laypeople alike, knew little of what caused the illness, or how to properly treat it.[5] These so-called cures were largely ineffective and based on individual doctors' and healers' instincts. Thus, medical treatments ranged from humble and palliative to heroic and extremely toxic; none of those available were very effective.

The more humble therapies were primarily futile, but not too sinister. These were less likely to severely exacerbate the disease; doctors and country healers variously used combinations of vinegar, cider, wood ashes, salt, honey, and various herbals. As we have seen in Orvis's journal, they also recommended dosing patients with a range of treatments such as "hot ashes combined in a tumbler of cold cider." More ambitious physicians attempting to demonstrate "professional" and "scientific" approaches to the treatment of disease might prescribe the use of drugs and other substances, either ingested or injected. Laudanum, emetics, and opium were the chief medications prescribed. Even more toxic were the equivalent of alchemical medicine; these featured the use of toxic and heavy metals such as mercury. Few doctors advocated the most effective treatment available: the careful rehydration of patients.[6]

The inevitable result of these inadequate treatments was a perennial harvest of infants and elderly from among the stricken that Orvis and her contemporaries could not help but be aware.

The single-most dreaded of the epidemic diseases of Orvis's day was smallpox. Not only was smallpox highly contagious, it was very often fatal; even when it was not mortal, this terrible disease had the potential to severely disable and disfigure its victims. As we have seen, the arrival of smallpox in Vermont triggered an immediate and vigorous response to preserve the common good. In response to the two major outbreaks in Bristol, the town fathers moved quickly to isolate the victims to prevent the spread of the airborne virus. They also made inoculation available to townspeople at these same sites to create a larger pool of immunity among members of their community. This response was no doubt a result of the combination of the perennial reappearance of the disease, especially in frontier communities, but also a horrific and relatively recent outbreak that killed hundreds of patriot soldiers, camp followers, and a few British troops in southern Quebec in 1775–76 during the ill-fated American attempt to invade and capture British Canada. A witness, Dr. Lewis Beebe, described the scene:

[7 June 1776]

Here in the hospital is to be seen at the same time some dead, some dying, some at the point of death. . . . Visited some of the sick in the hospital was moved with a compassionate feeling for poor distressed soldiers. . . . [who are] left to take care of themselves.

[17 June 1776]

Scarcely a tent upon this isle but what contains one or more in distress and continually groaning and calling for relief, but in vain! Requests of this nature are as little regarded as the singing of crickets in a summers evening . . . The most shocking of all spectacles was to see a large barn crowded full of men with this disorder, many of whom could not see, speak, or walk. One, nay, two had large maggots, an inch long, crawl out of their ears, were on almost every part of the body.

[3 July 1776]

Death is now a daily visitant in the camp.[7]

There were certainly Revolutionary War veterans in Addison County, Vermont, and Saint Lawrence County, New York, who witnessed the horrific conditions of that outbreak. They brought home descriptions of the corpses with terrible lesions and the daily burial of an almost endless supply of bodies hurried into mass graves with little ceremony at Quebec City, Fort Chambly, and Fort Saint Jean, Quebec.[8]

Even those who had not been eyewitnesses heard the macabre stories through the military and civilian grapevines; terrible suffering, lingering death, and piles of wasted bodies dominated the accounts. Moreover, survivors carried the scars from the terrible disease for all to observe for their entire lives. Closer to home and more recent, the 1798 epidemic activated a swift and concerted response. This was born of an older mentalité that recognized the high rate of infection—some claim 100 percent from the respiratory strain—that smallpox contagion brought.[9] The tried and true method of containing an outbreak by quarantine had been practiced for as long as English colonists occupied the New England territories. As a child, Orvis probably heard stories of the pest house erected on a corner of her grandfather's Bristol farm in 1798, in response to the medical emergency. Certainly, she knew a number of her neighbors and relatives acquired their immunity as a result.

The same year Orvis recorded the cure for "Cholera Morbus" in Parishville, Bristol was visited again by smallpox. Just as the original 1798 epidemic was brought to the village by a businessman who traveled from Canada, the 1820 epidemic stemmed from a similar expedition made by a journeyman clothier, Philip Vadakin. Upon his return to Bristol in January 1820, he attended a Sunday meeting, tended his shop, and consequently came into contact with, as well as potentially infected, a substantial number of townsfolk. Again, the village authorities quickly moved to isolate or inoculate as many individuals as possible who were exposed. A new pest house intended to isolate the infectious was built away from the village; several area physicians were called into assist, and the actual death toll was contained to Vadakin. As in 1798, many were infected, either by inoculation or exposure, and the survivors developed immunity. Moreover, the 1820 outbreak was tempered by the availability of a cowpox-derived vaccination technique developed by Edward Jenner in 1798.[10] Despite this, outbreaks of smallpox did continue to erupt in communities across the frontier. In Parishville, the disease made its appearance in April of 1829, although Orvis did not elaborate on the effects of this particular episode.

In addition to smallpox, Orvis witnessed many other waves of epidemic disease first in Vermont and then in New York. Between 1803 and 1820, there were repeated epidemics of "canker rash" (scarlet fever), measles, mumps, and whooping cough in Bristol. As in the case of many of these diseases, those most affected were infants and small children since they were the "virgin soil" the disease took root in. However, the elderly and infirm could also fall victim.

These diseases also appeared in Parishville; such visitations occurred with frightening regularity. Throughout the period of the journal (and long after its close), there were constant reminders of the danger to the neighborhood children as infants and young toddlers of friends, relatives, and neighbors often succumbed despite the valiant efforts of their mothers. Even before her first child was born, Orvis knew the risks. In May 1823, only a few months after moving to Parishville, Orvis noted that there were "mumps in the town."[11] Three days later she noted that her new neighbors, the Chase family, had lost an infant.[12] While she did not expressly connect the arrival of mumps and the death of the Chase baby in the document, these two events were likely related.

By the end of July, several people died from mumps and complications associated with the disease, including a young neighbor that had visited earlier, Lucinda Thomas. Other victims were variously, and sometimes permanently, affected since mumps had the potential to cause sterility in affected males. The annual cycles of scarlet fever, whooping cough, mumps, and measles threaded their way through the settlement, spreading quickly from one home to the next, through contact at the common school. One particularly virulent episode of measles occurred in the spring and early summer of 1826. In March, Lucius Brooks, Orvis's young cousin, became ill. Following this first notation of a sick relative, Orvis chronicled the spread of the disease as she noted that the (Samuel Sr.) Eastman, Sampson, Oliver, Hazen, Selah, Wells, Chase, and Converse households were all afflicted. In each home there were multiple cases; by the time the disease burned itself out several months later, many families sustained losses. From that one outbreak there had been at least ten deaths, half of them infants. For Orvis, this was especially troubling as her new daughter, Mary Elizabeth, was less than two months old. In this case, the Eastmans were very lucky; Mary Elizabeth did not succumb, although Orvis still suffered an important loss that spring.

Shortly after the last reported death from measles in late June, Orvis's Aunt Brooks became seriously ill.[13] Her final illness seems not to have been associated with the measles epidemic; rather she seems to have been suffering from a fever associated with childbirth. If so, Brooks was the exception to the other adults who passed away that spring; several other families lost adult members in the measles outbreak, including the Sampsons, Hazens, and Selahs.

Although Orvis often noted neighbors and relatives' maladies in her journal, after her children were born, she became even more absorbed by such concerns. In May 1824, as her first child was born she noted both her relief at surviving delivery and the worry associated with her role: "*thanks to my God it will never be a mother*" (my emphasis).[14]

Her comment reveals the depth of her anxieties and connects them to her gender. Men simply did not have the same apprehensions as women and for very explicit reasons. While they certainly loved their wives and children, it was their wives who invested their whole bodies into the enterprise of family building. As we have already noted, women spent most of their adult lives gestating, birthing, and caring for their children in an uncertain dangerous world. Orvis clearly felt the weight of that great responsibility and was reluctant to bequeath it to a daughter. Eventually daughters were born to the Eastmans, but for that first moment of motherhood, Henry's sex seems to have been a comfort to her. A man would not carry her burdens.

While the first year of caring for Henry was no doubt fraught with "first-time-mother" jitters, it also seems clear that she developed a vigilance for the quality of his health (and all his siblings) that seems to border on the obsessive. Eventually, Orvis experienced the same loss as many families in her neighborhood: the 1841 death of her sixth child, Joseph; his illness the result of one of these childhood plagues.

Other illnesses that beleaguered the Orvis/Eastman household are as familiar as the perennial colds, influenzas, and nonspecific fevers that still make the rounds more than two hundred years later. For instance, in 1807, a virulent strain of influenza that was widespread and deadly flashed across Addison County (New England, generally). Periodic waves of influenza made their way from the port towns into the hinterland, usually via travelers carrying the viruses. During the War of 1812, there were several waves of an unspecified "spotted fever" that caused "many deaths in Bristol" and seemed to affect a broad spectrum of victims since, as one antiquarian wrote: "no sex, age or condition was exempt."[15]

Aside from epidemic disease and viral outbreaks, another potentially mortal contagion, endemic both in the Vermont and New York backcountry, was pulmonary consumption (tuberculosis). Consumption is a disease that mainly affected the lungs, but could spread to other systems of the body and cause a systemic failure generally. The broad-spectrum effect of "consumption" was a progressive weakening of the body with bouts of respiratory difficulty until the victim finally succumbed to a secondary lung infection. In Orvis's day, there were no treatments for consumption and little understanding of the disease. Physicians believed that the disease was caused primarily by poor diet, poor hygiene, and environmental factors such as "impure air" or "unhealthy climate." Treatment was as varied and decidedly unhealthy as those intended for *Cholera Morbus*.

In an 1835 treatise on pulmonary consumption, Sir James Clark noted specific therapies in common use. These included ingesting toxic substances such as mercury, iodine, antimony, and alkaline—or, the use of purgatives and emetics. There was also a common belief in the efficacy of bloodletting, the application of counterirritants such as blistering, and an assortment of inhalation therapies; inhalation of tar vapors was considered efficacious, for instance. The less invasive treatments included imbibing mineral water (especially sulfurous) and bodily immersion in ice cold water. The cumulative effect of these "cures" was almost certainly not a return to good health.[16]

Orvis certainly knew people who developed the disease. In May of 1827, she noted that Mr. Wing (possibly a relative through the Rogerses) had died of consumption. Later that same year she got a letter from Vermont with news of the death of her Aunt Lovina Brooks's father, John Hawkins. Within the immediate family circle, Orvis's maternal uncle, David Brooks became ill in 1825. In the case of David Brooks, the opinion of his family was that his "consumption" was the result of his settling in the unhealthy Cuyahoga County, Ohio, territory. Five years after Brooks emigrated, he informed his family via letters that he was ill. Orvis received one of Brooks's missives and noted it along with other family illnesses in her journal:

> *Pleasant. Washed some. Ironed, made a shirtee. received a letter from my Father stating that Brother Eleazar had lost the use of the left part of his face and Sister Elizabeth was sick and had been seven weeks. Heard Uncle David Brook[s], Ohio, was sick of a consumption. Spent most of the day in tears. While my friends experience loss of health I enjoy it without returning any thanks to my God for his mercy.*[17]

Closer to the Eastman home, and perhaps to her heart, was the illness and death of Adolphus Taylor, husband of her old friend Orra Copeland and her own first love. Taylor contracted the disease and died prematurely at the age of forty-three. Since Taylor's 1841 demise occurred after the close of the journal, we do not have Orvis's firsthand comments on her loss, but given her continued relationship with the Taylors, she would have been aware of his illness and mourned his untimely death.

Disease was not the only harbinger of mortality in Orvis's experience. Accidents and other events brought their own measure of sorrow into her life and that of her family and neighbors. Just a month before Orvis commenced her journal in 1820, her cousin Amos Brooks drowned in a mill pond in Ferrisburgh.[18] Drowning in raging spring torrents were frequent in a time when country bridges were often constructed of tree trunks covered with wooden planks—or rivers were forded directly. In the space of just a few years, Orvis recounted a near-drowning incident involving herself, a Nicholson cousin swept away in the Boquet River in the spring flood of 1821, and a neighbor drowned at the fordway crossing of the New Haven River at Beaman's Hollow. Other unexpected fatal and near-fatal accidents also took their toll on Orvis's friends, family, and neighbors.

While attending school in Middlebury, a friend and former beau, Elisha Dunham, fell from his horse and died from internal injuries.[19] In another accident, a journeyman chair caner in Bristol was nearly killed in pursuit of his raw materials:

> *Pleasant shower. starched Ironed and mended. wove five yards. Mr. James Taylor came here to bottom chairs. In getting his bark a limb fell upon his head, knocked him down and broke in to [two]. Wonder it had not killed him.*[20]

While Dunham's internal injuries were impossible to treat given the medical expertise at the time, even simple injuries could mean serious trouble. The lack of antibiotics or treatments for infections in Orvis's time would have guaranteed that even simple cuts and scratches could lead to terrible consequences if bacteria or gangrene got a foothold in a body. An overnight guest in 1828 left Orvis's bed clothes so soiled that she washed on a day not normally devoted to laundry:

Washed. An old soldier spent the night. Was obliged to wash my coverlet on his account. He had a number of wounds.[21]

The image of this poor man's suppurating wounds almost a decade after the end of the War of 1812 offers a particularly poignant tableau. The plain fact was that there was little in the way of specific treatments that could heal open wounds. Thus, each injury that penetrated the skin was a possible entryway for infections that could mean the loss of a limb, if not a death sentence.

Death could also be a result of moral turpitude. Orvis was undoubtedly exposed to the enthusiastic rants—written or spoken—of evangelicals who decried the general sinfulness of American society and the need for a renewed salvation, or face terrible death. One of the particular social ills targeted by this kind of jeremiad sermon was overindulgence in alcohol. Temperance became the watchword of aspiring middle-class men and women and paralleled the rise of evangelical philosophies. In her case, Orvis feared her husband's intemperance would be his undoing. Throughout the first few years of her marriage, Orvis commented on her husband's love of drink, her fears for his health and her fears of the effect it would have on their children. For his part, Eastman seems to have ignored his wife's warnings. Militia training days were excuses for Eastman and his brothers to overindulge at Durfey's tavern. This state of affairs did not change until Eastman succumbed to the persuasion of the awakener message. It is also likely he was drawn to the righteousness of Temperance at the same time. But Orvis did not miss an opportunity to reinforce her desire for his continued sobriety. One such observation percolates to the surface in 1830:

Wrote late at night to J.B. Isham, Vt. Mr Ira Farnam died last Tuesday at Hogansburgh in consequence of ardent liquor, a warning to all.[22]

Chronic illnesses also made life difficult. Uncle Eleazar Orvis suffered a stroke that compromised his left side. Unable to shift his own body, he became a terrible burden on his already sickly wife. Before her death, Orvis's aunt suffered through multiple miscarriages and seemed not to be able to recover her health. Her husband's stroke added to her physical decline.

Even less serious injuries were still a major concern to Orvis's contemporaries. Broken bones that did not break the skin, sprained limbs, and other minor injuries had the potential to become serious impediments to normal activities and a drain on family resources. Any impairment of the physical body was serious since farm life demanded an active and vigorous constitution.

For Orvis, pain was a constant grief. Her persistently infected teeth caused her to suffer almost constantly from abscesses and toothache. In fact, the remedy of pulling affected teeth seems to have resulted in the loss of nearly all her teeth before she was thirty. As noted in her diary:

Finished the kersey. put in a Cotton web for Dr. Sprague. he extracted a tooth for me. came very hard, the only one remaining. glad to get rid of it.[23]

Throughout the decade covered by her journal, Orvis noted various problems with her teeth and the frequency of oral infection probably affected her health in less obvious ways. Dentistry in Orvis's time may have had some tools for dealing with her problems, but in rural New York the only treatments for her bad teeth was removal; the only relief from the pain and swellings of abscesses were poultices and topical applications of dubious value.

Beyond illness and injury of the body, there were also those who suffered from mental illness. While psychological problems were not an obvious or even recognized health issue in Orvis's time, the results of mental illnesses can still be observed. The most conspicuous examples of mental disorder in the journal are the suicides she noted. At least three suicides occurred in the ten years she kept up her regular writing. The first was an acquaintance of her grandfather's from his time in the militia, a Captain William Bailey. Although Orvis was sufficiently moved by his act to remark on it, there was no extended commentary on this: "informed by a traveler that Capt. Bailey of Plattsburg murdered himself with a knife last Tuesday."[24]

The second suicide was a neighbor, Ephraim Munson. A New Haven man, Munson's suicide elicited a more wordy and emotional response. This time, Orvis expressed shock and empathy for Munson's family.

> *Mr. Ephraim Munson, Newhaven, last evening after supper went to the privy, took his dull pocket knife and cut his throat from ear to ear at four places. Mrs. M being anxious told her son to go and see to him. He went to him. he did not speak. took a light and behold, he gasped the last breath, his hands supporting his head. His wife held his bleeding head until the neighbors came to her assistance. Oh my God preserve his family for thy sake.*[25]

The horrific image of a man driven by mental illness or sheer despair to use a pocket knife to end his life is particularly shocking. Orvis's prayer for his family's preservation was likely born of the knowledge that they had not only lost their husband and father, but also were now tainted socially by this grievous act of self-destruction. Suicide and mental illness carried the kind of social stigma that ruined families generally.

The third victim, John Bastian, shot himself.[26] This death seems to have had the least impact on Orvis. She did not know him, nor did she seem to have any attenuated connection other than to hear the report of his death. The fact that Bastian killed himself on a Sabbath day seems to have been the most shocking element of his death. Yet Orvis, still made note of his passing. The mysterious nature of mental illness was feared widely in Orvis's time, and the victims were often hidden in people's attics with the other shameful family secrets.

The sum of all of the illness, suffering and death that Orvis witnessed and chronicled in her journal, clearly helped to shape her understanding of the world. To be sure, she acknowledged certain truths as she understood them—that life could be cruel, short, or unfair—but she seems not to have acquired a particularly morbid frame of mind. Instead, she incorporated the details of these events in her writings as part of the larger fabric of births and deaths, illnesses and recoveries, stagnation and growth. This is not to say that she was unmoved by sad events; rather, she understood and interpreted them within the framework of daily life, her faith, and the cultural milieu in which she lived. The nineteenth century was a time when life was precarious—even when Americans were not at war. As a pioneer living on the edge of the raw frontier, Orvis was aware of this and likely witnessed more than her share of this uncertainty. Moreover, as a woman, Orvis faced death every day. Her acceptance of the inevitability of her own death was as sure as the old soldier whose wounds left stains on her coverlet. Each of her fourteen pregnancies and every illness that swept through the town threatened her health, and was potentially mortal. Yet, Orvis seems to have been able to balance those dangers with an innate appreciation of the beauty of life that surrounded her and the preciousness of the people she shared it with. Once such observation made near the end of her life is a case in point:

> *took a very high position on Mount Pleasant. Such splendid scenery I never saw before. Such beautiful springs of crystal waters so much of grandeur & sublimity of towering heights. Lengthened space above, beneath & all around. Seemed really enchanting. The eye could not be satisfied with seeing for itself, but oh how I did wish my family could all (and very many others) behold this beautiful scenery.*[27]

Conclusion

"beneath the spreading Oak and Hickory"

After 1830, Orvis gave up her regular journaling. The demands on her time and energy effectively curtailed the habit. She likely kept up some correspondence with family and friends when and where she could, but none of those letters have yet come to light. Then, in 1855, Orvis took up her pen for a short burst of writing when she and Eastman set off on a trip to Wisconsin. This short travel journal briefly chronicled their tour and its highlights. Four years later a second excursion home to Vermont prompted her to a similar effort. Perhaps the trip to Wisconsin and then to Vermont gave her time to write again. Being away from the farm and her housekeeping cares may have yielded Orvis time to write for those few weeks on each trip, however briefly. Moreover, she may have wanted to preserve these precious visits with faraway relatives for later perusal. Whatever the case, Orvis wrote two final postscripts that give us a last glimpse of her life and thoughts.

To prepare for her first trip in 1855, Orvis purchased an *American Railway Guide for the United States* for "one shilling."[1] This expedition to relatives who lived in the newly minted state of Wisconsin may have been the first long trip in the company of her husband since they traveled from Vermont to Parishville in 1823.[2] It is also possible that Orvis and Eastman previously traveled north into Ontario to visit with her brothers Silas and Eleazar Orvis, but there is no evidence of such a trip. There are references in the journal of several visits by them to Parishville while on route to and from Vermont. In fact, Orvis and Eastman made a short visit to Pickering on the way to Wisconsin.

Back home, most of the children remained behind on the farm likely under the supervision of the eldest siblings still "at home." Sister Mary had already married and left home; she lived in nearby Colton. Henry, although also married, may still have resided in the family home with his wife, Sarah Harrington. This arrangement was probably convenient for Eastman and Orvis. There were seven younger siblings to care for and who must have required a substantial investment of domestic labor. Beyond the household, there was a substantial farm to care for. Eastman cultivated more than fifty acres of improved land with an annual production of 300 bushels of Indian corn, 200 of oats, and 300 of "Irish" potatoes. In addition to the chores of plowing and planting, there was a great need for harvest labor. The livestock also required care; there were four horses, a team of working oxen, and nine milch cows, as well as assorted other farm animals. All would need to be fed, and the "freshened" cows milked. The liquid milk would also have to be processed into butter or cheese and this was no small task. According to the agricultural statistics of 1850, the farm produced over 500 pounds of butter annually from its small herd.[3] As Orvis and Eastman did in their turn as unmarried children, the young members of the Eastman family carried on in their parents' absence.

On September first, the Eastmans drove their wagon to Ogdensburg, where they joined Silas Orvis for the first leg of their journey. This stage of the trip required traveling up the Saint Lawrence River to Oswego via ferry and then sailing down Lake Ontario to Toronto. Next, the travelers boarded a local train to Whitby, the small community near Pickering where the bulk of the extended Orvis family lived. From the 5th to the 12th the couple moved about staying with various siblings and cousins and generally visiting. On the 13th, they again took to the road, this time traveling by train to another lake port, sailed across Georgian Bay and into Lake Huron. Their ship traversed the Mackinac Straits and entered Lake Michigan. They finally disembarked at Sheboygan, Wisconsin, on the 15th. Orvis did not enjoy that portion of the trip; she was seasick most of the time and commented wryly that she was "very sick indeed."[4] Once on dry land, the couple commenced their visiting schedule with Orvis's half-brother Isaac. In 1855, Issac Orvis was deeply involved in the Underground Railroad. His work placed him in danger of arrest and put him in conflict with the relatively new Fugitive Slave Laws. Whether or not Orvis was aware of his work, she did not comment on it.

Between September 15th and October 4th, Orvis and Eastman continued to visit with relatives who were now settled in a territory more than nine hundred miles distance from Eastman's Parishville homestead. While in Wisconsin and Illinois, Orvis met grand- and great-nieces and nephews for the first time, and renewed ties with siblings, cousins, and old friends. They went sightseeing and visited the graves of family passed on. Her beloved brother Eleazer and his wife Emily were laid to rest in the Avoca Cemetery in Fond du Lac, Wisconsin. This visit prompted an emotional outburst commenting on her feelings of loss:

> *[Here] at the graves of Eleazer Orvis & Emily E. Orvis, beneath the spreading Oak and Hickory his nephew and niece & the grandchildren of Brother Silas. Cynthia Daughter of Loren Orvis. Here too are the great grandchildren of Grandmother Brown all slumbering in the silent graves while the living relatives are far away.*[5]

Aside from the joys of visiting and the pathos of reminisces of lost family members, Orvis and Eastman had entered into a new world of travel that was very different from earlier times. Consider the differences between this trip and Orvis's first journey from Vermont to New York in 1821.

In that first trek from Bristol to Hopkinton, Orvis walked nearly the whole trip. Lake Champlain had been frozen and she had walked across on the winter ice. While this might seem an extreme kind of travel, for the times, it was typical. The ice saved the necessity of the cost of a ferry during the months when the lake was liquid. Moreover, winter travel guaranteed that muddy roads that passed through swampy hollows and wound along river edges were frozen hard and covered with snow. These conditions made such journeys faster, relatively safer, and more efficient. Even so, the entire trip out to Hopkinton, about 140 miles total, took four full days of travel and required her to walk most of those miles over rough terrain.[6]

In 1855, the trip out to Wisconsin took the same number of days, four, but covered six times the distance (900-plus miles). Clearly, times had changed.[7] In the intervening years, the Champlain, Erie, and Oswego Canals were constructed and opened. And almost as soon as the canals were opened, railroads augmented and then superseded them. Fulton's inventions had revolutionized travel over the waterways. Now, steamboats plied the waters of Lake Champlain, the Great Lakes, and navigable watercourses such as the Saint Lawrence, Hudson, and Ohio Rivers. Train travel accelerated the pace of change and also the comfort of travel. Moreover, communication had also changed. While Orvis no doubt wrote to her relatives of their impending visit, she could also have sent a telegram. Morse's telegraph had resulted in miles of wire strung across great distances and changing the rhythms of information exchange. At the same time, these technological and social shifts took place in the wider world, great personal changes had taken place for Orvis and her family as well.

By the time of that first postjournal expedition, the Eastman's youngest child, her eleventh, was now twelve years old. In fact, Orvis was already a grandmother once and the arrival of her second grandchild in November 1855 followed closely on her return to Parishville. The original log house where most of the Eastman children had been born and where Orvis fought so valiantly to make a civilized and neat home was now greatly modified. In the years between, Eastman expanded the hewn-log "cottage" into a two-story frame dwelling with plastered walls and clapboarded exterior. Presumably the furnishings had also become more refined and adapted to the sensibilities of their middle-class status.

The farm had also prospered. Certainly the income from the farm allowed Eastman and Orvis to be generous to their children. At the time of their marriage, the Eastman children were presented with "going to housekeeping goods"; the actual lists recorded in the back of Orvis's original journal. The Eastmans also provided an education for those children still at home; the federal census reports show all attended school. In short, the work and worry of thirty-three years had finally produced an abundance that enabled the couple to leave on this extended tour.

The short travel diary Orvis kept of this trip probably does not do justice to the excitement and wonder that she felt traveling out to a new territory. The complete account is contained almost entirely on one sheet of paper in close-written concise sentences. But those short phrases still reveal a wealth of experiences. Traveling across Ontario on a train to the shores of Georgian Bay, the couple witnessed the broad expanse of the agricultural frontier created by Upper Canada Loyalists in the aftermath of the American Revolution. Sailing across the length of Georgian Bay, up Lake Huron, and through the Mackinac Strait, they passed some of the most beautiful and historic country in the Old Northwest. While we do know that Orvis suffered from seasickness and missed some of the trip due to illness, it is hard to imagine that the woman who devoured so many travel narratives would have failed to enjoy this journey.

Once in Wisconsin, the pace of the trip was fairly rapid. The Eastmans traveled from Sheboygan through Fond du Lac to Oakfield, Wisconsin, where they visited with family members scattered across the county, including Orvis's younger half-brother, James. Proud of their new state's public buildings, the Orvis clan took the couple on a sightseeing tour, including the brand-new state-built Waupon Prison.

A combination of nostalgic "rambles," riotous family gatherings, sightseeing tours, and a visit to the state agricultural fair rounded out the trip. The travel narrative ends with the Eastmans arriving in Gardiner, Illinois, to visit a contingent of the extended family, the Clapps, Orvis cousins who left Bristol and Monkton to immigrate to Illinois in the 1830s. We are left wondering if the couple retraced their steps home via the Great Lakes and Canada, or if they returned home via train connections through Ohio and western New York. In this, the travel notes are silent.

This was the first of two trips, the Wisconsin and Illinois tour was followed four years later by an excursion to Vermont. This particular trek home was Orvis's third experience of crossing the lake back to her birthplace. Without the benefit of anything more than the short travel journal she kept, we do not know if the impetus for this journey was to fetch her stepmother, Lillis Brown, back to Parishville, or if Orvis intended this to be her own nostalgic tour. Perhaps both. What we do know from her descriptions is that she retraced her youthful journey from Starksboro to Bristol to Middlebury, and back to Ferrisburgh. At each juncture, she took time for "rambling" in areas she frequented as a young girl, and her narrative waxes poetic with her joyful memories. For instance:

> *[T]ook a long ramble alone over the gardens, rocks, hills, and rills. The old rocky cliffs I had so often clamber'd over were the same. The rocky seats so many in number where I once delighted to sit, to read, & sing yet are inviting as ever, as old friends. The old fruit trees yet leaf, but not much fruit. The old thorn trees are full of mellow fruit while an hundred locust trees shade the pathway down to the road. . . .*[8]

For more than two weeks she traveled the familiar roads of northern Addison County, reconnected with friends, visited family members, and made memorial visits to places from her past. At the end of two weeks, she began her journey home to Parishville in company with "Mother" Brown.

As with the trip to Wisconsin, the manner of Orvis's travel was significantly different from her first foray into the wilds of central New York. This time, she and Mother Brown traveled in comfort and walked only from buggy to platform to wharf. They boarded the Rutland Railroad, which delivered them to Burlington. On the waterfront, they embarked on a Delaware and Hudson steamer to cross Lake Champlain. On the west side of the lake, they were met and then carried the five miles to Peru, New York, where they visited with Lorenzo Orvis, "Mother" Brown's fourth son. Lorenzo married a Keese from the Quaker Union there and now lived and worked on her father's farm. The two women were then conveyed to nearby Plattsburgh, where Orvis and Brown continued by train to Saint Lawrence County. The total trip lasted only a day and a half, with the train from Plattsburgh passing directly through to the depot where Eastman was waiting to carry them ten short miles home. Life was decidedly different in 1859.

While on her visit to the Eastmans, Mother Brown may well have been called on by the Ontario Orvis relatives, including Silas, Orvis's eldest brother. Certainly Brown would have exchanged visits with family and friends originally from Ferrisburgh, but who had settled in Saint Lawrence County over the last four decades. These would have included the extended Eastman family, Delongs, and Durfeys. Since Mother Brown eventually traveled back to Ferrisburgh where in due course she passed away, it may be that Orvis made one final trip home. No record exists of that journey if it took place. Eight years after the visit to Vermont, Orvis was also gone. She died at her home in Parishville at the age of sixty-seven, presumably surrounded by her husband and living children—and probably tended by a loving neighbor in the same way she had tended hers. Her husband laid her to rest in Hillcrest Cemetery adjacent to the Baptist Church she resisted joining so many years before, but was now a member in "good standing." Buried next to her thirteen-month-old son Joseph, and marked by a modest stone marker, Orvis ended her life in the same gentle, unassuming way she lived. Because of this comfortable anonymity, except for the historical accident that preserved Orvis's written words, we would never have known anything about her life. Even with those documents we know only a fraction of her life, and even this is imperfectly understood. And we know only an outline of her later experiences, although official records fill in some of the gaps.

At the time of Orvis's death, all of her children had married except James and Joseph, and they married in the next decade. Many of them remained close to home, settling in the towns surrounding Parishville, if not directly in the neighborhood. Her beloved first son predeceased her; Henry died of camp fever during the Civil War at Baltimore in 1862. His widow and three children lived in the nearby town of Stockholm. After her marriage, Mary Elizabeth resided in Colton with her blended family, including two children from her husband's first marriage. Lucinda, Martha, and Phebe all married local men and settled close to home as well, Lucinda just next door to her brother James, who stayed in the old homestead. By 1868, when she died, Orvis was a grandmother more than a dozen times over. Orvis and Eastman's children and grandchildren helped to expand the growing communities surrounding Parishville. The original homestead was occupied by family members into the middle of the twentieth century. Grandson Frank Eastman (son of James) inherited the homestead from his father and lived there until his death in 1936. One can imagine that Orvis would have felt great pleasure to see the successful results of her diligent care. Her last travel diary implies that despite the years of toil and certain loss, Orvis retained her romantic, even poetic, way of viewing the world. Thus, it is not difficult to imagine that if she had written a memoir, Orvis would have reprised her accomplishments with pride, but also humility, as she credited her faith. As she exuberantly wrote in her journal: "Just like a story or song I pass my life."[9]

The Journal

The sweet, single life
July 1, 1820–February 5, 1823

BRISTOL, VT Commencing July first, 1820

Sat. 1st Sewing on silk frock. received a new pair of shoes. sent back to Mr. Walker. in low spirits. the fruit of melancholy.

Sun 2nd Attended church. heard a sermon delivered by Mr. Dodge. went to Sabbath School, readEvening Amusements" and "Twin Sisters."[1] received a visit from Mr. A[lva].S[prague]. Miss [Orra] Copeland from Mr. [Adolphus] T[aylor].[2]

Mon 3rd Received and refused an invitation to visit at Mr. Cooks; on East Street in Newhaven. Rode in company with Miss Amelia Annin to Monkton [VT] Mr. Samuel Clapps. Worked at Millinery and Mantua making. Visited by Miss Nancy Nash carried her to Mr. Williams. Went to Mr. Benjamin Clapps.[3] Staid all night. Amelia and myself had a pleasant visit. very warm.

Tues. 4th Independence. Celebrated at Vergennes. Worked at two bonnets and gown made one ruff. rode home, called at Gen. Dunton's.[4] Being warm sat up and read the life of Baron Trenck. Mr. Taylor and Miss Copeland returned at twelve from the visit at Mr. Cooks, Newhaven. Retired at twelve with low spirits. The fruit of disappointment.

BRISTOL

Wed 5th Sewed until about noon. Took a horse, borrowed a wagon, drove to Mr. [Benjamin] Clapps, Monkton. Went by way of the village, exchanged horses.

Phebe Orvis's journal has been reproduced as faithfully as possible. Inconsistencies that are reproduced in spelling, use of punctuation, and capitalization are intended as a faithful transcription of the original manuscript.

Thurs 6th Drove to Ferrisburgh in company with Mrs. Clapp. Went about six miles round. arrived at Cousin Frederick VanVliets and took dinner. Very warm forenoon. A high wind and rain ensued for about an hour. Visited at Cousin Sarah [Brooks] Rogers. Returned to F.V.V. [Frederick VanVliets] and made a bonnet. Staid overnight. The air became cool after the shower. Retired much fatigued.

Fri 7th Called at Cousin S[arah].R[ogers]. and Cousin Enoch Brooks. Arrived Father's [Loren Orvis] found them in good health and spirits. Visited at Mr. Stephen Fishes. Had a pleasant visit with Miss Lydia Fish. came to my brother's Tarr'd [tarried] all night.

FERRISBURGH

Saturd 8th Pleasant. Started for Bristol. Called at Mr. Silvanus Smiths. Changed horses at Uncle [Samuel] Clapps in Monkton. Called at Mr. B[enjamin]. Clapps engaged to spin two or three weeks, saw Miss Harriett Charter and Miss Amelia Annin.[5] Urged hard upon my tarrying all night, not consistent arrived at home, was told if I left home and went out to work, I would be deprived of a home here. Sent Mr. C[lapp] word I could not come. Walked to the village. Purchased six yards and half of fustian for a gown. Accompanied by Miss Sally Gaige as far as Susan [Moor]s. Went to springs, drank a quart of the water, returned to Mr. Annins had an agreeable visit with Miss Harriet Charter. Was informed of the particulars of her mind respecting matrimony. My feelings injured.

BRISTOL

Sun 9th Arose this pleasant morn, visited the springs. Miss Charter and myself attended meeting. Staid at Mr. Gaiges until meeting time.[6] Called at Esquire Halley's at intermission, saw Mr. Taylor. took tea at Mr. Annins. Attended my classes at Sabbath School, saw Mr. James Kimball. Heard Mrs. Copeland very sick. Spilt ink on my white frock. Almost exhausted this evening, sick.

Mon 10th Finished my web of Diaper.[7] Put in another. Visited by Mr. Arnot, Miss [Elizabeth] Prime. Mrs. Bradley and daughter, been quite out of health, retired to rest about two hours. Instead of relieving, made me worse. Cut out two shirts.

Tues 11th Wove but little today, rode to see Mrs. Copeland. Found her much better than expected. Mrs. Church buried today. Staid at Mr. Annins all day.

Wed. 12th Wove some. Baked pies. Visited by Mrs. Eastman, Mrs. Eddy, had a very hard shower with thunder and lightning. Wrote a letter to Uncle Phineas Durfey. Retired at a very late hour. My thoughts hoving to the ends of the earth.

Thurs 13th Visited by Miss Sally Prime, Miss Electa Prime, Miss Amelia Annin, Mrs. Eliza Prime of Bristol. Miss Amelia Langdon, Miss Laura Doubel, Ladies from New Haven. had a pleasant visit. Although, they are in affluent circumstances.

Fri 14th Visited by Miss Susan Ellsworth, Miss Clarissa and Nancy Nash. heard from Monkton and Newhaven. Received a letter from Uncle David Brooks, Ohio, Cuyahoga County, he informs us that it is a good country but unhealthy. Thunder, Lightning and rain. High spirits.

Sat 15th Saw Mrs Abigail Pierre, heard from Newhaven, Miss Jerusha Sprague's health is very poor. Mr. Sidney Pierre has received no benefit by visiting Saratoga Springs. Saw Mrs. Pierce of Starksborough. Starched ironed clothes. High spirits.

Sun 16th Attended meeting at Newhaven Mills. Walked to Mr. Handys' at noon. rode home with Miss Sylphina Hanchet, and took tea, introduced to Mr. Phelps and Calvin Butler. received a pressing invitation to go to Mr. Harris. rode home from Mr. [Joseph] Berrys with Miss Annin, Mr. Drake & Mr. Austin to the Springs. Saw Mr. D. Giles, called at Mr. Pettibone's to see Miss Almira, found her very sick. Introduced to Mr. Elijah Smith of Monkton. Returned home late.

Mon 17th Weaving. [for] Mrs. Hawkins. Mr. Jewett been here informed us of Mr. Henry Warner's death. Uncle John been to Vergennes. Washed a little. Walked to Mr. Howdens, returned home. went to Mr. Dunshees, rode from there to Mr. Annins and cut out my silk frock. Staid all night [with] Amelia, very tired indeed. good spirits.

Tues 18th Wove almost all day for one yard. Amelia been here. Orra [Copeland] has gone home with her. Mrs. Lata, L. Taylor been here and Miss Electa Prime. wrote Miss Annin. Alone this evening, which is seldom. Serene air.

Wed. 19th A fine shower this morn. lowry day. Mrs. Shotwell & Mrs. Barnard called. took tea. Miss Hilpa Nash married to Mr. China. took up a paper this evening, read of the death of Frederick Pickle (N.Y.) aged one hundred. At 94 cradled 500 sheaves of rye, in a day. at 97, he went into the wood, and split 100 cherry rails in less than a day. In Ireland, Theodore O'Sullivan, aged one hundred and fifteen years, he died while sowing oats in the field with one of his grandchildren singing one of his fav. songs.

Thurs. 20th Weaving and spinning some. Dr. Stearns has been to see Lovina.[8] She is very feeble. Uncle John has been to hire a girl. could get none. Sewing on my silk frock this eve. retired early.

Fri 21st — Pleasant with heavy dew. washed little, wove little, put in a web of Kersey.[9] wove a yard, sewed some. Boiled out some yarn. Orra and myself went to the river and rinsed it. went Raspberrying brought home a load of pines, washed all the floor and Orra the shop. Miss Elvira Hand, Miss Betsy Rich, Miss Babbett called this afternoon. retired much fatigued.

Sat 22nd — Wove four and half yards and spun little. visited Miss Laura Eastman's school in company with Mr. Taylor and Orra. Miss E's health very poor. She rode to Esq. Halleys with us and took tea. found Miss Mandana H. [Hawley] unwell, became acquainted with Miss Lucinda Pierce. Strong request to visit her at Dr. Newcombs. received a letter from Miss Annin was informed of Miss Charter's ill health. weary of the vanity of the world.

Sun 23rd — Pleasant morn, Cloudy eve. read a few pages in the Twin Sisters. drove to meeting called over to Mr. Gaige's at noon conversed with Miss Miranda Parmalee, engaged a correspondence with her. also Miss Sylphina Hanchet, Mrs. Susan Moor. Miss Sally Gaige, and Catherine Gaige, Rachel Dayfoot. Mrs. Munsill all intend visiting me on Tuesday. few scholars at Sabbath school. Wrote to Miranda Parmalee.

Mon 24th — Rainy, carded and spun 14 knots of tow yarn wove seven ½ yards of Kersey.[10] Baked pies, sewed some. Dr. Warner called. Grandma'am sick with a bleeding sore on her ankle.

Tues 25th — Lowry. Put in a web of Kersey. wove three yards. washed all the floors. visited by Miss Catherine and Sally Gaige, Miss Rachel Dayfoot, Ladies from the [Bristol] village. Miss A. Annin, Cleora Carpenter from the north of the town. Sewed on my frock. visited at Mark Moors this eve. staid at Mr. Annins, received a billet from Gen. Dunton to be ready to attend the court on Friday. Received a letter from H. Charter. the other Ladies agreed to correspond with me. sick and tired.

Wed 26th — Came home and wove 4½ yards, made four [pillow] beers in a harness. visited by Mrs. Howden, Mrs. Halley. Agreeable weather.

Receipt for Leaven . . . make light emptyins of hops and rye flour then stir in Indian meal and dry them. Soaked in milk when used.

Thurs 27th — Wove three yards, put in a web of Forty slay.[11] Starched, ironed, Plated. Gen. Dunton, Mr. Severance, Mr. Meader. Misses Clarissa and Hilpa Nash called here today. saw in the Paper the marriage of three Priests, the execution of Hull and Hutton.[12] called over to Mr. Primes, Mr. Pettibones, Mr. Dunshee.

Fri 28th — Wove some, washed some. Mr. Annin accompanied us to Mr. Nortons. Took dinner. Attended court at Mr. Torman's. Mr. T's witness absent. was finally settled. Miss Copeland, Miss Charter, Miss Drake, Mr. Taylor and myself rowed out on the pond. a hard shower gently wet us to the skin. Just as we returned, Mr. Thaddeus Dunton returned from Virginia, joyful scene. we all visited at Mr. Carpenters slept with Harriet [Charter]. happy season, conversed freely, respecting her union with Mr. [Thaddeus] Dunton

Sat. 29th — Mr. T. Dunton brought me home this morning. visited by Mrs. Willy, Mrs. Walbridge, Mrs. Ashley, Harriet C[harter]. staid all night. sent a letter Miss Parmalee by Edward D[unshee]. Very unwell indeed.

Sabb 30th — Quarterly meeting at Barnumtown. Attended Sabbath School. out of health Visited the springs with Mr. and Mrs. Prime. Orra carried Miss Charter home. Visited by Mr. Alva Sprague. Miss Copeland by Mr. Taylor, Miss Charter by Dr. Dunton, Miss Mandana Halley by Mr. Seymour. Pleasant visit indeed. retired at half past one o'clock.

Mon 31st — Wove some. sewed some, Baked pies. taken with a hard cough and sore throat. wrote a letter to Miss Annan. visited the springs, called Harriet C[harter].

August 1820

Tues 1st — Poor health, sewed some, wove little, heard from the village, Mr. Henry Kilburn, after having traveled nine hundred miles round the world has returned to Bristol and thinks it the best place.

Wed. 2nd — Finished weaving my pillow cases. Put in a web of Diamond Key sowed some.[13] bought one pound of cotton yarn. one dipper, one skimmer of Mr. Weaver. Uncle John sold six bushel of green pears at Vergennes today. Ocean B. Prime, Orra and myself been after choke cherries. cut out [shirt] waist.

Thurs. 3rd — Cool weather. Drove to Mr. Shotwells, Mr. Barnard's to Newhaven Mills Mr. Nashes Carding Machine. Ephraim Monsons Store Miss Hannah Bradley, Miss Abigail Todd started for Georgia[, VT], received a letter from Amelia. visited by Rev. Mr. and Mrs. China.

Fri. 4th — Cloudy with rain. Weaving and sewing. Mrs. L. Taylor, Mrs. Kimball called from Middlebury. very hard cough. dejected spirits.

Sat. 5th Rainy day. wove some, my cough dry and hard. Mr. and Mrs. Clapp here tonight.

Sund 6th Drove to meeting. had such a cough I could hear nothing. sewing. called Mr. Gaige's at noon, saw Miss Charter, received a letter from Miss Miranda Parmelee. attended Sabbath School. Mr. and Mrs. Taylor staid until dark. went to the river. retired early but could not get but little sleep hard cough.

Mon 7th Cool morn. Mr. Nash, Miss Sally Lorea called Mrs Dunshee very helpless. wove two yards. finished my web. Mrs. Walker has a daughter.

Tues. 8th Wove four yards. visited by Miss Amelia Whitney. Mrs. China called took tea with us. bought me a pair Morocco shoes much disappointed with them. knitting. My cough looser today but very hard indeed. Warm day.

Weds 9th Wove five and half yards. sewed some. Visited Mrs. Dunshee found her no better. Baked pies. Mrs. E. Scot's son weighed seven pounds. Cough very hard.

Thurs 10th Wove seven yards, visited at Mr. [Spafford] Grouts in the evening. great party all from the village some from Newhaven. very rainy. retired twelve.

Fri 11th I took horse and wagon in company with Miss Copeland. Drove to the Borough in Middlebury. called at Mrs. Gowdy's shop. Mr. Stewarts Store, Mr. McDonald, Mr. Hough Mr. Hegers, Mr. Woods, Mr. Gison, Mr. Hooker and Brewsters, bought a thimble. Mr. McDonough purchased a comb and Lemay. Mrs. Kilburns Shop, Orra bought a bonnet. had to wait for it to be trimmed. Went to Mr. S. bought white crape made it for ruff. had two crimped. Saw a gentleman from Georgia. called at Miss Olmstead saw Mr. Calvin Cook. called at Mr. Tars to see Miss Alpha and Almeda Olmstead. Drove through the river and spent the afternoon at Mr. Nashes saw Mr. and Mrs. Munsill. invited to visit them, hard shower, called at the carding machine. came home heard we had fourteen visitors. cough, pain in my head. dejected.

Sat. 12th Wove four yards and put in a web visited Mrs. Dunshee. found her better. saw Mr. Taylor. Uncle John went to Vergennes & sold six bushels new potatoes. went to fathers, found them well excepting sore eyes. very unwell.

Sun. 13th My cough much worse. ate a melon, apple, green corn the finest we had this year. attended Sabbath school disappointed of company. on account of "__________," a wild disagreeable melancholy.

Mond 14th Washing starching. Ironing, sewing. Wove six yards besides. Uncle J[ohn] been to Middlebury with green sauce. very much fatigued.

Tues. 15th Wove five yards. sewed the rest of the day. very rainy. hard cough.

Wednes. 16 Commencement at Middlebury. Mr. Taylor & Miss Copeland have gone. I wove five yds. took a horse and waggon. Drove to Mr. Annins, asked Amelia if she would ride to commencement with me. called to Gen. Dunton and took Miss Charter. Went to Mr. Clapps on errand. came back to Gen. Dunton's took tea. Mr. Carpenter just arrived from Ohio. Excellent visit. visited at the village at Mr. Gaige[']s, came home in a rain storm wrote to H[arriet].C[harter]. tired, sick[,] wet.

Thurs. 17th Rainy, wove three yards. washed all the floors, clothes, sewed some. Went to Mr. Annins. staid all night. out of health. good visit.

Fri. 18th Received a letter from Miss Jerusha Sprague. wove five yards. attended church meeting at Mr. Dunshees. very sick. wrote a letter to Uncle David Brooks. Ohio. in the evening Dr. Stearns came.

Sat. 19th Rain, wove three yards. visited by Miss Sally and Alpha Olmstead, Miss Almeda Cook from Middlebury. Strong invitation to visit them. Cousin Frederick VanVliet and wife from Ferrisburgh. heard that Cousin Amos Brooks was drowned the first of June in a mill pond. Starched, ironed, excellent visit, very rude affairs

Sund 20th Been very unwell indeed. not able to attend meeting. F[rederick]. VanVliet, returned home, Mr. John Crane, Miss Copeland, called, took tea. Quarterly meeting at Middlebury. Miss A. Todd, Col. Nash called eve

Mon 21st Wove five yards of Kersey. Baked, spun thirteen knots. Lovina sick visited this eve by Mr. Sand, T. Grout, R. Dunshee. T.G. [T. Grout] intends departure for Canada.

Tues 22nd Wove three and half yards, put in a web. Amelia Annin spent the night agreebly.

Cure for the Choleras Morbus "Put one spoonful of hot ashes into a tumbler of old Cider. give the patient three table spoonfuls of it. the cure will be affected in half of an hour."[14]

Wednes 23rd Sent to Vergennes for a quart of French Brandy, pound loaf sugar for my cough. Wove five yards. sewing, written a lengthy letter to Miss Charter concerning Matrimony. called over to Mr. Grouts. very weary.

Thurs 24th Wove four and half yards. visited by Mrs. Drake. Miss Elizabeth Prime.

Fri 25th Put in my web. Scoured the house. Mr. J. Taylor and wife called. Mrs. Nash, Miss Todd, Mrs. Shumway, Miss Fanny Carpenter, Ferrisburgh, in pursuit of Cyrenus, her son which ran away. Mrs. Trip buried. weary.

Sat. 26th Wove five yards. finished my silk frock. visited by Mrs. Grout, Mr. Eastman.

Sund 27th Cool morning. attended meeting dressed in silk. attended Sabbath School. Spafford Grout here this evening. visited by Mr. [Alva] Sprague.

Mond. 28th Washed this morn. wove four yards. wrote a long letter to Miss Abigail Lewis, Co. of Essex (N.Y.) gathered plums.

Tues. 29th Wove five yards, Starched, Ironed. saw Mrs. Taylor. Mr. R. Spooner. staid overnight. Orra gone to Mr. Annins. Mr. Weaver called.

Wednes 30th Wove five yards. wrote a letter to Mrs. Nicholson. Grandmother and Uncle John started for Lewis, [NY]. Miss Amelia Doubel. Miss Electa Prime. Mr. [&] Mrs. Pier this afternoon. good spirits. fine weather.

Thurs. 31st Company this eve from the North Part of the town, village and this street, some from Monkton. Mr. Seymour from Newhaven. fine visit indeed. heard of Mrs. Eastman. T[haddeus].D[unton]., H[arriet].C[harter]., A[melia].A[nnin]. stayed.

September 1820

Fri. 1st Wove but two and half yards. washed the floor, been very unwell. visited all day Mr. Dunton came after the Ladies, staid, took tea with us.

Saturd 2nd Did the house work washed all the floors, from top to bottom. wove three yards and half. Our people came home[,] brought cousin Lucinda Nicholson with them, also Brother E., Sister H., Cousin Sarah Roger, Miss E[lecta] P[rime], N[ancy] D[unshee] called. Captain Mathews died today.

Sund 3rd Wrote to Sister Betsy, visited the springs, drank two quarts of the water. heard from Cousin Philena, she married Hiram Adams of York, Genesee County

Mon 4th Put in a web. walked to the village heard a preparatory Lecture by Mr. Rison. the members of Starksborough Church attended. very tired.

Tues 5th Freemens meeting.[15] great party at Dr. Newcomb's at the village. wove four and half yards. the heat intensely hot. visited the vineyard[.]

BRISTOL

Wednes 6th Very warm, wove five yards, sowed some, Uncle J[ohn]. been to Vergennes. Mr. Robert Dunshee. Mr. Ocean B. Prime visited this eve.

Thurs 7th Wove three yards. put in a web. washed some. visited by D. Warner and wife. Mr. Pier and wife, Mrs. White staid all night. heard of the death of Mrs. Giles child. made a ring of my own hair.[16] depressed spirits.

Fri 8th Wove five yards. visited by Mrs. Susan Moor. Mrs. Jewett, Mrs. Laura Munsill, Mrs. Harriet Ellsworth. strong request to visit them. agreeable visit. ironed this eve. much fatigued.

Sat 9th Wove five yards. Starched, ironed, plated ruffs, read seventy pages of the barbarity of the English, Mr. Pettibone, Mr. Rowley Kilburn, Mr. Lorenzo Day, Mr. Severance, Mr. Robert Dunshee, Mr. Marcus Moors. here this afternoon to eat melons. Uncle John gone to Camp meeting at Charlotte. weary.

Sun 10th Remarkably dry and warm, visited this eve by Mr. Sprague. gave him dismission, Miss Copeland by Mr. Taylor. Dr. Warner called drunk. about two o'clock, very unwell, dejected.

Mon 11th Wove six yards. visited by Mr. Martin Larrabee and wife from Greenfield, Massachusetts. staid all night. Mr. Bush., Mr. Chamberline from Ferrisburgh. Miss Jerusha Sprague. Clara Allard called. good spirits.

Tues 12th Wove four yards put in a web, rained all night and all day.

Wednes 13th Wove seven and half yards. received an invitation to quilting. from Eddy's, two quilts and twenty four ladies. Miss Nancy Dunshee staid all night. Mr. Jewett called this evening. Severe headache, hard cough, depressed spirits.

Fri 15th Wove eleven yards and put in a web through the harness. Mrs. Carpenter very sick, received a letter from H[arriet].C[harter]. Mr. Larrabee, Mr. Otis, Mr. Walker, Miss E. Prime, Miss Mahalia Gaige called today. Mrs. White staid all night heard of the death of Miss Ruth Slocum of Monkton. severe headache, face much swollen by coughing. cool evening.

Sat. 16th Wove 2 yards. washed little, coloured red, washed the floors. trimmed silk cape, plated my crape ruffs, went to Mr. Pettibone's Mr & Mrs. Howden, Mrs. Prime visited here. walked two miles to Mr. Whitneys. agreeable visit with Amelia. tired.

Sund 17th Very cloudy. attended meeting at Newhaven Mills, Mr. Holt delivered a sermon, walked to Mr. Jewetts at intermission. agreeable visit with Miss Nancy Nash. took tea at Mrs. W[hitney]. attended conference Mr. Hunter took the lead. A Mr. Todd just arrived from the city of Washington, gave an account of the awakening in the College of Yale, Newhaven, Connecticut, which was very interesting. Mr. Edward Dunshee published to Miss Miranda Parmalee. Miss Pamelia Hamblin had a fit at meeting. sick.

Mon 18th Shower this morn. wove seven yards, sowed some, Nancy D[unshee]. called. severe headache.

Tues 19th Wove four yards, put in a web, through the harness. waited for a reed.[17] made [shirt]waist, headache.

Wednes 20th Put in my web through the reed. wove six yards made stand cloth. accompanied by Mr. John Seymour of Lanesborough, Newhaven. requested permission to visit me. saw Mr. Taylor. became acquainted with Mr. Murray of Williston now living at the village, clear and cold. retired at 3 o'clock. almost tired.

Thurs 21st Hard frost. wove seven yards. Mr. Pier, Miss Mason, called. Mr. Taylor gave us an invitation to visit at Gen. Duntons. I refused. Orra accepted. Mr. Smith Farmer and wife came back from Ohio today. also Mr. Plumley died. hard cold. dejected.

Fri 22nd Had a large wash, washed all the floors, very tired. wove three yards. cousin Lucinda had three fits occasioned by the Whooping Cough. held her through the day and night, face swollen, parched lips, sick.

Sat. 23rd Very unwell, lame, wove five yards, Ironed. altered my Bombay frock. Mrs. Clark called. visited by Miss Amelia Annin.

Sun. 24th Shower. read considerable. Conference at the School house. E[liza] Prime N[ancy] Dunshee insisted on my accompanying them. obligated to refuse. visited by Mr. John Seymour of Lanesborough Newhaven. wrote to Miss Annin at twelve. retired at half past[.] Mr. Hawkins sick.

Mon. 25th Wove five yards, put in a web. knit some but very unwell. A[melia] Prime [called].

Tues 26th Cool. Put in a web. wove five yds three quarters. Mr. Seymour gone to St Albans. A[melia] A[nnin] staid all night.

Wedn 27th General [Militia] Training at Vergennes. wove four yards. put in a web. washed clothes and floors. Mr. R[obert] Dunshee visited this (p.m.) tired. hard cough.

Thurs 28th Wove two yards. cut and made Lucinda a frock. company from Lewis [Essex County, NY] Aunt Lucinda Nicholson and Mother, Mr. David Sykes and wife and child. his nephew, David Baldwin Sykes. received a friendly letter from Miss Abigail Lewis. heard of the death of Miss Esther Armstrong.

Frid 29th Wove 1 yard. paring apples today. our company started for Barnet [VT]. unwell.

Sat. 30th Wove three yards. Starched Ironed. Plated ruffs. knit some, washed two frocks. sick.

BRISTOL
October 1820

Sund 1st Attended meeting, called at Mr. Ingraham's at intermission. Uncle [Benjamin] Clapp at our house and Mr. Nightingale. went home with them. sick.

Mond 2nd Visited this afternoon at Mr. G[eorge]. Bacons. Orra came after me and L.M. fine visit. Saw Miss Charter, Mr. David Haskill of Madrid [NY] sick.

Tues 3rd Wove two yards prepared for wedding [of Edward Dunshee and Miranda Parmalee]. accompanied by M.T. Mr. Milton Caldwell Miss Laura Munson. waiters of the Bride and Groom. Mr. Beach of the Liquor. about one hundred and fifty spectators. likely for a shower. started for home. called at Mr. Gaiges Inn spent the evening. the rest of the company called. heard of marriage of Mr. Chancy Fitch to Miss Sophia Ketch Newhaven. Mr. Clark Cady to Miss Naomi Mills, Munger Street [Middlebury]. Mr. S[eymours]. birthday. dressed in silk.

Wed 4th Rainy. large party at Mr. Dunshees of Married people Second Part. party Mr. Hawley's at the [Bristol] village. married at Starksborough Mr. [original blank space] Miss [original blank space] Fuller. Wove five yards. starched Ironed, plated ruffs, wrote a lengthy letter to Miss Abigail Lewis. weary of parties.

Thur 5th Wove three yards. Put in a web of Kersey. Rainy. Orra gone to carry Mrs.[Lucinda] Nicholson to the Lake. she saw Mr. N[icholson] & his family. well. dejected.

Fri 6th Wove out my web. Put in Blanket. Mr. Severance & [Mr.] Otis. called on Mrs. Taylor. went home with her. staid all night at Mr. Annins. received a letter from Miss Charter. Ladies from the village at Mr. Moors sent for me. refused.

Sat 7th Wove four half yards. spun some. finished my stocking. saw Miss Mason. frost.

Sun 8th Cloudy. Heard Elder Stearns preach two fine sermons. to Mr. Kilburn's at noon. Mr. J. Annin and [his] Mother arrived in town. read some. in low spirits.

Mon 9th — Wove but little. Rainy. Mr. Sweet arrived from Rhode Island. Mr. Annin this eve.

Tues 10th — Very rainy. washed clothes, floors. etc. Mr. Samuel Dolbear came here to work.

Wedn 11th — Rained all day. wove some. sewed the rest of the time. heard of Mr. Flint's child dug up by Mr. Joseph Wards, Mr. T[haddeus] Hoyt. Mr. A. Squire all fled.

Thurs 12th — Election [Day]. took the wagon accompanied Grandma'am to Mr. Shotwell's, Mr. Mason's purchased a trunk. went to Col. Nash's., esq. Mr. Jewett insisted upon my visiting them this afternoon. went to Mr. Spencer's. returned to Mr. G.'s several of their friends supped upon a baked pig. I had as lives eat a sheep. Mr. and Mrs. Taylor visited here this evening. Mrs. & Miss Langdon.

Friday 13th — Frost. Wove few yards of Check. Mr. Taylor & Miss Copeland started their journey. read considerable. enjoyed myself well.

Satur 14th — Pleasant. wove out my web. put in a coverlet for Sally Brooks. Mrs. Bradley, A. Prime called. Composed an Acrostic on Amelia Annin.[18] alone but happy after indulging in tears.

Sund 15th — Rainy. Read an inaugural Oration delivered by Mr. Joshua Bates professor of Middlebury College. 26 pages. 18 pages of Amelia Seymour. Practice of the Sandemonians, 22 pages, 16 pages of tract. written an Acrostic and adieu. read a magazine. rained all day and night.

Mon 16th — Rained all night. great damage. the water rose so high at the village it carried off two Blacksmith shops at the washing dock[,] two Barrels, a wash tub full of clothes for Mr. Barnam. At the third bridge it tore away the dam, took part of the bridge, undermined Mr. Taylor's house. They were obligated to move out in the night. wove three yards on a coverlet. been to Mr. Annins. bade my friend Amelia adieu. rainy.

Tuesd 17th — Cold windy. wove out my coverlet. put in a web, tired[.] a gentleman took dinner by the name of Rockwell, Cornwall, [VT]. the Annins started their journey. walked across to Mrs. Sprague's, Newhaven, made Bombazett pocket. The river at the Mills took some houses & half an acre of land. left the saw mill past the middle of the river opposite. converse until day.

Wedne 18th — Very hard frost. came home almost sick with a lame side. Wove four yards. tired. Two Mrs. Heady's called. uncle sick. low spirits.

Thur 19th Pleasant shower. starched Ironed and mended. wove five yards. Mr. James Taylor came here to bottom chairs. In getting his bark a limb fell upon his head, knocked him down and broke in to [two]. Wonder it had not killed him. Ordination at the village of Deacon Rider. Elder Green passed the examination. Elder Dodge preached the sermon. seven elders attended Mr. Rider very high spirits.

Fri 20th Hard frost. Wove seven yards. Mr. and Mrs. Hill of Starksborough, Mr. Bell of Weybridge, Mrs. Nash of Newhaven brought weaving. Mr. Weaver called. washed clothes and floors. very weary indeed.

Satu 21st I suspect I was born 19 years ago today. Pleasant frost. Wove 3½ yards bought a pair of Shoes for Mrs. Copeland. to [too] small. Walked to Mr. Follit's. staid a short time rode with Mrs. Mrs. Rathburn to Mr. Cranes. found Mrs. Copeland dangerously sick. I shingled off her hair, had her head shaved and a blister drawn on it.[19] Went to Gen. Dunton's. staid all night. took a hard cold, very sick in the night. excellent visit with Harriet [Charter]. High spirits.

Sund 22nd Uncle came after me. dressed in silk for meeting of the Friends at the schoolhouse. took supper at our house. heard Mr. Dunbar preach at the Methodist Chapel. Mr. Winter Halley published to Miss Polly Seymour of Newhaven. enjoyed myself well.

Mond 23rd Wove five yards. spun 7 knots. Mrs. Nash and Daughter took tea. Sally Prime commenced spinning here today. George Hall died.

Tues 24th Wove 6 yards spun 7 knots. Orra and Adolphus came home had a good jaw. Mr. Mrs. Bush, Mrs. Mr. Clapp. Miss Lucy, Miss Becky Anstead.

NEWHAVEN

Tues 24th Heard from Mrs. Copeland, no better. Lovina blessed with an infant daughter. have a very hard cough.

Wedn 25th Snowed about twelve inches deep. wove out my web. Put in my coverlet. Mr. Spencer Monson, Miss Zilpha Pettibone called. made a cap this eve.

Thurs 26th Out of health. wove but a trifle. Mr. [Winter] Holly and Miss [Polly] Seymour entered the Matrimonial State. Miss M[iranda] H[awley], Mr. H. N. waiters. good spirits.

Frid 27th	Wove three yards on Coverlet double twisted. F.P. S.G. F.G. called[.]
Sat 28th	Wove out my coverlet, put in two blankets. took waggon, Drove to Mr. Nobles, Mr. Howdens, Col Nash Esquire. at Jewetts took tea. White flannel done. Left Grandma'am, took Orra, proceeded to Mrs. Cranes found Eunice [Copeland]. no better. watched with her. slept none. read Monima, A Beggar Girl.[20] froze very hard indeed.
Sund 29th	Saw Miss Charter. returned home about noon. Mr. Packard, Mr. Griswold. Miss N[ancy] D[unshee], E[liza] P[rime] called this evening. Mrs. Frolla Smith, daughter.
Mond 30th	Wove five yards of Blanketing. worked a large washing of clothes. A[lva] called. J. [Uncle John] been to Vergennes. prepared my cloth for whitening. tired.
Tues 31st	Wove five yards of Blanketing. E[liza] P[rime] James Taylor. rain. indisposed.

November 1820

Wednes 1st	Wove six yards, ironed. Rainy morn, pleasant eve. Mrs. A. Dunshee, Mr. S[ylvanus] Smith and wife visited.
Thurs 2nd	Wove three yards. finished my web. put in a coverlet. a jolly pedlar called. heard from Mrs. Copeland, better. Mr. John Prime and wife, Mr. Edward Dunshee and wife visited us this eve. heard of Mr. Plumleys marriage. strange man.
Fri 3rd	Wove but little. sewing[.] rain[.] heard from Mr. Sprague and Taylor. melancholy.
Saturd 4th	Frost, washed clothes, all the floors chored. Mr. Dolbear taried overnight. why is it that I dislike him, why can I not feel towards him as he does towards me? Uncle, Grandma'am been to Middlebury, tried to appear familiar in vain. very tired.
Sund 5th	Went to the chapel. disappointed of preaching. took tea at Mr. Gaiges. Rain snow altogether. Mr. Harvey Griswold published to Miss [original blank space], Castleton.
Mon 6th	Weaving coverlet. good visit with Uncle Clapp. Grandma'am rode to the mill with him. How happy might I be had I a contented mind.
Tues 7th	Pleasant. washed Ironed. sewing. Why am I discontented? wickedness
Wed 8th	Weaving. aired all my clothes. put them away. Miss N[ancy] D[unshee] [&] Mrs. Drake called.

Thurs 9th	Wove all day. Grandpaw arrived from the west out of health. received a letter from P[hineas] Durfey, E[lisha] Brooks of Parishville. all well.
Frid 10th	Cool. Finished my coverlet began another made four small caps for Mrs. Clapp. Dr. Day called this evening. our people making cider. frost.
Sat. 11th	Took the wagon drove to Lanesborough Street, hired Board at Dr. Stearns. called at Esq. Hoyt's introduced to Miss N. saw Erastus Dean. Miss Harriet [Charter] staid all night with me. severe pain in my head.
Sund 12th	Snowed all day all night. read Dr. Watts sermons. Gorge, N.Y.
Mond 13th	Snowed all day clear at night. Mr. Hawkins carried H[arriet Charter] home
Tues 14th	Wove on a coverlet all day. pared apples at night. tired
Wed 15th	Pleasant and cold[.] L. Day called. Dr. Stearns called. told I could board with him as long as I wished. paid him three dollars thirty three. John, Orra gone to Vergennes purchased her pelisse cloth. sewing.
Thurs 16th	Pleasant. Mr. Hotchkiss came after a loom. Grandma'am coulouring. Red & yellow. attended a conference at Mr. Dunshees. very muddy. low spirits.
Frid 17th	Pleasant. finished my coverlet and fringe. put in a blanket. sewing.
Sat 18th	Frost. walked to Newhaven Mills. sold my gowns, cloth. called at Col. Nash. Mr. George Jewett brought me home. dejected.
Sund 19th	Rain. at home. read considerable. took a walk to the river.
Mond 20th	Wove one blanket. sewing this eve. quite unwell. low spirits.
Tues 21st	Wove the other blanket. Found my flannel shirt. strung my beads. had a new lock put on my trunk. high winds and rain . . . So slides time away faster than we prepare for death and Eternity.
Wed 22nd	Cold, put in a coverlet. set it to work. Accompanied Grandma'a'm to Monkton. called to Mr. David Clapps took tea at Samuel Clapps. sold Mr. Copeland a pair of shoes. sewing.
Thurs 23rd	Washed. Ironed. stiffened my crape on my hat good spirits.

Frid 24th Been to Middlebury. purchased Plaid Bombazett five dollars. Cummings Geography and Atlas.[21] Rhetoric by cash. Reckoned and settled with Mr. Thayre. returned after dark.

BRISTOL

Sat 25th Cloudy rode to Vergennes staid four or five hours. left my trunk at Dr. Stearns. visited my Fathers. almost sick.

Sund 26th Rainy visited my brothers, cousins, FVV [Frederick Van Vliet]. unable to get farther. [came to] Dr. Stearns. felt very disagreeable to be out of my health at a boarding house.

NEWHAVEN

Mon 27th Attended the Ladies Quarterly. School taught by Miss Lucy Burnap.[22] enjoyed very disagreeable feelings from various courses. first on account of my being an entire stranger to most of the Ladies and they to me. second being entirely unacquainted with the manner and customs of the school. third have not attended any kind of school for some years which of course rendered me more ignorant than others of the school (These reflections I conclude effects of injured pride.) However, I am extremely pleased with Mrs. Burnap. her dress is plain, her manner easy and agreeable and excels on piety which renders her exemplary and amiable. The school commences by reading two verses a piece of Scripture. Miss B. makes an introductory prayer next attend to writing Hebromon, in geography, a lesson in Cummings' Geography. parsing English grammar in the afternoon. Rhetoric, Logic, Philosophy, other studies. have singing instead of reading before prayer in the evening. toothache.

Tues 28th Attended school almost for nothing. almost distracted with the toothache, not able to study. Miss Prudence Hills had one drawn, one dug out. homesick.

Wedn 29th Attended school this forenoon not able to compose. Drew a short extract. returned to Dr.'s. distracted with the sick headache together with the toothache not able to get up[.] after puking and taking Essence felt more relieved[.] Esq Hoyt, Miss Sarah Matticke of Montpelier. Miss Delia Hoyt called this eve to see me, hearing that I was out of health. after soaking my feet and taking more essence, retired.

Thurs. 30th Snowed some. rather better but very weak learnt a lesson in grammar, worked on Geography. Miss Prudence Hills spent the evening with me. she had another tooth drawn. my friends displeased with my frock. went in to the store and exchanged it for plain this evening. Snow

December 1820

Frid 1st — Been sick all night. at a loss which to do: go to school or take an Emetic? went to school. Miss P[rudence] H[ills] sick obliged to go home. became acquainted with Miss Mandana Holly. stomach sick. eat nothing today.

Sat 2nd — [No entry]

Sun 3rd — Heard Mr. Hopkins preach from these words "As I live saith the Lord I have no pleasure in the death of the wicked but that they turn and live."[23] Attended conference at the Schoolhouse in company with Miss Louise Hurlburt. very discontented. homesick. wrote to Miss Copeland, Miss B. Sexton and Miss S. Eastman to me.

Mon 4th — Attended school. recited a lesson in Self knowledge. Painted the atlas with one colour. received a letter from Miss Copeland. Mr. Taylor called this eve. the first person that I have seen that I am acquainted with. Miss Aurelia and Mandana Squires came here to board. Miss Maria Wilcox spent the night with me.

Tues 5th — Little snow, recited a lesson in Geography. one on the Atlas. Painting. received invitation to singing by Mr. P. Refused. introduced [to] Mr. B. Grant.

Wed 6th — For the first time wrote a composition. on Composition. Two lessons geography one grammar. Miss Mills exchange boarding awhile went to Mrs. Phelps to study with Miss Jerusha Hoyt. Mr. Taylor accompanied.

Thurs 7th — Painting, Starched Ironed. Miss Hoyt insisted upon my visiting her again, the last night being Society meeting. thirty Compositions read today.

Fri 8th — Recited two lessons in Geography. had the toothache all day. Mr. Elisha Dunham brought here with one rib broken, dreadfully bruised. life is doubtful.

Sat 9th — School kept but half day. accompanied to Bristol by Mr. Taylor. found them well. Miss Copeland and myself conversed almost all night for I had been from her the whole of one fortnight. am I glad to get here.

Sun 10th — Snow of considerable depth. returned to Newhaven. heard Mr. Hopkins preach from Ezekiel Thirty-third. Eleventh . . . Turn ye, Turn ye, why will ye die O house of Israel. saw Miss Sylphina Hanchet at Mrs. Phelps. insisted upon my visiting her at Mrs. Spragues, East Street. Miss Maria W[ilcox]. insisted on my spending the night with her. I did. my old tooth threatened to jump out of my head.

Mond 11th	Sewing. out of school. entered a letter in the [Post] Office to Mr. Durfey, Miss Betsy Erskine boarding at Esq Sextons. fine young lady.
Tues 12th	Boarding to Mr. Hills. two lessons in Geography Mr. T[aylor]. called for me to attend Singing school at Dr. [Stearns] not there. knitting no place today.
Wed 13th	Sewing. recited two lessons in Geography. an Irish Pedler came in to our room to trade. Julia Barros visited here this evening.
Thursd 14th	Wrote a composition on Modesty. heard thirty and a Dialogue written by scholars. recited once through the Atlas. Oblige to go from school on account of the toothache. went in to the store purchased a handkerchief, half Quire of Letter Paper. One Hair comb. wrote a letter to Miss Copeland broke my large Hair comb P. and myself rude couple.
Fri 15th	Attended school this forenoon. Dr. Stearns called at noon told me I must go and take care of Prudence for she had taken an Emetic after I had gone to school she was all alone. found her in a state of delirium. Miss Patty Hoyt called. strong invitation to visit her. wrote until twelve O'clock at night. read a number of letters of P[rudence]'s.
Sat. 16th	Learnt through the Geography. received a letter from Miss Copeland.
Sun 17th	Read considerable Scripture. also the Prince of Abyssinia which pictured out the many situations of life but found no solid happiness in any.[24] toothache very hard.
Mon. 18th	Commenced a review of Geography. finished writing Astronomical Geography. Passed in Pope's Essay. lesson map
Tues. 19th	Took a review of Alexander's grammar. went through this forenoon Commenced Rhetoric. recited four lessons today. very tired.
Wed. 20th	Recited four lessons. Sewing. out of school. cut out my frock. playing on the Harp. called over to the store. bought three skeins of silk, Cambric for Ruff, Linen for gown, side comb. Mr. Taylor called eve.
Thurs. 21st	Pamelia Moore went home. visited there one thousand eight hundred & thirteen. Mr. T[aylor] called. recited Rhetoric. disappointed in my Boarding Place.
Fri. 22nd	Thanksgiving. Two hundred years since Columbus Landed on America shores. Heard a discourse by Rev. Josiah Hopkins. invited to Esq. James Sexton's to

supper. disappointed of going to Bristol[.] saw Miss Lucretia Gowdy [and] Miss Marsha Ann Saterlee from Middlebury. Ladies of this street took a ride to Town Hill. retired at one. sick.

Sat 23rd Rode home with Mr. Hawkins. Froze my feet. visited Mrs. Dunshee found her in low circumstances. Mr. Taylor called.

Sun 24th Deep snow fallen. Cold is extreme. Blustering. The roads almost impassable. Miss Copeland visited by Mr. Taylor. writing a piece.

NEW HAVEN

Mon 25th Returned to Newhaven but not able to attend school. 18 inch snow.

Tues 26th Recited one lesson in Self knowledge, one in Astronomy. sewing.

Wed. 27th Wrote a composition on Geography. one in Rhetoric. Presented with skein of flax by Mr. Samuel Washburn. excellent visit at Mrs. Phelps. retired late. Cannot study any. out of sorts. recited 27th

Thurs 28th Mr. Loyal Phelps found my penknife which I lost last eve. P[rudence] Hills spent the night with me. she has eight boils. Ten O'clock before eat. Could not have breakfast because there was not fire enough to get it. fine Boarding Place. Mr. Sexton very anxious to have me board with him the other half quarter. Tracing and Painting. Ruff Pattern.

Sat. 29th Painted the map of Parish's Geography. Cousin F.V.V. [Frederic Van Vliet] called just as school was out, his wife, her sister. rode to Bristol with them. Carried home my trunk. found Orra and Uncle John sick. visited at Monkton with them this eve. returned Bristol.

Sun 30th [No entry]
[Date discrepancy in the journal; no entry for December 30th and 31st, 1820]

January 1821

Mon 1st Cousins returned home. almost sick. watched with Mr. D.

Tues 2nd Washing. Mending. Boarding with Lovina. became acquainted with Mr. Everett Hall. calculating to attend his school.

Wedn 3rd — Attended school recited a lesson in Geography. began Arithmetic Just before noon. Worked out fifty sums. prepared supper. after school Lovina and myself washed both Linen and woolen clothes[.] visited to Mr. Hall. all the Atlas. retired at two o'clock. very cold weather.

Thursd 4th — Attended school recited one lesson in Geography. learning the rules of Arithmetic. worked forty-two sums. Orra gone to Middlebury with Esq. Howden. A Ball to Mr. Eddy's - 2 o'clock.[25]

Frid. 5th — Cold and blustering after supper. Ironed. made a cap for Mrs. Copeland. very tired. retired at one o'clock. late evening.

Sat. 6th — recited arithmetic and geography. watched with Mr. and Mrs. Dunshee. very unwell myself. Mr. and Mrs. Brigham staid at our house.

Sun 7th — Sacrament Day. staid at home. Mr. Hall gone to Middlebury this eve. Mr. Prime called. Mr. Mrs. Hawkins visited Sally.

Mond 8th — Attended school. Mr. T. Grout returned from Canada.

Tuesd 9th — Attended night and day school. received a letter from Sister B.

Wedn 10th — Attended school. washed this eve. Mr. Briggs. Mr. Prosper Durfey, Mr. S[eymour] called brought me a letter from Mr. P[hineas] Durfey from Hopkinton. he informs me I must prepare for a journey to the west for he should be out in ten days. of course I cannot go to school but one day more.

Thursd 11th — Attended school perhaps for the last time in this house. recited a lesson in Geography. one in astronomy. married in Newhaven Mr. Ira Gifford to Miss Lucia Fuller. Mr. Loren Ashley to Miss Elldridge. Mr. Seth Langdon to Miss Laura Squires. low spirits.

Frid 12th — Reckoned, settled with Mr. Handy. Esq. Jewett. came home spun twelve knots of worsted. visited at Mr. Follits. snow little. disagreeable taking leave.

Saturd 13th — Very cold. spun twenty five knots. Mr. Sprague, Miss Jerusha [Sprague] been here. J[erusha] says if I go to Hopkinton she will. we therefore agreed to go.

Sund 14th — Very cold. Mr. W[illiam] Dunshee and wife came to town today from Sangersfield heard Mr. Dodge preach this eve from these words "As I live, saith the Lord, ye shall live also." perhaps the last time

Mond 15th Visited at Mr. Dunshees. pleasant visit with Mr. & Mrs. Parmelee Mr. W[illiam] Dunshee and wife. Heard that My old mate Miss Rosetta Beardsley was attending the Academy at Thetford [VT].

Tuesd. 16th Sewing today visited by Mr. & Mrs. Follit, Mr & Mrs. Terry of Plattsburg [NY] three quarters of mile this side of the Saranac, my old friend.

Wed 17th Returned to Newhaven school. visited Mr. Taylor's school this afternoon read, spelt, parsed with them. saw some of their compositions. Mr. [Taylor] this eve at Dr. Stearns.

Thurs 18th Carried my globe to school. Miss Burnap says it must be framed first. Recited a lesson by course two on the Modern Map, one on the Ancient. Mr. Hawthorn Houghton visited here this eve. plated shirt ruff for Mr. Houghton. he says he is well acquainted with Miss Rosetta Maria Beardsley, Thetford. sick.

Frid 19th Attended school. Dr. took another boarder, Miss Freelove Spinks. received an invitation to visit with the Ladies at Capt. Wheeler's thought it to [too] far to walk. Mrs. S.T[aylor] called over Mr. Bingham's. accompanied home to Mr. Sextons spent eve. the young company took a ride to Middlebury. tore my frock.

Sat 20th Finished the Ancient Atlas. this forenoon. drew a pattern for Capes. Took a ride to Bristol with Mr. Taylor. took Orra with [me] visited Gen. Dunton. fine visit A[dolphus] T[aylor] & O[rra] C[opeland] visited L. Taylor. staid Mr. C[opeland][.]

NEW HAVEN

Sund 21st We all attended meeting at Monkton. called at Uncle Clapp's, returned to Gen Duntons. spent the eve Mr. Calvin Edward's. Returned home, found Mr & Mrs Durfey had arrived. exchanged handkerchiefs with Mr. T[aylor], bade him adieu. retired absorbed in grief.

Mond. 22nd Cold, South wind. rode to Middlebury. visited at Mr. Olmstead's. Isaac O[lmstead] died the last of November. Settled with Mrs. Gowdy. dressed in silk. Mr. Clerk. Mr. E[astman] and P[hineas] Durfey called this eve. almost sick

Tuesd 23rd Visited at Mr. Gaiges and Mr. Needham's Quarterly school. Catherine presented with a string of beads Saw sample of her pelisse. a Ball there this eve. we called at Mr. Moors spent the evening very cold. Excellent sleighing.

Wed 24th — The coolest day I ever knew. The young people visited with me, bade me adieu. agreeable visit with Mr. Edwards. it is disagreeable to part with friends and not know of ever seeing them again. tore my frock and shoe sole.

Thurs. 25th — Cold and Blustering, P[hineas] D[urfey] and myself traded some at the store. paid Miss Burnap. took tea at Mr. Silas Eastmans took my leave of street.

Friday 26th — Uncle John Nicholson visited us all. visited Mr. Clapps. Adaline [Clapp] fine girl.

Sat. 27th — More moderate air. mended my Bombazett frock. all hurry and confusion.

Sund. 28th — Snowed little. parted Mr Mrs N[icholson] rode to Father's [Loren Orvis]. all the young people there.

Mond 29th — Wrote to Sister [Harriet] Chamberlin. visited my Brothers, Cousins and took my leave. spent the night at F.V.V. [Frederic Van Vliet] very sick in the night indeed.

Tues. 30th — Returned home to Bristol. thaws considerable. saw Mr. David Haskall of Madrid at Vergennes. visited this P.M. at Rev. Mr. Hopkins. tired. sick.

Wed. 31st — Mr. Taylor Miss Copeland took a ride to Starksborough. sleigh turned over.

February 1821

Thurs 1st — The snow almost all gone. Uncle John returned from Crown Point. Froze some but very pleasant washed this morning. Attended School to write. went to Mr. Grout's at noon staid and visited Mrs. Munsill.

Friday 2nd — Rode in a waggon to Col. Nash's. settled with him. Mrs. N.'s health very poor. Mr. and Mrs Lee, Mr. and Mrs. Durfey of Lincoln visited.

Sat. 3rd — here Mrs. Olive Eddy. Brother Eleazar. Sister Harriet, Ferrisburg[.]

Sund 4th — Very little snow it is doubtful whether I get out of the state or not. Uncle Clapp & family visited here. Orra came back. E. better. took a walk river.

Mond 5th — Pleasant as Spring. visited by Mr. Mrs. Hopkins Mr. Andrew Squires, Mrs. Charlotte Durfey. Mr. [William] Miller departed this life today. had my shoes mended, packed my clothes for my journey. Mrs. Dunshee rather better I never expect to see her more.

Tues. 6th Took leave of my home that has sheltered me nineteen years to see a new country. left them in tears. as we rode slowly in a waggon in the winter season everyone at their window of my acquaintance it appears as if I were following some friend to the tomb. Uncle John went with us as far as the Creek at Vergennes. Mr. Watkins started with them left his portbagg had to go back. we proceeded alone. He overtook us at Essex, village situated very pleasant on the Lakeshore. we crossed the Cracks, the last. the horses broke through. put up at Drews Inn the first time I ever staid at a Publick house. rode fifteen miles on the ice. different strangers.

Wed 7th Little snow. concluded to try bare ground rather than risk the Lake. Started with Mrs. C[harlotte] Durfey on foot. I walked as far as Sheldon Inn four an half miles, then rode half mile to J. Jones Inn in Willsborough village. Walked to the top of Willsborough Mountain, two miles more. tolerable sleighing down the mountain. Called, took dinner at Buckminsters Inn, Chesterfield. passed Ceylons Forsyth's. Bozworths. called at Hays. Lost a horseshoe after passing the Gate. called at Buck. to get a new one on. Charlotte and I walked four miles farther to [Stephen] Stackpols [Forge] Mills in Peru [Altona]. Passed Cochrans Inn, put up at Stoddards. walked full twelve miles, the most beautiful country I ever saw. passed five or six ponds. our feet blistered. so lame we could hardly get to our bed. such a noise we slept little.

Thursd 8th Colder. found some snow. rode ten miles to Bankers, Plattsburg, Clinton County. took breakfast. passed Daniel Townson's Inn called at Robinson's ten miles from Bankers Corners. Peru is the handsomest place I ever saw but here in Chateauguay the road is strait, handsome[.] passed three encampments, many chimneys are still remaining. ten miles called at Bare's put up at Robert(s) in Moor Town. slept with a girl from Montreal and Miss Submit Rockville of Malone. very tired.

Frid 9th Took breakfast at Mr. John Varnals. introduced to Mr. Eastman of Hopkinton. called at Amsted's [Hotel], Malone village[.] the handsomest bridge I ever saw. fine village. walked one half mile put up at Fosters Inn, Malone. snowed some.

Sat. 10th Snowed little. crossed Deer River in Dickinson. rode six miles to Chandlers, took breakfast. Mr. John Stearns came to meet us. met Ira Brown and Mother. passed [James] Trussels, [Thaddeus] McLaughlins Inn. arrived at Uncle's at nine O'clock. Introduced to Miss Susan Davis, an agreeable girl. Miss Orrilla Squires, saw Mr. Levi Squires, Mr. Timothy M. Hopkins, Mr. John Osgood. trimmed Harriet's Bonnet and Cloak. how disagreeable to be among strangers.

Sun 11th Pleasant morn. Surprised to see the gentlemen take the same liberty to call on the Sabbath as any other day. Attended a Deacons meeting at the Schoolhouse, three quarters of a mile. introduced to Miss Rachel Squires Miss Sally Remington. Susan [Davis] proposed a walk to a Beaver Brook. Mr. Martin Delong and wife, Mr. Joseph put up here from Bristol on their return from Canada. wrote three letters.

Mon 12th Rainy all the snow is gone from the road. washed. sowed the rest of the day. introduced to Mr. Tinkham. several gentlemen staid late, drinking, carousing, the Beaux are as awkward as they are ignorant.

Tues 13th Attended Mr. Hopkins school. the strictest school I ever saw. passed two lessons in grammar. introduced to Miss Betsy Eastman, a lovely girl to appearance but so extremely reserved, I find it difficult to form an acquaintance. Introduced to the two Mrs. Coveys. received an invitation to Singing School. I complied with reluctance. rode all in a huddle on an Ox Sled drawn by horned horses. I was pleased with the wonderful style but as for myself, I never rode on one before. I find it is common. Chaise. low spirits.

Wedn 14th Snowed very fast. put [on] a face as long as my arm. P[hineas] and J[oseph] Durfey, S[tillman] Remington, visited school. Stillman [Remington], Mr Hopkins visited here this eve. Mr. Stearns, Miss Davis gone.

Thursd 15th Mrs. Eastman visited us. Finished my stocking. J and S came home. snow considerable deep. travellers tried to pass counterfeit bill. Uncle followed them to Fosters, 14 miles, took their great coats.

Frid 16th Attended school. received an invitation to a party at Mr. Jack Durfeys by Mr. Remington. Considerable hard feeling because Harriet [Durfey] did not go. I don't feel very guilty about it for I did not think of her going.

Sat. 17th Snowed almost all day. Saw Mr. Timothy Soper and wife from Vt. returning home to Canada. I enjoy myself unpleasantly among strangers.

Sund 18th Snowed some, Read the Life of John Murray.[26] Uncle Elisha Brooks and cousin Lucius came here. Introduced to Mr. Jacob Drum, Mr. James Davis, Miss Anna Drum from Fort Covington took a ride with eight others in one sleigh. J. Drum, J and S. Davis, Sally and Stillman R[emington]. L Stearn(s) H[arriet] Durfey very good ride to Conference at Mr. Baldwin(s) but such conversation was enough to make one shudder as I heard coming home.

Mond 19th Washed. introduced to Mrs. Remington. saw Dr. [Gideon] Sprague, my old Schoolmaster. Rode on a sled to sing[ing] school. Mr. R[oswell] E[astman] made apology for [original blank space].

Tues 20th The snow all gone. rode to school and home again. singing school hard cold.

Wed 21st Froze. Attended school. mended for Mrs. Stearns. gave me a ruff. dejected.

Thurs. 22nd Pleasant. Not able to go to school. Starched. Ironed. plated ruff. Mr. Blood from Madrid, Mrs. Durfey visited at M. Coveys. left alone. made cement.

Frid. 23rd Snowed considerable. visited by Miss Sally Remington, had a silk handkerchief stolen. exhibition at the white house. stormy, else I should [have] gone. Cannot be at home.

Sat. 24th Doing chores and knitting. introduced to Miss Lydia Squires. dejected spirits.

Sun. 25th The house full all day. Mr. Ira. Brown, my old friend, came here had a fine visit. just from Vermont on his return to Canada. Mr. Ben Soper and wife three children, Mr. Storrs Mrs. S[torrs] left her gold beads. read John Murray.

Mond 26th Washed. Knit the rest of the day. The ground bare. it looks dismal to me.

Tuesd 27th Attended school. Mr. Howlen Delong came. staid two days. wrote one letter. Orra Copeland, Miss Catharine, and Sally Gaige. Susan Moor, Harriet Charter.

Wed 28th Pleasant. Ironed, braided twelve yards of Straw. Mr and Mrs Eastman visited us.

March 1821

Thurs 1st Rain. made a pair of Trowsers. Mr J[oseph] and C[harlotte] Durfey visited us.

Frid 2nd Sewing. Attended Spelling school, old and young spell together.

Sat 3rd Pleasant. Sewing Ratinett for Harriet. alone again today.

Sund 4th Pleasant. Attended meeting this forenoon. returned at noon. dejected. took a walk to the wood. sought relief by tears. Oh that I had a friend.

Mond 5th Pleasant. worked. Accompanied by Mr. Stearns to a party at Mr. Stillman Remington's, his freedom treat. Introduced to Miss Eliza Talcott. became acquainted with Miss Laura Smith. fine girl. enjoyed myself disagreeably. a stranger in a strange company [home] 2 o'clock.

Tues 6th Pleasant finished the frock. very melancholy. visited at Mr. J[oseph] Durfey. Town meeting. received a letter from Miss Orra Copeland. Mr. Dunshee died fourteenth of February. Dr. Thomas married Betsy Gazely. low spirits.

Wed. 7th	Snowed little. rode on horseback to Parishville. Uncle Elisha Brooks visited at Mr. Joel Hawkins this evening, their youngest son is sick.
Thursd 8th	Pleasant. saw Miss Talcott. Introduced to Miss Harriet Hayden. came home.
Fri 9th	Pleasant. Tended Barr. braiding fine straw. the young people visited here this eve. they danced considerable. For myself I was very disagreeably entertained. my feeling repose flies far from me.
Sat. 10th	Pleasant. finished braiding, doing chores the rest of the time. almost sick.
Sun 11th	Pleasant. read the most of the day. sick all night. Oh, could I see the [original blank space].
Mon 12th	Washed alone. Done all the floors. Aunt Ruth [Phineas Durfey's wife] very sick. far from the tents of joy and hope.
Tues 13th	Rainy. Starched, Ironed, plated ruffs. a gentleman from Ogdensburg took supper. left an advertisement. 60 Dollars reward, six persons broke jail on the eleventh.
Wedn 14th	Cold, but pleasant. Spun a run of tow candle wicks. visited Mr. Remington. unwell.
Thurs 15th	Rainy and muddy. Spun thirty knots of linen. number of travelers called.
Fri. 16th	Snow. Spun thirty knots. Col. [Alexander] Macomb called.[27] Went to Mr. Eastman's to singing school. most disagreeable company. Electa Gilbert staid all night. rude girl, strange, too.
Sat 17th	Snow. Spun thirty knots. Uncle Phineas hunting today.
Sun 18th	Very cold and Blustering. melancholy reigns continually.
Mond 19th	Very cold. spun but little. sowed some. [Uncle] Phineas [Durfey] forty three years of age.
Tues 20th	Washed alone. visited by Miss Betsey and Molly [Mary] Eastman and by Mr. and Mrs. L[evi] Squires. snow. finished my stockings.
Wed 21st	Tended Bar. number of travelers called. done house work. sewed.

Thurd 22nd	Very pleasant. arose at half past three o'clock. dressed in silk visited the Miss Spencers at Potsdam village. most part of the way woods. Potsdam is a flourishing village pleasantly on the Racket River. arrived very early in the morning. introduced to Mrs. Peas, Mr. Henry Clark of French Mills, Dr. John McChesney, Miss Laura Pier, Mr. Shepherd, Mrs. Bigelow, Mr. & Mrs. [Charles] Eastman, Miss Ingerson, Dr. Holmes. visited Mr. Moran, Horatio Munson. saw Mr. Mrs. Pier. pleasant visit at Mr. Bigelows this evening. Miss Spencer very anxious I should assist her in the millinery for two or three weeks. called over to the store. tired out and sick.
Frid 23rd	Pleasant. Mr. E[astman]. called on us this morn. Miss Esther and myself took a ride with Dr. Mc. called at Mr. Aikins introduced to Miss Aikin. rode four miles farther. returned. introduced to Miss Ives. returned this afternoon to Hopkinton on bare ground. Aunt Rebecca Brooks, Miss Talcott came to visit me. was gone. tired indeed. dejected.
Sat. 24th	Some rain and snow. spun thirty-three knots. Mr. Durfey sick with a Boil on his wrist. Lonesome tired out of health and low spirits.
Sund 25th	Snows but melts as fast as it comes. Loitered at home all day.
Mond 26th	Cold. washed alone. sewing. The little girls visited here this eve. low spirits.
Tuesd 27th	Considerable snow. spun thirty knots. introduced to Mrs. Warner the weed from the village. Lee and Roswell E[astman] returned.
Wed 28th	Spun this forenoon. attended Exhibition at Mr. Sam[uel] Goodells five miles from this. Mr. Leonard Mr. Henderson fought. Mr. L[eonard] was shockingly bruised. visited Mr. Lee Eastman at a party at Mr. Joseph Durfeys. being dressed in silk took hard cold. Dangerous entertainment.
Thursd 29th	Spun thirty knots. wrote a lengthy letter to Miss Clarissa Woodward of Ticonderoga. the gentleman from the village had a spree.
Frid 30th	Spun thirty knots Mrs. Covey, Mrs. Tinkham visited here. had a sore brake in my head. discharged at my nose. Mr. Clark from the [French] Mills. sick.
Sat 31st	Spun some. Tended Bar. Mr. Durfey started for the [French] Mills. Bought two handkerchiefs of a couple of Canadians. Mr. George staid about two hours. Brother Eleazar here. sick. and tired out. He had been confined for three weeks at William Cunningham's at Hallowell. Good and travelling now[.]

April 1821

Sund 1st — Saw a French family pass. My Brother made me a present. handkerchief. he visited at Elisha's. read a book of letters. reposed in tears and sighs.

Mon 2nd — Washed alone. Brother's health some better. Mr. S[amuel Eastman]. Mr. R[oswell Eastman]. Mr. J[ames] S[prague] called this eve.

Tues 3rd — Wrote a letter to Miss Copeland, one to Miss Charter. retired at one.

Wed 4th — Pleasant. Brother took his leave this morn. for Vermont. began spinning Tow. spun forty knots. visited by Mrs. Peck. Mrs. Baldwin. Mrs. Eastman. Mrs. Remington. became acquainted with Mr. Lane of Rupert [VT] going to the Upper Province Ontario, Can.

Thurs. 5th — Pleasant. Spun forty knots. Mr. Roswell Eastman cut his knee. bought of a Peddler six yards of Calico, one hair comb. tired. sick.

Frid 6th — Very unwell. spun but thirty knots. did some chores. Mr. Ballard tarried.

Sat 7th — Spun thirty knots washed floors sowed some. Mr. Nutter called from Potsdam.

Sund 8th — Rainy, Mr. Durfey sugared off this Sabbath. how offensive to their God.

Mond 9th — Pleasant. spun 30 knots of Linen. Ten travelers called. boatmen. Barnard McGovern went with them. Mr. Smith to the Academy of Potsdam.[28]

Tues 10th — Pleasant cool. washed. visited at Mr. Eastman's with Aunt. tarried overnight. pleasant visit with Betsey [Eastman], a lovely girl of 15.

Wed. 11th — Came home this morn. spun thirty two knots Starched. Ironed. Plated ruffs. unwell. Mr. J. Stearns called this eve. injured feelings.

Thurs. 12th — Carded and spun thirty knots of Tow. Cool air some snow this P.M.

Fri. 13th — Carded and spun thirty knots. Cool but pleasant very tired and melancholy.

Sat. 14th — Pleasant, Carded and [spun] only twenty knots. Mr. Hallock, an enlisted sailor has been away nine years. called on his return to his parents in Genesee [NY]. Pain in my head.

Sun. 15th	Cloudy and cool. have still violent pain in my head. weak. melancholy.
Mon 16th	Pleasant. visited at Mr. Coveys. Miss Sarah Remington, Miss Burr M. Eastman staid with me this eve. I waited upon them at home.
Tues 17th	Very cold. Spinning. washed the floor this eve.
Wed. 18th	Cold, some snow. Carded and spun twenty-eight knots. Mr. L. Squire, S[eth] Abbott called.
Thurs. 19th	Cold day. spun but twenty-eight knots. very unwell. three travelers.
Fri. 20th	Pleasant, spun thirty knots and finished the two. Cut out two Calico aprons. almost finished one of them. Drew some flowers. tolerable spirits.
Sat. 21st	High winds. some rain. washed alone. Starched & Ironed my Calico frock. boiled sap this P.M. I never did this kind of work before and many others that I do now to keep peace. Mrs. D[urfey] sick all day. not far from my [mother.]
Sun. 22nd	Cold and cloudy. some snow. read considerable. cut Mr. Remingtons hair this evening. my sinking spirits scarcely admit my thoughts to roam.
Mon. 23rd	Very windy some rain. boiled sap. done Sugaring. very tired indeed.
Tues. 24th	Election. Spun 21 knots of thread. six of [embroidery] floss. Mr. Raymond & Mr. H. Weed. Dr. Brooks. Dr. Sprague cut out the skirt of my gown.
Wed. 25th	Second day of Election. washed. Sally Remington and myself walked one mile and half introduced to Miss Matilda Witherell from Vt. Miss Post, Miss Gould staid all night with me. gentleman disappointed, some mad.
Thurs. 26th	Last day of Election. Harriet and myself were alone all day. Worked on my gown some. took a walk to the wood to relieve my wounded feelings. I went to J[oseph] D[urfey] a few minutes but all did not drive away those gloomy feelings. severe pain in head.
Frid. 27th	Pleasant. expected company. none came but my good friend Betsey. she was so good as to spend the night with me. Mr. H. Myres spent the night from Ferrisburgh. Heard Cousin S[arah Van Vliet] married to Mr. D. Hazard. Mr. Lee Eastman arrived from Fowler. good visit. indeed. tolerable Spirits.

Sat. 28th Warm. Pleasant. sowed some. studied some Rhetoric received my H. book.

Sun. 29th Rainy all day. very lonesome. L.E. [Lee Eastman] S.R. [Stillman Remington] J. S.[tearns] called Mr. D.[urphey]. sick all day yesterday, today.

Mon. 30th Rainy all day. washed alone. warped a web. sowed onions did the chores. raked and swept the door yard until dark. dreadful pain in my side tonight. took some spirits of Turpentine to prevent finding me out.

May 1821

Tuesd. 1st Cloudy, some rain. finished my frock. Put in a web of Diamond Kersey. great difficulty in doing anything with it almost twisted it.

Wed. 2nd Cold and frosty. wove all day for two yards. very unwell. discouraged.

Thurs. 3rd Very cold and windy. Mr. Roswell Eastman came here this P.M. the first time he has been from home since his lameness. called over Mr. E. this eve'g. Julia C[ovey] Sally R[emington] spent the night with us. B[etsey] E[astman].

Frid. 4th Very cold. windy. Bad weaving. my worthy Miss E[lizabeth] E[astman] visited me again this P.M. Miss Chloe Squire. Miss Rachel S[quire] took a walk to the south also Sally R[emington]. very urgent to have me spend the night with her. Uncle Elisha Brooks at work here today pleasant visit indeed.

Sat. 5th Very cold. wove some. washed the floors. Mr. E. Sampson, Jr. J. Rivers called.

Sun. 6th Rainy A.M. Pleasant P.M. read through the Book of Exodus.

Mon. 7th Pleasant. visited by Mrs. Tinkham, Mrs. C[harlotte] Durfey. went home with her to spend the night. Maria came after me to go home to see Mr. Taylor my good friend from Vermont. brought me a letter from Orra [Copeland] one from Harriet [Charter] all well but Grandma'am. had a pleasant visit with him. retired at two.

Tues. 8th Pleasant. Mr. T[aylor]. Took his leave. went home with Sally R[emington], Joseph D[urfey] put my [original blank space].

Wed. 9th Smoky.[29] weaving. visited this P.M. by Mr. R.E. [Roswell Eastman] severe pain in my head.

Thurs. 10th Very smoky. very unwell. received an invitation to visit at Mr. J[oseph] D[urfey] refused. took a walk to the north slash & the Miss E[astmen]s called for me to go and spend the night with them. obliged to refused. several fought fire until 1 p.m.

Frid. 11th Very rainy introduced to Mr. Andrew Squire of Orwell. Mr. R[oswell] E[astman] and myself had a hard scuffle for a few letters. I conquered at last.[30]

Sat. 12th Pleasant. wove three yards engaged in school for four months for one dollar and twenty-five cents per week.[31] Mr. Hiram Frank staid all night from Vermont. heard of the death of Mr. Ellsworth. Marriage of Miss Filomena Mason to Mr. Van Rensselaer Allen & Eleanor Burrows to Mr. Bond.

Sund. 13th Pleasant. Mr. F. took leave this P.M. agreeable visit. heard very practical ideas.

Mond. 14th Pleasant. saw Mr. Miron Munson just from Vt. brought me a letter from Orra [Copeland] heard of the death of Mr. Hiram Scott. Grandma'am very lonesome. she writes she is no better. Mr. R[oswell] E[astman]. visited this P.M. Not happy.

Tuesd. 15th Fine growing season. S[ally] Remington myself visited Mr. E[astman]. she spent the night with [me].

Wed 16th Dry. windy. worked at the door yard until I almost fainted. took cold.

Thurs. 17th Finished weaving. very glad of it. sewed some. toothache. almost sick.

Frid. 18th Rainy A.M. worked at the schoolhouse. cleared the door yard. ready for school. so tired. could not get home. spent the night with B.E. [Betsey Eastman], R.E. [Roswell Eastman] hurt his knee as bad as ever. had a great visit. but slept none.

Sat. 19th Starched. Ironed. plated ruffs. Inspected by Mr. S. Remington. Mr. Elias Post, Mr. Abbott. Mr. J.D. [Joseph Durfey], C.D. [Charlotte Durfey] Mr. and Mrs. [Phineas] Durfey, spectators[.] I never felt more disagreeable in my life. received a pleasant visit from Mr. Taylor, very unwell indeed hardly able to sit up. retired at one o'clock.

Sun. 20th Rainy day. Mr. T[aylor] wrote to Orra.[32] have the toothache very hard. sick at the stomach very sick this evening. almost fainted or rather a fit.

Mond. 21st Rainy. Mr. T[aylor] took my ring & left his watch. he walked to the schoolhouse with me. began a school for the first time. put all my scholars into their ABC's.

	very still school. only ten scholars. returned home. went to bed sick. very muddy and wet. took cold. all for the best.
Tuesd. 22nd	Pleasant. plated ruff before school. much pleased with my employment. Mrs. Charlotte Durfey took tea with us. gave me an invitation to board with her.
Wed. 23rd	Very pleasant. washed this morn. commenced boarding at J.D. [Joseph Durfey] one mile and quarter from school. took a walk to the wood. found the smaller [unreadable].
Thurs. 24th	Pleasant. took a walk to the wood at noon for exercise. Mr. R.E. visited my school, presented me with a key. Mr. Warner's house raised this P.M.[33]
Frid. 25th	Cloudy. saw Mr. Pierce. informed of his [impending] return to Vt. wrote to Mr. Dunshee, Orra [Copeland], Harriet [Charter], Jerusha Sprague. went as far as Mr. E[astman]'s spent the night.
Sat. 26th	Rainy. Trimmed the schoolhouse with popple and cherry [blossoms]. returned to uncle [Durfey]'s.
Sund. 27th	Rainy. Attended meeting. Mr. J[ames] S[quire], S[tillman] R[emington], L[ee] E[astman], A[ndrew] S[quire], Mr. Spencer called.
Mond. 28th	Rainy. morn. returned to J.D. informed of Censure on account of writing.
Tuesd. 29th	Rainy morn. girls forbidden to bring work by the inspector S.R. [Stillman Remington] took my usual walk to the wood. called to Mr. E[astman]'s, took tea. Betsy went home with me. staid all night. we took a Clandestine walk to West Parishville to take a view of her Brother's farm. High spirits.
Wedn 30th	Pleasant. Four visitors, just as school was out. enjoyed myself well with them.
Thurs 31st	Pleasant. finished my Bombazett Petticoat. wore my new gown for the outing at Mr. Squires. Retired not dejected.

June 1821

Frid 1st	Pleasant. Melancholy possess my mind and gloomy prospects rise. returned home to J[oseph] D[urfey] all gone from home. Mrs. Remington sent for me to visit her. Chose to enjoy myself in melancholy. but know not from what it proceeds. sewing for C[hloe Squire].

Sat 2nd Pleasant. Mr. Remington. Mr. Lee Eastman, call. After school trim the house, bushes. Called over to Mr. Squires. Spent the night tolerably.

Sund 3rd Pleasant. Walked to the village in company with Miss C[hloe] & R Squires. Betsey Eastman. Mr. Green [minister] preached from I of Peter 4–17:

> For the time is come that judgment must begin at the house of God. And of it first begin at us what will the end be of them that obey not the Gospel of God.

Took supper at Mr. Squires, called Mr. E[astman]. Mary spent the night with me. Mr. Otis Kent playing fiddler this eve. A number of gentlemen called.

Mond 4th Pleasant. [Militia] Training. Received invitation to a dance by Mr. L[ee]. Eastman. Walked to Mr. E.('s) at noon. Very rude to appearance but it left an inward sting behind. Dressed in white. the party broke up at three. How disagreeable to my feelings but they know it not.

Tuesd 5th Pleasant. took tea at Mr. E. Spent the night at P. Durfey's. Sally and I took a walk.

Wed. 6th Pleasant. washed before school. picking wool for Aunt Ruth [Durfey]. Very tired.

Thurs 7th Pleasant. To work at wool, do many chores, all this slavery for nothing.

Frid 8th Warm. Pleasant. PM Thunder and lightning. scrubbed my school floor.

Sat 9th Taught school this forenoon. took dinner at Mr. E's. trimmed the house with popple trees. Elder Green preached from these words. . . . "Continue in Love one to another." introduced to Mrs. Hannah Squire. Spent the night agreeably with my dear Betsey. retired at one o'clock.

Sund 10th Pleasant. Mr. & Miss B.E. to Parishville. six miles on horseback. threw from the horse. tore my silk frock sadly. called and fixed it at Bakers Inn. Attended meeting at the Academy. Introduced to Miss Phebe L. Brownall. Walked to Mr. Hazens with her. Miss Judah Howards died today. Supped at Col. Hards. Accompanied Miss Talcott to Uncle Brooks. Took supper. Saw two wild deer, one tame fawn, one woodchuck. Rode very fast, very tired. Found uncle sick. gentlemen L.R., D. Eastman R & L. Squire. J. Stearns. called. I felt as though I was a burden to society at least to Mrs. D[urfey]. retired and gave vent by tears.

Mond 11th Pleasant. visited at school by Sally R[emington]. received a Letter from Fort Covington. Miss Susan Davis. Lend may. Poor stuff indeed.

Tues 12th — Warm. Cut out a gown for S.R. [Sally Remington] Visited her. Took Cambric shirt to mend.

Wed 13th — Cloudy. walked to Mr. E. [Eastman, Sr.] at noon. William sick. visited Mrs. Tinkham.

Thurs. 14th — Rainy. R.E. [Roswell Eastman] visited my school. Miss B.E.[Betsey Eastman] quite sick. rained so I could not conveniently get home. staid with Betsey.

Frid. 15th — Very Rainy. returned to J.D.'s [Joseph Durfey's] Went home with Mrs T. [inkham]. read letters from Miss Fanny Darwin. also her experience. hard pain in my side. dejected spirits -the tatting tongue lies not dormant.

Sat 16th — Pleasant. took my leave of Mr. J[oseph] Durfey's called at Mr. Covey presented with a Peony the only one I have seen in this country. called at Mr. Remington. made a trifling mistake in Sally's frock which incurred the old Lady's displeasure. indulged a few tears and went along to school about eleven o'clock. Mr. Ocean Prime and Robert Dunshee called from Bristol. dismissed my school. returned to uncle Durfey's with them. received a lengthy letter from Orra [Copeland], one from Betsey Hills one from Mrs. Miranda Dunshee, one from Amelia Annin in Petersborough. Lost my penknife [at] party. made a gown for Maria [Durfey]. very good visit. very warm.

Sund 17th — Pleasant. Lent my Bonnet to J.D. wrote a letter to the gentlemen. one to Miss Phoebe Brown, Pickering [Ontario]. very warm.

Mond 18th — Rainy. Gentlemen took their leave. commenced boarding at Mr. Eastmans. saw three deer. Lee and Samuel killed two of them. tolerable spirits.

Tuesd 19th — First day of Second election at [uncle] Phineas Durfey's. made waist. agreeable place.

Wed 20th — Rainy. received a Bonnet and gown pattern from Potsdam. pain side.

Thursd 21st — Pleasant. heard from Bristol. drew a likeness. wrote a letter. entered the Office at Mr. Dunshee. weighed one hundred twenty. good spirits.

Frid 22nd — Pleasant. washed some. washed school house at noon. Strawberries ripe.

Sat 23rd — Pleasant. requested to spend an evening with Mr. S[amuel] E[Eastman] surprising indeed. took a walk to the South wood with Betsey. read until Dark. Discomposed.

Sund 24th Pleasant. Miss B[etsey] and myself staid at home alone. the Ladies called over here at noon. took a walk after meeting. pleasant visit.

Mond 25th Pleasant. washed. starched my clothes before school returned to P.D.'s [Phineas Durfey's] went to Mr. J.D. [Joseph Durfey] read a letter from Mr. T.M. Hopkins. heard Alvin Squire near. Rainy day. starched. Ironed after this morn. walked to Mr. E. at noon.

Tuesd 26th Betsey came to see me after school. good visit. Basted a gown for Mrs. Durfey.

Wed 27th Cloudy. washed my Crape ruff, bonnet strings, gloves etc. Mr. Harvey Munsill called from Vt. Sent six letters by him. my feelings depressed.

Thursd 28th Pleasant. sewing. received a lengthy letter by the hand of Mr. Lee from My dear Orra [Copeland]. she [in]forms me her health is very poor. unwell.

Frid 29th Pleasant. Out of health. called over to Mr. E.'s at noon. saw Mr. Ellis from Potsdam. Basted a Dimity Petticoat of (for) Betsey. received an invitation to the Independence Ball. what can all this mean?

Sat 30th [No entry]

[July 1821]

July first Pleasant. Dressed in white. Attended Mrs. Henderson's funeral at the village. Walked to Mr. [Taylor]s at noon. Saw old Mr. Hawkins saw Mr. M. Mires on his return to Vt. Started to go to conference, went as far as Mr. E's staid until night there being no conference. hard pain in my head. retired but not to rest. Sick and weary of life. Oh, that I was prepared to leave.

Mond 2nd Rainy morn. washed before school. Mr. Lee Eastman spent the intermission at the school house. insisted upon my being present at the Independence if I would not join them. Uncle insisted upon my dismissing school and assisting them after school. Baked and fried cakes eve. Warm fore, warm. weather also. Almost melted. Tired of Balls.

Tues 3rd Cool. trimmed the Bar Room in high style. made the colour for the flagg for the Liberty pole. Baked pies. swept the door yard. waited upon twenty four Gentlemen and Ladies at supper in as good a style as possible. tore my white frock. sadly. several requests guests to join them. Mr. Hawkins, Mr. Lee called. went to Mr. E's to get rid of the noise. spent the eve with R[oswell] E[astman] if ever I was a slave for nothing it has been today. retired at three.

Wed 4th Slept none. went home at four. washed my clothes some, chored and cleared out for school. the gentlemen called this morn. some staid all night some to breakfast. I found a gold ring. almost broke. Miss Betsey and Mary Eastman visited my school. staid until almost night. commenced boarding to Deacon Seth Abbotts. very tired.

Thursd 5th Very cool. sewing. took my daily walk to the wood. leaning upon a rock, fell asleep. wrote to Miss Copeland. took a walk down to the Brook with Miss Sally Abbott. an agreeable girl. read in the eve. pain in my stomach. What a fool I have been to do as I have for nothing.[34]

Friday 6th Pleasant cool, dewing. took a walk to Mr. E's at noon. Elder [Hiram S.] Johnson Elder [Richard] Palmer and wife staid to Mr. Abbotts. fine visit with Mrs. P. heard from Mr. Taylor. went to Mr. Wrights to lodge. very unwell.

Sat 7th Pleasant morn. Rainy P.M. trimmed the schoolhouse in a style. washed it. Mr. R.E. [Roswell Eastman] called after school, returned to Uncles. very wet road. retired to my chamber. drowned myself in tears undressed not. wept myself to sleep. arose with a heat. ready to cuss.

Sund 8th Attending meeting. heard Mr. Richard Palmer preached from [original blank space]. Took tea to Mr. E.s to my shame walked to the south road. heard a sermon delivered by Mr. Roads from Romans VI:

> "Therefore being justified by faith, we have peace with God through our Lord Jesus Christ."

walked home with Mr. Samuel Eastman, [he] spent the evening. surprising that he should request my heart and hand at the first visit. What can all this mean? if this is the method he takes to gain my esteem he will meet many obstructions. I conclude there are some strange intentions.

Mond 9th Pleasant. Cool. washed this morn. finished [uncle] P[hineas].D[urfey].'s Cambric Shirt returned to Mr. Abbotts. Mr. A. was married nine years today. indulged myself in grief. what can I do.

Tuesd 10th Saphronia Eastman eleven years old this day. Miss B[etsey] E[astman]. and C[hloe] S[quire]. called at the schoolhouse. spent the afternoon at Mr. Squires. heavy heart.

Wed 11th Rainy. Mrs. E. sent for me to come there at noon. very unwell. staid late at the schoolhouse to indulge my tears alone. solitary object.

Thurs 12th — Rain. finished the other shirt. walked to P.D.s [Phineas Durfey's] at noon. took some tea. took a walk with Miss S. [Sally] Abbott. appeared my cheerful and lively self but one continued melancholy reigns within my breast no friend to unbosom my feelings to. no one to advise me or protect me from insults.

Frid 13th — Cloudy. my present feeling[s] are as though I had not a friend in the world. Miss Sally Abbott visited school. tarried to singing school. rode home with Mr. and Miss Remington. a number of the young people called there in the evening. I endeavored to hide my gloominess [but] my feelings are indescribable. Oh if I were in some desert, I think I could be happy.

Sat. 14th — Pleasant. cool. took a walk with Sarah to Mr. C.'s[.] washed starched and Ironed and plated ruffs. at uncles after school. Mr. Tupper called. took a hard cold. very unwell. melancholy.

Sund 15th — Pleasant. very melancholy. it is noticed. uncle proposed to walk to the west farm, reluctantly accepted. very tired. walked to the schoolhouse. heard a Lecture preached by Elder Lothrop.

Mond 16th — Pleasant and warm. finished my knitting. conversed with Mr. Remington of past offences. saw Mr. L.S., C.S., J.S. [Levi Squires, Chloe Squires, J. Squires] Just like a story or song I pass my life.

Tues 17th — Rainy. sewing. entered a letter to Mr. Hills, Portland. Mr. Remington visited my school. conversed freely with him respecting his views towards Miss Witherell. I find his feeling rather disturbed. my own also.

Wed 18th — Rainy. muddy walking. visited after school by S and R. E. [Samuel and Roswell Eastman] hard cough.

Thursd 19th — Pleasant. kept half day. walked to uncle's rode with Miss Anna Oliver to a party at Mr. Otis Squires. saw Miss Phebe Brownell invited strongly to visit her school. borrowed the Economy of Human Life.[35] returned to Mr. Abbott's. Tolerable visit. very lively but I deceived them. I did not feel so.

Friday 20th — Pleasant. began another stocking. went Raspberrying. Sally and I thought we must have something that was rotted, raked hay, poor.

Sat 21st — Cloudy. made Red and green ink. made thirteen certificates in imitation of Pink. trimmed the [school] house with bushes. Sally helped me clear the door yard, broke a rake, prepared my hat for Sally to wear. hard cold.

Sund 22nd — Pleasant. took a ride to Stockholm to meeting, about five miles, in company with twenty gentlemen and Ladies from Hopkinton. The meeting was led by a Churchman. walked to Miss Gurley's at intermission and took refreshment. Returned there after meeting. Had a very uneasy pace to Stockholm, the roads rough. Wore my white frock. Stepped in eight holes. bruised my arms most shockingly. I bathed well in vinegar until I retired which was early. great pain.

Mond 23rd — Better than I expected. washed my clothes. received a friendly letter from Mr. Taylor, one from Miss Copeland, Vt. She writes me her health is better. Mr. S.E. Called.

Tuesd 24th — Rainy Ironed. sewing. Mrs. A[bbott] and myself took a walk. raspberrying.

Wed 25th — Rainy. worked at my ruff. presented with a cucumber by Mrs. Wright the first I have seen this year. Mr. and Mrs. W. reprimanded me highly for not calling.

Thursd 26th — Pleasant. worked at my ruff. visited at school by Miss Dorothy and Barbara Dewey. Miss Julia Covey. Miss Anna Oliver. spent the P.M. at M(r.) Eastman. accompanied them to Mrs. Tinkham's spent the night very tired but little sleep.

Frid 27th — Pleasant and warm school visited by Miss Betsey and Mary Eastman. Chloe S[quires].

Sat 28th — Pleasant took leave of Deacon Seth Abbott. returned to [Uncle] P[hineas] D[urfey] to spend the Sabbath. informed by a traveler that Capt. Bailey of Plattsburg murdered himself with a knife last Tuesday. Cut Mr. Lee Eastman's hair. attended Conference accompanied home and spent the evening with Mr. Eastman. a traveler staid from Kingston. the gentlemen all called this eve. I suspect to shew their manners.

Sund 29th — or else they knew no better than to think it was good manners.

Mond 30th — Pleasant. washed went to Mr. Warner's to board. visited by Mrs. Squire & Mrs. Coolidge. making a cape. read the Journal of Mr. Fisk and Parsons.

July 31st — [No entry]

August 1821

Tuesd 1st — Pleasant very warm. unwell. walked to P.D. [Phineas Durfey's][.] sewed some. rode to Uncle Brooks, Parishville. As soon as I arrived here last night I lay down to rest being very tired. hard pain in my stomach and side. was in dreadful pain and distress through the night I think I never experienced such pain in my life.

every remedy that could be thought of has been applied to no purpose. everything I take immediately leaves my stomach. I am scarcely able to help myself any at all. heavy hands.

Wed 2nd Pleasant. Uncle heard that I was sick. came immediately to see me and insisted on having a Doctor. I think I shall soon get better without. I cannot have a Dr. Was bled at noon. this afternoon by the help of Miss Talcott and Miss Hayden walked to Mr. Newtons about 40 rods in an house. almost tired out. Miss P.B. [Polly Brownell] called.

Frid 3rd Rather better but very weak and feeble. no kind of appetite. by the help of a staff and Eliza, I walked into the field a little. Mrs. Durfey came to see me. Mr. Remington called. took my horse home. Miss Orrilla Squire called to see me I cannot walk alone yet, sit a little.

Sat. 4th Gaining slowly the Dr. came six miles to visit me. he left me physic and drops for my cough. he speaks very discouraging about me. sat up considerable but very feeble. no appetite. tolerable spirits.

Sund 5th Pleasant. Mr. Durfey took the pains to come on foot to enquire after my health. also Mr. Eastman staid five or six hours. a number called. the best of care[.] I have every one trying some experiment[.] not able to sit up much. I told uncle I thought I would try to get home soon.

Mond. 6th Pleasant. rather better Miss Phebe Brownell. Miss Sabrina Hoyt called to see me[.] I had taken a walk with Eliza. I think I shall return.

Tuesd. 7th Pleasant. tried to ride on horseback behind Eliza but not able. Harriet Durfey came after me, I started for Hopkinton. She rode behind to support me and Eliza at my side. called to Mr. Rose's and lay down and rested. I at last reached home better than I expected. I found Mr. Robert Dunshee and Mr. Lucius Loveland on their return to Vermont. I sent to the school house for a letter. finished and sent to Miss Orra [Copeland].

Wed 8th Very feeble today I thought best to ride out. I rode to Deacon Abbotts. it was too far. Mr. Lee and Miss Betsey Eastman. Mr. Andrew and Chloe Squire called over to see me this eve. invited to visit them as my health would admit.

Thursd 9th Pleasant. my health returns very slowly. left medicine and take Syrup. rode to Mr. Joseph Durfeys. head a fine sermon delivered by Mr. Parmalee of Malone from these words HEB [Hebrews] IV II:

> "For if the word profit them not mixed with faith in them that heard it."

He first shewed why it did not profit and then pointed out the consequence of not profiting by it. strong invitation to spend the night but I was tired and ashamed of lying in bed from home.

Friday 10th Pleasant. and warm. fine growing season. Miss Oliver left uncle's this morn. rode to Mr. Eastman's. spent the day and night pleasant visit. gain very slow. worked a pair of gloves for Mrs. Durfey.

Sat. 11th Read some in a History called Thinks I to Myself. returned home slowly on foot. very weak and tired. melancholy feelings. low spirits almost discouraged. Mr. Lee Eastman worked here.

Sund 12th Pleasant. cool. read considerable in the Bible. Mr. Lee and David Eastman, P. Durfey gathered choke cherries. Mrs. Durfey picked a pail full of Blueberries. I laid myself [down] and gave full vent by tears to see the examples set before their children. very unwell. No appetite. Mr. S.E. came and spent a few hours pleasantly. a number of gentlemen called this eve.

Mond 13th Pleasant. much better. washed a little. sewed some. spent an hour at Mrs. Remingtons. visited by Mr. Tailor of Stockholm. he returned my ring for his watch. Miss Oliver was thrown from a horse yesterday. broke [her] leg.

Tuesd 14th Mended silk and white frock. starched, plated ruffs. refused my invitation to Quilting and preferred solitude. Mr. T. [Taylor] took a friendly leave at eleven o'clock. he wrote part of a letter to Miss [Harriet] Charter. I finished it. enjoyed my melancholy being all alone excepting two travelers called.

Wed 15th Boarding at Mr. Caleb Wrights. began working my lace Cape. trouble with the rheumatism in my shoulder. saw Dr. Sprague. he almost discouraged me. I acknowledge I am not able to go to school.

Thursd 16th Smoky and warm. hard pain in my side and stomach. scarcely able to get to school. went home at noon and retired to rest. it appeared this afternoon as if I could not sit up until school was out. hard shower and thunder.

Frid 17th Commenced my school again. began Boarding at Mr. Wrights. fine Boarding place. good spirits to think I can again resume my school. read until dark.

Sat. 18th Rain morn. starched, Ironed, plated ruffs. received an invitation to take a ride to Parishville on the morrow by Mr. Lee Eastman. rode to P.D. [Uncle Phineas Durfey's] took clothing. returned.

Sund 19th Pleasant. Miss Lucy McAllister. gone home. dressed in silk. attended meeting at the schoolhouse. very tired and weak. a violent pain in my side and shoulder. retired after meeting to my chamber alone. almost lost in thought. What can I do?

Mond 20th Mr. Andrew Squires took breakfast here this morning. Uncle Durfey sent to have me come home if able for the purpose of learning to wind feathers for the Militia. Mr. S.E. L.E. B.E. J.D. [Samuel Eastman, Lee Eastman, Betsy Eastman, Joseph Durfey] called this eve. extreme headache, pain in my shoulder. bathed in Pepper and Vinegar. it was too much for me to come home. not able to sit up any.

Tuesd 21st Lowry. some rain. Mr. S.E. called. rode to school with Mr. J. Durfey. Kind while out of school. troubled with a Rheumatic pain in my side.

Wed. 22nd Cloudy very unwell today. Mrs. Charlotte Durfey. Mr. R. Durfey Mrs. Eastman, Mrs. Covey. visited my school. visited at Mr. W[itherel's] after school. excellent visit. pressing invitation to visit them. tolerable spirits.

Thursd 23rd Cool and clear. worked at my Cape. Miss Matilda Witherel visited my school. walked to Mr. Durfey's with her this eve and spent the night. worked some at feathers. Dr. Sprague. Mr. Seth Abbott spent the evening. pleasant visit with Matilda. Conversed freely of her late suitor - S. R. [Stillman Remington]

Frid 24th Called at Mr. E.'s Miss Betsey spent the forenoon with me at the schoolhouse. at noon we went to Mr. Wrights she being out of health retired. spent the night. Mr. Remington brought me a red feather to have one made. spent the eve.

Sat. 25th Pleasant. finished my cape. went home at noon. took my leave of Mr. Wrights. returned to Uncle's. Miss Julia Covey and Miss [Diadama] Dewey spent the night with me. good visit but I have such a continual pain in my side that I can[not] be lively.

Sund 26th Rainy day. out of health. received a visit from Mr. Eastman this evening.

Mond 27th Heavy fog. washed, finished one red top feather for Mr. Remington. engaged another. commenced boarding at Mr. Squires, Mr. Lee and David Eastman spent the eve. at Mr. Squires. I do not feel at home here. as I do in someplaces. very alone.

Tuesd 28th Returned to Mr. Squires. Met Dr. Sprague. he gave me about twenty pills with a strict charge to obey his orders. obliged to lie down to rest as soon as I get home. I do not regain my health as I should. I suspect. do nothing.

Wedn 29th — Rainy P.M. Miss Betsey Eastman called over to the school house insisted upon my spending the week with her. Took a Military Frock to make for Mr. Lee Eastman. fringed it this evening. I feel rather delicate about boarding here.

Thurs 30th — Pleasant. Sewing while out of school. not able to do much. called to uncle's.

Friday 31st — Pleasant. hard cold. Uncle John Brooks came in from Vermont. rode home with him received a letter from Miss [Orra] Copeland. heard Mrs. Carpenter had a fine son born the twenty-third of this month. B and D [Diadama] Dewey and J. [Julia] Covey called to visit me.

September 1821

Sat. 1st — Pleasant. Mr. E[astman] called this morn. visited my school this P.M. saw Mr. Adolphus Hawkins from Vermont. Miss Maria H[opkins]. retired drowned in tears with a bursting heart.

Sun 2nd — Pleasant. rode to meeting uncle gone to Mr. Perry's. saw Mr. Timothy M. Hopkins, Mr. Horace Lampson of Crown Point. Miss Betsey Eastman and myself had the ill manner to leave meeting to indulge our tears. meeting was out before we could retreat. we fastened ourselves in the room, remained until we could retire without discovery. We walked down the North woods, there gave full vent to our grief. But by being dressed in white was discovered. Mr. S.E. [Samuel Eastman] anxious to know the cause of our abrupt departure. came to inquire the cause of our grief but did not succeed. we separated and went home. Mr. Hopkins visited and took his dismission from Miss Eastman. Mr. Lee Eastman requested me to take a walk to Mr. Coveys. refused on account of my health. melancholy.

Mond 3rd — Rainy. washed. rode to school with uncle Brooks. called to Mr. Wrights and took my clothes. spent the night with Betsey. good visit. both in good spirits. retired late.

Tuesd 4th — Rainy Sewing. calculating to return to Mr. Squires but Betsey came after me with a horse. we rode down to uncle's. I have this evening the most trying scene of the kind that ever I experienced. hard case. I must either relinquish my resolutions of matrimony or make one miserable leave his friends forever or else my heart melts at the thought. but still I cannot resign willingly. what shall I say or do? Heart sick.

Wed 5th — Rainy. enjoyed myself tolerably well after school. so rainy expecting to stay at schoolhouse. Mr. Roswell Eastman came after me with a horse. melancholy eve.

Thursd 6th	Rode to school with Betsey. rode home with Adolphus Hawkins. finished Lee's frock. received an invitation by Mr. E[astman] to visit at Mrs. Remingtons. refused. spent the eve.
Frid 7th	Wrote a letter to Miss Copeland. one to Miss Abigail Lewis of Lewis. the music met here this eve. conversed with Aunt respecting my opinion of matrimony with Mr. E[astman] as he has offered.
Sat 8th	Mr. Brooks took his leave of us this morn. took some cord to make. good deal of trouble in making it, being unwell. it worried (me) much. made twelve yards of it. made six Tabersille for hats. Starched. Ironed. Plated Mr. Durfey's shirt. R[oswell]. returned home at ten. spent an hour with Mr. E. informed of his disagreeable feelings. all I can say will not remove them. for my own part, I wish I had never been born.
Sund 9th	Rainy. very uneasy. discontented. took a lengthy walk in the unknown wood, the rest of the time on the bed. received a letter from Miss Charter. her health poor. dejected.
Mond 10th	Training. Made one pair of tawrills. put on the Cord to another. very tired, indeed. when I reached the schoolhouse called over Mr E's at noon. made me promise to return to tea. Miss Mary E[astman] visited my school, went home with her. we had a good supply of Melons. Reluctantly took a ride with Mr. Lee E. to Mr. Post's, four miles. Had a good visit. I suppose for my part I was as near death as alive and wished to be nearer. introduced to Miss Emily Weed, Miss Betsey Johnson, Miss Harriet Sawyer, Miss Maria Hopkins, Miss Phebe Harwood, strong request to visit them. very tired.
Tuesd 11th	Very weak and tired out. Mr. Tinkham's people took their leave of this place. rainy P.M. spent the night at Mr. Wrights[.] very bad ulcer in my mouth.
Wed 12th	Rainy. rode to school. spent the night at Mr. Squires. very low in health.
Thursd 13th	Cool, called over to Mr. E[astman] visited with the Ladies at Mr. E[astman]'s. Miss [Diadama] Dewey and myself. took a candle and went to the schoolhouse. spent the evening in reading. the other girls came to frighten us but we neither saw nor heard them. we went to Mr. E[astman] dress in great coats, hats. walked out to see them. but missed them. spent the night. almost tired out after my folly but I did it to deceive them of my dejection.
Friday 14th	Pleasant. Miss Sally Remington visited me at school this P.M. visited this eve at Mr. E. large party devoured watermelons in abundance. retired at two.

Sat. 15th	Pleasant bought me a pencil and bread server. made a few small pockets for the girls. Harriet visited me at school. Alas, What a wretch I am. wretch indeed.
Sund 16th	Aunt Ruth very sick. A.M. wrote an address to my scholars. Attended Meeting this P.M. Mrs. E. sent me her cloak. very hard. staid until dark. conversed with Mr. E. found his feeling indescribable. took hard cold.
Mon. 17th	Dismissed my school for the last time. Miss Betsey Eastman, Miss H[arriet] Durfey, Miss Sophia Remington visited my school. returned home almost crazy with toothache. spent the night in sleepless agony. very weak.
Tues 18th	Scarcely able to sit up long at a time. ript the trimming from uncle's Military clothes. purchased me a large comb 4/6 [4 shillings, 6 pence] Mr. Frank spent the night with us. his health is very poor. rather consumptive.
Wed 19th	Washed my clothes and wove fleeces of wool. called over to J. Durfeys - made a ruff for his shirt. my face swollen so that I can scarcely see out of my eye. and very painful. I think I was favoured before my school closed.
Thursd 20th	Worked for Charlotte [Durfey] this A.M. Rainy P.M. returned to P.D. All the gentlemen called eve.
Frid 21st	After a sleepless night, I arose picked & greased my wool. did some chores. saw Mr. Storrs, Canada. Mr. Booth of Ferrisburgh [VT] took tea at Mrs. R[emington's]. accompanied my dear Betsey to J.D. my teeth troubled me so I could not visit.
Sat. 22nd	Not able to do anything. Betsey staid with me until night. Mr. E. called. My face swollen so that the ulcer cannot be lanced. I can scarcely endure it.
Sund 23rd	The ulcer broke and discharged plentifully at midnight. having been without sleep so long almost worn out with pain. I slept a little this morn. staid with the children for Mrs. Durfey to go to meeting. returned to uncle's. dejected.
Mond 24th	Rainy. washed, Baked and fried cakes. very weak and lazy all the time.
Tuesd 25th	Fixing uncle for Training. made his Epaulette shorter. Starched Ironed Plated ruffs for his shirts. did chores. went to J.D. and knead[ed] her bread and washed ten pounds of butter, her finger being sore. returned to uncle's. made a blue flagg. an eagle, thirteen stars. made a sheath. put on cockade and feather.
Wed 26th	Pleasant. General training Potsdam. did the chores. scoured the floors. visited with the married Ladies at J. Durfeys. unwell.

Thursd 27th Sewing on Mrs. Durfeys Bombazet gown. visited Mr. C[ovey] toothache staid J.D.s [Joseph Durfey]

Frid 28th Rainy. finished the gown. staid until ten o'clock. returned to uncle's. visited by Mrs. Eastman, Miss B[etsey] E[astman], Mr. Remington. C[harlotte] Durfey. tolerable spirits.

Sat 29th Pleasant. made an Apron. did good many chores. dressed chickens. Mr. S[amuel] E[astman]. J[ames] S[quires] all night.

Sund 30th Rainy. the gentlemen took breakfast Mr. Smith Durfey, Mr. Henderson staid several hours. Julia and Datha [Diadama] staid almost all day. have the toothache. hard.

October 1821

Mond. 1st Mr. S[amuel] E[astman, Jr.] called this morn. made some persons dreadful cross. spinning worsted, chores. toothache.

Tuesd 2nd Rainy. finished spinning, twisting. washed floors, sewed some. toothache continually.

Wed 3rd Went to J.D.s about eleven. put in a web of woolen. wove two yards. cut out two caps. made one. very agreeable people. but I am contented nowhere. Rain.

Thurd 4th Wove three yards and half. attended a Quilting at Mr. Coveys they had three. one for the married Ladies, one for the young Ladies and one for the small girls. I staid untill eleven o'clock and left them dancing. went home alone with dejected spirits and wounded feelings. I think now I will not attend another party.

Frid 5th Wove seven yards. Rainy night. Mr. Durfey out hunting. took cold yesterday. toothache.

Sat 6th Wove six yards. toothache. unwell beside my mind greatly agitated with the [tricks] of others and for want of counsel and Consolation, a Mother, a friend to place trust.

Sund. 7th Rain. took a Clandestine walk alone to the west. saw perhaps the place of my future abode, but God grant it may never be my lot. "But not my will but thine be done." If such should be my situation grant that my time may [be] devoted to my Redeemer and all other duties to my companion in life. returned to P[hineas] D[urfeys], read the Shepherd of Salisbury Plain.[36] visited by Mr. E[astman]. painful scene endeavored to dissuade him from harbouring such feelings but all in vain, left him agitated.

Mond 8th I returned to J[oseph] D[urfey]s wove out my web. Mr. E[astman] called. staid about four hours. washed some Worked a pair of gloves for Charlotte. returned to uncles. pared apples.

Tues 9th Rain. rode to carding machine. visited Mrs. Perry introduced to Mrs. Woodward. returned to the machine. took some rools. took tea at Mrs. Posts. returned at dark. tired. cold.

Wed 10th Rainy morn. called over to J[oseph] D[urfey], Mr. Covey A.M., Mrs Sprague, Mrs Laughlin. visited Mr. C's borrowed B.E. Wheel [Betsey's spinning wheel] spun ten knots of my wool, visited with the girls at Mr. E's. pleasant visit. Betsey and Mary staid with me until twelve.

Thurs 11th Rode to Mr. Laughlin's entered the Capt. returns to Major Orvis. on my return was thrown from the horse. without any material injury. spun twenty knots of warp. much fatigued. pain in my stomach and side.

Frid 12th Very rainy season. had the toothache all night and day. my face swollen full. together with my fall, confined me to my bed in great pain.

Sat 13th Rainy. the farmer appears to have lost his labour, his crops are spoiling. tried to work this P.M. Baked and churned. I generally suc[c]eed in keeping it to myself.

Sund 14th Very rainy. my tooth continues to ache. Very discontented and lonesome. drowned my cares in sleep for a few hours. spent one hours agreeably with Mr. E.

Mond 15th Rainy. spun 35 knots of warp. visited by Miss Sarah Remington all night. tired.

Tuesd 16th Rainy. unwell. spun but thirty knots. the Mrs. Durfeys visited at the village. spent the night at Mr. Eastman's agreeable visit had the toothache very hard cold.

Thursd 18th The most pleasant there has been this sometime. spun 18 knots, finished my wool. read a Valedictory address of Gen. Washington. went home. washed yarn. took cold.

Frid 19th Hard frost. very cold. Cloudy. spooled and gulled my yarn washed three blankets.

Sat. 20th Cold and Pleasant. did chores called over J[oseph] D[urfet] put in a web of 35 yards. returned to uncle's. hard pain in my stomach. lonesome and melancholy.

Sund 21st	Pleasant. This day arrived at my twentieth year. read in the forenoon. spent four hours in the wood. attended conference at the schoolhouse. visited by Mr. E. agreeable visit. Miss Julia Covey spent the night. good spirits.
Mond. 22nd	Cold and Pleasant. returned to J[oseph] D[urfey]'s. wove six yards. knit this eve. visited by Mr. S and Miss B.E. agreeable visit Miss Julia [Covey] spent the night good spirits.
Tues 23rd	Pleasant, cold. wove six yards. went to uncle's. cleared the Barr Room of old bushes. milk tables and trash about the quickest. accompanied home by Mr. Seth Abbott. Julia spent the night. strange people in the world.
Wed 24th	Pleasant. wove six yards made a sheet. Charlotte [Durfey] thirty-one years old. Mr E[astman] gave me an invitation to visit Mr. Wrights on the morrow.
Thursd 25th	Pleasant. wove four yards. walked to Mr. Wrights. spent the eve accompanied home by Mr. E. Agreeable visit retired at three. low spirits.
Frid 26th	Low spirits and ill health. not able to weave but four and half yards.
Sat 27th	Very pleasant. wove seven yards. lonesome. spiritless. melancholy.
Sund 28th	Pleasant morn after a rainy night. rode to the village. excellent meeting called over Dr. Spragues at intermission. tore my silk frock. came home tired. saw uncle Elisha Brooks. exchanged beads[.] Oh that I were in some lonely desert far from the frowns of the peevish. Mr. S[amuel] E[astman, Jr.] called. staid until nine. soon retired and relieved my heavy heart of its melancholy burthen [burden] by tears and sighs until late hour.
Mond 29th	Pleasant. high winds. put in the blankets. went to J[oseph] D[urfey] wove two yards. finished my web. washed some. ironed. came home very tired. visited by J.C., G.C., S.R. [Julia. Covey, Gilbert Covey, Stillman Remington]
Tuesd 30th	Wove four yards on my Blanket visited by Mrs. Abbott. Mrs. Durfey Mr. Covey, Mr. E. called. Mr. Levi Squires insisted upon my selling my Geography. dejected.
Wed 31st	Pleasant very cold. Mr. E called at the shop. staid until noon wove three yds. received an invitation by Mr. J. Vrooman to a party. Mr. E. obliged to refuse.

November 1821

Thursd 1st	Very rainy. hail and snow. Mr. E[astman] called. staid until one. Mr. L.E. [Lee Eastman] called twice. wove four yards. made up my school bill. knitting evenings.
Frid 2nd	Pleasant. wove five yards. and finished the Blankets. very tired. sewed on them this evening. Miss B. Eastman spent the eve. insisted upon my spending the night with her. I did. fine visit. retired [at] one.
Sat 3rd	Rain. sewed on my flannel petticoat. Mrs. E. colouring red. retired early in melancholy.
Sund. 4th	Cloudy. the men are spending the Sabbath in husking Mr. E. called. spent 6 hours.
Mond 5th	Washed. called over J.D.s took care of the children. spun some washed. read some.
Tues 6th	Returned to uncles. pressed and bound my gown. Charlotte visited us. bought two Books from Joseph Durfey and Wm. E. Eastman. endeavour to be lively.
Wed. 7th	Scoured all day. finished my coat. this evening. fried cakes.
Thurs 8th	Grated between 3 & 4 pounds of potatoes starch. Mended. melancholy the rest of the day.
Friday 9th	Cloudy. scoured the doors and ceilings. mended the rest of the day. very tired.
Sat. 10th	Cloudy, doing chores all day. Mr. S[amuel] E[astman], R[oswell] E[astman], L[evi] S[quires] called this evening.
Sund 11th	Some snow. attended meeting A.M. cold. came home at noon. indulged my tears five hours.
Mond. 12th	Cloudy. went to Mr. Eastman's. prepared harness for Kersey. Put in a web wove yard and half. Mr. E.'s health very low.
Tuesd 13th	Wove four and half yards. knit evening. agreeable company.
Wed 14th	Cold. rainy. weaving. enjoy my health and spirits well.
Thurs 15th	Wove all day for almost nothing. Betsey and myself work together and slave.

Frid 16th	Finished the kersey. put in a Cotton web for Dr. Sprague. he extracted a tooth for me. came very hard, the only one remaining. glad to get rid of it.
Sat 17th	Wove three yards on the cotton very tender. I have an excellent home here.
Sund 18th	Rainy and muddy. read tracts. enjoyed good spirits and company.
Mond. 19th	Unwell. wove but little. Miss Lucy McAllister took tea with us. S.E. [Samuel Eastman] sick.
Tuesd 20th	Wove all day. my health is far better than it was when I came here by not being exposed to the inclemency of the weather. My cup [overflows] with blessing[s].
Wed 21st	Pleasant. received a letter from Miss Copeland, Bristol. one from Miss Sprague. one from Miss Hanchet, Newhaven, all in tolerable health. weaving.
Thursd 22nd	Wove all day for a little. snows some every day just enough to wet.
Frid 23rd	Finished weaving. for this year. Miss Betsey disappointed of [her] boarding place.
Sat. 24th	Snow all gone this morn. put in a web for Betsey. returned to uncle's. did chores until late all the thanks I get for what I do is a frowning sigh.
Sund 25th	The snow fell ten inches deep last night. continues to fall. retired at dark.
Mond 26th	Washed, visited Mrs. Remington. studied in Willets Geography.
Tuesd 27th	Cut out two aprons. made one. Mr E.'s health very poor. called over to uncle's picking dead geese this eve. the gentlemen and Ladies from the village took a ride over here. agreeable visit. Mr. Storrs staid here from Canada.
Wed 28th	Did the chores. returned to J[oseph] D[urfey]'s to work for Charlotte. returned to [uncle] P[hineas] D[urfey]'s. spent the eve with Dr. Sprague and wife. returned to my home.
Thursd 29th	Cut out, partly made my flannel gown. engaged to work for Charlotte two weeks sewing fulled cloth. she is agreeable company for me.
Frid 30th	Sewing on Mr. D[urfey]'s coat what I get besides chores. rather dull spirits. my feeling[s] are such of late I know not where to find myself.

December 1821

Sat. 1st	Sewing, knitting, whatever is wanted. called over to uncle's for cloth.
Sund 2nd	Thawed all day. read considerable, toothache again.
Mond 3rd	Sewing. washed Mr. E. called this eve. retired at 1. toothache very hard.
Tuesd 4th	Sewing. visited by Mrs. R. Durfey. tolerable spirits to appearance.
Wed 5th	Mrs. D. thinks I make good improvement sewing thick cloth. toothache.
Thursd 6th	Mr. Durfey caulked the house with moss on account of my taking cold. took [original blank space].
Frid 7th	Pleasant. almost discouraged with my teeth. Mr. Wright called. hard toothache.
Sat 8th	Sewed some but have the toothache very hard. head disordered by it.
Sund 9th	Sewed on my gown. took the Belt from the Bombazett gown.
Mond 10th	Washed. Mrs. Eastman visited here this A.M. at Mr. Remington P.M. insisted very hard for me to accompany them. declined. as soon as I was left alone I unburthened my injured feelings by tears. finished my frock crape.
Tuesd 11th	Very stormy indeed. obliged to go to uncles very early. cut out and partly made two gowns. toothache very hard. How vain are all things here.
Wednes 12th	Thanksgiving. finished the gowns. visited by Miss B and M E. [Betsey and Mary Eastman] this evening. Mr. E, Julia Covey, Mr. R.E. [Roswell Eastman] G.C. [Gilbert Covey] N.P. [Noah Post] pleasant visit.
Thurs 13th	Returned to J[oseph] D[urfey]'s cut out a flannel frock for Charlotte. Sewed all day. Mr. and Mrs. Rockwell called a few hours. agreeable women indeed.
Frid 14th	Clear and cold. Finished the gown, worked on Pantaloons. toothache.
Sat. 15th	Finished the pantaloons. worked on a coat for Lucius [Durfey][.] Mr. E. called here. made bread.

Sund 16th Pleasant. Read considerable. A letter from Mr. T. Hopkins, Mr. and Mrs. D[urfey] Visited this eve at P[hineas] D[urfey]s. Pleasant visit with Mr. E[astman]. Retired in tolerable spirits.

Mond 17th Washed. Visited at Mr. David Coveys. worked on my ruff. Sewed eve.

Tuesd 18th Cold. Housework. sewed. Finished Lucius' coat. Mr. E[astman, Jr.] called. Melancholy.

Wed 19th Cold and windy. Mrs. D[urfey] gone all day. Mr. D[urfey] this eve at Mr. Chester Rockwell's did the wash. Twisted and washed ten knots of yarn. pieced the outside of a quilt. Mr. E[astman, Jr.] called. I spent the eve alone excepting the children. Retired at twelve.

Thursd 20th Very unwell this morn. Sti[t]ched the forepart of a coat. Did the wash.

Frid 21st Cold. Housework and sewing. Toothache. Melancholy. Where are my distant friends, far from me and I fear will be this winter. Oh my mother, where are you?

Sat 22nd Housework. Finished Mr. Durfey's coat. Miss Betsey visited me. She was thrown from her horse. Hurt her side. She spent the night.

Sund 23rd Clear. cold and pleasant. Rode to uncle's with Mr. E.[astman, Jr.] and B[etsey] E[astman]. Attended meeting at the village with Mr. Durfey. Indifferent. Melancholy.

Mond 24th Stormy eve. Mr and Mrs. Durfey started for Madrid [St. Lawrence County]. Left the care of the house to me. Mr. J[oseph] D[urfey] with Miss B[etsey] E[astman], R[emington] E[astman] Mr [Samuel] E[astman, Jr.] spent the evening. agreeable.

Tuesd 25th Only one traveler called for Breakfast. altered my blue frock. toothache hard.

Wed 26th Altered my Bombazett frock. very melancholy. toothache. Mr.[Phineas] D[urfey] returned Miss Betsey called spent the night with me. her feelings are not very pleasant.

Thursd 27th Cold and stormy. Cut out the facing of a great coat and made the buttonholes for Joseph. worked all day for her. returned accompanied by Mr. Eastman to Mr. J[oseph] Durfeys.

Friday 28th Sewing. Mr. D[urfey] killed his swine today. had to do some housework.

Sat. 29th Very cold. sewing and housework. Harriet D[urfey] spent the night with me. brought a letter from Mr. Adolphus Taylor, Stockholm, tolerable spirits.

Sund. 30th Cold and stormy. read the Book of Ecclesiastes. Mr. Ephram Sampson married this eve to Miss Laura Smith. melancholy tears flow easy.

Mond 31st Clear and pleasant. washed. strung my beads. carded Bats for a quilt.

HOPKINTON

January 1st A.D. of our Lord 1822.

Tuesd 1st Pleasant. agreeable weather. Twenty years this morn since my mother left this world. Ah! where is she? Is not her spirit hovering o'er my head entreating her infant daughter to reclaim her wandering steps? yet little does she realize it. received a morning invitation to visit at Mr. Eastmans this eve by S.E. [Samuel Eastman] Mrs Durfey and myself prepared a quilt and for company. Mr S.E. [Samuel Eastman, Jr.] D.E. [David Eastman] called. Introduced to Mr. John Kelly, [of] Fowler. but what was my embarrassment and disappointment aggravation! the gentleman did not call for me. what am I to think of this treatment? Mr. Seth Hawkins, Mr. Reuben Post called. strong request to take a ride to Capt. Durfeys. refused. retired with a heavy heart. ashamed ignorant of my crime and also of the cause of neglect.

Wed 2nd Blustering. the Ladies old and young came very early. saw Mrs. Kelly, Miss Rosalina Wholeman. introduced to neither. the gentleman spent the eve. for my part I felt very disagreeable indeed though I endeavoured to disguise them. Mr. L.E. [Lee Eastman] paid for making his frock. 60 cents. Mr S.E. [Samuel Eastman Jr.] informed me the reason of his neglect. an ignorant mistake which is still worse. Mr. Buzzee. Charlotte [Durfey] came to spend a few hours.

Thurs 3rd Very blustering, the cold extreme. preparing another quilt, ironing, Etc. Visited at Mr. Eastmans, a number of others. a disagreeable evening to me. if I could retire to some cavern to screen me from the world, how soon would I do it, but I must not think so. not harbor such feeling.

Frid 4th Cold. low spirits. the coldest day that has passed this year the schoolhouse burnt in the east part of Hopkinton [modern Nicholville]. working my ruff. Mr. E[astman, Jr.] called this A.M. staid until twelve at night Mr. R[emington] returned. Mr. D[urfey] sick.

Sat. 5th Cold, finished my cuff. called over to uncle's found them sick and lame. went to J[oseph] D[urfey]'s.

Sund 6th More moderate. Attended meeting. refreshing ser[m]on but alas how soon it is forgotten. Mr. Samuel Hurlburt. Hinesburg, Vt. gave us an account of the conversion of three thousand souls in Vermont within eight months. saw Mrs. Peery[.] Mrs. Durfey gone to watch with Mrs. Sheldon. Mr. L.E. [Lee Eastman], G.C. [Gilbert Covey], D.D. [Diadama Dewey], J.C. [Julia Covey] spent the evening D.J. staid all night. the girls were very rude. absent minded.

Mond 7th Worked for myself today. enjoyed myself tolerably well. Mrs. D. sick.

Tuesd 8th Stormy. returned to uncle's. the neighbors invited to spend the eve. to our surprise Uncle John Brooks and Grandma'a'm arrived from Vt. informed that uncle had been blessed with another son. Cyril.

Wed 9th Cold. rode and visited with them at Uncle Brooks. rode with Mr [&] Mrs Durfey to the Village. called at Mr. Hawkins. pleasant visit with Grandma'm.

Thurs 10th Returned home Mr. E[astman, Sr.] and wife visited us. pleasant visit with S[amuel] E[astman, Jr.] Retired four.

Frid 11th Rode to Potsdam, purchased a dictionary saw Mr. Wm. Clark, Stockholm heard from Mr. Taylor returned home sleigh-sick. Old Mr. Covey spent the night.

Sat. 12th Very unwell. sewed on Joseph [Durfey]s coat. our people took their leave this morn. Mr. E[astman, Sr.] called. His health is very poor indeed.

Sund 13th Very cold. melancholy. indulged a few tears. the girls called for me to attend the conference at the schoolhouse. was none. accompanied home by Mr. R[emington] E[astman], Mr. H[opkins] Miss P[rudence] Chandler called. Toothache. what a relation.

Mond 14th sewed and tended Barr. superstition, what a torment to tranquility.

Tues 15th Sewing. knitting. tended Barr. not very well. Mr and Mrs. Covey to work here. Uncle Elisha [rooks] came for me to go to J[oseph] D[urfey]'s good visit with Rebecca. spent night.

Wed 16th Returned J.D. called over to Mr. Es. [Samuel Eastman Sr.'s] S[amuel] E[astman, Jr.] came home with me. Mrs. E. Wright, Lisbon had her arm badly torn. attended the wedding of Mr. Edmund Hayden and my agreeable friend Eliza Talcott. dressed the Bride. spent the cold night at Elishas had my ring and comb marred, and broke.

Thurs 17th Mr and Mrs. Hayden. Mr. Ruel Hayden. Miss Sally Abbott spent the night with us. thanks to my God I am not bound with matrimonial bonds.

Frid 18th Took leave of uncle's, visited at Mr. Roses. rode with them to Mr. Durfey. strong request to visit with them. finished Harriet [Durfey]'s overshoes. uncle gave to the French Mills. Aunt out of health. Mr. E[astman, Jr.] called and that riled her amazingly. she gave him an insulting Lecture. she cried, talked and acted like a mad fool all night. I did not pity her at all. only her temper.

Sat. 19th Done all the work. Baked Pies and biscuits. Etc. went to Mr Coveys put in a web of Diamond Kersey. uncle returned. purchased the girls a frock.

Sund. 20th Attended meeting at the schoolhouse. Mr. E[astman, Jr.] spent the night until four. agreeably presented with a silver dollar. ashamed of accepting it. took leave for eight weeks. Miss Julia spent the night. determined not [to] tarry long with their family on account of the ill treatment of Mrs. Durfey to Mr. D[urfey].

Mond. 21st Rain. did the chores and a large washing ironed some sewed considerable. heard from Ferrisburgh by Mr. Samuel Cole. Charlotte [Durfey] spent the night.[37]

Tuesd 22nd Cold. very stormy. sewed all day on Joseph's coat. Mr. Canada & Miss Witherell called. insisted upon my returning home with them. took tea at Mrs. Remington. Bought me a green veil and a pocket handkerchief, hemmed it. Mr. Proctor's family put up here. this gentleman weighs three hundred and seventy-five. Rode with Mr. R[emington] E[astman, Miss M[ary] E[astman] to watch with Mrs. Wright of Lisbon. how thankful ought I to be.

Wed 23rd Very cold. Mr. S[amuel] E[astman, Jr.] came after us. spent the day and night but the slavish fear of my aunt under which I labor rendered it unpleasant indeed.

Thurs 24th Very cold indeed. tolerable visit. returned to uncle's informed that Mr. Cole had been robbed of his Cider by Mr. Asa Squires, Gilbert Covey, Nathaniel Baldwin, Aurelius Remington. G[ilbert] C[ovey] owned [confessed] it.

Frid 25th Cold. saw Mr. Silas Eastman and wife of Newhaven, Vt. visited by Miss Orrilla and Lydia Squires. Harriet went home with them. E.G. spent night.

Sat 26th More moderate. prepared breakfast for four from Plattsburgh. The Ladies were sisters to the Late Flavel Clerk Williams. fine visit with them. Rev. Mr. Cook, wife, two sisters from Genesee. washed floors starched, ironed ruffs. Miss B[etsey] E[astman] and myself went to watch with Mrs. Wright. did not need us, returned.

Sund 27th Attended meeting at the schoolhouse. read considerable. Mr. H[iram] Mires, J. Mills staid here. prepared supper for James and Jeffry Davis, French Mills. disagreeable feelings.

Mond 28th Washed. My eldest Brother [Silas Orvis] and family arrived A.M. in health. Mr. Cole returned. Court held until two o'clock. the house full. good visit with Sarah. very tired.

Tuesd 29th Washed again for my brothers family. Brother Eleazer and Rowland Brown arrived about noon. we visited at Elisha Brooks. returned at twelve. I sat and conversed until three. indulged a few tears and retired to rest. Canada fever.[38]

Wed 30th Stormy and cold Brother Silas [Orvis] took his leave for Canada in company with Mr. John Doty. hard parting with friends for the last time. washed for the others. Eleazer mended shoes all day for me. Elisha spent the night. Mr. Israel Birchard also from Canada to Ferrisburgh. conversed with my Brother [Eleazor] respecting his union with Miss [Elizabeth] Austin.[39] I pity their situation. we retired at four. I felt very disagreeable. perhaps the last opportunity I shall ever have to converse with either of my Brothers. this side of endless eternity.

Thursd 31st My Brother [Eleazer] Orvis and Mr. Brown bade me adieu and started for Canada, town of Pickering between Duffins and Lords Creek. my brother unhappily left his great coat. uncle Durfey accompanied them as far as Potsdam. settled with J[oseph] D[urfey]. Due to me three dollars eighty-two cents. tended Barr. did chores. out of health. Mr. E[astman, Jr.] called a short time.

February 1822

Frid 1st Started for the French Mills rode eight miles to Chandlers and boated fourteen miles to Wakefield's. rode ten miles crossed the line to Canada. traded ten dollars. put up at Mr. Pecks. almost sick.

Sat. 2nd Crossed the line before day. ten miles to Wakefields. one mile to Stoddards and took breakfast. rode to Chandlers. boated from there home. Mrs. Covey, Mrs Durfey, Miss Witherell, Miss McAllister spent the eve. very tired indeed. almost sick. frowns in plenty.

Sund 3rd Attended meeting at the schoolhouse perhaps for the last time. staid to Mr. Wrights P.M. returned home settled with Dr. Spragues. tired. sick and fatigued.

Mond 4th Washed. Mr. Sweet, Mr. Taylor, Mr. Eastman and wife, Mr and Mrs Bird seven or eight others spent the night. Mr. E[astman, Jr.], B[etsey] E[astman], J[ulia] C[ovey], E[liza] G[ilbert] spent the eve. Mr. E[astman, Jr. visits me perhaps for the last time. to part with some very disagreeable, others very agreeable. behaved as though some evil spirit ruled. sat up until day. very unwell.

Tuesd 5th Took leave of Hopkinton and its inhabitants. rode to Chandlers then to Potters 19 in Bangor. called upon Miss Harmona Eddy. rode ten miles to Smiths Chateauguay four corners. it appeared I could ride no further. my side swollen. Pained me greatly. Rode eight miles farther to Roberts which made thirty six miles. prepared supper for nine. upwards of sixty staid here almost discouraged. unless I am better in the morn.

MOORS, TOWN [MOOERS]

Wedns 6th Stormy. began to find myself on the road to Vermont. eight sleighs in company. rode eight miles to Oliverts. prepared breakfast for the whole. in good spirits rode ten miles to Robinson's, ten miles to Bankers. left Bird and Eastman. rode six miles to Gordon's, Plattsburg village. crossed on Cumberland head. snowed so we could scarcely perceive the Bushes in the cracks put up at Fletcher's on the Grand Isle. prepared tea. visited late with the Ladies. they were preparing for Installation tomorrow.

Thursd 7th Crossed the Lake. found it very rough, seven miles to Burlington. the handsomest situation I ever saw. Prepared breakfast for the last time on our short journey. I have not thought much about returning to my native place but from Burlington and Williston I could discover the Mountains rising with majestic grandeur, their snowy tops mingling with the clouds spread a delightful prospect of Nativity. called at the Hull's Inn, Hinesburg. Mr. Williams took his leave. very cold. called to Mr. Collins but arrived in high spirits at Mr. Sweet's.

Frid 8th Saw Mr. T[haddeus] Dunton, Mr C. Edwards, Mr. Taylor. went to Mr Strong's and brought my dear Orra and Eunice [Copeland] home. Mr. Sweet waited upon us home to Uncle Brooks. once more arrived safe in my native dwelling. Found them well. in high spirits. I think now I can never leave it again.

Sat. 9th Rode to Middlebury. purchased skin of Morocco. one pair of Beaver gloves, other articles for cash. called at Mr. Haynes. Mr. Samuel Dolbear called to see me. expressed great joy at my return, more than I did at his presence; called at my homestead. returned home to tea then rode to Mr. Follits for a pair of shoes had a fine visit. Mr. Spafford Groot. Mr. A. called.

Sund 10th Mrs. Barrows departed this life this morning. attended meeting at the Chapel. Nehemiah 8th. 10th. Mr. Taylor & Miss Copeland published. read several letters on Love. Mr. Hawkins visited Miss Polly Pettibone this evening. sick.

Mond 11th Washed. carded Bats. prepared a quilt. Mrs. Berry visited us this P.M. Mr. R.D. eve[.]

Tues 12th Very cold Mrs Hawkins and myself quilted all day. Miss Sally and Eliza Prime visited me this eve. Mr. Taylor returned. I find my journey almost to[o] hard. Sick.

Wed 13th Mr. Luman Monson. Married this day to Miss Sally Gaige. visited this P.M. by Miss Harriet and Lidia Burr. Miss Nancy Dunshee. Miss Amy Prime. Mr. and Mrs. Alden. called from Starksborough. Adolphus and Orra went to Middlebury purchased matrimonial articles. I indulged my tears plentifully.

Thursd 14th Quilted all day. received a pressing invitation to attend the [Taylor and Copeland] wedding at Starksborough. Mrs.[Eunice] Copeland came to tarry until they were gone. for my part I was very melancholy and lonesome and almost sick.

Frid 15th Very pleasant indeed. quilted all day. severe headache. Uncle Samuel & Aunt Olive Clapp visited us. felt indisposed to attend wedding. sick.

Sat. 16th Very windy. wrote two letters to Hopkinton. Mr and Mrs. Taylor took their leave. I would not be in her present situation for worlds. finished my quilt. Mr. C[opeland] returned.

Sund 17th Rainy. Attended meeting at the white house. heard Mr. Jours preach A.M. Mr. Parker P.M. went to Mr. Riders, intermission. Miss C[elia] Gaige insisted upon my spending the night with her. refused to read Shakespeare eleven at night.

Mond 18th Cold washed for Lovina. Mr. Storrs called visited by Mr [&] Mrs Clapp [unreadable] my quilt. spent the evening alone until twelve. very tired. my health is declining.

Tuesd 19th Warm. visited at Edward Dunshees agreeable visit. spent the night. N.D.

Wed 20th Warm. cut out my Calico Wrap. visited with N.D. M.D. at Mr Annin Mr. Moors P.M. rode to E.D. spent the night with Miss Prime. Alma blessed with daughter.

Thurs 21st Old Mr. Hall buried today. Lewis Mason married yesterday to Miss Sally Hawkins. Rainy. returned home. Avery Huntington here all night. strange person.

Frid 22nd Stormy. sewed little. the two Mr and Mrs. Follits visited us. Uncle John Nicholson, Mrs. Doan, Mr. Lee spent the night. I was very sick all night. my health fast declining. my friends think best for me to spend a few days in Lewis on account of my health. Mr. N[icholson] says he will fetch me home when I wish. consented.

Sat 23rd Very cold. started for Lewis. called to Rich Inn, Verjennes [Vergennes]. crossed from Ferrisburgh, Panton to Northwest Bay, five miles. crossed the largest crack that I ever saw on the ice. called at Newels. saw Dr. Wilson, Wm Livingston, my old acquaintance in Lewis. arrived at uncle's. pleasant situation on the Boquet. joyful meeting with my nearest and dearest aunt I have & her sweet babes.

Sund 24th Read some. rambled some. conversed considerable with Mr. Samuel Mason, strange. wrote a letter to Hopkinton. agreed with Mr. Smith to fetch my clothing to me.

LEWIS [NY]

Mond 25th Assisted Lucinda washing. visited by Esq. Nicholson and wife. Mrs Sykes. introduced to Mrs. Woodruff. Mr. N. insisted that I should return home with them. uncle being gone to Willsborough I refused to go. my health is better. pleased to find myself with Aunt.

Tuesd 26th Cold. enjoy myself perfectly well. I think I should like to spend the spring.

Wed 27th Warmer. sewing. introduced to Mrs and Miss Lovina Weaver, Mr. Bliss. took a lengthy walk down the ice. find it failing fast. received a very polite request to visit with the Ladies at Mr. Woodruffs. uncle returned from Willsborough, he was informed that Mad Dogs were very plenty in that Quarter. Miss Betsy Holcomb married this eve to Mr Patterson.

Thursd 28th Thawing fast. visit the river often[.] it begins to break up[.] finished my wrap[.]

LEWIS [NY]
March A.D. 1822

Friday 1st Mr Noah Lee called. made a tablecloth. chores. I am afraid my friends' wishes will be granted that the snow will go off and leave me here.

Sat 2nd Very warm. rain. the water begins to overflow the ice. made my sheet spread them out to whiten. Miss Sophia Lee walked two miles to visit me.

Sund 3rd Pleasant. Mr. Nicholson, Miss Lee, myself started to attend meeting W.P. Uncle led me across. it was venturesome indeed. I was some frightened. the foam of the torrent lay rolling beneath my feet threatening to devour us while my head appeared to be soaring on air. Sophia came near plunging. walked one mile, heard Mr. Armstrong from these words,

> What if a man should gain the whole world and lose his own soul?

introduced to Mrs. Lobdell. Miss Peggy Knapp. when we returned to the river we saw Lucinda in tears on the opposite rocks waving us not to approach. the ice had flown down against the poles. expected every moment to see them give away. raised to the depth of twenty feet just in the place where there was a young lady drowned last season. Mr. Mason, Mr. W's family came to cut poles, chained the poles, made a bridge so that we could get on to them and came across to us tolerably well. We were obliged to divest ourselves of all our loose clothes, shoes Etc and with trembling steps braved the awful torrent. arrived with joy on the opposite shore very tired. with wet feet we arrived at the house. Being dressed only in silk and standing so long on shore, took cold.

Mond. 4th Took a wearisome walk two miles with Sophia to Mr. Woodwards. visited her A.M. P.M. at Dr. Livingston's. Every one soliciting for me to spend the night. Mr and Mrs Pratt gained the agreeable visit for I have thought of late I never should enjoy the happiness of visiting my amicable friends in Lewis. Sophia and Rhoda Lee came and spent the night with me. fatigued.

Tuesd 5th Mrs Pratt went with me to Mr. Lee's and staid all day. we were all very rude indeed. Mr. Gales Frisby left his school. expressed himself as unfortunately in love without acquaintance. requested an introduction. we had a great deal of sport about it. Mr. Stephen Blackman carried me home to the poor creature's mortification[.] I find my health every day regaining.

Wed 6th Warm. dipped sixty five pails of water from the river. washed. took a lengthy walk through the snow in the wood[.] took a severe cold, throat sore and swelled. the snow has left the roads entirely and I am here happy.

Thursd 7th Colder. assisted Lucinda took my knitting. chose an alcove of rocks where I spend much of my time. [Here] the least movement forwards I could mingle with the foaming flood. Here in this dangerous situation, I sing to the roaring of the falls, raise my thoughts to my God or direct them to my distant friends and wish them as happy as I am. here away from [the] home [to which I] can't return.

Frid 8th — Pleasant. visited with Lucinda at Mr. Woodruffs. cut and basted gown for Mrs. W. almost sick with my cold. very anxious to get home to see my Parents have not seen them for more than a year. but I must not complain nor allow myself to be uneasy. It is all for the best I suppose.

Sat 9th — Pleasant. I and Lucinda took a walk to the summit of Bald Hill. received letter from Hopkinton, some clothing. every effort tried for fear of my being homesick.

Sund 10th — Pleasant. hard cough ventured to cross the poles alone. Lucinda accompanied me to meeting. Mr. A. preached from these words:

> Behold how they love one another A.M.
> Adam where art thou, P.M.

introduced to Miss Sally Cowan. Saw my dear friend and correspondent Abigail Lewis. she returned and spent the night with me. she has been very sick. she could not enjoy herself as I could wish. the place I had chosen for pleasure was where her sister was drowned. wet, muddy.

Mond 11th — Cloudy, some rain. Miss Lewis reluctantly took her leave. washed. broke into the river. took an addition to my cold. Mrs. W[oodruff] visited us. almost sick.

Tuesd 12th — Cloudy. very sick this morn. put in a web. Ironed. uneasy for fear I shall not get home.

Wed 13th — Pleasant. Cold. hard cold and cough. low spirits I should like to spend the summer here if my situation was such that I could, but it is not.

Thursd 14th — Cold. Mended for Uncle all day rather homesick. uneasy. visit the river often.

Frid. 15th — Pleasant and is like to be. Mr. N[icholson] gone to Willsborough. very anxious to see my Parents. it appears as though I could not stay until the Lake breaks up. But I will endeavour not to be so foolish again.

Sat. 16th — Pleasant morn. Miss Lewis came requested me to accompany her to Mr. W[oodruff']s. Excellent visit. read several letters of my own Composition. Aunt informed me of her numerous trials of matrimonial concerns. which were hard things to judge of. I added to her joys and lessened her sorrows as much as possible[.] I know not what to tell the poor girl. precarious situation.

Sund 17th Pleasant. Walked to the house of worship at Lewis corners where I had long been deprived of the privilege. Mr. Stone preached. called to Mr. Sykes saw many of my youthful companions as once were. Went home with Mrs. Charlotte Nicholson. spent the night. introduced to Mr. Ralzy Morse, an agreeable young man, Dorset. very pleasant visit[.] very hard cough. wearied from cold. rain this evening.

Mond. 18th Pleasant. took leave of Mr. N[icholson']s family. spent day and night at Mr. Sykes, miss Lewis returned. Visited Mr. George Smith. introduced to his Lady. high spirits. all of us.

Tuesd 19th Pleasant took my leave of Mr. Sykes family. walked to Lee's. Sophia accompanied me home. called at Mr. W[oodruff]'s. Abigail went as far as Mr. Moor's. High scrape. rather tired when I came to uncle's but high spirits.

Wednes 20th Washed woolen and linen clothes for Lucinda. Before I had finished Uncle came in. "Well, Phebe," he says "if you cannot possibly stay this summer, I will go home with you today for the ice is now fast rotting." We soon took our leave and started for Vermont. When we arrived at Northwest Bay, we were told that it was impossible to cross before morning. at Barber's the lake was breaking up. of course, we must cross at the bay. put up at Stephen's. Perhaps before another setting sun I shall repose in a watery bed. then farewell, my friends.

Thursd 21st Pleasant morn I arose at the sound of the Pilot's horn at four we drove our waggon, hired a passage to Vergennes for seven cents per mile. With one gentleman whom I had seen at Hopkinton, I walked down to the ice. Saw them pass two Cutters, one Double-loaded sley, one waggon. three horses six men and 41 handspeaks, bars of iron, boards, ropes, [all] fastened for the purpose of saving us. It appeared more like a funeral procession than a ride but by bridges, we arrived on shore in safety after riding five miles on floating ice as it were. proceeded to Verjennes [Vergennes] rode to Fathers with Cousins P.F.V.V. [Peter and Frederick Van Vliet] whom I had not seen for a year. Mr. N[icholson] walked to Bristol. Mr. Wm. White to Miss Sally Burr. Mr. Israel Birchard to Miss [original blank space] Tiff. retired early in tolerable spirits being once more in Vermont.

FERRISBURGH

Frid 22nd Snow'd some. marking and knitting. indulged a flood of tears. homesick.

Sat 23rd Stormy but insisted upon returning to Bristol. Abraham [her brother] came with me, glad to get home.

BRISTOL

Sund 24th	Pleasant Mr. Hawkins went as far as the Lake and Grandpaa' went home with my Brothers. I took a ramble to view the purling rill, the rocky hills where I spent the playful moments of Childhood. happy creature.
Mond 25th	Beautiful day. carded and spun thirty knots of tow. very tired
Tuesd 26th	Beautiful weather. heard of the death of Miss Eliza Downing. thirty knots.
Wed. 27th	Pleasant high wind. spun thirty knots. weary of spinning. absent minded.
Thursd 28th	Rainy. spun thirty knots. alone evening entirely tolerable health and spirits.
Frid 29th	Cold carded and spun thirty knots of rope yarn. Mr. Eddy sick.
Sat 30th	finished spinning my bed cord. warped it. walked to the village spent the night at Mr. Gaige's. called over to Mr. Munson's and Munsill's.
Sund 31st	Pleasant morn. snowy eve. Mr. Dodge preached read Proclamation by the Governor.[40] Richard Skinner introduced Mr. Horatio Murray. Mr P. Hawley spent the eve. violent cough all night racked my stomach.

April 1822

Mond 1st	Walked home. took breakfast at M. Moors. called Mr Annans
Tuesd 2nd	Mr. Rich died last night. took the waggon accompanied Grandma'a'm and Betsey to Chapmans store, Newhaven. Cold wind. carded some wood. Mr. Purrington called. Mr. Fulton spent the night. Mrs. Pettibone called.
Wed 3rd	High winds. washed for Lovina. Spun. doubled twisted eight knots of Worsted. made an Indispensable. invitation to visit Mr. Arnold. hard cough.
Thurs 4th	Carded and spun a wool for stocking. Mr. Mills, Mr Berry called this eve.
Frid 5th	Snow. finished my yarn. made another Indispensable. spun thirty knots of Linen for Lovina. Uncle came home sick with a cut on his thumb.
Sat. 6th	Spun thirty knots[.] Mr [&] Mrs. Otis, Mrs Chase visited. received 12½ cents from Mr. Eastman. my brother Isaac visited us. had bad news from Brother. hard cough.

Sund 7th	Cold. wind. Dr. Thomas called to uncle. [And] to our extreme joy our long absent David Brooks, Ohio, whom we suspected was dead [arrived home]. Cousin V[an] V[liet] received a letter from Miss Betsey Hills, Mr. Eastman. answered it.
Mond 8th	Rainy. spun forty knots. Uncle D[avid Brooks]. visited Mr. Clapp. Uncle J[ohn Brooks] better. hard cough.
Tuesd 9th	Spun thirty knots. uncle gone to Middlebury. visited by Miss Sand Mrs. E. Prime N. Dunshee. insisted very hard upon my visiting them. almost sick.
Wed 10th	Fast day. cold spun thirty knots. Mr and Mrs Clapp visited us. unwell.
Thurs 11th	Requested to engage in a school in Monkton. refused. spun thirty knots. sick.
Frid 12th	Spun thirty knots. finished spinning for Lovina. sewing P.M. uneasy.
Sat. 13th	Rainy. worked at my quilt. good spirits. nothing to trouble me. request [original blank space].
Sund 14th	Rainy. wrote a letter to Miss Betsey Eastman. [One to] Mr & Mrs. Dufrey. one to me [from] Mr. Elisha Brooks. Mr Clapp came after [Cousin] Olive [Clapp]. kept [to] my chambers all day.
Mon 5th	Pleasant. Uncle David Brooks took his leave this morn. probably for the last time. cleared and washed the shop. visited at Widow Eastman's called over to Mr. Ellsworth. found Mrs. E[llsworth] no better. strong invitation to visit at Mr. Scott's. my health is poor.
Tues 16th	Put in two Coverlets, twice. Mr Annin & Mr Case called this eve. insisted hard upon my engaging in the school of this District for five months. reluctantly engaged for the low price of one Dollar per week.
Wed. 17th	Cloudy. weaving very tired. Miss Sally Prime called upon me. hard cough.
Thursd 18th	Wove but little, finished piecing my quilt. doubled twisted stocking yarn.
Frid 19th	Rainy. low spirits. lazy and dull. sewed some[.] what hinders my happiness?
Sat 20th	Cloudy. wove a little more. cut outside of a Comforter. Tolerable spirits.
Sund 21st	Cool. Attended meeting at the Chapel. called over [Mr.] Gaige's saw Mr. Sprague. Mr. Terry Gaige had his skull fractured yesterday. read considerable. in Mrs.

Ramsays History.[41] Dr. Day came after me to go there for one day until he could get some other girl. found his wife [Mrs. Day] very low. worked until 12 o'clock.

Mond 22nd Baked. Ironed. waited upon her all day and very tired. Read Pocket Magazine.

Tues 23rd Beautiful day. Mr. Hawkins came after me this morn. borrowed Campbell's Narrative.[42] wove little. happy in the enjoyment of friends.

Wed 24th Weaving. sewed some. spent the night agreeably with Miss Betsy Berry at Esq Darrow's. I am easy and contented alone and in good spirits.

Thursd 25th Pleasant A.M. rainy P.M. sewed some and wove some. the happiest of the happy if it were not for the neglect of duty to my God.

Fri 26th Very warm. wove considerable. it is the most tender weaving imaginable.

Sat. 27th Warm. weaving. picked six geese. Mrs Nash called bought twelve lbs. flax.

Sund 28th Very pleasant after a shower. finished reading memoirs of Mrs. Ramsay. took an agreeable walk to the river where I have not been for a year. Oh how changed many of the places where I have read and sang hours, my voice reaching with the rolling waves are now no more, they have plunged the stream while I view the place of past scenes. I think the comparison may be applied to mankind. sometimes the current move easy and beautiful but soon it rushes with impetuosity, renders the Sublimity strikingly majestic, trees torn from their native soil, are tossed to and fro, rising and plunging with the furious torrent. So is man. Sometimes his circumstances are flattering, his mind is easy, he slides sweetly along the stream of life. But alas! soon some sudden and unseen affliction hovers around him and tost [tossed] him upon the billows of despair unless his hope is rested upon the rock of salvation where he is safe [from] all harm. but if his afflictions are placed upon the fading this of this world. perhaps a little property, perhaps a dear friend or relative, perhaps the partner of his joys, the companion of his bosom is torn from him. then he thinks his cup is full his burthen is greater than he can bear. thus he is afflicted, he strives to regain his former security of pleasure but the stream of time swiftly carried him down unless some kind assistance comes to his relief. Attended Conference.

Mond 29th High winds. wove all day. sewed evening. tolerable health and spirits.

Tuesd 30th Laboured hard. at last finished the rotten coverlets. Miss Z[ilpha] Pettibone called.

May 1822

Wed 1st	Warm, windy. wove the fringe. took a ride to Ferrisburg. out in a very hard shower, being dressed in thin silk, took cold. very we took dinner at Fathers. spent the P.M. at V.V. [Van Vliet']s Polly very unwell. spent the night agreeably at Sarah Hazard's. retired at two. almost sick.
Thurs 2nd	Cloudy. called to Vergennes five miles. traded some passed the gate, took the turnpike. called H. Hawkins, Waltham. Bated at Mr. Peck's Inn. called at the Papermill. Took dinner at Mrs. Bell's, Weybridge. sold my coverlet. rode to the Borough called at Gibson's. Heart's, Brewster's Stewart's Hagar's Printing office. purchased Blank [book], Dictionary. Mrs. Kilburn's shop Mr. Hayne's Inn. Saw Nancy and Clarissa Nash. Called Mr. Handy's to get the waggon mended. arrived at home after shopping and riding twenty six miles found a house full of visitors. Aunt Clapp very sick. sick myself.
Frid 3rd	Hatcheled my flax. sewed some. retired sick. a restless night, lame indeed.
Sat 4th	Coloured otter. sewed some. washed little but very unwell. Mrs. Jewett visited.
Sund 5th	Cloudy. very lazy today. read little. slept some. walked some. idle creature.
Mond 6th	Cloudy. Began my school. found an ignorant unmannerly sett. If I cannot make them more agreeable, I shall leave the school. heard from Aunt Olive, rather better. my summer's task looks hard but away with such feelings. they are not profitable, I will not harbor them any more.
Tuesd 7th	Pleasant. Spun a run of Linen beside(s) my school, Mrs Arnold sick.
Wed 8th	Pleasant. sewing. my school more agreeable today commenced boarding Mr Annins, commenced reading Shakespeare. poor health.
Thurs 9th	Sewed but little. very unwell. agreeable boarding place. saw Mr Crane.
Frid 10th	Unwell. called home at noon. found my dear friend Harriet Charter at Mr. A[rnold's] pleasant visit after being long separated. cut out cape.
Sat 11th	Pleasant. sewing and visiting. very tired at night. read Shakespeare Plays, though it appears it is almost useless for me to read on account of Memory. Harriet [Charter] and I visited Mrs. Arnold, found her better but low.

Sund 12th Pleasant read Mr. Bently's visit to his friend Mr. Clifford, an interesting account of the Piety, Charity, Government Education of their family.[43] saw Miss Betsey Sprague and Sinai Munsill at the Springs. walked north for an hour. we returned home went in the cabinet shop chamber. selected each of us a rocking chair, sat and conversed until all that is wanting to complete our felicity is a contented mind. God grant that we may earnestly pray for it until we obtain it.

Mond 13th Pleasant. spent the evening at Mr. Pettibones. finished my VanDyke[44]

Tuesd 14th Pleasant. cut out the skirt of my frock. washed a few things. Mr. Hohn Simmons came here, an Irishman. spent the night at Dr. Moors.

Wed 15th Rainy. commenced boarding at Mr. Dexters. sewing on my frock.

Thurs 16th Arose and visited the springs before light. drank some water from Saratoga. Cut out the skirt of my white frock.

Frid 17th Rainy. called to see Miss Catherine Gaige. my face badly swollen with ulcers. great many kinds of work to attend to at school.

Sat. 18th Called received a new Pattern for gowns. Cut out mine and a cap.

Sund 19th Melancholy. my face very troublesome. rode to see Mrs. Ellsworth found her better, but in low circumstances. took a walk to the river.

Mond. 20th Washed some. cut out ruffs and indispensables for the girls. called to Dr. Moors. very urgent for me to spend the night but positively refused. very absent minded. distant friend employ.

Tuesd 21st Rainy. Mr. Dexter carried me to school. my little Mary Clapp came to spend two weeks with me at school whom I have not seen for 14 months. called at home after school. starched. spent the night.

Wed. 22nd Rainy attended a splendid exhibition at the white house, [Bristol] village. a vast concourse of people. the Galleries in danger of breaking down the crowd was so great. it seemed as if I should have fainted after spending eleven hours. I returned home threw myself upon the bed fatigued and weary of life I think I had better been reading my bible than to have gone. discontented.

Thursd 23rd Sewing. took a shirt to make for M. Hawkins. returned to Mr. D.s

Frid. 24th Rainy. sewing. Esq Barrow lent me the Travels in China containing Descriptions. Observations and Comparisons.[45] made and collected in the course of a short stay at the imperial Palace of Yuen Minyuen. A subsequent journey from Peking to Canton. four hundred twenty two pages. weary of my school.

Sat 25th Finished the shirt. Mr. Fletchers house burnt. heard of the death of Mrs L. Taylor. left two Babes to her bereaved companion. indulged in tears. home.

Sund 26th Pleasant. reading History. disagreeable feelings unworthy to live and obtain so many mercies with so much unthoughtfulness.

Mond 27th Warm returned to Mr. Dexter. visited by Mrs. Mason, Filura Allan.

Tuesd 28th Sewing. spent the time agreeably. visited the Springs. daily reading.

Wed 29th Sewing. visited the springs twice today. S. Prime insisted that I should spend the afternoon at M. D[exter's] with the Miss Doubbs, Town Hill.

Thursd 30th Visited spring. bought imitation shell comb. took leave of Mr. Dexter. Commenced boarding across the river. Silvester Scott took a tedious walk up the Cobble. although lived so near I never visited before.

Friday 31st Sewing. gathered fir for the schoolhouse. washed at night. returned home.

June 1822

Sat 1st Wove all day for three yards of Kersey. everything out of order. rather been in school two days. I am almost thinking distant friends have forgotten.

Sun 2nd Disappointed of preaching. took a letter from the [post] office from Miss Betsey Eastman, Hopkinton. entered at Monkton. a shower obliged us to call Dr. Moors. Miss Olive Kellogg brought a child of illegitimacy into the world last evening. shocking. Wet my silk frock sadly. took a pleasant ride to Monkton to visit Mrs. Clapp. introduced to Mr. Daniel Nimblet returned at dusk. wrote to Miss Betsey Eastman. retired late.

Mond 3rd Wove one yard before school. washed P.M. Mr. Fulton spent the night.

Tuesd 4th Wove three yards. Training. good spirits. Ironed. ungrateful child.

Wedn 5th Wove three yards, sewed some. read a tract. enjoyed myself well in health.

Thursd 6th Wove out my eleven yards. returned to Mr. Scotts. cut and basted a gown for Sally Brooks. read ninety pages Travels of Cyprus.[46] tolerable health.

Frid 7th Returned home this morn. cut a frock for Betsey read 100 pages Geography.

Sat 8th Rainy. Moors carried to school waggon. went home at night. Mr Follet called, spent an hour or two. very absent minded on Saturdays. weary eve.

Sund 9th Pleasant. Mr and Mrs Lee called. Drove to meeting heard Mr. Dodge preach A.M. called over Mr. Munsill's intermission. heard Mr Elijah Crane at the Chapel P.M. from these words: Romans IVXX:

> We staggered not at the promise of God through unbelief: but was strong in faith giving glory to God.

our girls rode home with Mr. Howden. I took Miss Lydia Buss. rode to her Fathers to tea. read The Life of a Hermit. visited the burial place. heard Mr. Crane preach at the north schoolhouse. read tract titles:

1 The repentance of the happy death of the celebrated Earl of Rochester
2 Exhortation to a Prisoner
3 A persuasive to Public Worship.
4 The True Riches.
5 A letter addressed to a member of his congregation upon removing from his pastoral care.

How wretched am I for not profiting by what I read and hear. why do I not practice it? Lidy [Lydia] spent the night.

Mond 10th Took the waggon after school. Drove to Lanesborough Street purchased a few trifles. left Grandma'a'm. proceeded to Town Hill Left my bonnet to be whitened. returned took tea at Mr. Eastmans. had to promise to call again. Mr. Squires died last night aged sixteen.

Tuesd 11th Sewing. after school Drove to Newhaven Mills to Mr. Beaman's store. took tea at Col Nash's. rained enough to wet us. took a walk

Wed 12th Ironed my clothes I washed yesterday. returned to Mr. Scott's finished my Calico Bonnet. Mrs. Case blessed with a daughter. melancholy.

Thurs 13th Pleasant. out of health this morn. visited P.M. Mr. Howden introduced to Miss Jones of Barnamtown Miss Harriet and Lida Buss. Miss Eliza Prime. spent the eve. melancholy on account of health.

Frid 14th Went home at noon. returned to Mr. Scotts. read fifty pages. melancholy.

Sat 15th Returned early. surprised to see Mr. [Samuel, Jr.] Eastman from Hopkinton. received two letters. dismissed my school at noon. indisposed. retired at twelve.

Sund 16th Staid at home all day. Mr. Eastman's health is very poor indeed. for my part I was uneasy. indisposed knew not what to say or do. retired dejected. Why am I thus lonely when surrounded by friends?

Mond 17th Rainy morn., Mr Eastman took leave to visit his friends in Lincoln. Commenced boarding at Esquire Moors. Took an atlas to paint of Miss Eliza Howdens Took a walk to the springs with Miss Pamelia Moors. Miss Polly and Zilpha Pettibone Miss Catherine Gaige. another spring been dug today. I fell in two or three feet, was caught out by Zilpha before I sank. no bottom but blue clay. cold.

Tuesd 18th Painting. took a walk to the burying ground this eve. indisposed[.]

Thursd 19th Pleasant. making dimity flounce starched. ironed. finished Betsey's gown.

Frid 20th Finished my Petticoat. Marcus Moor(s) took an Emetic. almost took his life.

Sat 21st Sewing. Shower. pleasant visit with Susan P.M. went home at four[.]

Sat 22nd Washed before school. Ironed. plated ruffs. read The Natural and Artificial Productions of the United States.[47] great curiosities abundant. indisposed.

Sun 22nd Dressed in white. Amelia light crepe. Minerva black silk. walked to meeting. Mr. Dodge preached from these words A.M. "Pray without ceasing"[.] P.M. "For by the cause of swearing the land mourneth" Mr. John H. Kilburn published to Miss Rachel Dayfoot. had a pleasant visit with Mrs. Carpenter Miss Charter. at noon returned to Dr. Moor(s). very tired. they are the most profane irreligious pack that ever I saw. retired to the hall and gave vent to my feelings by tears and prayers for their conversion. accompanied Mark and Susan to the Springs retired early. reposed in sighs, tears, and groans. injured.

Mon 24th Hard rain. Left Dr. Moors. called at home exchanged my wet clothes for dry. Commenced boarding at Mr. Thompsons. Read the affecting story this eve. "The sorrows of Werter."[48] He at last shot himself for Charlotte who was married to Albert. Mr. Wm Rugg drowned at Beaman Hollow.[49]

Tuesd 25th Pleasant. after school drove to Newhaven Mills. purchased a ruff returned home. left Grandma'a'm. Drove to Town Hill for my bonnet. disappointed again. left my trimmings. Miss Z Pettibone rode with me. very tired when I returned.

Wed. 26th Washed. Ironed. sewed some. Picked geese received a letter from Mrs Orra Taylor returned to Mr. Thompson's. high spirits. very tired[.]

Thursd 27th Pleasant Mr. Mrs Amidown visited today. Miss Electa Prime spent the night with me. pleasant visit one year and half separated.

Frid 28th Returned home. Mr. Eastman returned with poor health. sewing.

Sat 29th Accompanied on a visit to my parent. found them in tolerable health. I was very tired and lonesome, I know not why.

Sun 30th Attended Friends meeting. returned to Bristol, fine ride, agreeable company. spent the time pleasantly until two.

July 1822

Mond 1st Indisposed. Mr. E. gone to Middlebury. Washed my clothes after school. Took another shirt to make. my cup with blessings overflowing[.]

Tues 2nd Ironed. Mr. E. visited school. took short walk Miss Charter spent the night. brought a number of letters. rainy night.

Wed 3rd Rain Mr E. took leave. returned to Mr. Thompson's spent the night with Harriet at Mr. Annin's. Why is my heart so far from thee?

Thurs 4th Independence. Very warm. visited by Mr & Mrs Amidown. Eliza visited the spring with Harriet. called to Mr. Annin's. rather melancholy.

Frid 5th Very warm. finished Mr. H.'s shirt. took another to make. spent the night with Miss Nancy Dunshee. the young people generally attend the Baptists[.]

Sat 6th Finished the shirt. finished my white frock. ironed. cut out a wrap for Mrs. Thompson. Drove to Hawley's store with Lovina. Very lonesome this eve.

Sun 7th — Drove to meeting. wore my white frock for the first time heard two excellent sermons by Mr. Chase[.] "He that saveth me will my father honor." He first showed what the sermon was, then the honor. returned to Mr Thompson's. very lonely. I know not the reason of my dejection. very disagreeable.

Mond 8th — Rainy. took trousers to make. Mr. E. called. his health a trifle better. bought a string of white beads, one thimble. spent the evening agreeably.

Tuesd 9th — Cool. the old lady rather affronted. finished the trowsers. very sober indeed.

Wed 10th — Rainy. washed, starched ruffs, visited by Miss N[ash]. Miranda Dunshee made a pillowcase. read this eve. why this melancholy gloom?

Thurs 11th — Rainy afternoon. walked to the village with Mr. E. disappointed of preaching. Miss Rachel Dayfoot married [to John H. Kilburn] this P.M. Drove Mr D[unshee]'s wagon home my white frock badly torn. Painted. very sick night indeed.

Frid 12th — Cut out my pink. washed little. almost sick. low spirits on account of friends.

Sat 13th — Unwell. wrote a lengthy letter to my distant friend, Betsey Eastman.

Sund 14th — Pleasant. Attended meeting. heard Mr. Ingleson "Except a man be born again he cannot see the kingdom of Heaven." Dressed in silk. visited by Mr. E. some part of it very unpleasant indeed. in danger of [original blank space].

Mond 15th — Rainy A.M. assisted Mrs. Thompson making harness until a late hour. appeared in high spirits. far different were my feelings.

Tuesd 16th — Pleasant. Mr. E. boarding at uncles. made a towel at noon. finished the harness at night. sewed some. Miss Z[ilpha] Pettibone Miss P. Moor[s] called.

Wed 17th — Took a morning ride to Beamans store, Newhaven. bought velvet for an indispensable, six thread buttons. took leave of Mr. T[hompson]. took a wrap to make. called over to Mr. Scotts. accompanied Miss Delaney StrawBerrying on the cobble. With difficulty obtained leave to return home. read forty pages Travels of Cyprus. agreeable visit. was weighed 116. good spirits.

Thursd 18th — Made four towels. Mr. E.'s health very poor. I fear it will never be better. washed after school. Uncle Clapp called. his health poor. good health and spirits.

Frid 19th Rode out this morn with Grandma'a'm to the village. unwell this A.M. Marked for towels. picked currants. today. lost my comb good spirits. crowned with joy.

Sat 20th Sewing. Mrs. Follit visits here. I should enjoy myself perfectly well were it not for Mr. E's miserable health. homesick and uneasy. Alas and did my bleed.

Sund 21st Took a pleasant walk. happy am I in the enjoyment of such a friend for life.

Mond 22nd Washed. Commenced boarding at Mr. Drake's. sewing. called over home and returned to Mr D's. Uneasy. disagreeable place. discords. riots.

Tuesd 23rd Pleasant. spinning linen. visited Esq. Darrows. went home a few minutes.

Wed 24th I never was so insulted as I have been this morning. I shall not board here any longer unless I can be treated with decency. Rain P.M. wrote until almost dark.

Thursd 25th Rainy day. Mr. E. visited school A.M. wrote until almost sundown. Returned to my home with reluctance. Spun this eve. Why am I this uneasy? All the day.

Frid 26th Cool. finished spinning my three runs of linen. washed the schoolhouse. took a hard cold. returned home. almost sick. pain in my side. restless night. Lovina almost sick.

Sat. 27th Pleasant. picked currants for wine. sewed some. ironed. Mr. E. remains in miserable health.

Sund 28th Rainy. took a pleasant walk with Mr. E. almost sick with a cold. spent the day in idleness.

Mond 29th Washed. sewing. called over to Dr. Moors. spent the night. at Mr. Annins. Miss P[rime]'s.

Tuesd 30th Sewing. called Mr. P[rime]'s, Mr. Dunshee's visited Mrs. Scott. found her better than I expected but very feeble. spent the night with Sally Prime. saw Mrs. Clerk. hard cough.

August 1822

Thurs 1st Pleasant. took a walk with Mr. E. to the springs. Lovina sick. saw Mr. Spofford Grout.

Frid 2nd Very warm. wrote a letter to Miss Betsey Eastman. hard thunder and lightening. my cup with blessings overflows and joy exalts my head.

Sat. 3rd Sewing. wrote a letter to Mr. Phineas Durfey, Hopkinton. took a ride to Mr. E. to General Dunton's, a great number of workmen and others prevented Our visit being agreeable. the girls were very rude indeed. I was rather dejected.

Sund 4th Hard rain, thunder and Lightening this morn. Mr. E. very unwell today.

Mond 5th Sewing. Rainy P.M. called at home. spent the night at Mr. Annin's.

Tuesd 6th Sewing. troubling perplexities on every side. I trust I shall live through it. engaged a table and stand of Mr. Annin's. Commenced boarding at Esq. Howden's. showered for the first time in my life. in low spirits. and health.

Wed 7th Showered this morn. called over home at noon. insulted accused of faults I am not guilty of. my feelings injured. but I am used to it. Sewing. finished Mr. T[hompson]'s wrap. melancholy.

Thurs 8th Sewing on my pink frock. called home at noon. saw Mrs. Hawkins, Mrs. Severance. Esq. Darrow and wife visited Mr. Howdens. Mrs. Berry very sick. melancholy feelings.

Fri 9th Warm. Mrs. Scott rode over. very feeble. visited with Mr. E. at Mr. Thompsons. took a walk to Dr. Moors. I spent the night in great distress at Mr. Thompson's.

Sat. 10th Returned home. read the Masonic Chart or the Hieroglyphical Monito[.]r[50] Mrs. Scott rode as far as here, very feeble. took an agreeable walk in the orchard, with Mr. E.

Sund 11th [No entry]

Mond 12th Washed a great washing for me before school. tolerable spirits. Mrs. Hall died about two o'clock at night. returned to Esq. Howdens. spent the eve. at Mr. Berry's.

Tues 13th Rainy. Returned home prepared for funeral. awful sudden and shocking.

Wed. 14th Pleasant wore my frock for the first time. Funeral attended by a great number of people. Mr. Ingleson preached a fine sermon from these words[.] "Be ye also ready." Returned home almost sick today. took a walk to the orchard. altogether probably the last I shall have with Mr. E for I must soon take my leave of this worthy friend. tolerable spirits.

Thursd 15th Mr. E took his leave and departed with Grandfather. rainy. Returned to Esq Howden's. made a pillowcase. May God protect my friends this night while I remain safe.

Frid 16th Pleasant. made pillow case. spent the night with Miss Sarah Eastman at Mr. Eddys. Took a walk to the river but very lonely indeed, I cannot tell why it is so.

Sat. 17th Received an invitation to spend the Sabbath at Mr. Scotts. preengaged. Returned to Esq Howdens. dined at Esq Darrows made pillow case. read the Vicar of Wakefield.[51]

Sund 18th Pleasant walked to the mill to meeting. disappointed of preaching. called over Mr. Case's at noon. Took a lengthy walk after supper on the hills. with Miss Buss she was visited by Mr Tracy of Monkton. was introduced. became considerably acquainted with the gentleman. I think Miss Lidie's rather indifferent towards him.

Mond 19th Commenced Boarding at Ephra Halls. great distance to board but agreeable. very tired. Knitting. Mr. John Hall, Jun. very sick. distressed family without a mother.

Tuesd 20th Cloudy. made another pillowcase. Miss Buss spent the night with me, very tired.

Wed. 21st Commencement. Number flocking to Middlebury while I am confined in school. but I shall feel as well as they tomorrow. twenty different kinds of animals produced the show. made the greater part of a pair of trowsers.

Thurs 22nd Finished making my linen. made a small pair of trowsers. spent the night agreeably at Mr. Dexters. Mr. Hurlburt of Shoreham was married Tuesday to Miss Amanda Rutherford, Starksborough. Thanks to my God I am not in their situation. I wish I was more reconciled to this kind of enjoyment.

Frid 23rd Visited the sick this morn. why was not I called to this bed of pain and distress instead of this young man? Made another pair of trowsers. returned to Mr Hall's. saw Miss Charter a few minutes this morning. her feelings are indescribable. Been writing to her what time I could get and extracting letters that are warm.

Sat 24th — Took leave of Mr Hall's. Returned home at night to my old chamber again in good spirits. wrote a letter to Mr. Eastman and Miss Betsey. Miss H. Durfey, Mr. Phineas Durfey. Alone and happy I sit and write to distant friends while probably they are slumbering in soft repose. retired late.

Sund 25th — Attended meeting at the village. Called at Mr. Munsills at noon heard of my friend's (Miss Charter's) health and spirits, so inexpressible. I left our people. walked to Gen Dunton's. conversed with her awhile and returned home. which made five miles I have walked. very tired but my feeling for my friend is more distressing than weariness. Mr. Ingleson preached from this[.] "Search the Scriptures." He first showed how and then why we were to do this and how great were our privileges which we so much neglected.

Mond. 26th — Pleasant. toothache very hard. Ague in my face. bound head with tea leaves on my face. almost to a blister. spent the night unpleasantly at Mr. Scott's. restless night.

Tuesd 27th — Learning to spin worsted. took a Vandyke and Cap to make for Miss Clapp. Commenced boarding at Mrs. Berry's. sewing and knitting. Mr. Loveland buried today. 82 years old.

Wed 28th — Cloudy. sewing. called over to Mr. Hall's. left one Dollar to send to Mansfield, Connecticut, for sewing silk. Mr. Horace and Holly Trask, Benjamin McKnight. Lidia Buss. E. Howden visited us this eve[.] L. spent the night. very rude.

Thurs 29th — Sewing. finishing writing my Diary the second time seventy four pages. tiresome job done. I shall now have more time for letters and certificates. took a walk this pleasant eve with Miss Beverly and visited Mr. Howdens old people.

Frid 30th — Pleasant finished Mrs. C.'s cape. Cyrus sent for me to go home he broke his leg bad. drove to the village for a cap pattern. watched with Cyrus. toothache hard this morn.

September 1822

Sat. 1st — Pleasant called over Dr. Moors with Miss Charter. returned to my chamber in good spirits.

Sund 2nd — Cloudy. walked to the village with Miss Charter. heard Elder Sawyer preach. took tea at Mr. Annan's. returned home. took a walk to the Vineyard with Lovina. Five young Beaus were found last night gathering melons. uncle shot among them. they undertook to cross the wall. several stones rolled on them. they were all known.

Mond 3rd Sewing. called over Mr. Thompson's. walked after school to the village to Church meeting. hard shower returned home very tired with severe pain in my side. low spirits.

Tuesd 4th Sewing returned to Mrs. Berry's. Betsey took a walk with me to Mr Hall's. took cold. Freemen's meeting. received a few clothes from Hopkinton. disappointed of a letter from that place. rather melancholy in consequences. it is wrong.

Wed 5th Rainy night. called to Mr. Eddy's Mrs. Miller's Mr. Thompson's. took a jacket to make. spent the night with Mrs. M. called Mr. Dunshee's after school. tolerable spirits.

Thursd 6th Sewing. called home at noon. found a house full. Mr and Mrs. White, two children. Dr. Rise. Mrs. Warner. Capt. Dayfoot. spent the night at Mr. Howden's. conversed with Miss [Charter] respecting her present suitor she wished me to advise her what to do and not.

Frid 7th Returned home at noon saw Mrs. Hawkins. Mrs. Otis, Mr and Mrs McHard. almost sick. obliged to attend school. Grandma'a'm insists on my weaving for her tomorrow.

Sat. 8th Wove ten yards today. picking wool this evening. very tired. but I have where I can retire to rest while my saviour while on earth had not where to lay his weary head. How thankful ought I to be for the many mercies I enjoy.

Sund 9th Very pleasant. took a very pleasant ride indeed. attended Friends meeting, Starksborough. took a view of my father's former situation — the place of my birth. Had a pleasant visit with my father and uncle Philander Orvis and family. whom I have not seen before and while the rapturous thought of my native place all those scenes new to me. yet the trembling tears to think of the cause of leaving it would present itself. Bereft of a Mother, carried away a tender infant almost twenty-one years ago and now returned only to say that I have seen the place where I first lived. How gloomy the thought it appears like a dream. returned home through Lincoln. called at Mr. Hawkins. severe headache. tolerable spirits. returned to my home contented.

Mond 10th Pleasant. wove two yards. washed some before school. picked six pounds of wool after. visited by Mrs. Darrow. retired at twelve. five hours alone.

Tuesd 11th Pleasant and warm. Finished picking, greasing my wool. dined at Mr D's. took a walk with Miss Mary Drake to Mr. Case's. M.D. spent the night.

Wed 11th Sewing. commenced Boarding Mr. Ellsworth. great distance to walk. Miss Mary Drake spent the night with me. Mrs Hall sent for me.

Thurs 12th Finished my stocking. cut out a white wrap for myself. spent the night with Miss Susan Ellsworth. sewing and knitting. Why do I not hear from Mr. E[astman]?

Frid 13th Went home. prepared for visitors. disappointed. spent the night agreeably with Mrs. Hall. Mr. H gone to Troy. we were alone all happy and contented.

Sat. 14th Sewing. Cloudy. made a belt to my silk frock. Spent the night at Mr. Case's, very tired indeed. my school's increasing and presents to make.

Sund 15th Walked to Newhaven Mills with Mrs. Hall. called over to Mr. Smith's at noon. Mr. Hopkins preached well but my side pained me so that I sat very uneasy. spent the night with Mrs. Hall. Miss L. Buss spent the night with us.

Mond 16th Returned to Mr. Ellsworth's. Why is my heart so far from thee my God?

Tuesd 17th One year ago today my school closed at Hopkinton. work at likenesses all the time.

Wed 18th This day closed my school. presented thirty-three likenesses of gentlemen and Ladies. returned home. washed all my clothes. knit two inches on my stocking. evening.

Thursd 19th Starched. Ironed. Mr. J. Hall so far recovered as to call on us. visited at Esq. Jewetts with Grandma'am brought home my rolls.[52] spun ten knots. evening almost sleepless night.

Frid 20th Spun twelve knots. walked to Uncle Clapp's, five miles in the Course of the day. called to Mr. Annin's. Mr. Follits. Mrs. F. would not let me depart until I agreed to spend three or four days with her. rainy p.m. called to Gen Dunton's. took tea with difficulty. went from there until morn. I surprised uncle's family by appearing [on] foot and alone. introduced to Mr. J. Jones. Mr. Amasa

Wheaten, Mrs. Gaige. very tired indeed. pain in my side.

MONKTON

Sat. 21st Cloudy assisted in preparing dinner for twenty men. supper for thirty. visited by Mrs. Gaige. found myself extremely weary at night. pained side. I have been on my feet all day and obliged to almost fly some of the time.

Sund 22nd Very unwell returned home with uncle dejected. I cannot think why I do not hear from distant friends. returned to Mr. Follits. conscience smitten Sabbath.

Mond 23rd Spun forty knots of warp. very tired not being used to spinning Mrs. F. very unwell indeed.

Tuesd. 24th Spun forty knots of warp very tired indeed but I must try to wash if I possibly can.

Wed 25th Spun forty knots of warp almost discouraged spinning I think I shall try weaving.

Thurs 26th Spun eight knots. walked. had the toothache all night. took the colt and waggon. returned. called. carried Mr. F[ollit] to the village. took a letter from the [Post] Office from Mr. C[opeland]. took about fifty yards to weave. engaged to take the pay in grain and share making. carried my patent pumps to make. carried Mrs. F[ollit] home. returned myself. visited by Miss Pettibone this eve. my mind confused greatly. rather dejected and weary.

Friday 27th Put in a web of flannel. Wove ten yards. Made up my school bill. Heard Mr. Calvin Edwards was married last eve to Widow Copeland. Confusing.

Sat 28th Wove two yards and a half. Took the wagon. Drove to the village. Carried home the web. Went around by Mr. Follits. Called there and at Mr. Arnold's. Mr. Dexter took dinner. Engaged to weave forty yards more work or die this fall. Returned home. Put in a web through the harness. mended some.
Break off my fetters Lord and show the Path in which my feet should go. If snares and foes beset the road, I fly to hide me near my Lord.
Rain.

Sunday 29th High wind, read some. rambled considerable about the river. In quest of solitude. retired early. Mr. Felton and Miss Rachael Maria Eddy spent the night. raining.

Mond 30th Arose at half past three o'clock morning. spun ten knots. put a web through the reed. wove six yards. spun ten knots in the evening Grandfather came home from the west this eve with the news of good health. almost hard cough Lucinda has lost her infant. [Grandfather] brought me a letter from Miss Harriet D[urfey]. Miss Lucy McAllister. one from Mr. Eastman which informed me his health is better than it was when he left me. joyful news. God grant its continuance.

October 1822

Tuesd 1st Arose at three spun eleven knots. wove six and half yards spun eleven in the eve.

Wed 2nd	Arose at three spun ten knots wove seven yards spun six eve tired out. retired early.
Thursd 3rd	Arose at four. spun five knots, wove six yards. spun a few minutes. tired out.
Frid 4th	Arose at three. spun ten knots wove out the web. put in a web of checks, very tender. wove two yard on that. spun ten knots evening almost sick.
Sat. 5th	Arose at three. spun six knots, wove one and half yards. starched. ironed. took horse, waggon accompanied the girls to Ferrisburgh spent the night at Mr. Hazards.
Sund 6th	Drove to Father's, visited them until five. took a lengthy walk with sister to the Creek. very tired. returned to rest awhile. received a request to attend my sister's wedding. returned home at half past eight in the evening. dangerous.
Mond 7th	Fatigued and lazy. wove six yards and half. grandfather no better[.]
Tuesd 8th	Wove five yards put in a web called over Esq. Darrow. returned home early.
Wed 9th	Arose at two. unwell almost all night. retired again until morn. concluded no tasks. spun and put in a web of linen. wove two and half yds. drove to Newhaven. bought of Mr. Beaman one pair gloves 4/5 one pr stockings 3/9 called at Esq. Jewetts & Mrs. Berry's. spent the night at Mr. Edward Dunshee's. he has the new house painted very nice.
Thurs 10th	Wove eight yards finished web. Miss Delany Scott, Sally Dunshee Amanda Eastman called over to Mr. Brooks. I accompanied them to Mr Hall's. lengthy walk. very rude. returned, spent the night with Miss Zilpha Pettibone. unhappy girl. I pity her. very tired.
Frid 11th	Put in another linen web. wove only four yds, almost sick. attended an Apple paring Bee. with about thirty others. very melancholy. took my opportunity, came home alone.
Sat. 12th	Wove six yards linen. wrote a letter to Mr. E. and Miss B. Eastman very tired.
Sun 13th	Spent the day wickedly. wrote to Miss M[aria] Durfey. Mrs. Orra Taylor unwell
Mond 14th	Arose at three. Mr. Hawkins started for the St. Lawrence Co. this morn with Mrs. Hawkins. Wove ten yards. finished weaving linen. very tired. prepared apples today. until morn. Mr. Lee married.

Tues 15th	Arose at three. worked at apples until eight. drove to Mr. & Mrs. Arnold rode with me to the village. paid me four dollars at Mr. Hally's store. carried her home. returned. Put in a web through the reed. picked geese and the remainder of the wood. Mr. J.T[hompson] paid me one dollar and half in specie this eve. Miss Charter gone to Castleton.
Wed 16th	Wove seven and half yards five quarters wide. mended considerable tried.
Thursd 17th	Wove seven yards, finished the web. carried it home. took tea at Mrs D[unshee] rode with Mrs. Allen. called to Mr. Thompson's obliged to spend the night heard widow Hall was married last eve to Mr. Whitman. I suspect Mr. Ellsworth was married this eve. to Miss Louisa Hazard, Wallingford. agreeable visit retired late. I find I work too hard.
Frid 18th	Warm shower. spun thirty knots. very lazy indeed. knitting eve. rainy.
Sat 19th	Warm shower. spun thirty knots. twisted eight of thread. lazy and tired out. finished my twentieth pair of stockings.
Sund 20th	Rainy. read considerable. spent some hours in sleep. determined rid of laziness.
Mond 21st	Spun seventy knots as warp only. not as hard twist. taking Vitriol. This day I am twenty one years old and nothing done for my maker and suffered to live happy.
Tuesd 22nd	Rather cold. spun but thirty knots of Warp. toothache very hard. Mrs. Charlotte Scott spent the day and night with me. Miss Abigail Jewett. Miss Harriet Nash called. brought me sixty yards more to weave. A party of married people. Mr. Dunshee's.
Wed 23rd	Cool. But pleasant for the season. Spun thirty five knots
Thursd 24th	Arose at four. spun five knots. Put in a web, wove. Attended quilting at Mr. Edward Dunshees. spent the eve at Mr. J. Dunshee's agreeably. while the rest of the party at E. Dunshees engaged in a dance. house full. I had no work with me. sewed for Mrs. Dunshee. She gave me a small stick of twist. she said I must keep it for Button holes to my old pantaloons. returned home at ten. Being dressed in silk without great coat, took cold.
Friday 25th	Cold. wove five yards, tender web. rather unwell. sprained my side. Quilting. Mrs. Nash brought me forty yards more. Miss S. Prime called this eve. hard frost.

Sat. 26th Arose at three. wove eight yards. washed some. Ironed and mended some.

Sun 27th Pleasant cool. spent at home. What shall I render to my God for all his gifts to me? Mrs. Dunshee published to Mr. Solomon Lord.

Mon 28th Arose at two. spun ten knots. very high winds. wove six yards, spun ten evening.

Tuesd 29th Arose at three. spun ten knots. wove two and half yards. finished the rotten web. wove eight yards on another. hail rain and snow.

Wed 30th Arose at three. wove seventeen yards. finished the web. cloudy[.]

Thursd 31st Arose at three. spun twenty-two knots. put in a web Cut and Basted and partly made two frocks for Miss Polly and Betsey Hall. spun ten knots this eve finished my wool I am tired of spinning nights very dark P.M.

November 1822

Frid 1st Arose at three. spun doubled twisted yarn for a mop. prepared four pair of stockings for dressing. visited at Esq. Jewetts. A.M. Called over to Col. Nash's became acquainted with Mrs. Wilcox. returned home. wove one yard tender. left it almost sick. headache.

Sat 2nd Few flakes of snow fell. Wove only four yards. obliged to leave work and retire. I have laboured too hard but have been taking Vitriol and Esther's Bitters in hopes that I could still labour. sick night.

Sund 3rd Pleasant, rather better but not able to sit up all day. I think I shall work tomorrow. I engaged so much that I cannot get along without.

Mond 4th Wove seven yards. not very well yet. sewing this eve. a few flakes of snow.

Tuesd 5th Wove seven yards. winding this eve. severe pain in my head. sore throat. Miss, Mrs Pettibone spent the day two other Ladies. Mr. Lord — Mrs. Dunshee married today.

Wed 6th Very unwell. pain in my head and throat. wove one yards. rode out. Drove to Mr. C.'s Store. traded three Dollars sixty four cents. returned. called Mr Dexter's. Returned. not able to sit up. With difficulty, speak or swallow. it appears like the quinsy.[53]

Thursd 7th Very unwell, throat worse. when I can sit up, I try to weave. wove three yards.

Frd 8th Rainy night. Cloudy day. rather better. wove six and half yds. spun four knots.

Sat. 9th Arose at four. Wove six yards, finished the web. Drove to Col. Nash's Esq Jewetts. My Brother came after me to attend my sister's wedding. Grandmother said at first if I went I never need to return. at last she told me I might go. for my part I was indifferent about it. almost sick. Melancholy.

Sund 10th Returned to Fathers. found them all at work. Mr. [Nicholas] Austin spent the evening.

Mond 11th Made my sister's wedding night cap, lined my white belt. assisted the other four in beating crackers. rather unwell. Here I am, my work at home. I am almost discouraged.

Tuesd 12th Rainy night and day. ript my silk frock. ironed it turning it and altering. pain in stomach.

Wed 13th Sewed some on my frock. some on Harriet [Orvis]'s. went with Father to Vergennes. purchased aCassimere. handkerchief. nine pairs of hooks & eyes. for cash - one Dollar seventy-five. Mrs. Powel. Mr and Mrs Carpenter arrived. finished H's crape [Harriet's crape frock] this eve.

Thursd 14th Finished my frock. Rained all day very wet and muddy. we repaired to the Meeting house all covered with mud. The Bride and Groom and waiters rode in covered waggons. When the ceremony is performed the Groom takes the Bride by the right hand and says[.] "In the presence of this assembly I take this friend Harriet Orvis to be my wife. Promising through Divine assistance to be unto her a dutiful and affectionate husband until death separates us." She then repeats the same unto Nicholas Austin. Soon after, a paper is signed by all the relatives and others if they wish. soon after [they] return home with their guests[s] which dined. were about fifty, forty to dine. for my part this eve I am unusually melancholly. not a few tears. I receive numberless invitations from them all and am not situated either to visit or receive.

Frid 15th Pleasant. we again collect to Nathaniel Austins to Dine and to tea. very splendidly treated in the best style. persuaded to spend the night with Elizabeth [Austin].

Sat 16th Pleasant. Sewing returned to Father's after dinner and from there to Bristol received a pair of Morocco Shoes. very tired indeed. no letters. what can be the reason?

Sund 17th Pleasant. took a walk on the rocks. melancholy. wrote a lengthy letter to Mr. Eastman. Mr. Ephraim Munson, Newhaven, last evening after supper went to the privy, took his dull pocket knife and cut his throat from ear to ear at four places. Mrs. M being anxious told her son to go and see him. He went to him. he did not speak. took a light and behold, he gasped the last breath, his hands supporting his head. His wife held his bleeding head until the neighbors came to her assistance. Oh my God preserve his family for thy sake.

Mond 18th Cloudy some rain. put in a coverlet twice. wove two yards on it. rainy eve. laid out and commenced piecing my Bed Comfort. Mr. Forman Mrs. Otis, Miss Hinsdale took tea with us. entered a letter.

Tuesd 19th Agreeable weather. finished Mrs. Dunshee's coverlet. Miss Olive Kellogg. visited us. Lazy.

Wed 20th Cloudy, some rain. Put in a cotton web for Mrs. Jewett and myself wove only one yard very fine and poor shuttles. Sewing mornings and evening. rather lazy.

Thursd 21st Rainy day. wove only three yards and half. finished my Bed comforter on the outside. Betsey and myself have made a number of paper bags for garden seeds this evening. I have thirty kinds.

Frid. 22nd Lowry, bought a few needles of a blind Peddler. wove four and half yards. rainy night. spun fifteen knots this eve. tolerable health and spirits.

Sat. 23rd Lowry. wove four yard and half yrds. finished my cloth spun ten knots. twisted of thread. Hatchelled two pounds of Flax. Heard from Monkton.

Sun 24th Pleasant. reading. took a favorite walk to the river. lonely.

Mond 25th High wind wove seven yards. walked to Mr. Dexter's called over to Mr. Hall's. Mr. Annin's, Thompson's, Prime's, so many entreaties to visit people and no time for it, I am tired of hearing them. returned home. cut out two flannel frocks made the waist to one. very tired.

Tuesd 25th Arose before day. wove only four and half yards. washed little sewed some. rained this eve. cut out two frocks for B.S. figured Bombazett. very tired.

Wed 26th Pleasant. wove four yards. finished the Cotton. Mrs. Jewett visited us. received a friendly letter from Mr. Eastman and his returned with it. Made my sheet.

Thurs 27th Some rain. some snow. wove out the Blanket I put in yesterday put in mine this evening. marked my flannel sheet. made almost my flannel petticoat.

Fri 28th Cloudy. Drove to Middlebury. accompanied by Lovina and Sally D. Bought at the Looking Glass Factory a plain gilt for one dollar fifty in cash. Traded four dollars seventeen cents by order at Hough's Store. visited the Cotton Factory. purchased one tea kettle, one small Pot and Spider of Philip Heart by cash. one spelling book by cash at Hagar's Book Store. one Bible, Box of wafers by credit. Tired of shopping without cash. Took tea at third store with Mrs. Crane. returned home by Curby Street. dark getting home. very muddy indeed. headache.

Sat. 30th Rainy. began a wool coverlet for myself. wove two yards. Ironed some. Perused my spelling book this evening. very different from others. tired.

December 1822

Sund 1st Rainy. Reading my new Bible. God grant that I may never fail one day of my life from reading it. Mr. Elisha Dunshee published to Miss Mary Drake. A still match.

Mond 2nd Wove three yards on coverlet. sewing on the girls' frocks. very tired.

Tues 3rd Finished my coverlet. wove three yards on Grandma'a'm's. sewing.

Wed. 4th Finished the coverlet. Put in a blanket for Mrs Thompson. sewing.

Thursd 5th Thanksgiving. Sewed all day on the girls' frocks. made them too small. Mrs. Pettibone spent the night. brought my Bonnet home. Almira P. borrowed to wear to the Splendid Ball last evening at Mr. Dunshee's. Mr. E.D. & M.D. [Elisha Dunshee, Mary Drake] married this eve. almost sick. melancholy.

Frid 6th Finished the girls' frocks, perfectly suited. cut out, partly made a cape.

Sat. 7th Wove Mrs. T.'s Blanket. too much for health. my left side swollen greatly.

Sund. 8th Pleasant. Ah! how many pleasant Sabbaths I have misspent of late.

Mond 9th Cold. called over to Mr. Thompson's and Prime's. This morn washed the furniture and East Room. Put on a quilt alone. sewing this eve for Lovina.

Tues 10th Cloudy, some rain. Marked the border, quilted the foot, part of the side. washed all the crockery in suds. Miss E[lizabeth] A[ustin], D.S., P.S. called to see me at noon. I work alone. sleep alone. I take great satisfaction in being alone.

Wed 11th	Very pleasant. Marked the middle of my quilt in flowers. visited by Miss L. Buss, Miss N. Dunshee Miss E. and A[lmira]. Prime. assisted me some on my quilt. Miss P and A Pettibone spent the eve. E[lecta] P[rime] the night. I receive but little company on account of Grandmother's aversion to it especially three years past. very tired.
Thurs 12th	Pleasant as summer. work alone late evening. very tired indeed.
Frid 13th	Pleasant quilted until eleven at night. took of my quilt. almost sick.
Sat. 14th	Rainy. Prepared and quilted my Bed Cushion. I think I will not work so hard another week. Very soon, Mr Severance to work here.
Sund 15th	Pleasant. very cold. read my Bible almost all day. Cyrus Brooks ten years old today. high winds. Little Polly very sick.
Mond 16th	Arose at three worked all day to get bindings for my quilts. bound the bed Cushion. very cold. high wind.
Tuesd 17th	Arose at three. unable to work. obliged to retire again. Bound my quilt, slow work. the snow has fallen to the depth of one inch. Made two holders this eve. rather dull[.]
Wed 18th	Scoured and Painted my Bedstead Venetian Red. rode to Newhaven called over to Mr. Beaman's store. 1/2 yard Calico 3/8 yards Green crape. 1½ Italian Braid. settled with Col Nash, Esq Jewett. very rough riding. visited Mrs. Pettibone's. ripped my coat up.
Thursd 19th	Sewing on netting. made some. made my coverlet. Col. Nash and wife dined with us. Col. wished [me] to call on them and he would make a present. Grandmother conducts so unpleasantly that I have cried almost all this P.M. who can live with her agreeably.

Extract from the American Repertory & Advertiser.

Grubs in Sheeps head. This grub proceeds from a large Bee which lays its egg in the nostrils of sheep. by the last of Aug. or first of Sept. may fin[d] between the mostrils and windpipe from 25 to 100 white grubs with black heads and black streaks on the back. in June a streak cross wise. july and August are as large as a pipe stem near an inch long. four large teeth as hard as bone. they leave the sheep, casting of their skin, become a bee. the symptoms appear toward spring; floss of flesh, running at the nose, snorting. Etc. some instances spring about wild and frantic, drop drown dead. Remedy: take half pound of Scotch snuff, pour two quarts of boiling water on it, stir it until cold. Inject a tablespoonful up each nostril with a syringe. repeat three or four times from the middle of Oct. to the first of January. half an ounce of Assefaetida pounded in a little water added to the snuff makes it more effective. this remedy was obtained by dissecting the heads of sheep.

J.N. Z.A. D.D.O.M.S.

Frid 20th Pleasant. sewing A.M. Washing P.M. sewing eve. A & P Pettibone[.]

Sat 21st Pleasant. removed from the chamber to the Eastroom. Square room. for the first time had the privilege of a lower room. killed swine. assisted the girls some.

Sun 22nd Pleasant. walked to the village. heard Mr. Dodge preach. called over to Mr. Gaige's. insisted upon my spending the night. Mrs. Brigham invited to tarry with her to singing school. took tea at Mr. G's accompanied to school by Mr. Frederick Smith, Newhaven.

Mond 23rd Pleasant. spun 26 knots of Linen. starched this eve. Cousin Enoch Brooks spent the night.

Tuesd 24th Spun 16 knots. visited at Mr. Annin's. walked to the village, took a letter from Miss Charter. returned and spent the night with C. Gaige at Marcus Moor's. toothache very hard.

Wed 25th Pleasant. toothache all day. returned home P.M. finished spinning linen. sat up all night with Lovina. Dr. Rise spent the night. she came near leaving the world.

Thursd 26th Christmas. took care of Lovina and Children. Almira P. [Pettibone] washed. very tired.

Frid 27th Pleasant. done house work. took care of two cross children, Lovina[,] and Baked. toothache hard.

Sat. 28th Pleasant doing housework. Lovina rather better. Uncle Clapp's family spent the night. toothache very hard. Why is my heart so far from thee, God, my chief delight? Dejected.

MONKTON

Sun 29th	Pleasant[.] took a walk with Aunt[Clapp] to the river. returned to home with them.
Mond 30th	Pleasant. sewing my flannel. visited with Mrs. Bacon at Mr. Williams. introduced to Mrs. and Miss Williams. pleasant visit. toothache. large ulcer broke. Mr [original blank space] Collamore married to Miss Abigail Latin. Midd. [Middlebury] almost sick.
Tuesd 31st	Stormy, some snow, high winds. Mr. Alva Smith married P.M. to Miss Sally Creed. Thomas Gifford published to Alvira Handy. requested to attend a party. not able. pleasant visit with Olive. Toothache very hard. two doll fifty Cts [$2.50] due me by Mrs. C[lapp] agreed to Balance for a pair of Shoes. Alas My Bible is at home unread not one day. Melancholy. Mr Rise to Miss Gaige.

January 1823

Wed 1st	Pleasant. sewing but little. how I dread to see it snow. how can I leave friends. twenty-one years ago my dear mother left me. Oh that I were ready to follow.
Thurs 2nd	Returned home with O.K. [Olive Kellogg] out of health. visited Mr. Prime's, spent the evening. insisted on my spending the night. my head ready to burst with pain.
Frid 3rd	Pleasant. Put in a web of kersey. Bags. wove four yards[.] washed floors. attended singing school at Mr. Dunshee's Hall. thaws. very sober today. reasons unknown.
Sat. 4th	Cold. wove four yards. Quarterly meeting commences. absent minded. Mr Matthew Nichols spent the night.
Sund. 5th	Cold. spent the day at home. drew notes of five tunes. rather dejected.
Mon 6th	Very cold. washed. wove out the web. Put in mine. a little snow every day.
Tues 7th	Very cold. making my flannel frock. hard cold. absent minded. melancholy.
Wed 8th	Cold. wove two yards. put in a carpet. sewing evenings. unwell. hard cold.
Thurs 9th	More moderate. wove four yards. finished my checkered. altered my Bombazett.

Frid 10th Wove one yard carpeting. Mr. William Eastman spent the day to collect my school bill. Took a ride this eve to Chapman's store, Newhaven. saw Mr. Timothy Hopkins. pleasant visit for the opportunity. paid Mr. C[hapman]. 6 dollars.

Sat. 11th The coldest day that has passed this winter. wove all day for almost nothing. almost sick with cold. Ironed[.] Ah whither am I going to leave Celibacy soon. Oh, awful the thought. why have I been so weak as to engage for life in so dangerous an engagement. Oh my God support me through this most trying scene. How incapable am I of filling the place of a companion.

Sund 12th Cold snow some. received a visit this P.M. from Mr. Harry Java. Stormy P.M. George Dayfoot published to Miss Laura Munson. Alas, I soon experience the same ceremony. soon leave my relatives and new modes of living among strangers. how singular to leave all for one of the other sex. Attended singing school at the village. an agreeable letter from Miss Betsey Eastman. received a pair of shoes.

Mond 13th Pleasant. Altered my red flannel frock. toothache very hard. very lazy.

Tuesd 14th Pleasant and cold. sewing. spent the P.M. at Mr. Annin's, the eve at the schoolhouse. I find it more difficult to sing on second Treble than on the air. cumbered about many things. but oh one thing is needful.

Wed 15th Cold, made a harness 36. finished my Cambric nightgown. good spirits.

Thurs 16th More moderate. finished my carpet. Attended singing school P.M. Esq. Jewett, Evening at the schoolhouse. But oh these seasons must soon close with me.

Frid 17th Pleasant. washed some. double and twisted 27 knots of worsted thread. Etc. very tired.

BRISTOL

Sat. 18th Thaws fast. gluing and preparing many things. washed floors. attended singing school, village. I had to take the lead on the second treble.

Sund 19th Rainy. snow gone. attended meeting by waggon. more than sixty singers. I never sung on the second before Mr. Dodge preached from these words Luke XII, XIII:

> Master, speak to my brother, that he divide the inheritance with me.

P.M. II Samuel XII 7th:

And Nathan said to David thou art the man.

Mon. 20th	Wet wove ten yards of Blanketing. earned one Dollar. absent minded.
Tuesd 21st	Thaws continually. wove seven yards, all the yarn. Uncle and Aunt returned from Ferrisburgh. received a letter from my dear Brother [Loren], Upper Canada. Mr. G. Dayfoot married this eve to Miss L. Monson.
Wedn 22nd	Sewing. settled with Mr. Monson, Mr. Beaman. purchased snuffers and divers articles. my great coat ruined. Mr. T. Gifford married this eve to Miss A. Handy.
Thurs 23rd	Little more snow. sewing all day. sleep departs from my eyes and slumber from my eyelids on account of my debts and want of furniture that I have not.
Frid 24th	Sewing. finished my Cambric Cap. What can be the reason of the delays of my absent friends. Heard of the death of Mrs. Maryann Van Vliet.
Sat. 25th	Cold. finished weaving. made a net for worsted. read several letters of Ira A. Demon. Mr. Esthers purchased the half a bushel of them for Roger.
Sund 26th	Cloudy. spent the day at home. melancholy. Mr. & Mrs Lee called. Attended Sabbath school.
Mond 27th	Sewing spent the A.M. at L. Dunshees. rather out of health dejected.
Tuesd 28th	Cold. Called over to Mr. Chapman's. Took up my due bill. bought trimming for my great coat, candlestick. Etc. engaged Miss Prime for a few days.
Wed 29th	Sewing on my great coat. out of health. To what am I hastening[?]
Thurs 30th	Sewing Two o'clock. retired. Expect Mr. E[astman] daily.
Frid 31st	Sewing. Mr. Eastman arrived in tolerable health. Sally [Prime] returned home.

February 1823

Sat. 1st	Took a ride to Lincoln. three couples of friends married. spent the night at Mr. Lee's. very melancholy indeed at the approach of matrimony. Cold.
Sund. 2nd	Very cold. attended meeting for the last time at the village. Published.[54] Horrid. spent the evening agreeably with Mr. E. out of health[.] tore my silk frock.

BRISTOL

Mond 3rd Stormy. visited my father and friends. dejected and rude. Saw Mr. J. [James] Brown from Canada. presented with two shuttles, one rolling pin by Mr. Austin. very tired indeed. have had but little rest.

New modes of living among strangers
February 4, 1823–October 6, 1830

Tuesd 4th Cold. rode to Middlebury. purchased my wedding articles of Mr. Kilburn. Mr. E paid for them in cash. visited the factory. returned home to tea. called over to the village. settled with N. Follit. almost sick.

Wed 5th Pleasant. what a dreadful day is this. Miss [Sally] Prime waited upon me today and this eve and Mr. Henry Byington Mr. Eastman's waiter to the marriage ceremony performed by Esq. Pier (he presented me with the dollar). Farewell to a sweet single life, I can no more enjoy you. Packed my goods ready to depart. What a change to relinquish parents and friends all for one of the other sex. Surprising and unpleasant.

Thursd 6th Very cold. took leave of my friends. left my companion to drive my two cows and proceeded with his father. called at Hull spent the night Barney Inn, Burlington village. very tired. almost sick.

Frid 7th Very cold indeed. Mr. E. overtook us this morn rode nine miles on ice spent the night at Newcomb's. became acquainted with Mrs. Cook. very tired.

Sat. 8th Cold. spent the night at Mr. Whipple's. almost sick and discouraged.

Sund 9th Pleasant. arrived at Mr. E's[.] Oh[!] how disagreeable is the thought that I am wedded for life and so ignorant of labour. how incapable of filling my station. Harriet Durfey called over to see me. very tired and melancholly.

Mond 10th Two years this day since I first saw my partner, visited the place of my future abode. Called upon the Mrs. Durfey. Mrs. C. Mr. E returned. heard from Canada. returned to Mr. E's. hard cold. very unpleasant I am.

Tues 11th Spent the day at Mrs. E's. introduced to Miss Thankful Knowlton. Mr. Moon.

Wed. 12th Called P.D. [Phineas Durfey][.]Moved home for so I must call it. endeavouring to regulate thoughts.

Thursd 13th	Pleasant. Baking. washing floors. Etc. Mr. Haskall called. hard cold. Mr. E. almost sick.
Frid. 14th	Pleasant. Made twelve doz. candles. Etc. well contented and prosperous.
Sat. 15th	Snows fast. work at a little of everything and understand nothing. I have more to do with than I expected, besides an agreeable partner.
Sund 16th	Very pleasant, cold. Mr. Durfey, children called on us. Mr. E's people this eve, six of them. how disagreeable to my mate and no longer their age.
Mond 17th	Snows fast. Baked, washed. Roswell [Mr E's brother] came to work here. finished two bedsteads.
Tues 18th	Snows and blows. scoured some. starched. Etc. Uncle Brooks returned from Vermont. brought me one dollar fifty cents in cash. Mr. E. presented me with a lb of tea. L & R [Lee and Roswell] to work today. had one window put in. Lame side. endeavour to serve them.
Wed 19th	Snows. Mr. Lee E. came, broke something almost every day. the two Mr and Mrs. Durfeys [Phineas and Joseph] called.
Thurs 20th	Stormy. almost sick. toothache hard. pain in my side. sewed some. scarcely sit up.
Frid 21st	Stormy. Mr. E. called. Miss J. Covey borrowed my shoes. Mr. J. Stearns called from Vermont[.]
Sat. 22nd	Pleasant. Baked, Etc. very unwell. hard keeping it to myself for Mr. E will know it.[55]
Sund 23rd	Very pleasant. sick day and night. almost discouraged. But that will never do.
Mond 24th	Pleasant. rather better. Mrs. E. made me an agreeable visit. Mr. Wing called. lame side.
Tues 25th	Visited by two Mr and Mrs. Durfeys. Mr and Mrs Covey. Miss B.E. better.
Wed 26th	Washed. took cold, very lazy. Mr. Chittenden called. unwell. toothache. very cold.
Thurs 27th	Cold and stormy. Baked. Mr and Mrs. Sampson spent the eve with us.

Frid 28th Cold indeed. Baked pies. toothache very hard. Mr. E. [Sr.] called. sewed some this eve.

March 1823

Sat 1st Very cold, snow very deep. toothache all night almost discouraged of living.

Sund 2nd Stormy and cold. toothache all day. Our moments fly apace nor will our moments stay.

Mond 3rd Very cold. washed. Mr. L.E. [Lee Eastman] called. I enjoy myself tolerably well. toothache some.

Tues 4th Cold. walked to Mr. E's [Sr] Hopkinton Town meeting, had a pleasant visit indeed.

Wed 5th Pleasant. I see the effect of ignorance in its most hideous shape.

Thurs 6th Thaws fast, rain. Mr and Mrs. Taylor visited us from Stockholm. visited this eve at Capt. Durfey's [Phineas]. lost my gloves. a Catamount came near the road.

Frid 7th Colder. our friends took their leave. visited by Mr & Mrs Flowers, Miss Janes, Mr. and Mrs. Rockwell. fine visit. I begin to esteem strangers as neighbors.

Sat. 8th Pleasant. Baked. David Eastman here tonight. Alas, and did my Saviour bleed and die.[56]

Sun 9th Attended meeting. heard Mr. Road [Rhodes] preach. introduced to Mrs. Talbot, Ogdensburg. Mrs. Chittenden saw Mrs Cook. happy child. If I gave attention to my maker that I do the world. . . .

PARISHVILLE

Mond 10th Cold, Pleasant. Walked with Mr. E. to Mr. J.D. [Joseph Durfey] Introduced to Mrs. Umphry [Humphrey] spent the P.M. with the elderly Ladies. the eve at J.D.'s At our return found Mr. E and [Daniel] Kelley [an in-law] from Fowler. spent the night.

Tues 11th Rainy. A pedlar of Essence dined with us. commenced making soap for the first time in my life. Bought half oz. Camphor.

Wed 12th Pleasant. D[avid] E[astman], J. Osgood work here. rather unwell. good spirits.

Thurs 13th	Pleasant Mrs. Durfey's for me to accompany them on a visit. my attendance to soap forbade me. Uncle Brooks and wife made us a short visit. finished my soap. Mr. E's health poor.
Frid 14th	Pleasant. Harriet D. [Durfey] Visited me Baked bread & pies. washed floors.
Sat. 15th	Visited Mr. E's this eve very tired indeed and monstrous lazy.
Sund 16th	Pleasant. walked one mile to meeting. Mr. Putnam preached Introduced to Mrs. Dustin. returned very tired indeed. read nary a word.
Mond 17th	Pleasant. done large washing. took Cold. almost sick.
Tuesd 18th	Pleasant. mending what time I get besides other chores. two boarders.
Wed 19th	Pleasant. mending. toothache. Starched. Ironed, no ambition.
Thurs 20th	Some snow. mending. Time flies swiftly onward to eternity.
Frid 21st	Little more snow. mending. made two false caps. Pleasant.
Sat. 22nd	Pleasant. mending. visited at uncle Durfey's unwell. borrowed tracts.
Sund. 23rd	Cloudy. some snow. took a walk to the wood. read tracts. fatigued
Mond 24th	High winds and rain. washed, Baked pies and bread. picked one fleece of wool. three Boarders. very tired, almost sick. Dislike to be alone with so many of the other sex. no company for me. disagreeable.
Tuesd 25th	Pleasant. melancholy. indulge my tears at leisure. How can I live and enslave myself for others? greased my wool. carded and spun only ten knots of wool. toothache almost all the time.
Wed. 26th	Pleasant. carded spun about twelve knots more of worsted. very slow at work.
Thurs 27th	Pleasant. carded, spun ten knots. mended almost sick. two boarers. all the time.
Frid 28th	Pleasant. spun some. an old drunkard called while alone. toothache[.]
Sat. 29th	Pleasant. Baked. finished carding wool. combed flax for thread. toothache.
Sun 30th	Pleasant. read awhile then took a walk with my partner. toothache[.]

Mond 31st	Pleasant. high winds. washed spun one skein. toothache every night[.]

April 1823

Tuesd 1st	Pleasant. Baked. finished spinning wool. I have more chores than I thought.
Wed 2nd	Pleasant. Hatchelled all my flax. Fifteen or twenty pounds. Saphrona E. [Eastman] [.] Mary came to see me. walked with them in the mud as far as J. Durfey's. C [J. Durfey's wife, Charlotte] gave me a few pickles. returned very tired. a few drops of rain. toothache continually.
Thurs 3rd	Pleasant A.M. Spun one runn of Linen. Rainy P.M. my wheel turns very hard.
Frid 4th	Pleasant. spun one runn of Linen. very tired. hard work for me to spin.
Sat. 5th	Pleasant cleared my house. moved one Bed upstairs. uncle called. high spirits.
Sund 6th	Pleasant day. Rainy night. took a ramble with Mr. E. Six gentlemen called on us. Uncle sent us some Poultry. How wicked do I spend my days.
Mon 7th	Rainy day. small washing. mended E's coat. very unwell indeed.
Tues 8th	Spun thirty knots. very tired. no faculty to get along. God grant that I may improve.
Wed 9th	Spun but little. made twenty lbs of Sugar. almost discouraged about spinning.
Thurs 10th	Spun one run. Made twenty lbs more. I find my health declining.
Frid 11th	Spun one run. Ironed. I find I grow more vile every day of my life. Pleasant.
Sat. 12th	Pleasant. very muddy. walked to Uncles. D. spent the P.M. & night at Mr Eastman [Sr.]'s. spent the time agreeably with Betsey. heard unpleasant news concerning Mr. Perry's stealing. Mr. Hopkins lost a child. Mr. Kent Esq. Merrills died this eve. Ah, why was it not I, unworthy wretch.
Sund 13th	Pleasant. heard Mr. Putnam preach from these words "Teach us, make haste and come down for today I must abide at thine house[."] returned home very tired indeed. Our moments fly apace nor will our minutes stay.
Mond 14th	Pleasant. gathered some sap. spun one run. rather discontented lonely.

Tues 15th	Pleasant. spun little. finished sugaring. visited by Miss Julia Covey.
Wed 16th	Very warm. six men folks to wait on. I should be discouraged were it not for the unbounded goodness of my partner. visited by Mrs. Rockwell. Mill [Miss] Janes. Miss Newton. Pleasant visit. good spirits.
Thurs 17th	Pleasant. spun 27 knots. very tired. I spend time almost for nought.
Fri 18th	Pleasant morn. Rainy P.M. Baked spun one run retired late.
Sat 19th	Pleasant. washed some and floors. sewed some spun 18 knots. very tired.
Sund 20th	Rainy. spent my time a part of it in sleep. Oh what a wicked creature I am, neglect my maker as I do. Lord forbid that I should continue to live in sloth, may I not renounce the things of an earthly nature, and seek superior bliss? God grant that we may live no longer in such a stupid Backslidden condition but may we both run the race that is set before us with alacrity, till we arrive on Canaan's happy shore
Mond 21st	Rainy. washed. spun ten knots. work but little for myself & less for my God.
Tuesd 22nd	Rainy. spun twenty three knots. I feel unable to spin any or too lazy.
Wed 23rd	Rainy. A.M. Pleasant P.M. spun 13 knots Mrs. D. and myself visited at Mr. N. Rockwell's.
Thursd 24th	Pleasant. spun little. Ironed. mended Etc. When shall I see and know all I desire or need.
Frid 25th	Showery. visited by Mrs Sampson. spun 15 knots. toothache all night.
Sat. 26th	Pleasant. finished my chores. went to uncle's. begg'd garden seeds, currant Bushes Etc. Baked pudding & pies. visited by Miss B. Easman. almost tired out. head and toothache.
Sund 27th	Another sabbath misspent. we took a walk to the millseat, also Mr & Mrs Dufrey took tea with us. B.E. [Betsey Eastman] returned with them. head pains me very much indeed.
Mond 28th	Washed and Baked, mended some. ten in the family days, seven nights.
Tuesd 29th	Pleasant. carded tow. spun Linen. very feeble. Mr. E's health very poor. hard work.

Wed 30th Pleasant, warm. carded some. sowed Onions. carded some. spun some. eleven in the family[.]

May 1823

Thurs 1st Pleasant. spun seven knots. worked in the garden some. visited Mr. Flower's[.] melancholy.

Frid 2nd Rainy. P.M. spun some. mended some. washed floors tired of such a family.

Sat. 34rd Pleasant. spun some. carded some. Baked, washed floors. heard some of Mrs. E's [mother-in-law] curses. Took a real feast of tears. the more I do, the more I may and this is the thanks I get.

Sund 4th Snowy morn. cold wind. spent the day in the house. low spirits.

Mond 5th Cold, a few flakes of snow. washed. Spun 14 knots of tow. Mr Weed called.

Tuesd 6th Pleasant. spun only 18 knots. very unwell. discouraged about spinning.

Wed 7th Pleasant. spun ten knots. Visited by the Miss Eastmans & Miss Knowlton. took a pleasant walk with them to Mr. Rockwell's[.] called to Mr. Flowers. accompanied the Miss E's as far as J.D.s [Joseph Durfey's]. returned home very tired.

Thursd 8th Rainy. spun 13 knots. almost sick. mended some. carded. rainy night.

Frid 9th Rainy. spun 18 knots. unwell and lazy beside. What will become of me.

Sat. 10th Rainy P.M. Miss L. McAllister called to see me. Baked. Churned. wash.

Sund 11th Rainy. read the scriptures considerable. took a lengthy walk to the Brook. returned very tired. what do I render to my God for all his gifts.

Mond 12th Pleasant. mended some. washed. visited at Mr. Coveys. doubled yarn. received a contusion in my side by the cellar. almost tired out.

Tues 13th Rainy. carded tow A.M. greatly distressed by my fall. while alone. Mrs. C. [Charlotte] Durfey spent the P.M. with me. fainted twice.

Wed. 14th Rainy Mr. R. [Ruth Brooks—Mrs. Phineas] Durfey spent the P.M. sat up to tea. fatigued.

Thurs 15th	Rainy. kept my bed all day. my partner labors with unwearied attention towards me in every respect. he is an excellent nurse
Frid 16th	Rainy. rather better. Mrs. Rockwell spent the P.M. washed floor for me.
Sat. 17th	Pleasant. both Mrs. Durfeys spent the P.M. washed for me[.] I am blessed with the best companions and neighbours. severe pain in my head.
Sund 18th	Very pleasant. walked out by the help of Mr E. severe headache
Mond 19th	Cloudy. kept my bed most of the day. B.E. [Betsey Eastman] came to spend the week.
Tues 29th	Sat up almost all day. knit a little. very feeble.
Wed 21st	Cloudy. rather better but very weak. How ungrateful am I to my God?
Thurs 22nd	Cloudy, rainy nights. Mrs. C. Durfey[.] Mrs. Covey visited and Baked for me[.]
Frid 23rd	Cloudy some rain. washed a few clothes and ironed. very tired Uncle Brooks called.
Sat 24th	Rainy. spun 13 knots. washed floors. ironed. mended some. very tired indeed.
Sund 25th	Rainy night, pleasant day. took a walk, the rest of the time reposed. fatigued.
Mond 26th	Some rain. washed. spun 11 knots. M.E. [Mary Eastman] came to spend the week. Mr. E sick.
Tues 27th	Pleasant. spun little. visited H.D. [Harriet Durfey] took a walk to the Millstream[.] caught a fish. Mr Amos Sampson was trapped, had 25 pounds of water taken from him.
Wed 28th	Rainy. spun 20 knots. carded. Mr. E's health is very poor. God grant his life.
Thursd 29th	Rainy. spun 20 knots. visited by Mrs. E. took William home sick [mumps in the town].
Frid 30th	Cloudy. spun 12 knots tow. carded. received a letter from Mrs. Taylor[.][57] her daughter was born April 4th. melancholy. churched mended etc.
Sat. 31st	Pleasant. Baked pies, pudding. washed floors. sewed. the Sawmill raised.

June 1823

Sund 1st	Pleasant. dressed in silk. walked to uncle Brooks. Attended meeting P.M. returned at night. Mr. S. and wife called an infant of Mr Chase buried today.
Mond 2nd	Pleasant. washed. visited at C. [Chester] Rockwells. introduced to Miss Bell. very tired.
Tuesd 3rd	Very warm, Mr. E. almost sick. spun some. slept some. idle and uneasy.
Wed 4th	Pleasant. Spun A.M. Baked pies, Pudding. visited by B & M E. [Betsey and Mary Eastman] J. C. [Joseph and Charlotte] D & R D [Ruth Durfey]. Laura Bell, Louis Newton. knitting. very tired. the musketoes very plenty.
Thursd 5th	Baked. spun 16 knots. boiled and rinsed yarn. alone today, somewhat lonely.
Frid 6th	Pleasant. sized my warp. walked to uncles[.] D spooled my yard. went to Mr. E warped. took tea. called to Mr. Cs [Covey] introduced to Miss. Josett Mayhew, beamed my web. JD. returned home. Aunt almost sick.
Sat. 7th	Pleasant. A.M. Ironed. spun 10 knots. Mrs. S. called. Mr. E. burned his slash[.] walked to J.D[s] put my web through the harness. rained so that I tarried.
Sund 8th	Pleasant, cool. Mr. E came, I returned. took a walk to the wood. almost sick.
Mond 9th	Pleasant. washed. visited with H.D. [Harriet Durfey] at Mr. C. [Chester] Rockwells. called over to M. Sanders.
Tuesd 10th	Pleasant. began my web, wove 1 yd 1/3. spent the night at Uncle's. very tired.
Wed 11th	Pleasant and warm. wove four yards. every thread out of order, slow weaving. Mr. E. came, I returned home with him. How happy am I, blessed with such a friend.
Thursd 12th	Pleasant Morn, Rainy P.M. Went out to J.D.['s] late. Mr. Ira Brown and his mother called to visit me. returned with him. Mrs. Powel's health is very poor. Received a letter from Miss Elizabeth Austin [note: her new sister-in-law]. Pleasant night.
Fryd 13th	Rainy. our company took leave at ten accompanied them as far as Mr. Rockwells. to Mr. Sampsons. took a pair of Bombaie trowsers to make. frost[.]

Sat. 14th Pleasant. mended some almost finished the trowsers visited Mr. Flowers inst[illegible] roads.

Sund 15th Pleasant. visited Mr. Sampson. attended Conference at the schoolhouse.

Mond 16th Pleasant. washed. Baked[,] Etc[.] Mr E and myself watched with Mr. Sampson.

Tuesd 17th Rainy night. rode home almost sick. toothache very hard. a Bee for hay.

Wed 18th Pleasant, warm. Braiding [straw]. visited by Mr & Mrs Eastman. violent pain in my head.

Thurs 19th Pleasant went to J.D[.'s] wove three yards[.] Mrs. R.D. [Ruth Durfey?] visited us. cool evening

Frid 20th Pleasant. wove four yard. visited at P.D. [Phineas Durfey's]. plated shirts for training. lonely creature.

Sat. 21st Rainy. finished my web. twisted thread. called over to P.D[.'s]. returned home.

Sund 22nd Pleasant while I stand Idle all the day long. God forbid it to continue.

Mond 23rd Pleasant. washed. Baked. dressed pigeons. very tired toothache all day.

Tues 24th Pleasant went to Mr. E.['s] picked two fleeces of wool. Picked strawberries etc.

Wed 25th Pleasant. cut out two shirts, one pair of trowsers, the first in my life. washed. Miss Bell visited me and spent the night. cut and Basted a frock for her.

Thursd 26th Cloudy P.M. sewing. went after the cows to Mr. E.['s]. they had strayed 4 miles, spent the night at J.D. tooth[ache] very hard every night. rain towards morn.

Frid 27th Sewing. visited at M. [Martha] Sampson. hard toothache all night. what can all this mean?

Sat. 28th Pleasant. sewing rode to uncle's. gathered currants. returned home melancholy.

Sund 29th Pleasant. unwell this morn. walked to meeting, three miles. took tea uncle's.

Mond 30th Washed visited at Mr N. [Nathan] Rockwells. had my shoe mended. very tired.

July 1823

Tuesd 1st	Pleasant. I find nothing but wickedness in my head.
Wed 2nd	Pleasant. Baked. sold one loaf. all here today Harriet called P[.]M.
Thurs 3rd	Pleasant. we took uncle's horses, rode to Stockholm. visited my good friends Mr [and Mrs] Taylor. walked one mile. hear Elder Road [Rhodes] "Who then can be saved[.]" These people live in the enjoyment of religion. Oh that we might follow their example. very tired.
Frid 4th	Independence. wrote a Letter to Aunt Lovina. returned, called to Mr. Simons, G. Sampsons. heard from Lewis, rode to Uncle's. assisted them on waiting [on] company. They have a dance, twelve couples obliged to spend the night. how different are the mind of this company and the one we visited yesterday. Oh that all might know the Lord.
Sat. 5th	Pleasant rode home as soon as light. we were unable to do anything.
Sund 6th	Cloudy. wrote a Letter to Aunt Nicholson and Abby, [at] Lewis.
Mond 7th	Pleasant. not well. visited Mr. N[athan] Rockwell very sick. Braded seven yard.
Tues 8th	Pleasant. washed large wash. scoured shelves. cleaned all day very tired.
Wed 9th	Pleasant[.] sewed a hat for the first time. H.D. washed here. aunt gave me a sheet. Why am I so favoured of God. Very warm.
Thurs 10th	Pleasant. great want of Rain. Baked, sewed some. toothache.
Frid 11th	Pleasant. great want of rain. Ironed we watched with Mr. Sampson.
Sat. 11th	Almost sick. Mr. Kelly [Kelley] visited us. Mr. Abbot's house raised. Cloudy.
Sun 12th	Cloudy but only a few drops of rain. attended conference at the schoolhouse. almost crazy with the toothache. Mr. K [Kelley] spent night.
Mond 13th	Cloudy. very feeble. mending. our people began haying. drytime.
Tuesd 14th	Sewing. doing all the time I am able. I have no strength to work.

Wed 15th	Fine shower of rain. had a window put in the chamber. moved all the [illegible]. cleared the chamber, a very hard job. Mr. Sampson died today. ordination Hopkinton.
Thursd 16th	Pleasant. Baked. washed. Attended funeral. Mr. Pettibone preached from these words. "Man diethe but after this the judgment." Oh that all might profit by this man's death. a number called to tea. I am almost tired out, toothache besides, heard from Stockholm.
Frid 17th	Pleasant. drove to Mr E, took 7 pounds of wool to spin. picked and greased it.
Sat. 18th	Pleasant. walked to uncle D. picked currants to dry. Miss Mayhew spent the night with us. toothache very hard, it gives me no rest day or night.
Sund 19th	Pleasant took a walk to the Mill, rode on the pond. Mr & Mrs D took tea here. Miss Mayhew returned with them. I went to a party on the Sabbath.
Mon 20th	Pleasant. Picked berries. toothache almost all day. Maria staid all night.
Tues 21st	Pleasant. almost sick toothache this P.M. it seem as if I should die[.]
Wed 22nd	Unable to sit up. very warm indeed, and dry. toothache to distraction[.]
Thurs 23rd	Very weak this morning both Mrs Sampsons visited me. Baked pies walked to the sawmill with them. caught four large fish.
Frid 24th	Rainy. sewing. called over to C. Rockwells Mrs Bran [Brand] is dead.
Sat. 25th	Rainy. sewing. finished haying here yesterday. picked green beans.
Sund 26th	Cloudy unable to go to meeting. Mrs. C.D., J. Mayhew called, took tea. they were very wet. picked cucumber read the Scriptures[.]
Mond 27th	Pleasant. Baked pies. visited by both Mrs. D's Mrs. Covey. agitated.
Tuesd 28th	Rainy staid to J.D. doubled twisted stocking yarn. returned.
Wed 29th	Spun ten knots of wool. toothache continually. hard shower Rain. had a large wart. toothache almost to distraction.

Thurs 30th — Baked. spun little. Mrs B. Mrs. S. took dinner. visited with Aunt at Uncle D's. Miss Lucinda Thomas buried today. Sewing.

August 1823

Fryd 1st — Rainy. visited at Mr. Coveys. the Mrs Rockwell Mrs T. Mrs S. Called. Mr B staid all night. toothache all the afternoon. hard shower.

Sat 2nd — Pleasant. Scoured the floor. rode to the village. Had a tooth pulled.

Sund 3rd — Pleasant. Again read the sorrowful tale of "Lucinda; or the Mountain Mourner[.]" Took a walk. not well. disappointed of . . [original blank space]

Mon 4th — Pleasant. Calculated to attend meeting at Hopkinton our cow[s] rambled. before they were found, it was too late. took a walk. Rain. washed. spun six knots. hard shower, thunder and lightning.

Tues 5th — Pleasant. spun 24 knots, very tired. My wicked will not relent . . .

Wed. 6th — Pleasant. churned spun 26 knots I am not fit to live or die[.]

Thurs 7th — Spun 24 knots. dressed pigeons. Lucy McAllister called. all alone. Mr. E gone.

Frid 8th — Spun 28 knots. ironed. Pigeons. it is tiresome for me to spin but . . .

Sat 9th — Pleasant. Spun 20 knots. Baked pies, cake, Bread. Etc. Mended some.

Sun 10th — [No entry]

Mon 11th — Washed. Rainy. Spun ten knots alone today. enjoy myself well[.]

Tues 12th — Pleasant. Spun thirty knots. churned. alone but not lonely. Happy[.]

Wed. 13th — Pleasant. Spun thirty knots. Why am I not more faithful to my God?

Thursd 14th — Pleasant. Spun thirty knots. Mrs. Sampson took tea with me. Went to Uncle's after the cows Mr. E was to [too] fatigued to return with me. Staid all night. very tired read but little. how good are my friends to me.

Frid 15th — Returned home. hard to work for eight men. Spun ten knots. very tired.

Sat 16th — Ironed. walked to Mr. Wright's. their babe died suddenly last night.

Sun 17th Pleasant. rode to uncle's. walked from there to Hopkinton. Elder Road [Rhodes] preached A.M. Mr. Pettibone Funeral sermon P.M. rode to uncle's. walked home. very much fatigued, headache, took cold.

Mond 18th Washed. prepared dinner for ten men. took cold. the first corn.

Tues 19th Pleasant. ten men again. unable to sit up much today.

Wedn 20th Pleasant. seven men. Picked pigeons. visited at Mr. Rockwell's.

Thursd 21st Pleasant. Baked. picked black berries. done but little all day.

Frid 22nd Pleasant. spinning little. How little do I do in the cause of my Redeemer?

Sat. 23rd Pleasant. Churned. Ironed. spun some. Harriet D. spent the night.

Sun 24th Pleasant. took a walk to the mill. how wickedly do we spend time.

Mond 25th Pleasant. washed. Lord help us to live more to thy law.

Tuesd 26th Pleasant. spun only twenty. twenty knots not worth keeping.

Wed 27th Pleasant. spun thirty knots. I wish I were not so afflicted. cold.

Thurs 28th Pleasant, dry season. spun thirty knots, very much fatigued.

Frid 29th Pleasant. Mrs. C.D. [Charlotte Durfey] S.S. [Sampson?] visited me. walked to the mill. Baked.

Sat. 30th Pleasant. Ironed. mended some. visited at M. Rockwells. introduced to Mr and Mrs. Douglass from Cornwall. saw Miss Janes. Washed[.]

Sund 31st Cloudy, some rain. wrote to Grandfather. which letter I have lost

. . .

September 1823

Mon 1st Pleasant. training day. spent the day at Uncle Brooks.

Tues 2nd Pleasant. Washed. Mr. Hopkins called from Newhaven [VT][.]

Wed 3rd Pleasant. Baked. not enjoyed myself very well. spun ten knots

Thursd 4th	Pleasant. spun thirty five knots[.] tolerable spirits and health
Fryd 5th	Pleasant. Spun twenty knots. twisted eight. It takes all my time. done.
Sat. 6th	Pleasant. Ironed, mended. Visited by Mrs and Miss B. Eastman Mr. D both Mrs Durfeys. visited the Mill. the first it sawed today. frost
Sund 7th	Cloudy. Uncle [Phineas] Durfey called. tired[.] spent the day idle & dull.
Mond 8th	Cool & Pleasant. washed. spun ten knots picked on trace seed corn.
Tues 9th	Pleasant spun twenty. twisted. one day nearer my last end.
Wed 10th	Pleasant. warm for the season. spun ten knots. Ironed. Harriet came, informed me that Grandfather had arrived. rode home with her to see him. walked home. visited by a number of young people for a melon party. took leave at two. retired almost sick spent[.]
Thurs 11th	Pleasant, warm. spun one run. very unwell. lazy and dejected.
Fryd 12th	Pleasant. spun ten knots. Baked. wrote to Bristol. Grandpa'a.
Sat. 13th	Cloudy some rain. finished my wool twisted 12 knots. gathered and scoured 23 runs of yarn. Mrs. E. called. very tired indeed.
Sund 14th	Cloudy. some rain. Oh that the lord would guide us in the way of peace. Rectify our feet, return our first love to him.
Mon 15th	Washed, spooled and warped my web. at C. Rockwell's. had company. cold.
Tuesd 16th	Pleasant. walked to Uncle Durfeys wove four yards. finished her web. walked home in the evening with Mr. E.
Wed 17th	Rainy, walked to J.D. put in a web, wove two yards. unwell.
Thurs 18th	Cloudy. wove nine and half yards. sent for home. very tired.
Fryd 19th	Pleasant. walked to J.D. wove one yard and half. finished her web. called over to uncle's, put in my web. visited with the ladies. borrowed Aunt's loom. Mr. E. carried it home. walked home. took cold.

Sat. 20th	Baked. washed floor. mended. almost sick of our profanity[.]
Sun 21st	Cloudy. very unwell all day. darkness veils our minds. frost
Mond 22nd	Pleasant. prepared dinner for fifteen. nine Friends. wove 3½ yds frost
Tuesd 23rd	Pleasant. Baked pies and cake. knit some. wove some. Mr E. gone to Lewisville [Louisville] to Training. staid alone for the first time of life.
Wed 24th	Pleasant. Churned. wove five yards. Mr. E. returned at one at night.
Thurs 25th	Pleasant. wove some. almost sick. disagreeable conversation daily.
Fryd 26th	Cool. wove little. I get but little time to weave. I am the bold sinner.
Sat. 27th	Cool. assisted Mr. E in the field some. wove some. very tired of a large family.
Sund 28th	Pleasant. Mr and Mrs. Sampson spent almost all day I wish not to have my neighbours call on me on the Sabbath. indisposed[.]
Mond 29th	Cloudy. cold, few flakes of snow. washed. knitting, sewing.
Tuesd 30th	Cloudy. Why am I continually in darkness of mind.

October 1823

Wed 1st	Pleasant. walked to Uncle D's, quilted all day. came home 12.
Thursd 2nd	Pleasant. husked corn this A.M. visited at S. Flowers P.M.
Fryd 3rd	Pleasant. almost sick. I am good for nothing and deserve calling down[.]
Sat. 4th	Pleasant. Cold. cut out my flannel. mended knit[.] Etc.
Sund 5th	Pleasant Cold. took a walk in the wood. guilty wretch.
Mond 6th	Pleasant. washed. Baked for company. knitting. very tired.
Tuesd 7th	Pleasant. visited Mrs R & F. L, J. & HL., Mrs C., Mrs. P. S. finished sock.

Wed 8th	Cold. windy. assisted husking A.M. quilting P.M. at Mr. E's.
Thursd 9th	Cold. twisted yarn all day. very tired. took cold. dull spirits[.]
Fryd 10th	Cold. hard frost every night. mending Ironing chores all the time.
Sat. 11th	Walked to Mr E's. Wound a coverlet. called over Mr. Wrights rode home.
Sund 12th	Ah God wilt though warm the heart of my companion [with] thy love.
Mond 13th	Rainy day. Baked. knitting and mending enjoyed myself alone.
Tuesd 14th	Pleasant. knitting A.M. P.M. spooled 14½ runs of yarn for A. Squire.
Wed 15th	Pleasant. walked to Mr E's. warped two webbs. returned home H.D. with me. put in my web. wove one yards. very tired walking.
Thurs 16th	Pleasant. wove twelve yards. how kind is my God to provide friends.
Fryd 17th	Cloudy. Cold wind. wove eight yards. finished the web. my God is good to me in every instance. Why then do I slight him so? Oh my God assist me to bear the Cross daily assist my companion for thy sake.
Sat. 18th	Cold and cloudy. washed the floor. Baked. Mrs. E visited me A.M. visited at uncles with the Mrs. Spragues. heard directly from Newhaven. fine visit. received an Eighteen Reed.
Sund 19th	Very pleasant. read my Bible with delight today. Enjoyed my mind better than usual will the Lord grant its continuance.
Mond 20th	Washed. visited at M. Rockwells. enjoyed tolerable spirits.
Tues 21st	Rainy. Harriet D. came. assisted me in making [loom] harness.
Wed 22nd	Cool. finished the six harnesses. put in a coverlet. perplexed. Lucy McAllister spent the night, pleasant visit. Cold.
Thurs 23rd	Rain little. visited at Uncle D. he is out of health. returned.
Fryd 24th	Pleasant Aunt D spent the day. walked to the mill. set my web. . . .

Sat 25th	Pleasant. Ironed. Mended[.] Etc. not well. dress a chick of our raising.
Sund. 26th	Snow little last night. read some but darkness pervades the mind
Mond 27th	Pleasant. Washed. visited by Mrs. Rise. Mrs. L. Mr. Sampsons house raised.
Tuesd 28th	Cloudy, cold. weaving slowly. knitting. mending some. low spirits
Wed 29th	Cloudy. frosty nights. weaving. rather out of health. Baked. Not worthy to live.
Thurs 30th	Beautiful day. weaving some. visited by H.D. Mr. Merrill's of Castleton, a peddler, spent the night with us. heard from and wrote to H. Charter. purchased three of flannel. a very agreeable person.
Fryd 31st	Beautiful, weather. weaving. very melancholy this eve.

November 1823

Sat. 1st	Pleasant A.M. Rainy P.M. toothache. ironed. wove but little[.]
Sund 2nd	Pleasant. cold, some snow fell last night. time hangs heavy.
Mond 3rd	Cloudy. wove some. Mr. E. took a fat Buck. cold weather[.]
Tuesd 4th	Cloudy. finished Aunt's coverlet. partly. made it. washed floor[.]
Wed 5th	Cold. cloudy. spent the day agreeably at Uncles. traded 2's [2 shillings?] with pedlar.
Thurs 6th	Few flakes of snow. carding tow. assisted Mr. E in securing his Flax. took cold, very lame. Rheumatism. Baked Pies. cold.
Fryd 7th	Little more snow. Baked bread Pies[.] etc. carded some. knit some
Sat. 8th	Cool. mending washing floors etc. Mr. Parish called. very familiar
Sund 9th	Beautiful day. took a walk to the north wood. stupidity.
Mond 10th	Washed. cut out a pair of trowsers. partly made Flannel shirt[.]
Tues 11th	Little snow. spun eight knots of Candlewick. knitting. mending.

Wed 12th Spun twenty knots of tow. finished my Blue stockings. toothache.

Thurs 13th Snow. made a pair of leggins. mended fore day. spun fifteen knots[.]

Fryd 14th Cold. some snow, some rain. visited by Harriet D. knit a cap for Mr. E.

Sat. 15th Cold and snow. mended almost all day. washed floor[.] dressed chickens[.]

Sun 16th Cloudy and cold. and still colder is my stubborn heart.

Mon 17th Clear and very Cold. made a net for Aunt Durfey. visited this eve at Mr. Flower's. fine visit with Lucina Janes. Mrs. A. Rockwell Blessed with a female infant. returned at twelve. we are blessed highly.

Tuesd 18th Arose, did my chores before light and went to Mrs. R. staid with her all day.

Wed 19th Some snow. Baked, prepared for company. finished Mr. E's shirt. very tired.

Thurs 20th Thaw, muddy. visited by Miss Janes, H.D., B and M Eastman. B staid. Mr. S. Abbott, an Frenchman spent the night. very tired.

Fryd 21st Rainy sewing visited Mrs. Sampson Broke very tooth of my comb[.]

Sat. 22nd Sewing. called over to Mr. Rockwells. Mrs. R not so well. will God support her.

Sund 23rd Beautiful day, but my mind is continual darkness. Will God lighten it.

Mond 24th Washed. Baked. prepared dinner for six men. very tired wolf hunt

Tues 25th Stormy P.M. spent it with Mrs. R. finished my shirt.

Wed 26th Rather stormy. began a pair of socks mending[.] Etc[.] tolerable spirits

Thurs 27th Rainy another hunt to no purpose. spun some visited by Mrs. Risdon.[58]

Fryd 28th Very cold. made eighteen Doz of Candles. finished one sock. lifted too hard.

Sat. 29th Few flakes of snow. not very well. mending called over to Mr[s.] R. found her better.

Sund 30th Cloudy. Attended meeting at the schoolhouse, heard Elder Roads [Rhodes] and Elder Simons, preach from these words: "What is truth?" but conveys no light to my darkened mind. Lord will though lighten our understandinge. Give us a spirit of prayer more to love thee.

December 1823

Mond 1st	Cloudy, Washed and baked. very tired indeed, not worth keeping[.]
Tuesd 2nd	Cloudy. visited at Mr. J.D. Mr. Remington's Uncle D and Mr. Abbott spent the night. finished the other sock. sat up almost all night.
Wed 3rd	Pleasant. call over to [Mrs] R.A.M. Mrs. R. better. ironed. mended some.
Thurs 4th	Cloudy, finished spinning tow. knitting. called over Mr. S.
Fryd 5th	Very cold. spun 13 knots of Linen. this P.M. why am I suffered to live [?].
Sat 6th	Snow. spun 17 knots. washed floors. visited Saphona E. Sylvia R[.]
Sun 7th	Snows some. Dr. S. rode out in his Cutter. the girls gone home, while I sit by the cold streams of Babylon with my harp hanging upon the willows. And must I here remain, God forbid!
Mon 8th	More moderate. baked. sewing, Etc[.] But done nothing for God.
Tues 9th	Cold Stormy. visited at Uncle's. sewing. Mrs R. Remington was blessed with a fine son Sabbath eve; Called to see it. Tolerable health[.]
Wed 10th	Stormy. sewed all day. finished Mr. E.'s Pantaloons dejected[.]
Thurs 11th	Cold. tolerable sleighing. visited with the Ladies at M. Rockwell's assisted about supper. became warm, rode out, took cold. almost sick.
Fryd 12th	Stormy. visited by Aunt D. Grandpaa called. my cold is very hard.
Sat. 13th	Stormy. almost sick. Julia C visited me. we called over to Mr. Sampsons[.]
Sund 14th	Stormy. almost sick but must attend to others more so.
Mond 15th	Washed. Stormy. sewing P.M. very unwell indeed. melancholy.
Tuesd 16th	Snow[.] visited Uncle Brooks[.] spent the night with Mrs. Rockwell. slept none, long night. almost sick with my cold. Mrs. R. better[.]

Wed 17th Cold. Bakes. spent the eve at Esq Sanfords. called . . .

Thurs 18th Pleasant. Thanksgiving. spent the P.M. and eve at Mr E's.

Fryd 19th Snow very deep. finished my twenty-first pair of stockings.

Sat. 20th Stormy. finished my apron strings. Attended a quilting at C Rockwells. Grandfather [Brooks] spent the night with us. Snow deep.

Sund 21st Snow. spent the day in Stupid thoughtlessness. two Frenchmen called.

Mond 22nd Continues to snow. finished my Aprons Etc. dull, melancholy.

Tuesd 23rd Snows and blows. spinning linen but get along slow indeed.

Wed 24th Snow. cold. spinning. frying cakes. very lame. Rheumatism.

Thurs 25th Snow. Christmas. Elder Roads [Rhodes]. Took supper with us. paid him this eve[.] Mr. Oren Andrews married to Miss Sally Remington.

Fryd 26th Cold. Snow very deep indeed. Mr and Mrs. D[urfey]. Dr. Sprague and wife visited us this eve. spent the night at Uncle D[urfey]s.

Sat. 27th Cloudy thaws, rain some in the eve. assisted them in dressing geese. gave me one. Mr E came for me in the eve. good spirits[.] rec'd shoes

Sund 28th Colder. Lee and David Eastman returned from Fowler in health.

Mond 29th Moderate rainy eve. washed. Had our house tightened. Mr. Enos Merrills spent the night. heard from and wrote to Harriet Charter of Castleton [VT]. F.F. took Jonathan Alexandria to Board. made head dress for Capt. D. formerly from North Carolina. has been a soldier. A Prisoner of war.

Tues 30th Thaws. spinning. Mr E purchased me a Brass and Horn Comb[.] Price 75 cts[.] Lanthorn, grater, Almanac[,] Etc[.] four Deerskins. How am I blessed with friends.

Wed 31st Stormy. thaws slowly. spinning. Baking. well suited with my lot.

January 1824

Thurs 1st Colder. knitting. walked to Capt D dressed Harriet for the Ball. 22 years ago my dear mother was dressed for the last time, for the grave. visited at Mr. Coveys P.M. Mr E making a partition to our house. nice.

Fryd 2nd Cold. pasting windows. mending Etc[.] our house is very comfortable.

Sat. 3rd Snow. spinning. making two small petticoats for unknown.

Sund 4th Pleasant. But my mind is unpleasantly stupid.

Mon 5th Cloudy. spent the day at Capt. D's [.] killed our swine and [illegible word here] [.]

Tues 6th Cold. Try'd thirty pounds of Lard. very lame with the Rheumatism.

Wed 7th Moderate. Baked. called over to Mr. Rockwells. dressed the sow[.]

Thurs 8th Blustering wind. washed floor. visited by Mr and Mrs Eastman [in-laws][.] Mr Judd, Mrs Rockwell, Mrs. Sampson. Capt. D and Grandpaa [Brooks] called[.] headache.

Fryd 9th Cloudy. Spinning thread. visited at Mr E. rained so hard we tarried all night.

Sat. 10th Wet. snow. spun little. called over to Mr Mott's. almost sick, dull headache.

Sund 11th Rain, Hail and snow. very unwell. almost discouraged of health for this season.

Mond 12th Very cold. washed a large wash but very unable to do it. I am not worth keeping.

Tuesd 13th Rain, Snow, almost all kinds of weather. finished all my spinning etc.

Wed 14th Sewing small things. Boiling yarn, cloth etc. purchased three yards cotton cloth[.] (60: 5 cash 55 note)[.]

Thurs 15th Snow little. Mr. E. very unwell[.] washed out my clothes. Ironed washed floor. fired cakes prepared meat for sausages. Bought earthen ware of Mr. Swift, one dollar seventy.

Fryd 16th Snow. Ironed. knitting etc. Mrs. S visited me, come holy spirits.

Sat 17th Cold. unwell. Mrs S visited again. double yarn. come shed abroad[.]

Sun 18th Clear and cold. Lucius Brooks called. not well. my mind heavy[.]

Mond 19th Cold Excellent sleying, the sleighs passing and repassing.

Tues 20th	Cold. Grandpa'a called to make his last visit. Mr & Mrs Durfey dined with us I fear I never more shall behold my aged Grandsire.
Wed 21st	Cold. Stormy Grandpa'a [Brooks] started his journey to Vermont, may health be preserved[.]
Thurs 22nd	Cold. Sewing, chores etc. if it were not for my wicked heart could ask no more.
Fryd 23rd	Clear and cold[.] made my sausages. and many other chores[.]
Sat. 24th	Very pleasant like spring. the feathered songsters warbling[.]
Sund 25th	Beautiful day. Uncle & Aunt Brooks made us a short visit attended a Lecture at the schoolhouse by Mr. Pettibone. unwell[.]
Mond 26th	Rather stormy. washed. heard that my Sister [Harriet] intended visiting me.
Tuesd 27th	Colder. Baked pies, cakes, gingerbread etc. scouring. very unwell[.]
Wed 28th	Cloudy visited at uncle Durfey's. bought half pound of tea.
Thurs 29th	Cold. Baked, sewed some. Ironed. cut out Shirtees etc
Fryd 30th	Cold, snow. Cut and made a small nightgown and blanket.
Sat 31st	Cloudy. washed floor, finished the third cap, two blankets.

February 1824

Sund 1st	Very cold. Idleness makes my heart her safe retreat forever.
Mond 2nd	Cold, stormy. finished knitting socks, one suspender. Commenced making soap, followed it close until almost sick.
Tuesd 3rd	Very cold. knitting, sewing, starching. very busy but not for God.
Wed 4th	Stormy. Washed floors, attended my soap. my Brothers and Sister Austin [her married sister, Harriett Orvis Austin] arrived. Aunt D spent the day. received a letter from Miss Abigail Morrison. Betsey Brooks sick.
Thurs 5th	The coldest day and night that has been this year. Brother sick. took a sweat but not able to pursue his journey. sick myself.

Fryd 6th More moderate. visited at Uncle Brooks. very sick on my return[.]

Sat. 7th Pleasant. Baked, sewed little. very unwell Uncle B called Uncle D's family visited us this eve. Brother returned with them.

Sun 8th Snow fast. at the request of our friends we spent that P.M. at Uncle D's. they returned with us prepared for their departure.

Mond 9th Pleasant. Our friends took their leave perhaps for life. presented us a small bottle. cleaned my house and sat down to wait returning health. mending, very dull.

Tuesd 10th Washed woolen clothes and floors. visited Mrs. S. Rainy eve.

Wed 11th Rainy. very high winds as has been known in the place. spun ten knots of my new flax - very short but white & good.

Thursd 12th Cold, frozen hard. the snow fled. the Chipping Squirrel [chipmunk] makes his appearance. washed large wash of linen. one year this day since we took possession of our cottage. ah what have I done[.] Ah nothing for my maker and but little for my partner. Spun only 73 runs wove seventy yds, one coverlet, knit 3 pair of socks etc. I hope more for both this year[.]

Fryd 13th Cloudy high winds. Spun 15 knots. Baked visited by Mrs. S. finished small Shirt Lord, how kind art thou to me.

Sat. 14th Pleasant. Ironed, spun fifteen knots. burnt our Bacon to a crisp[.]

Sun 15th Cloudy, read but little very drowsy kept my Bed most of the day. Surely, Oh lord thou art giving me my portion in this world. only one thing lack I: that is that my dear companion and myself may live to thy honour and glory which will render us happy in this world and to enjoy what thou hast given.

Mond 16th Pleasant. spun 24 knots. Carded some. Uncle Brooks had another daughter born Saturday night. May she prove a blessing.

Tuesd 17th Snows very fast indeed. all day. spun 17 knots of tow carded all.

Wed 18th Stormy. sewing all day. not very well but better than I deserve[.]

Thursd 19th Stormy. Sewing. visited with Mrs Durfey at Mr[s] Sampson's.

Fryd 20th Pleasant, thaws. Baked. sewing. Mr & Mrs [illegible word]took tea with us[.]

Sat 21st	Cold. Sewing, washed floors. nothing to molest or make afraid[.]
Sund 22nd	Stormy. Joseph D. spent the most of the day. while his Pa'a worked at the Mill. what an example this for his child.
Mond 23rd	Stormy, sewing. What stupidity prevails among the sons of Men[.]
Tues 24th	Washed. very cold this eve. greatly distressed with the Rheumatism.
Wed 25th	Cloudy. working at Leather mittens. very thick, hard sewing.
Thurs 26th	Stormy. Rainy P.M. visited at Mr Sampson's[.] finished one pair of mittens.
Fryd 27th	Snow, rain and hail, sun shine and high winds. the most blustering day I ever saw. Finished another pair of Mittens, made with a welt.
Sat. 28th	Stormy. ironed. made another pair of mittens. Baked pies, washed floors etc.
Sun 29th	Pleasant. read the Life of Washington.[59] my dearest companion and friend very sick last night and today. Lord will though support his sinking spirits and raise his thoughts to [the] awaken his mind from sleep.

March 1824

Mond 1st	Beautiful day. mending. A travellor called and spent some time.
Tuesd 2nd	Pleasant. Town meetings. walked to Mr D's spent the day with Harriet. returned, visited this eve at Mr Sampson introduced to Miss Virginia Werden, Mrs. s.' sister.
Wed 3rd	Pleasant. Made ten doz of candles. visited with the Ladies at J.D.'s. very disagreeable visit. out of health and almost humour[.]
Thurs 4th	Pleasant. Baked. almost sick. cut out two frocks, sewed some.
Fryd 5th	Pleasant. thaws fast. sewed little, washed floors. lay in bed the most.
Sat. 6th	Cloudy, rather better today, thaws very fast indeed. sewing little.
Sund 7th	Cloudy Snowy night. Mrs. Flower, Mrs. Converse both blessed with a daughter last night. God grant that they may be useful to the world.
Mon 8th	Storm of snow A.M. Pleasant P.M. Finished blue frock. Slothful[.]

Tues. 9th	Pleasant. washed began footing a pair of stockings. Alexandria [Alexander?] left the mill[.]
Wed. 10th	Pleasant. mending coat. Mr[&] Mrs Wright Called[.] Alexandria drunk[.]
Thursd 11th	Pleasant. made six squares. Ironed knitting etc. how disagreeable is drunkeness[.]

MONKTON

Fryd. 12th	Pleasant[.] made four squares but I am so afraid of being seen making such things and so many coming in it keeps me continually upon the spring.
Sat. 13th	Cloudy some snow. Finished one stocking[.] I can do nothing as long as this man of sense he's drowned in Liquor. Oh Lord wilt thou not put an end to his love of ardent spirits and quicken him with thine holy light?
Sund 14th	Pleasant almost out of patience with the praise of drunkeness[.]
Mond 15th	Pleasant. sewing. Alexandria took his leave. visited at Uncle D's Mr E came after me with a Cutter. received our new kettle-five pails. Two gentlemen from Malone spent the night by the name of Sperry.
Tuesd 16th	Pleasant, cold. sewing visited Mrs Sampson[.] Miss Werden home - sick.
Wed 17th	Cloudy snowy eve[.] visited by Mrs S [&] Miss W. H.D. [Harriet Durfey] sewing, knitting[.]
Thurs 18th	Cloudy[.] Hatcheled my flax[.] 13 lb[.] carded some. knitting evenings. Mrs Humphrey brought a fine son weighing nine pounds.
Fryd 19th	Cloudy carded and spun twenty knots of tow[.] visited the eve at Mr S.
Sat. 20th	Rain, Hail and snow last night. some this A.M. P.M. Pleasant, high winds. Spun ten knots[.] carded all my coarse tow. almost sick. discouraged.
Sund 21st	Pleasant. very cold[.] wrote an answer to the Letter I received yesterday from Orra Taylor[.] Why do I have friends while so undeserving of any favors?
Mond 22nd	Washed, cut straws for a hat. visited by H.D., L. McAllister at Mr S. this eve.
Tuesd 23rd	Snow last night and this morn. Brewed. Baked[.] spun twenty knots[.] V. [Virginia Werden] visited.

Wed 24th	Pleasant. carded and spun twenty knots. How good is God to me.
Thurs 25th	Carded and spun thirty knots of tow. finished the coarse part. very tired.
Fryd 26th	Pleasant. Mr E tapped trees. spun only ten knots. very unwell today.
Sat. 27th	Pleasant. walked to P.D. sized my Bedtick yarn. spooled & warped at Mrs Remingtons. H.D. brought me home on horse back. very muddy.
Sun 28th	Pleasant. unwell. how negligent of my duty to my creator and my God.
Mond 29th	Rainy. drew in my web. wove one yard. Sugared off about ten pounds of sugar.
Tues 30th	Pleasant. wove six yards of Kersey and wound my quills. great hurry and of still [original blank space]
Wed 31st	Pleasant wove two and half yards. finished my web. made it up. visited at M.S.

April 1824

Thurs 1st	Sugar'd off about twenty lbs of sugar spun one run of Linen. boiled yarn.
Fryd 2nd	Stormy. spun twenty knots. prepared mince for Pies. found all musty.
Sat 3rd	Pleasant. Baked, fried cakes, etc. trimmed and tucked my silk frock for Harriet. lent my other dresses for exhibition. retired very late.
Sun 4th	Pleasant. spent my time ill. walked to the Saw Mill. Oh that I might live more to the Glory of God and my own happiness. H.D. returned home.
Mon 5th	Very pleasant. finished a white frock and cambrick nightgown.
Tues 6th	Rainy. spun one runn of Linen. Boiled yarn. sized and spooled part of my web. sugar'd off this eve. the Butterfly begins to flutter & frogs to sing.
Wed 7th	Cold and pleasant. washed. starched. Ironed. very tired and lame worked tonight.
Thurs 8th	Pleasant. Ironed and plated ruffs. finished spooling. went to Mr Rockwells to warp her Barrs not at home. Mr E floored the Cellar. toothache.
Fryd 9th	Pleasant walked to Mr Remington's. warped my web bought a new reed. Forty "Slaie" spent the P.M. at Uncle's, walked home in the mud. Quite too much mudd.

Sat 10th	Very warm and pleasant. very unwell. Sugar'd off, I suspect for the last time this year. visited by J.D. H.D. drew in part of my web.
Sund 11th	Rainy unwell gathered a few greens. a few pale flowers have peeped forth their latent beauties. Cow calved. working a Lace Cap this eve. Oh did we but enjoy Religion, how happy might we live.
Mond 12th	Rainy. Put in my web, not able to weave much. was called upon to attend Mrs. Sampson's confinement. slept none all night. Oh my god what a trial. soon ah soon I must be another victim perhaps of Death. Lord help me to prepare for it.
Tuesd 13th	Stormy at eleven o'clock A.M. Mrs S. brought forth a daughter this P.M. mended some. An Irish man his wife and two little children came in all wet and muddy. spent the night[.] Why was it not my lot thus to wander far from friends as this Mrs. Smith.
Wed 14th	Cloudy and cool. wove only one yards. almost sick. two travellars spent the night from Peacham, Vermont, one an Irishman by the name of Smith.
Thurs 15th	Rather sultry. scoured tubs, made vinegar. cleared the cellar etc. very tired. Uncle Brooks took dinner with us Mrs. Cook, Mrs Chittenden called.
Fryd 16th	Snowed little. wove one yards and half. Fried cakes. I have enough to do besides weaving. bad weather very fine. I think I cannot finish it. Cool[.]
Sat 16th	Some snow. some rain. wove one yard and half. sick all night melancholy.
Sund 17th	Cloudy. gloomy thoughts of my approaching fate. Perhaps this is the last Sabbath of my life. and wither am I going to death and hell. made four squares this eve. boiled five pails of sap. likely for rain.
Mond 18th	Very warm. boiled eleven pails of sap made Molasses. two squares. made little more vinegar. filled another straw bed of my own. cleared and swept the chambers tired almost out I. Fenner worked.
Tuesd 29th	Warm and pleasant. wove all day for two yards. almost discouraged.
Wed 21st	Rainy. unable to weave. only done a few chores. very unwell.
Thursd 22nd	Warm. wove half yd. Baked pies gingerbread etc[.] called over to Mr S. hem'd half my handkerchielf. my Cedar Pail almost burnt up.

Fryd 23rd — Rainy P.M. wove half yard. baked bread beans peas Etc. very tired. made two small caps, trim'd two. very unwell most of the time.

Sat. 24th — Pleasant & cool. wove little. hemmed the half of my handkerchief visited by Mrs S Miss Werden Miss B.E. another week is past and gone. rec'd a letter H. Charter

Sund 25th — High winds. Cloudy eve. I have been permitted to spend one more Sabbath, perhaps the last. Ah God wilt thou warm the heart of my companion with thy love?

Mond 26th — Rainy. very unwell. Cut out my web and had the Loom carried home. Aunt sent me some dried Apples. My God provides kind friends and companions. made a pair of Linen sheets.

Tues 27th — Pleasant. very lame. but with diligence and patience done a large washing. visited Betsey E. two workmen S.W.[,] B. Rowley[.]

Wed 28th — Cloudy. restless night. Rheumatism and cramp. hardly able to crawl in the morning but in the course of the day have mended and ironed a number of clothes. made one Cap two squares. Mr R's Barn raised.

Thursd 29th — Rainy. Washed floors fried cakes etc. sewed some[.] not able to do much.

Fryd 30th — Pleasant. large baking. gathered pine. trim'd the house[.] finished two squares.

May 1824

Sat 1st — Pleasant. mending. choring all day. sick all night. Cramps etc[.]

Sund 2nd — Pleasant. tolerable well A.M. distressed spell this P.M. but have no reason to complain. my God is still merciful and kind.

Mond 3rd — Rainy morn. Thunder & Lightning, afterwards very warm. finished green flannel frock. made two tyres, the eleventh cap.[60] mended some. sick night.

Tuesd 4th — Storms of snow. very unwell. A.M. visited by V Werden. B. Eastman. mended some. made one cambrick Bib. restless night but God supports me.

Wed 5th — Very cool morning. Pleasant day. two Mr. Moons worked here. enjoyed health today. washed floors. work'd on the fiftieth garment for my unborn. mended some. perhaps this is the last day of my life. God only knows.

Thurs 6th	Pleasant. knitting visited by Aunt R. Brooks. Mrs Rockwell. Mrs Flower. walked home with them. I felt so much better that I knew not hwen to stop. came home with more than usual spirits. retired but not much sleep. the pains of labor were upon me. restless night three o'clock in the morn my companion left me to procure assistance while I was left to the care of my Guardian protector and supporter. I felt as if I was as safe with him as under the eye of millions. I perused my Bible perhaps for the last time. A few hours may determine[.]
Fryday 7th	Rainy. Oh my god what a day is this and how hast though supported me through it. At half past ten A.M. didst thou make me the Mother of a lovely son weighing seven pounds four oz. thanks to my God it will never be a mother. since it has been thy will to restore me to my bosom friend with this little pledge of love instead of taking me from him, wilt thou grant us wisdom to bring it up in thy fear, teach him to remember his Creator in the days of his youth. greatly distressed through the night. F.H. Covey for a nurse.
Sat. 8th	Showers. As comfortable as could be expected. my pains are still hard. my babe rather troublesome. am weak, unable to attend him. my nurse not so faithful as I could wish. Almost out of patience.
Sund 9th	Pleasant. sat up to tea. Uncle and Aunt visited me. Mrs S. very good to call over and see me. tired almost out[.] my breast great trouble to me.
Mond 10th	Pleasant. in less pain, my breast worse. L. Newton V. Werden visited.
Tues 11th	Pleasant two small visitors. H.D. M.C. Aunt sent me some eggs[.] feeble.
Wednes 12th	Pleasant. sewed few stitches, eyes weak. Babe worrysome but tolerable well.
Thursd 13th	Cloudy. sewed little more. partly made crape cap. gain slowly.
Fry 14th	Snowed all day. gloomy day for May. sat up almost all day.
Sat 15th	Pleasant. walked to the door, not so well. my Babe unwell cross.
Sund 16th	Pleasant A.M. Cloudy P.M. much better. dismissed my nurse.
Mond 17th	Frost. tolerable smart. Mrs. S. took tea with [me] went down cellar, took cold.
Tuesd 18th	Pleasant. unwell. Ague fits. took a sweat. severe headache with fainting, better P.M. B.E. called Uncle Brooks. I am a weak frail creature.

Wed 19th Pleasant but cool. washed a few clothes for the Babe. very tired. Babe cross.

Thurs 20th Pleasant cold morn. H.D. called. carried my babe to Mr S. I walked and spent the P.M. sewed some. I fear my returning health will weaken my trust.

Fryd 21st Cloudy unable to to anything. but my chores and attend to my Babe.

Sat. 22nd Pleasant. finished the Babe's frock almost sick of life. discouraged lonely.

Sund 23rd Pleasant. B.E. took tea with us. slept some but endeavouring to nurse my Babe difficult[.]

Mond 24th Smoaky. the fire raging on almost every side. by wetting the roof of the house, preserved it. I could not assist but little[.] great deal of grain destroyed.

Tuesd 25th Cloudy. the shower last eve quenched the flames but it rages some today. Not able to do much. very drowsy and dull.

Wed 26th frost. Pleasant washed. very tired my Babe worrysome and not well.

Thursd 27th frost. Pleasant. Ironed knit some. I find I regain my strength daily.

Fryd 28th frost. spun three knots of tow. Babe unwell and troublesome.

Sat 29th Warm. Baked. spun ten knots. Bought a new frock for my Babe.

Sund 30th Pleasant. Miss J.B. Mayhew D. Dewey called. walked some wrote a Letter to my Father. My Babe unwell. severe headache.

Mond 31st Pleasant washed. visited by Mrs. S. my Babe worse, lies stupid.

June 1824

Tuesd 1st Cloudy. Ironed. mended some. visited Mrs. S.[.] Mosquitoes plenty.

Wed 2nd Cloudy some rain. visited at Mr Flowers A.M. Mr. C. Rockwells P.M.

Thursd 3rd Cloudy. cold, backward season. a just reward for our iniquities

Fryd 4th Rainy day. spun a little tow. how gloomy are my thoughts.

Sat. 5th	Pleasant and very warm. washed floor. visited by Mrs S. heard from VT.
Sund 6th	Pleasant, warm. heard Aunt D was sick. walked to see her. found her better than I expected. heard from Lewis. Heard of the death of Esq Pier in Newhaven.[61] my conscience will not uphold Sabbath visits.
Mond 7th	Very warm. how happy should we live if our hearts were as warm with the love of God as our bodies are from the heat of the Sun[,] But alas they are not.
Tues 8th	Baked. churned. spun some. the darkness of my mind forbids quietness.
Wed 9th	Washed. finished spinning tow[.] showers in the P.M. to water the earth.
Thurs 10th	Frost. commenced picking wool. have but little far better than none.
Fryd 11th	Cold. unwell, done scarcely anything. melancholly[.] wrote a Letter to Bristol.
Sat. 12th	Cold, frost. wrote a Letter to Mrs. Orra Taylor. Ironed picked wool. read some.
Sund 13th	Pleasant but still cold. another sabbath gone in the same stupid manner.
Mond 14th	Cold and rainy. sewed some. finished picking wool. ready for carding.
Tues 15th	Cold, some rain. Washed. my Babe worrysome. looks likely for snow[.]
Wed 16th	Cloudy and cold. Ironed. sewing for the Babe. few drops of rain[.]
Thurs 17th	Pleasant. Baked. Visited by Aunt Durfey. Betsey E. spent the night.
Fryd 18th	Pleasant. warm. walked to uncle's spent the A.M. P.M. at Mr. Wrights. found Mrs. W. in a bad state of health. called over to Mr. Abbots. returned home very tired indeed. how thankful ought I to be for my health.
Sat. 19th	Warm, rainy night. unwell. done but Little. Oh, of that little was for God.
Sund 20th	Some cloudy. read some of the rise and progress of religion Mr. D.E. [David Eastman] and R.S. took tea with us. Mr [original blank space] attended third meeting at Mr Harrington's.
Mond 21st	Pleasant. washed. my washing increase fast. spun ten knots linen.

Tuesd 22nd Cloudy. spun 25 knots of linen. how glad should I be to do it every day.

Wed 23rd Rainy went to gather pine and laurels with H.D. [Harriet Durfey]. became very wet, took cold. very heavy thunder Miss J.B. Mayhew knocked down.

Thurs 24th Some showers. Baked. nursed Mrs. Sampson's Babe while she attended the Festival of St. Johns. V. Werden spent the day.

Fryd 25th Showery. visited M. Rockwells. pleasant visit. spun some.

Sat. 26th Cloudy[.] not very well but have no reason to murmur.

Sund 27th Cloudy made another Sabbath visit at Uncle Brooks. came home. Mr. E. had to find his cows at Hopkinton village. I am resolved to stave off this sinful practice. Lord assist me.

Mond 28th Pleasant. washed a very large washing. very tired. alas how prone to sin.

Tues 29th Pleasant[.] My Babe unwell. troubled with Diarhea. Cloudy.

Wed 30th Very warm. spun some. very drowsy took a walk to the Mill. went out on the raft fishing. caught none. headache.

July 1824

Thurs 1st Pleasant. washed, bed clothes. starched. visited Anna Oliver at the shanty. our little dog broke his leg. corn taken from crib.

Fryd 2nd Rainy. Baked. Babe no better. Ironed. how little do I labour.

Sat. 3rd Cloudy. washed some. Ironed. Washed floors. mended some.

Sund 4th Pleasant. Independence. spent the day alone. Mr. E. attended meeting at Hopkinton. But returned stupid[.][62]

Mond 5th Pleasant. Attended Independence at Capt. Durfeys. Mrs. Taylor came to visit. we returned home. tired of company.

Tuesd 6th Rainy. washed some. visited all day. retired late. heard from Vermont of the Marriage and death of Mr. Terrel Sprague.

Wedn 7th	Rainy. accompanied Mrs. T. to Uncles. got very wet, took cold
Thurs 8th	Pleasant. Mr. Newton & Heart [Hart] to work here. Baked. almost sick[.]
Fryd 9th	Pleasant. spun twelve knots of wool. doubled & twisted it. washed some.
Sat. 10th	Pleasant. spun twelve knots. purchased steel yards and a basket.
Sund 11th	Pleasant. took a walk to the North. dull Sabbath or I am dull to improve . . .
Mond 12th	Washed. spun ten knots. my Babe is very good for the most of the time.
Tues 13th	Pleasant. Baked. S. Western to work here. spun ten knots knitting.
Wed 14th	Pleasant. Mr. Hutchins and Webb to work here. spun twenty knots[.]
Thus 15th	Pleasant. Mrs. Oliver to work for us. churned. spun ten knots. indulge tears.
Fryd 16th	Pleasant, dry weather. spun ten knots. How long shall stupidity prevail over our minds and keep us miserable victims of darkness.
Sat. 17th	Cloudy some in the evening. spun ten knots. ironed and mended[.]
Sund 18th	Pleasant. Harriet D. visited us. Mr. Kelly from Fowler. hard cold.
Mond 19th	Cloudy. J. Fenner to work here. washed woollen and coloured clothes almost sick with a cold but more sick of living so thoughtlessly.
Tues 20th	Pleasant. large washing. visited Mrs. Rockwells[.] finished footing a pair of socks.
Wed 21st	Starched. Ironed. made the Babe a cap, calculating to attend meeting.
Thurs 22nd	Cloudy few drops of rain. great men of muck[.] Mr. Pettibone ordained. disappointed of attending. spun ten knots. Baked.
Fryd 23rd	Pleasant. spun twenty knots. wrote a Letter to J.B. Visited Mr. Mott.
Sat. 24th	Cloudy, but no reain. spun ten knots. washed the house. Ironed mended.
Sund 25th	Pleasant. took a walk to the south. read but little. Oh God we need prayers.

Mond 26th	Rainy. washed, starched and ironed. sewed some. how can we live at this [original blank space]
Tuesd 27th	Pleasant. Churned. spun thirty knots of warp. Mr E gone to work with Father.
Wed 28th	Pleasant. spun only ten knots. visited with R. at Mr Sampson's. Beans.
Thurs 29th	Rainy[.] spun ten knots[.] unwell[.] melancholly and dejected. Cucumbers.
Fryd 30th	Rainy. A.M. Baked. mended. almost discouraged of ever doing good.
Sat 31st	Cloudy and Cool. made the Babe a shirt. mended. Ironed some. washed floors. visited by Mrs S. Miss W. how unfriendly is the world to me and I to my Saviour. Alas and did he die for such a wretch as I?

August 1824

Sund 1st	Pleasant. stupid and dull. Rosewell E. took some tea with us this eve.
Mond 2nd	Cloudy. great want of rain. washed. spun ten knots[.] how negligent.
Tuesd 3rd	Pleasant. Mrs S. came here and spun here and Virginia washed. spun 20 knots.
Wed 4th	Pleasant. spun twenty knots[.] very dull and unwell[.] B.E. called[.]
Thurs 5th	Pleasant. spun ten knots. had seven men to cook for, visited by Miss B.E., M.E., A. Harrington, Mrs. S., Miss W., B.E. spent the night.
Fryd 6th	Rainy. Baked and churned. prepared Breakfast for six more. unwell. visited Mrs S. spun fifteen knots. enjoy myself very unpleasantly.
Sat 7th	Some rain. great many chores to do today. B.E. and D.E. spent the night. my Babe is three months old this day and weighs fifteen lbs.
Sund 8th	Pleasant. read considerable but to no effect. B.E. spent the night.
Mond 9th	Rainy night. washed visited by Mr and Mrs Rockwell, both sick indeed.
Tues 10th	Cloudy. spun only ten knots. I care but little whether I work or not.
Wed 11th	Pleasant. Miss Werden started for Essex. accompanied her [as] far as Uncle Durfeys. gave her a comb. picked currants to dry. good visit with the Ladies. Harriet D. spent the night with me. very tired.

Thursd 12th	Cloudy, some rain. Baked. washed floor Mr Frank visited us melancholy.
Fryd 13th	Cloudy. spun ten knots raked some hay. Why is my heart so far from God[?]
Sat 14th	Pleasant. washed some. finished another pair of socks. visited by Mrs S., Mrs Remington, S.R. [Stillman Remington]. Starched and Ironed. our people finished haying.
Sund 15th	Pleasant. read to little or no purpose. God is not mocked. Why so dull?
Mond 16th	Pleasant. Baked. mended. Mr Frank called again[.]
Tues 17th	Pleasant. spent the day at Uncle Brook's[.] called to Mr Rockwells. found many sick. how unthankful am I for my good health.
Wed 18th	Rainy. spun fifteen knots. not well. my Babe unwell.
Thurs 19th	Cloudy, some rain. finished spinning my wool. fifteen and half runns[.]
Fryd 20th	Pleasant. Washed. scoured and sized yarn. starched and Ironed some. Visited Miss Betsey Eastman's school. she spent the night with us. visited after school at Mr Converse. oh sweet religion when Shall I inherit thee? Oh, come sweet Jesus come and warm my cold heart with heav'nly love. Oh pity my dear companion and bless my soul.
Sat. 21st	Rainy. Ironed. mending. my sweet infant unwell. Oh God wilt thou not save him from the errors of his Parents. Ah teach him to love thee with his whole heart, soul, might, mind & strength.
Sun 22nd	Cloudy. how heavy hangs the hours of darkness upon my mind.
Mond 23rd	Cloudy. Washed. Baked. But nothing done for my soul.
Tues 24th	Pleasant. took up the Chamber floor and cleared the house of some of the moths. Oh that I would lay up my treasure in heaven where moths doth not corrupt nor thieves break through to steal.
Wed 25th	Some rain with thunder and lightning. visited Mrs. S. severe headache.
Thurs 26th	Rainy. called over to see Mr[s] Rockwell. found her low in health walked to Uncle D spooled part of my web. Called to see Mr Covey. his mind greatly agitated. will God have mercy on this aged sinner.

Fryd 27th Cloudy. visited by Mrs S. mending. Oh that I could mend my ways

Sat. 28th Cloudy, some rain. walked to Uncles. spooled my web, warped it. to Mr E's and spent the P.M. agreeably. my eyes very sore.

Sund 29th Pleasant. how disagreeable are my feelings this day. tears will not silence my grief to see my dear companion pursuing the broad road with me, he calculated to have rambled blackberrying - were it not for me and makes light of my tears for him. Oh may our little son flee this path. called over to Mr. R's.

Mond 30th Some rain. Washed. unwell. Baked. slow to do good.

Tues 31st Rainy. Washed. for what use is it for me to live at this poor dying [illegible word] [.]

September 1824

Wed 1st Rainy, mending. my new loom is not wide enough for coverlets[.]

Thurs 2nd Rainy P.M. called over to C and A Rockwells. came home very tired.

Fryd 3rd Cloudy, Rainy eve. churned, mended, washed floors. visited by Mrs E., B.E., S.E., S.S. Mrs E. has a very bad thumb by a cut on the joint.

Sat 4th Cloudy, some rain. twisted yarn for Harness. visited Mrs. Rockwell.

Sun 5th Pleasant. My Babe weighs seventeen and half lbs. called over to Mrs R found her better. oh Lord will thou comfort her through death.

Mond 6th Pleasant. Mr. E. trained, Parishville. Baked Bread, Crackers, etc.

Tuesd 7th Cloudy warm. Took Mrs. R's Babe to keep until she performs her journey. Mrs. Lucas, Miss C. McAllister dinner with us. Called over to Mr R's. Mr S. Mr. E. started at twelve for Lewisville [Louisville] to Gov't training rainy staid alone. A[ndrew] Squire remarried.

Wed 8th Rainy. sewed some. visited by Mrs S. Mr Grout Prime called received a Letter from Sally Brooks. Mr E. arrived at 12.

Thurs 9th Washed. My adopted child is very troublesome today. want patience[.]

Fryd 10th	Pleasant. Ironed. Baked crackers[,] etc[.] Pies[.] visited by Mrs. Lucas.
Sat. 11th	Pleasant. mended some. made twenty Bar of Harness. good spirits.
Sund 12th	Pleasant[.] R.E.[&] Mr L. Mayhew called[.] went with Mary Lewis to the Shanty.
Mond 13th	Pleasant. Wahsed. rinsed clothes at the brook. finished harness.
Tues 14th	Pleasant. Baked bread and pies. get along slowly worked at my harness.
Wed 15th	Pleasant. finished my harnesses. sewed. some want patience much.
Thurs 16th	Cloudy. was it not for my wicked heart I could be happy in life.
Fryd 17th	Pleasant. washed my shelves and crockery floor Etc. visited Mrs. S. Sampson.
Sat. 18th	Pleasant, but a frosty morn borrowed a kettle. gathered weeds, coloured yellow.
Sund 19th	Cloudy. disagreeable feelings. my partner intended working in the field today and is greatly displeased at my objection. What shall I do? shall I encourage it and see my darling Babe do in like manner?
Mond 20th	Pleasant. Washed, Ironed. heard my Grandma'am' was bereft of her senses while I use mine as though I had none.
Tues 21st	Pleasant. mended all day. Oh that I had more love to God.
Wed 22nd	Rainy. But no showers of grace. nothing but clouds of darkness.
Thurs 23rd	Pleasant. Baked Bread, Pies. gathered herbs for colouring.
Fryd 24th	Frost. Pleasant. Washed Coloured Otter. How long shall I dwell in stupidity?
Sat 25th	Frost. Pleasant drew my web in through the harness. Ironed.
Sund 26th	Frost. Pleasant days but cool nights. and colder are our thoughts of eternity.
Mond 27th	Cloudy. Washed, Ironed, mended some. But nothing done for God.
Tues 28th	Rainy. mended considerable. drew my web through the Reed Etc[.]

Wed 29th Rainy. wove one and half yd. Baked pies. mended some. tired of [illegible word] the [illegible word]

Thurs 30th Pleasant. wove five yards and quilted. hard frost. began to gather corn.

October 1824

Fryd 1st Pleasant. wove four yards. mended some. Sick. the Other people ate.

Sat 2nd Pleasant. wove two yards, finished my web. Baked bread & crackers[.]

Sund 3rd Beautiful day. not well[.] uneasy. what am I living for, God knows.

Mond 4th Cloudy some rain. done nothing but chores and take care of my Babe.

Tues 5th Rainy. drew my web of Diamond Diaper through again, quilted eve.

Wed 6th Rainy. set my web to work mended some, I but very little[.]

Thurs 7th Cloudy[.] coloured yellow. H.D. visited me. heard from Vermont. rainy.

Fryd 8th Rainy[.] wove little. my web is not worth weaving so fine and tender.

Sat 9th Rainy. Find no time to weave. washed floor, etc. all chores.

Sund 10th Cloudy. feel very lazy and unwell. disagreeable indeed to be thus[.]

Mond 11th Rainy. wove little. made Henry a new frock. Blue. cut up mine[.]

Tues 12th Pleasant. Washing very large. rinsed them at the Brook. In the evening Baked.

Wed 13th Cloudy. Ironed visited at Uncle Ds. S carried Martha[.] I walked home.

Thursd 14th Cloudy, mending. chores without number. wove little piecing, one gown[.]

Fryd. 15th Rainy. made Henry another Blue frock[.]

Sat. 16th Homely weather, mending Mrs Es coat. elections job. my eyes sore.

Sund. 17th Cold. how are our Sabbaths spent? someone calls. Everyone of them[.]

Mond 18th	Cold and stormy. How negligent we live and still go on to save.
Tues 19th	Cold. The harvest is past, the summer is ended and we are not secure.
Wed 20th	Cold. wove a little. made Martha a shirt, Saphrona E spent the night.
Thurs 21st	Cold. twenty three years of age. Molly E spent the night.
Fryd 22nd	Cloudy. Baked pies visited by JB & RB. mended some etc[.] dull weather. warm.
Sat 23rd	Cold. Maria D returned. ironed, washed floors. one continued round.
Saund 24th	Cloudy Baked bread and pies. tired of two Babes alone. One ox hurt by the fall of a tree.
Mond 25th	Very wet and muddy. mending all the leisure time I have[.]
Tues 26th	Rainy. Washed. M.V., Stephen Eastman arrived from the Ohio[.] been absent five years. Mrs Lucas called[.]
Wed 27th	[No entry]
Thurs 28th	Cold[.] altered my Red flannel frock. visited by Mrs Sampson[.]
Fryd 29th	Rainy. washed yarn and Linen clothes. Mr E kills a Doe. very tired.
Sat. 30th	Cloudy. Ox killed. Baked pies, sewed some[.] Betsey E spent the night
Sund 31st	Cloudy. all of the Eastman boys here today[.] trappening[.] Oh that God would have mercy on their souls

November 1824

Mond 1st	Cold. Baked Bread and Pies. sewed some[.] The Ox weighs 952½ lb.
Tuesd 2nd	Snow some. Ironed, sewed some. Mrs. Covey called of Stockholm[.]
Wed 3rd	Snow some. Third day of Election. Mrs Rockwell returned[.]
Thurs 4th	Snow little every day. washed. Mr R[ockwell] [illegible word] us & to their Babe. Hard cold.

Fryd 5th	Snow. engaged to weave a Coverlet for Mr. Covey. Made Henry a shirt.
Sat. 6th	Snow rain and hail. visited at Uncle D's A.M. Mr E.'s P.M. washed[.]
Sund 7th	Snows some. L[ee] & D[avid] E[astman] called. all hunting stories Mr E. setting traps. etc, Oh god forbid that my little son should be trained up in this manner. how disagreeable. Mr Wm Perry called from VT. heard from Bristol. Grandma'a's [Brooks] health better.
Mond 8th	Some snow all day. washing and Ironing. knit some for Henry.
Tuesd 9th	Rainy[.] Baked pies[,] Bread. etc. all day doing little or nothing the ox sold.
Wed 10th	Some snow received an agreeable visit from Mr Wm Perry of Newhaven, Vt. wrote a lengthy letter to Vt boiling damaged beef.
Thursd 11th	Snow. Mr. P. left us for Vt. finished a stocking for Henry. very cold.
Fryd 12th	Cold. finished getting tallow out of beef, ten pounds. visited this eve at H.R.
Sat 13th	Cold. drew in a coverlet for Mrs Covey. Wove some Double Chariot Wheel.
Sund 14th	Cloudy. How great are the inequities of this people, the Sabbath a playday for hunting and the like. Oh God save my son.
Mond 15th	Stormy. wove all day for ¾ of yard. Babe unwell and worrysome.
Tuesd 16th	Rainy. visited by Silvia R. [Remington] Saphrona E. [Eastman] wove some.
Wed 17th	Snow wove little. have Mr E's folk to cook for this week[.]
Thurs 18th	Snow. Visited D. Dewey J. Covey, badly frightened by the coal pit. for fear Mr E had fallen into it. Baked this eve.
Fryd 19th	Cloudy, dull and cold. wove some knit some but nothing [for] God.
Sat 20th	Very muddy. walked to uncle D's. borrowed yarn for Mrs. C.[Covey] H.D. [Harriet Durfey] came home with me and spent the night agreeably.
Sund 21st	Pleasant. Oh how this day is profaned. our neighbours some tending coal pits, the rest driving runways for deer. God forgive them.

Mond 22nd	Rainy, very muddy. Walked to Mr E. warped two coverlet for Western & Rowley. Came home. wove some very tired almost sick.
Tues 23rd	Snow. wove some. knit some. wash floors etc. I am anxious to visit my friends in Vermont once more. I durst not expect it.
Wed 24th	Snow and rain. weaving little. finished Henry another stocking.
Thursd 25th	Snow. finished Mrs C's coverlet. Mr C came after it. paid $1.50 ct.
Fryd 26th	Some rain. washed. toothache, unwell. but my night is worse than day.
Sat. 27th	Rainy. Put in Coverlet through the harness. Baked pies, washed floors.
Sund 28th	Cloudy. spent the day in vileness, some shooting, some at work. Mr E has been to a wolf hunt, caught nothing.
Mond 29th	Cloudy some rain. Washed. lazy, very tired[.] not very well.
Tuesd 30th	Rainy. Drew in coverlet. wove little. my Babe unwell.

December 1824

Wed 1st	Rainy. Toothache all day. sick headache this eve[.] vomited felt better.
Thurs 2nd	Smoaky. Air. wove some. my Babe has one tooth cut through[.] gets up by chair.
Fryd 3rd	Smoaky indeed. wove one yard. received a pair of shoes to [too] small.
Sat 4th	Rainy A.M. very cold[.] some snow P.M. Baked Bread Pies [unreadable]
Sund 5th	Pleasant[.] very cold indeed. no one has called upon us today, uncommon.
Mond 6th	Misty weather. Washed[.] spent the eve at Mr S. The heaviest shock of an Earthquake on Saturday. last I ever heard. have the toothache.
Tuesd 7th	Flies of snow. knit some, wove some, not well. my Babe is seven months old, weighing 21, gets up by chair.
Wed 8th	Snow. Mrs Mott and her troublesome child spent the day. I worked for her until after crowing for day. Finished her gown.

Thurs 9th	Pleasant. Mrs Harrington spent the most of the day. I engaged to weave two coverlets for her. not very well, get along slowly.
Fryd 10th	Thaw some. wove but little. very dull and sleepy and lazy.
Sat 11th	Snowy. Ironed, washed floors, doors, windows, etc[.] mended some[.]
Sund 12th	Cold, the wintry blasts are creeping round as well as death.
Mond 13th	Rainy. saving punking for winter by striving[.] wove little. Mr E killed another of the innocent deer[.] My stomach sore.
Tues 14th	Cold, cloudy. washed. wove some. Miss Rowley & Western called.
Wed 15th	Cold. wove some. visited this eve by Mr. & Mrs Flower, Mr & Mrs S.
Thursd 16th	Cold. Pleasant. Baked largely. wove some the winter is beginning[.]
Fry 17th	Rainy. wove one yard and half on coverlet, very hard work.
Sat. 18th	Very slippery. wove one yard and half. finished coverlets Mr E killed one deer, wounded another. receiv'd a pair of shoes
Sund 19th	Cloudy. some snow. not very well. Mr E been and caught a deer[.]
Mond 20th	Cloudy. washed, mended. not well but better than I deserve[.]
Tuesd 21st	Thanksgiving. spent the day alone. Babe only. spent the eve and night at Uncles [Durfey]. very slip'ry.
Wed 22nd	Cloudy spooled and warped two coverlets visited at Mrs[illegible word][.]
Thurs 23rd	Cloudy. put in the web. my Babe is very worrisome indeed.
Fryd 24th	Cloudy. Baked pies. try'd to weave but it works very hard.
Sat. 25th	Cloudy. washed some, mended etc. Christmas day
Sund 26th	Cloudy, moderate weather. no prayer is heard within our dwelling, no praise to our Creator is wont to be made.

Mond 27th Rain little, then snow steadily all day. wove but little else.

Tues 28th Cloudy. wove a little. two workmen getting wood.

Wed 29th Beautiful day, tolerable sleighing. Baked. Mrs M.

Thursd 30th Pleasant. wove some. This year will soon close, perhaps life, too.

Fryd 31st Thawing fast. the snow almost gone. wove one yard on coverlet[.]

January 1st A.D. 1825

Sat 1st Twenty three years this day departed my mother. God grant that we begin and spend this year more to His glory than ever yet we have done. Mr E. finished coaling [charcoal making]. Washed all his clothes.

Sund 2nd Cold. once more began with the year to read my Bible through I hope to be faithful, to continue it every day.

Mond 3rd Very cold. E. Butchering today. Tried my lard, 32 lbs. very tired.

Tues 4th Pleasant. made 24 doz of candles. great many chores.

Wed 5th Pleasant. doing chore all day. visited at M. Rockwell's eve[.]

Thursd 6th Snowed very steady all day. mended some. sick night.

Fryd 7th Very stormy. mended all day. not well, took cold.

Sat. 8th Stormy. mending all day read the Watchmaker, a tract.[63]

Sun 9th Pleasant[.] Oh that I could say I live pleasantly but I cannot. we live as though we knew not God or cared for is love or his mercy which is great.

Mond 10th Pleasant. washed and Baked. visited this eve by Mr & Mrs Hall.

Tues 11th Pleasant trying to weave little. my Babe is very troublesome[.]‘

Wed 12th Pleasant. Mr. Flower & Rockwell worked here. Ironed & wove some.

Thurs 13th Pleasant. finished the coverlet. bought a Coffee pot of a Pedlar.

Fryd 14th — Some rain, Hail. alltogether makes it very slippery. put in Coverlet.

Sat. 15th — Foggy, thaw some. wove little. visited by H.D. my little boy begins to call paa' paa' paa'. I fear he begins so young he will talk as much as his Mother if he lives. I hope it will be more sensible.

Sund 16th — Cloudy, few drops of rain. visited at P.D.s this eve[.] he gave us another goose instead of one the foxes caught last night. My babe took cold.

Mond 17th — Pleasant. Baked, visited by Aunt Durfey, Aunt Brooks. cold[.]

Tues 18th — Pleasant. My Babe very sick, done nothing but hold him.

Wed 19th — Cloudy. My Babe no better, unable to sit up, very high fever.

Thurs 20th — Cloudy. My Babe's two upper teeth cut through. some better.

Fryd 21st — Cold, considerable snow fell last night. Henry better wove 1½ [yd][.]

Sat. 22nd — Pleasant. wove one yard [and] half. bought small ivory comb. chores[.]

Sund 23rd — Cold. wrote a letter to Uncle Clapps of Monkton. Wove this eve.

Mond 24th — Cloudy, likely for a shower. wove one yard [and] quarter snow this eve. Colder.

Tuesd 25th — Thaw some. finished weaving. moved back the Loom and partitioned it there. Moved the Bed into the kitchen. washed floors.

Wed. 26th — Pleasant. visited at Uncle Brooks', returned late at night. Sled[.] sick

Thurs 27th — Baked. Friends from Ferrisburg. Called over to Mr Rockwell's. visited at Mr Harringtown's. received 4 dollars [for weaving][.]

Fryd 28th — Cloudy. wrote a letter to Uncle Nicholson. visited at Uncle Durfey's. gave some wooden dishes to my Cousins. Mr Gage of NY buried today.

Sat. 29th — Washed clothes floors etc. mended some. very sore yes, bad cold.

Sund 30th — Pleasant. Happy is the man whose hopes rely on God.

Mond 31st — Stormy. of snow P.M. washed woolen clothes. rode to Hopkinton. purchased of J. Thomas one pot [$]1.50 one kettle 1.00 one bason 75 by cash three Dollars twenty five cents P.D.

February 1825

Tues 1st	Very stormy day and night. washed Linen clothes.
Wed 2nd	Very stormy. Mr S. to work at the house. do nothing but chores.
Thurs 3rd	Very stormy, snow deep. sat up very late. fried cakes.
Fryd 4th	Cold and stormy. Baked pies. my Babe is very cross today.
Sat. 5th	Blustering. Ironed, Mended books to occupy my cupboards.
Sund 6th	Very cold morn, moderated. our Red cow brought a fine calf.
Mond 7th	Rained all day hard and steady. sewed some.
Tuesd 8th	Clear and cold. scoured all my tin. regulated my new cupboard.
Wed 9th	Clear and cold. Baked Bread, pies, cake, etc. Mr. S had me a lantern[.]
Thurs 10th	Very pleasant. S. finished what we calculated to have done to the house at present. I cleared the house from the chamber to the cellar. retired very late. Oh that I would rid my heart from every sin and hateful vice and create love and obedience.
Fryd 11th	Pleasant thaw. Washed. disappointed of my friends not arriving[.]
Sat. 12th	Rained slowly, all day and night. Finished Henry's yellow frock. mended, Ironed etc. the road begins to be bare.
Sund 13th	Stormy little snow. read considerable of the proceedings of the children of Israel, how they displeased the Lord, as I do every day. How then can I stand at this awful Bar?
Mond 14th	Washed. visited at Mr E. received a Letter from Lucinda James.
Tues 15th	Agreeable weather, wrote to Miss James. pieced Bombazett for gown.
Wed 16th	Pleasant A.M. Stormy P.M. Worked on my gown, not worth it.
Thurs 17th	Beautiful A.M. mending all day. rainy P.M. My Brother at P.D.
Fryd 18th	Pleasant. Baked. my Brother [Nicholas] and Sister [Harriet] and Mr [Nathaniel] Austin, her father [-in-law], visited Uncle Brook's. spent the night. agreeable visit

but short. receiv'd Letters from Father, Abraham, Clarissa & Jacob [Phebe's young half-siblings] one runn of yarn from [Step]Mother.

Sat 19th Few flakes of snow. our friends took their leave. very unwell[.]

Sund 20th Very slippery. saw Betsey E. Visited at Uncle Durfey's this eve spent the night. uncle returned from Vt. received a letter from Sally Brooks, a few dried apples, box of sauce.

Mond 21st Snow some. visited by Mrs Rockwell. almost sick[.]

Tues 22nd Pleasant. visited by C. McAllister, Stephen Eastman.

Wed 23rd Pleasant washed C took her leave. Mr. Austin returned from Prescott. My brother had bad luck crossing the St. Law. Twenty-five Doll. duties to pay. wrote to father 24th.

Thurs 24th Thaws Mr A took his leave finally[.]

Fryd 25th Thaws and rains. sewing some. do little of anything[.]

Sat 26th Colder. mending, washed floor, etc. Stephen E Spent the night.

Sun 27th Colder. some one in almost all day. how many mispend the Sabbath in this part of the world of whom I am chief.

Mond 28th Moderate winter. Washed, ironed. Henry is worrysome.

March 1825

Tues 1st Snow. Town meeting. visited at Uncle Brooks Mrs. M. Dewey spent the night.

Wed 2nd Pleasant. Baked, fried cakes. prepared for company. Mrs Hawkins spent the night.

Thurs 3rd Pleasant. mending. Visited this eve at Mr. Rockwell's. Have a hard cold.

Fryd 4th Carded and spun a little wool. almost sick, very drowsy. Babe sick.

Sat 5th Pleasant. finished spinning wool. Mr. E. caught thirteen pounds of trout.

Sund 6th A few flakes of snow falling all day, soon melts.

Mond 7th Cloudy. Washed. rainy night, the snow almost gone.

Tues 8th Cloudy. Baked. spun six knots of thread, get along slow.

Wed 9th Pleasant. spun forteen knots of thread, boiled out.

Thursd 10th Very pleasant. visited at Mr N. Rockwell's. Bad cold.

Fryd 11th Very pleasant. visited at Mr. D. [David] Covey's. snowed at night.

Sat. 12th Pleasant. visited by Mr. Barns Hall from Vt.

Sund 13th Pleasant. read several tracts and the Indian Captive. Zadock Steele. He was taken by the Indians under refugees and Tories from Randolph, Vt., On the 17th day of October 1780 to Canada through a wilderness of three hundred miles in seven days, where underwent almost everything but death. They made their escape from Prison Island by digging under the Pickets with a Jack knife. Twenty feet underground, twenty two and half in length in two years. After enduring famine and distress, they arrived at home at Ellington, Connecticut.[64] wrote a letter to Mrs. Taylor.

Mond 14th Beautiful day. Mr. Hall took his leave. done a few chores.

Tues 15th Pleasant. Mr. E. commenced tapping the Maples today.

Wed 16th Pleasant indeed for the season. Wrote a letter to Sister Kelly [Kelley, sister-in-law] [.]

Thurs 17th Very warm, like May. Called over to Mr Rockwell. high spirits.

Fryd 18th Cooler, made forty lbs of Sugar. braiding straw, mending.

Sat 19th Pleasant. H.D. visited me. Returned with her, spent the night.

Sund 20th Pleasant and warm. returned with L. Newton. very tired. read some, but oh how miserably do I spend my time.

Mond 21st Beautiful season. washed, braded some. unwell.

Tues 22nd Pleasant. sugar'd off forty six lbs of sugar. called over to Mr. Motts. How far superior are my privileges and yet how unthankful to my God for them. Forbid it, Lord.

Wed 23rd	Pleasant. spun fifteen knots of Linen. Baked pies.
Thurs 24th	Pleasant. No snow to be seen, the Birds singing sweetly.
Fryd 25th	Pleasant. little rain at night. spun fifteen knots. swept. very tired.
Sat 26th	Rainy day. snow at night. made 60 lbs sugar. Vinegar[.]
Sund 27th	Snowed all day. read considerable but no prayers heard.
Mond 28th	Snowed most of the day. spun one run. P. Capel. came to board with us this week. an agreeable youngman.
Tues 29th	Pleasant. washed and baked. fried cakes etc. Very tired[.]
Wed 30th	Rainy. spun some. knitting drawers. little Henry begins to talk[.]
Thursd 31st	Rainy. Mr. Beba Abbott died today after an illness of three days. May we take warning by this.

April 1825

Fryd 1st	Some snow, thaws as fast as it comes. Baked. Henry sick.
Sat. 2nd	Pleasant. washed clothes and floors. Mr. C [Capel] took leave of us[.]
Sund 3rd	Pleasant. Read fifty chapters in my Bible. Frogs peep.
Mond 4th	Pleasant. To work in the sugar bush all day with little Henry.
Tuesd 5th	Pleasant. Boiled sap all day again. Welcome sweet spring with all thy share.
Wed 6th	Rainy. Boiled sap part of the day. spun fifteen knots. sick.
Thurs 7th	Pleasant. made about half barrel of Molasses, some vinegar[.]
Fryd 8th	Pleasant. worked some. made Henry a sun Bonnet. Leeks coming up.
Sat. 9th	Pleasant. Boiled a barrel of sap for vinegar. Finished for the year.
Rund 10th	Rainy. read fifty chapters in my Bible. toothache.

Mond. 11th	Pleasant. spun some. not well Henry unwell., worrysome[.]
Tues 12th	Few flakes of snow. Washed and Baked. Bought a reed 32 [dents].
Wed 13th	Few more flakes of snow to whiten the ground[.] began to wean my little boy. he is remarkably good about it.
Thurs 14th	Pleasant. spun one runn. my breast pains me[.] have a great deal of milk. I fear it will be hard drying it away. unwell.
Fryd 15th	Pleasant. spinning. I cannot but pity my little son[.]
Sat. 16th	Pleasant. very warm. worked in the garden all day. visited by Saphrona E. my darling babe is so busy to play in the dirt days. he cannot be comfortable nights.
Sun. 17th	Smoaky. Air. spent my time foolishly. S.E. gone home.
Mond. 18th	Pleasant. Washed. Very cold nights, freezes considerable hard.
Tues 19th	Cold. Baked. mending. spun some. have the toothache
Wed. 20th	Cold. froze all day. Mr. Wilson & Pillsbury worked here.
Thurs. 21st	Pleasant. Visited Mr. A. Rockwell. her health very poor.
Fryd. 22nd	Pleasant. the spring looks unfavorable but God is able to make it otherwise. if he sees fit. It is all for the best.
Sat. 23rd	Pleasant and warm. great want of rain. visited by Aunt Brooks and Miss Mary Lewis. toothache.
Sund. 24th	Smoaky, warm. Attended meeting at the schoolhouse[.] have sermons read. Lord wilt though strengthen these feeble efforts to some good purpose[.]
Mond. 25th	Rainy. Sewing on hat of straw. Oh that I were more industrious[.]
Tues 26th	Rainy. made soap. finished spinning flax. Cold for the season.
Wed. 27th	Cloudy. finished my soap. washed floor. Why am I so dull[.]
Thurs 28th	Some rain and snow. Baked. Alexandria returned.

Fryd. 29th Rain and snow. Cold. made a Beer of roots. mending.

Sat. 30th Snow A.M. Visited by Mrs. Mott. took a gown to make.

May 1825

Sund 1st Snowy and Cold wrote a letter to Uncle David Brooks, Ohio.

Mond. 2nd Cold. Washed. visited at Mr. Mott's, the Mrs. Converse. Mrs Osgood. took a frock to make for H. Mott. toothache. Obliged to whip my little Son several times a day and yet I do not know as it is best. Oh God wilt thou teach me to do him justice.

Tues 3rd Snow, finished the frock, carried it home. Mrs M. told me I should leave this place for a new country - one settled on each side. Oh that I were prepared to meet the Lamb of God.

Wed. 4th Cold. freezes hard evey night. picked greens but had been frozen.

Thursd. 5th The ground covered with snow this morn. rained & snowed all day. great wolf hunt. caught nothing but colds. Mr. E. very sick all night after such a fatiguing rout.

Fryd. 6th Cloudy and cool. scoured some. Trimmed the house with pine. Visited with the Mrs. Rockwells. Mrs. Flower at Mr. M.'s Mr. Eastman's health has never been so poor as it is today. since I knew him. Better P.M. Oh, that he was sick of this world and its alluring vanities and would seek God.

Sat. 7th Cool. pleasant finsiehd scouring the house. altered a gown.

Sund 8th Cool. attended meeting at the schoolhouse. heard a Mr. Wilkison, an English man, preach from these words: II of Corninthians XIII.II. Be perfect, be of good comfort[.] be of one mind. live in peace[.] Henry was so worrysome I did not hear much in the P.M.

Mon 9th Cool. Washed visited by sister Mary Eastman. Baked.

Tuesd 10th Cool. finished straw hat, mending, Etc. toothache. backward season[.]

Wed 11th Rainy. Baked Gingerbread etc. washed floors[.] worrysome child.

Thurs 12th Pleasant. visited by sister Betsey E. mending clothes not conduct.

Fryd 13th Pleasant. Betsey and myself walked and carried Henry to Mr. E. called over to Mr. Wright's. visited with the Ladies at P.D.s P.M.

Sat 14th Pleasant[.] very unwell[.] I not feel able to sit up. Turning my silk frock.

Sund 15th Pleasant. left our Babe with Mrs. Flower walked two and half miles heard Mr. W. [Wilkinson] preach A.M. from these words "Maybe to yourselves friends of the unrighteous Mammon that when ye fail they may receive you into everlasting habitations." Took supper at Mr. Flower's. borrow'd of Mrs. Dustin. a Book called Spiritual Babylon, with some remarkable signs and prophecies of the last day. By Elisah Peck.

Mond 16th Cool nights. washed. visited Sister Mary E. Henry troublesome.

Tues 17th Some rain. Turn my heart, Oh God, from alluring vanities.

Wed 18th Rainy. accompanied Sister Betsey to Potsdam. purchased trimmings for bonnet, left to bleach. called to see Miss Spencer. Mr. Partridge, Dr. Lymans. dined at Mr. Banks. walked to the Academy to Declamation. got very wet coming home. spoiled my wedding ruff and shoes. left Henry at home.

Thurs 19th Cloudy. visited by Mrs. Rockwell. very tired today. toothache[.]

Fryd 20th Pleasant. dropping Potatoes for Mr E. to plant, small help.

Sat. 21st Pleasant. P.M. showery morn. Miss Mayhew, Miss Covey, Miss McAllister called. finished planting potatoes. Black flies thick.

Sund 22nd Attended meeting at schoolhouse. Mr. W. preached. Married this P.M. Mr. Carlos Humphrey to Miss Julia Covey, both of Hopkinton[.] God bless them.

Mon 23rd Pleasant. washed, ironed. I believe I have grieved the spirit.

Tues 24th Rainy. Old Mrs. Covey came to tarry a few days. had another window cut out in the Bedroom. looks pleasant.

Wed 25th Pleasant. Baked beans, Pudding & Pies. Mr. W. called. Mr. Merrill.

Thurs 26th Cloudy. Mr. Wilkison preached here from these words: "Man dieth and wasteth away and where is he." He spent the night agreeably with us. Oh that God would give my companion the spirit of Prayer he needs.

Fryd 27th Pleasant. received a Letter from Mrs Taylor[.] she writes she has been blessed with a fine son, David Nehemiah.

Sat. 28th Pleasant. finished spooling my web. walked to Mr. Remington's. warped it. received my Bonnet from Potsdam.

Sun 29th Pleasant. warm. left my Babe at Mr. Rockwells, walked two and half miles. Mr. W. preached from the first Psalm A.M. preached their sermon at our schoolhouse. called to Dr. Broos, had a tooth drawn[.] very trying. Took supper at Mr. Harrigton's, very tired, bad cold.

Mond 30th Pleasant. Baked, churned, almost sick. Mrs. Covey returned home.

Tues 31st Rainy P.M. visited by H. Durfey made a collarett.

June 1825

Wed 1st Pleasant. walked to Mr. E's. picked wool, spent the night.

Thurs 2nd Rainy P.M. picking wool, took 25 lbs of poor wool.

Fryd 3rd Pleasant. bad cold. so Drowsy I can do nothing.

Sat. 4th Pleasant. Baked, washed floors. washed, Ironed some.

Sund 5th Rainy. Mr. E. attended meeting at Hopkinton.

Sund 5th Rainy. Mr. Mott cleared out with a borrowed horse and waggon yesterday in the night with his family.

Mond 6th Rainy A.M. spun twenty-four knots of tow. sowed peas.

Tues 7th Pleasant. Picking wool that I took of Lee Eastman.

Wed. 8th Some rain. Mr. E. attended the Burial of Mrs. Wright.

Thurs 9th Pleasant. Washed. very warm, want of rain.

Sat. 11th	Warm. A.M. heavy shower of rain with thunder and lightning.
Sund 12th	Pleasant and warm. Alone with my Babe. heard that many in town were shocked with lightning yesterday.
Mond 13th	Pleasant. picking wool yet. visited by Aunt Durfey. Mr E. kill'd deer
Tuesd 14th	Pleasant. finished picking wool. Fine growing season.
Wed 15th	Pleasant A.M. rainy night. visited by Miss J. Mayhew, Julia Umphrey. Greased my wool. Baked pies, washed.
Thurs 16th	Rainy. Put in my web, wove one yd and half. coarse.
Fryd 17th	Pleasant. Wove four yards. washed some. my work is a bug bear.
Sat. 18th	Pleasant. The commissioners laid out the road. Wove little. Received a Letter from Father, another from Brother.
Sund 19th	Cloudy. Wrote to Father and Mother, heard from Canada.
Mond 20th	Pleasant. very large washing. wove one yard. very tired.
Tuesd 21st	Pleasant. wove five and half yards and half crying.
Wed 22nd	Pleasant. finished my web. boiled it out. Went strawberrying to Uncle Durfey's Aunt gave me a present bought red [illegible word][.]
Thurs 23rd	Pleasant. cut out partly made tow trousers. Baked.
Fryd 24th	Pleasant. sewing. Mr. E. brought home rolls.[65] I carried the most of them to Mr. Rowley's to be spun, horseback.
Sat. 25th	Training. Finished trowsers, made part of a shirt. almost sick.
Sund 26th	Fine weather. a thousand blessings attending us.
Mond 27th	Pleasant. Began a fish net. crops look well after the shower.
Tues 28th	Rather cool. do nothing bu chores. people to work on Road.

Wed 29th Pleasant. To work on net. my God is good to me, very good.

Thursd 30th Warm. washed some. visited by Mrs. Eastman. Cold heart.

July 1825

Fryd 1st Very warm. Baked, washed. Cook'd dinner for a number of men. A.M. almost sick. P.M. cut out a pair of trowsers.

Sat. 2nd Warm. Visited by H.D. A.M. visited Uncle Brooks[,] P.M.[,][&] Roswell E spent the night with us. agreeable visit.

Sund 3rd Pleasant. we attend no meetings of late. I want to meet God at his home in my own heart but I wander far from him.

Mond 4th Independence. Washed. Visited at C. Rockwell's. all the children in the neighborhood under the age of twelve years. twenty girls, five boys; mine uneasy.

Tues 5th Pleasant. our people began haying. green peas.

Wedn 6th Warm. Sewing. How repidly does time glide away.

Thurs 7th Spun one runn. Making cheese, very small.

Fryd 8th Warm indeed. Cleaned my house. Oh that it was heart.

Sat. 9th Pleasant. Baked largely for company, disappointed.

Sun 10th Very hot. Want of rain. a rain of conviction, also.

Mon 11th Very warm. Fine shower to water the thirsty crops.

Tues 12th Pleasant. Sewing, Baking. all chores. no good done.

Wed 13th Pleasant. spun one run. Mr. E. gone to work for Father.

Thurs 14th Pleasant. sewing. What a stumbling block to the world.

Fryd 15th Pleasant. walked to Uncle Durfey's, picked currants.

Sat 16th Pleasant. Baked, washed floor. sewing, chores, etc. shower[.]

Sund 17th	Pleasant. Had a tooth drawn with a piece of jaw.
Mond 18th	Washed. H.D. [Harriet Durfey] came here. have cucumbers and String beans.
Tuesd 19th	Very warm. Heard that Miss Mary Dewey had departed this life leaving a son of illegitimacy. It is to be lamented that she has conducted so as to merit so shocking a death among strangers in a strange land.
Wed 20th	Very warm. Want of rain. Trying to pick corn.
Thurs 21st	Warm. spun thirty knots of warp. chores of all kinds.
Fryd 22nd	Look likely for rain. Called over to Mr. Rowley's. very tired
Sat 23rd	Very dry season. But did I deserve as good I should be glad.
Sund 24th	Very warm. Read the Life of John Fletcher of Switzerland.[66]
Mond 25th	Warm. Washed, made cheese. Mr. E gone. have all the chores to do.
Tues 26th	Pleasant. spun but half run. How slowly do I get along.
Wed 27th	Pleasant. A gentlemen spent the night from Grand Isle.
Thurs 28th	Pleasant. Have six cows to milk now. Visited at the Rockwell's.
Rdy 29th	Rainy. P.M. Almost tired out. things suffer yet for rain.
Sat. 30th	Shower P.M. Been pulling flax what time I could get.
Sund 31st	Pleasant. Want of rain. Green corn large enough to eat.

August 1825

Mond 1st	Pleasant. Baked. spun one runn it takes most of the A.M. for chores[.]
Tuesd 2nd	Pleasant. Washed, made cheese. visited at Mr. Flower's[.]
Wed 3rd	Warm indeed. spun ten knots visited by Rachel S. [Sampson], M.E. [Mary Eastman][.]

Thurd 4th	Some showers, spun ten knots. Visited by Mary Lewis.
Fryd 5th	Pleasant. spun ten knots. Visited by Mrs. E. We visited at Mr. Converse shamefully treated by Mrs. Sampson.
Sat. 6th	Pleasant. Made cheese. Ironed. Visited at Father E's.
Sund 7th	Rainy. Very unwell, we have ripe Water Melons.
Mond 8th	Cloudy. washed. spun twenty knots. Crops suffer for rain.
Tuesd 9th	Very hard shower this morn. Went Black Berrying[.]
Wed 10th	Cloudy. Washed, Baked, made cheese. Spun six knots. Mr. E gone to watch with Mr. S. Abbott. All alone to night.
Thurs 11th	Pleasant. Called over to Mr Rowley's. Visited at Mr. Harrington's. Oh, Lord, how unthankful I am.
Fryd 12th	Pleasant. Made cheese. spun a runn. almost sick.
Sat. 13th	Rainy P.M. Spun one runn. Ironed, very melancholy.
Sund 14th	Pleasant. Read again the life of that truly pious man John William de la Flechere. Rev. Joshua Gilpin
Mond 15th	Cloudy few drops of rain. Washed some. spun fifteen knots.
Tues 16th	Cloud but no rain. spun sixteen knots Mr. [blank space] Smith here
Wed 17th	Cloudy & cool. Made cheese. Baked. walked to Mr. Rowley['s] called to Mr. McAllaster. Ripe melons in plenty. Very tired.
Thurs 18th	Frost. Pleasant spun twenty knots sister Betsey returned from Potsdam. took tea. bought dye wood.
Fryd 19th	Frost. Pleasant. spun twenty knots. Went to the brook carried and scoured fifty seven runs of yarn. sized one web.
Sat 20th	Cloudy, little rain. Went to the Brook and did a large washing. come home, washed floor Mrs. Dewey took tea.

Sun 21st	Rainy. Read the Life of John Flecher by Rev. John Westley. Scriptures, I read in vain.
Mond. 22nd	Shower. Prepared tubs for butter and pickles.
Tues 23rd	Pleasant. spooled and warped a web. not well.
Wed 24th	Pleasant. washed, Ironed. My time is spent for nought.
Thurs 25th	Pleasant. borrowed a raddle of Aunt D. Ate ripe apples. Baked for compnay. Put in my web, wove one yard.
Fryd 26th	Pleasant. Wove one yd and half. Visited by the Miss Rockwells, Mrs. Flower. Mr Violetto hung at Malone.
Sat 27th	Pleasant. Mary Rockwell spent the day. Wove three half yards.
Sund 28th	Pleasant day, rainy night. Visited by Uncle & Aunt Brooks. Oh God wilt thou have compassion on them and us and Give us a spirit of prayer when we meet.
Mond 29th	Pleasant. Baked & washed some. Wove two yds. indisposed.
Tues 30th	Pleasant. Very unwell. visited by Miss Louis [Louise] Newton.
Wed 31st	Pleasant. Finished my web, spooled some. get along slowly.

September 1825

Thursd 1st	Pleasant. Finished spooling, warped. Called over to Uncle D.
Fryd 2nd	Pleasant but cold. Baked & washed some. visited by Mrs E., S.E.
Sat 3rd	Rainy. Gathered weeds for yellow dye. Stephen Eastman returned from Fowler in tolerable health. Headache.
Sund 4th	Pleasant. My bosom friend, one that ought to pray with me and teach me the way of life is hunting Bees. Oh, God, wilt thou hunt for his wandering heart and bring it home to thee. Must we so lives 'till death shall close our eyes. Oh God forbid but they will be done but do I entreat of thee have compassion on the tender Babe and keep him from the error of his Parents and may he lead a pious life for thy sake.

Mond 5th	Pleasant. Training. Visited all day at Uncle Brooks' with Mrs. Flower & Rockwell. Agreeable visit indeed.
Tues 6th	Cloudy. put in a web 5 quarters wide. wove one yd. H.D.[Harriet Durfey] L.N. [Louise Newton] visited.
Wed 7th	Cloudy. High winds, but very little rain. Made a flannel sheet. Henry is so cross I wove only one yd and half. This eve wove two yds. Baked. Stephen E. took breakfast with us. Sophrona took tea with me. Rainy.
Thurs 8th	Cloudy. very little rain. wove three half yds. sewing.
Fryd 9th	Cloudy and cold. Baked pies, called over to Mr. Wead's, Hopkinton Took tea at Uncle Durfey's. came home, mended some. Wove one yard this eve. one day more is gone[.]
Sat. 10th	Cloudy. wove some keep busy but brings little to . . .
Sund 11th	Pleasant. read and slept and so goes my Sabbath.
Mond 12th	Cloudy. wove eight yds. My babe better today.
Tues 13th	Cloudy, some rain. wove three yds. gathered Sorrel to set a Logwood dye. Visited by Sophrona E.
Wed 14th	Rainy. Gathered Sorrel. Baked for company. Sewed.
Thurs 15th	Cloudy. Colouring black but it is a tolerable Blue[.]
Fryd 16th	Pleasant. Harriet D spent yesterday, returned today. Finished spinning wool, forty knots. Washed floor[.]
Sat 17th	Cloudy. Wove three yards. Baked. Dressed chicken[.]
Sun 18th	Pleasant, but my mind is unpleasant. I have strayed from my God and dare not return.
Mond 19th	Cloudy. Made Mr. E a woolen frock. knit some. Visited by Mr. Robert Dunshee from Vermont, and Stockholm. Mr. H. Ellsworth to Miss A. Eastman Catharine Gaige to Mr. Perry.

Tuesd 20th — Rainy. Gathered herbs for colouring yellow. Mending.

Wed 21st — Some rain. finished colouring. mending. Baked etc.

Thurs 22nd — Cloudy. Washed at the brook. Rainy night, very wet.

Fryd 23rd — Rainy. mending visited by Mrs. Flower. cleared house[.]

Sat 24th — Cloudy. visited at Mr. E's. Cleared off. Hard Frost indeed.

Sun 25th — Very pleasant. Oh what will become of my husband, cutting corn. Reading the History of the United States.[67]

Mond 26th — Pleasant. Baked. H. Hulburt came to work at shoes.

Tuesd 27th — Cloudy, some rain. Binding shoes. visited by Mrs. E.

Wed 28th — Pleasant. Washed all day visited by Sister B.E. [Betsey Eastman] took cold.

Thurs 29th — Pleasant. Washed. Bound Boots. Visited by Mrs. Flower.

Fryd 30th — Pleasant. Baked, sewed some. Almost sick, little Henry sick.

October 1825

Sat. 1st — Pleasant. Hulburt finished work here for the present.

Sund 2nd — Pleasant and warm. Read the History of the United States[.] Mr & Mrs Oliver took supper with us. Oh the Sabbath.

Mond 3rd — Very warm indeed Baked. Spooled & warped my web of yarn.

Tues 4th — Warm. Hulburt came and made a pair of Moccasins.

Wed 5th — Pleasant. Drew in my web. finished a pair of socks. Heard from Fowler. Stephen E. brought word that Sister Kelly [Kelley] was dangerously sick. He spent the night. Will God be nigh unto her and speak peace to her soul which friends wish[.]

Thurs 6th — Pleasant, very warm. Washed wove three yards. hard cold.

Fryd 7th Pleasant. quite unwell A.M. wove three yards P.M. spooled, carded[.]

Sat. 8th Very smoaky and cool. Called to Uncle D.['s], Mr. Rockwell['s]. wove one yd. Almost sick and little Henry also.

Sund 9th Smoaky, hard frost. My husband been to a wolf hunt. Oh, that he was as eager to hunt the souls of men. Read History but it is not so good as my Bible.

Mond. 10th High winds, shower at night. wove one & half yd. mended. visited by Maria D. [Durfey], S.E. My teeth troublesome.

Tues 11th Cloudy. coloured Otter, poor colour. finished all my weaving.

Wed 12th Smoaky. rainy eve. husked nine bushel of corn. wove one yd.

Fryd 14th Pleasant, but very cold. Wove six yards. Toothache face swollen.

Sat. 15th Pleasant, cold. Wove two yds. Finished the web. mending. almost sick.

Sun 16th Cloudy very cold. finished the History of the United States. Toothache[.]

Mond 17th Cold & Clousy. Washed. toothache, face badly swollen, hard cold.

Tues 18th Cold. Spooled, warped, drew in a web. Ironed. Mr. E. finished husking.

Wed 19th Cloudy. Mr and Mrs. Hewet took breakfast here from Jay. Wrote to Mrs. Partridge, visited with Mrs. Rockwell at Mr. Eastman's[.]

Thurs 20th Pleasant. Baked, sewed. Some melancholy pervades my breast.

Fryd 21st Pleasant. Wove three yds. spooled a Blanket. Unhappy life, stupid.

Sat. 22nd Pleasant. Washed some. Ironed, made a shirtee. received a letter from my Father stating that Brother Eleazar had lost he use of the left part of his face and Sister Elizabeth was sick and had been seven weeks. Heard Uncle David Brook[s], Ohio, was sick of a consumption. Spent most of the day in tears. While my friends experience loss of health I enjoy it without returning any thanks to my God for his mercy.

Sund 23rd High winds, some rain. Wrote a lengthy letter to my Father.

Mond 24th Pleasant. Baked twice. Visited this eve at Uncle Durfey's.

Wed 26th Rainy. Wove three yds. My feet still continue very lame.

Thus 27th Rainy. Wove two yds and half. Finished my web. Attended quilting at Mr. Rockwell's. Mr. E killed two Deer this morn.

Fryd 28th Cloudy. Made seven Doz. of Candles. Chores visited this eve. C.R. [Rockwell].

Sat. 29th Cloudy. made Shirtee. Baked mince pies. washed floors etc.

Sun 30th Cloudy. Heard from Vt. in good health. Uncle Elisha [Brooks] called.

Mond 31st Rainy. Coloured otter. Drew in a Blanket. Wove one yd. sewed.

November 1825

Tues 1st Showery. cutting pieces for a quilt. Mrs. Chase dined here. Betsey E spent the day and night. wove one and half yds.

Wed 2nd Showers. Finished the Blanket. spooled & washed Mrs. C[hase]'s web[.]

Thurs 3rd Put in another Blanket visited by Louis Newton spent the night.

Fryd 4th Baked. wove one & Half yd washed some. Engaged good deal weaving.

Sat. 5th Cloudy. wove three yards. spent the night at Father Es[.]

Sund 6th Pleasant. Read some in the Apocrypha.[68] I know not what to think of it, whether it is of use to read it or not.

Mond 7th Pleasant. Finished the Blanket. last eve drew in a web, wove three yds Mr. Flower assisting Mr. E. in unstoning his well.

Tues 8th Very warm indeed. Wove four & half yds, finished the web. Visited by Mother E but nothing is said of our Lord and Saviour.

Wed 9th Rain. Some snow last night. very unwell this morn. spent the day at Mr C. Rockwell's. Mr. E gone to Election. Sewing.

Thurs 10th	Colder. making slip and drawers for Henry.
Fryd 11th	Cold. Washed. I have so much to do and do so little, I am discouraged.
Sat 12th	Cold and cloudy. Made attempts to clean some part of my house.
Sund 13th	High winds, Cloudy. Read some, but no prayers do I hear. Called to visit a little cousin which is not likely to live until morning. Mr E went, I tarried alone through the night.
Mond 14th	Stormy. Rose to Uncle B's on a man saddle, fell off backward with my little Boy without injury. was bled. Worked on grave clothes, sat up all night. I know not how to pity these parents.
Tues 15th	Pleasant. returned home dined at Mr. Flower's. Mr. Wilkinson buried a child today and yet mine is spared. Almost sick. sewed little.
Wed 16th	Cloudy. How stupid are my senses to good work.
Thurs 17th	A few flakes of snow. Baked. Oh God wilt thou quicken our drowsy spirits and raise our thoughts to Heaven.
Fryd 18th	Cold. cut out, partly made me a flannel frock.
Sat. 19th	Cold and stormy. Finished my frock. My God is good to me.
Sund 20th	High winds, rain & snow. Walked through the snow to Uncle Brooks', their little girl is rather better today.
Mond 21st	Cold. Cloudy. Scoured, washed floors. My little son almost sick. Miss Almira Parkhurst came to sow [sew] for us this week.
Tuesd 22nd	Pleasant. it [takes] me most of my time to take of my little Boy.
Wed 23rd	Pleasant. Sewed some. Baked pies. Reading Memoirs of Henry Obookiak a native of Owyhee, also a member of the Missionary Society, died at the age of twenty-six.[69]
Thurs 24th	Stormy. Thanksgiving Day, but not in heart I fear.
Fryd 25th	Pleasant. visited by Mother E and Sophrona. Visited this eve at Mr. Flower's. Sewed considerable today, finished.

Sat 26th — Pleasant. Miss P. [Parkhurst] finished sewing for us, paid her in cash.

Sund 27th — Pleasant. Almost sick. Roswell & David E. [Eastman] took supper with us. Miss P Gone. Uncle Brooks called, his child no better.

Mond 28th — Pleasant. Put in a coverlet for Mrs. Rockwell. Sophrona came to spend the week. Mr. E. finished his well again.

Tues 29th — Pleasant. Wove half coverlet besides many chores.

Wed 30th — Pleasant. Finished the Coverlet. visited by Mother E. almost tired out.

December 1825

Thurs. 1st — Pleasant. warped thirty yds Diaper & coverlet. put it in. Mr Peck to work here making a couple cherry bedsteads.

Fryd 2nd — Rainy. Wove but little very slow work indeed. Fine work.

Sat. 3rd — Mr. P. gone home. Washed floors. Wove some, almost sick.

Sund 4th — Pleasant. Read my bible considerable but heard no Exhortation, no prayer, no religious conversation. I fear I never shall have the sweet satisfaction of hearing a single prayer from the lips of my husband. Oh stupidity.

Mond 5th — Cold winds. Visited by Mrs. Cornstalk, wove but little.

Tues 6th — Some snow. Not well but my health is far better than I deserve.

Wed 7th — Cloudy. I find coverlets almost too hard for me at present.

Thurs 8th — Cold. Finished the coverlet and glad am I. Looks likely for snow.

Fryd 9th — Very high winds . Piecing lining to a puff'd quilt alone today.

Sat. 10th — Little snow. Sewing. how unhappy do we live and nothing (I think not) but the one thing needful. that will sweeten all things and without this I can enjoy nothing as I wish.

Sund 11th — Stormy A.M. Pleasant P.M. one poor travellor called. I had the pleasure of giving him a meal which is highly gratifying to my feelings, to impart a trifle to the poor but still there is an aching void that lives continually in my breast. His parents are careless about the things that be his and their everlasting peace. no example worthy [of] his imitation and, how can I bear to see the little innocent thus live? Oh God forbid wilt thou give us a praying spirit, family religion, a pious heart and may it ere long be our meat and our drink to do the will of our Father[.]

Mon 12th Very cold indeed. how thankful ought I to be for the blessings of God in providing a kind partner, food and clothing while some are destitute of both, have scarcely the necessaries of life while I have a plenty. Oh how undeserving am I for it.

Tues 13th Very cold, indeed. Fourteen degrees colder than it was last winter.

Wed 14th More moderate. Washed. Visited by Mr & Mrs Oliver. fatigued.

Thurs 15th Cloudy. Assisted at Father E's, spent the night. They killed fourteen hogs. Worked quite too hard. Very lame, Rheumatism.

Fryd 16th Lowry. Returned home almost sick. yet I have many mercies.

Sat. 17th Cloudy. Baked, Ironed, mended, etc. welcome Saturday evening.

Sund 18th Very wet and muddy. Called over to Uncle Brooks', his darling babe appears fast approaching the shadow of death.

Mond 19th A few flakes of snow. Drawing in a web of double Prussian Diaper.

Tues 20th Pleasant. wove little. slow work and thrity yds long for Mr E. D.R. [D. Remington].

Wed 21st Windy. Wove one yd. washed some. Visited this eve by Mr & Mrs Rockwell, Mr & Mrs Flower. Snow some this evening. dejected.

Thurs 22nd Very cold. Mr E. killed our red cow. tried thirty-two Lbs of tallow.

Fryd 23rd Windy & cold. Made twenty-seven Lbs of Candles. hard cold.

Sat. 24th More moderate. Baked mince, pumpkin pies. etc. Sister Polly came from Potsdam and spent the night with us. Very tired.

Sund 25th Rainy. Finished reading my Bible through within a year.

Mond 26th Some snow. arose very early, washed some, mended the day.

Tues 27th Cold and stormy. Mr E. killed our three hogs. Mrs. E. assisted me. The two smallest weighed six hundred forty-nine Lb. tried my lard.

Wed 28th Moderate. Worked hard at chores that belong to butchering. Lame indeed[.]

Thurs 29th Stormy. Washed. Mr E bought a yearling heifer six Dollars fifty cents. He received ten Dollar in cash for Pork. dull and lame.

Fryd 30th Cold. Mending all day. very late at night. Snows or Hails fast.

Sat. 31st Icy rain. Washed some, Baked etc. this year is gone and not one good deed have I done while thousands have gone to Eternity.

PARISHVILLE
January 1826

Sund 1st Rainy. twenty four years this day since my Mother left this world of trouble. Perhaps I shall soon follow. Rainy, very icy indeed.

snowed all night. went to Father Eastman's, spent the evening agreeably.

Mond 2nd Snow'd all day. wove one yd of Prussian Diaper. Very tired.

Tues 3rd Snow considerable depth. Wove one yard more; slow going.

Wed 4th Pleasant, colder. Wove one yard more. I find but time to weave.

Thurs 5th Pleasant. sewing all day. very dull and lame and drowsy.

Frdy 6th Cold. washed large washing, Linen clothes. very tired.

Sat. 7th Thaws some. Baked, Ironed etc. Very lame. Welcome Saturday.

Sund 8th Rainy. Visited Uncle Brooks, his child no better. called to C. Rockwell[.] Spent the evening became acquainted with Miss Polly Stone. Louise Newton came home with us.

Mond 9th Pleasant, some rain, thaws fast. washed. Louise scoured the rest of the day. Visited by B.E., Miss Hannah Layman; this eve by Miss Stone, the others spent the night merrily.

Tues 10th	The snow all gone or mostly. The Ladies returned home. almost sick.
Wed 11th	Mending, wove some. Deep snow fell this night unexpectedly.
Thurs 12th	Snowed some. Wove all day for less than a yard. When shall I pray?
Fryd 13th	Snow some, white frost. The winter thus far is very unsteady.
Sat 14th	Moderate. One week more is gone and nothing done for my God.
Sun 15th	Pleasant. Read the Fool of Quality again.[70] Perhaps I am wrong.
Mond 16th	Stormy. A pedlar took dinner with us, traded some. Wove little.
Tues 17th	Cold, stormy. Wove little. Fried cakes. A number called Mr. Wilkison.
Wed 18th	Pleasant. Wove some. Baked. Very tired. Mr. Oba Hoit ordained, Potsdam.
Thurs 19th	Cold. Uncle Clapp. Mr. J. Bacon, R. Dunshee. called from Vt. Grandmother is very sick & almost the rest of the family. Wove one yd and half. Mr & Mrs. Kelly called from Fowler. Very tired.
Fryd 20th	Pleasant. Worked very hard. A.M. Visited Father E. P.M. sewing.
Sat. 21st	Pleasant. Almost sick. Took down the Loom. Visited by Mr. E. Mr & Mrs Kelly, L.E. [Lee Eastman], Mrs K. spent the night. She is very sick.
Sun 22nd	Pleasant. Mrs. Kelly much worse. Betsey spent the day & Night. Mr. K. a number called. Uncle Clapp returned. The Dr. speaks no ways encouraging of Sally. Sat up all night.
Mond 23rd	Pleasant high winds. Sally is some better. Mrs. E. spent the day. Sally went home with them. Mr & Mrs Brown. of Upper Canada. Spent the night. Visited at Uncle D's this evening. Received a Letter from Brother Eleazar, They have not enjoyed good health since they left us[.] My other relatives in that place are well. Almost sick.
Tues 24th	Snows some. Almost sick today. sewed a little H.D. [Harriet Durfey] gone to Vt.
Wed 25th	Colder. traded one Dollar by Cash yesterday figured mull for a cap. Sewing. My spirits are dull, powers drowsy.

Thurs 26th As cold I think as I could wish, blustering. sewing trifles.

Fryd 27th Moderate. Why should I be suffered to live any longer[.]

Sat. 28th Washed all day. Rheumatism, very hard in consquence. read a part of the Life of Sir William Wallace who redeemed Scotland three times from Edward, King of England, was at last betrayed by his servant and taken his head placed on London gate, his quarters placed upon the gates of the most popular cities of Scotland.[71]

Sund 29th Pleasant. Mr E attended meeting but Oh, my God, how innsensible.

Mond 30th Stormy. Spent the day at Uncle Durfey's, sewing not well.

Tues 31st The coldest day that ever was known, it is thought by some. My little son burnt his arm and was bitten by the dog over eye.

February 1826

Wed 1st More moderate but very cold. Mr. Kelly returned, carried us to Mr. E. spent the night. cut out two night caps. saw Mrs. F. Allen.

Thurs 2nd Some snow. Mrs. Kelly returned home with me. spent the night.

Fryd. 3rd Washed woolen clothes, floors Etc. Am so lame I can do but little[.]

Sat 4th Ironed, sewed some. Much to do. Mrs. Kelly sent a coverlet to weave.

Sun 5th Stormy. Read the Life of the Rev. Levi Parsons, A Missionary to Jerusalem who died at the early age of thirty nine.[72]

Mond 6th Stormy. Mr. E gone all day to Hopkinton. purchased one sett of plates[,] three tumblers, mending. making dish clothes, holders etc.

Tues 7th Stormy. Mr E attended the funeral of my niece Harriet Brooks who died yesterday after an illness of three months lacking three days.

Wed 8th Very stormy. washed all day. Very tired indeed, Rheumatism.

Thurs 9th Pleasant. Very lame and sick. not able to do but little of anything.

Fryd 10th Pleasant. Visited at Uncle Brooks. A lonesome family indeed.

Sat 11th Stormy. Lucius Brooks came here last night. has cut his knee bad this morn. Baked. Not well. Lucius homesick.

Sund 12th Stormy. the snow is very deep. Carried L. Home. Finished reading the Life of Mr. Parsons. I profit nothing by reading.

Mond 13th Pleasant. Oh God what a day of distress is this to me, yet thou hast wonderfully supported me and by thine assistance have been enabled to bring into this world of woe a lovely daughter to appearance (though untimely)[.] But what may be the fate and character of this innocent offspring I know not. Oh, my God, I beseech the[e] to enable me to live better, more exemplary before the world and the precious Babes which thou hast given me. Oh Lord wilt keep them as in the hollow of thine hand and from the errors of their parents, a stupid pair, what a cruel example for children. Miss L. Newton spent the night. great distress most of the night. snow fallen about six inches tonight. toothache. [in the margin: 8 lbs. this may be her baby's weight at birth]

Tues 14th Snows. sat up considerable but hard pains, singular chillness in my head. Harriet Durfey came to spend a few days with me. heard particulars from Vermont by her.

Wed 15th Pleasant. L. Newton went home this morn. Henry sick with a cold.

Thurs 16th Cold and cloudy. Harriet almost sick. My Babe took cold.

Fryd 17th More snow. Mr and Mrs. Brown returend from Vermont and spent the night Received a Letter from Sister Clarissa.

Sat 18th Pleasant. H.D. returned home. Sister Betsey came to spend a week with me. Finished my cap of figur'd Mull. Very tired.

Sund 19th Very Pleasant. Sat up all day. My eyes weak, distress in my head.

Mond 20th Pleasant. Uncle and Aunt Brooks visited me. Lucius has the measles.

Tues 21st Pleasant. Sew'd a trifle but my eyes are weak, yet God is kind.

Wed 22nd Cold and stormy. I get along well with my Babes and takes all my time.

Thurs 23rd Not so well today. My little ones have very bad colds indeed.

Fryd 24th	Pleasant. Visited by Mother E. Mrs. Rockwell, Mrs Flower. Very tired.
Sat. 25th	Thaws fast. Dismissed my nurse. the wind blew as hard as ever it was known to blow in this county. The snow goes fast.
Sun 26th	Pleasant. Uncle Brooks and Durfey called. My eyes are very sore.
Mond 27th	Spent the day alone excepting my little ones. Mr E. to work for Mr F.
Tues 28th	Continues to thaw. Roswell E. sick with the measles. all around.

March 1826

Wed. 1st	Thaws slowly. Mr. E. to work for Mr. Rockwell. M.E. called.
Thurs 2nd	Pleasant. Mr R & F to work for us today getting wood. The Rev Mr. Wilkinson and wife called today, agreeable persons to appearance. My eyes are so sore and swollen I cannot see very much, and yet I enjoy far more favors than I deserve.
Fry 3rd	High winds and some rain. Washed considerable. Headache very bad. Mr. E. finished drawing his year's stock of wood. has bad cold.
Sat. 4th	Rainy. I do not earn my board seemingly yet it saves one dollar per week by not hiring it done. I ought to be more easy.
Sun 5th	Pleasant, but my mind is troubled about my little ones.
Mond 6th	Pleasant. piecing a cradle quilt. Washed some. My babe cross.
Tuesd 7th	Very pleasant indeed. Mr E gone to Town Meeting. sewing.
Wed 8th	Rainy. Baked, starched & Ironed caps etc. Mr. Heady called informed me of the death of his wife. Very sharp lightning and thunder this eve.
Thurs 9th	Rainy. A Mr White and family called. They were moving. colder[.]
Fryd 10th	Pleasant, showers. Quiled a cradle quilt. My Babe is worrysome.
Sat. 11th	Pleasant. Walked to Mrs Rockwell's and carried my Babe. Very tired. spent the day with her. It is very sickly with colds & measles.

Sund 12th	Pleasant indeed. Uncle Brooks called, his family has the measles. Aunt Durfey very sick. Seven very sick at Father Eastman's of the measles, not but two of the family able to do anything.
Mond 13th	Pleasant. Washed. I dare not visit the sick on account of taking the disorder and my little babe should die.
Tues 14th	Pleasant. Stephen E. came home today unwell. Mrs K [Kelley, in Fowler] better.
Wed 15th	Pleasant. Walked to Uncle Durfey's, carried my Babe most of the way. it was too much for me. Found Aunt better but feeble.
Thurs 16th	Cloudy colder. Mrs. Sampson's child died last night. Braiding.
Fryd 17th	Stormy and tedious. Amir Otis and family, two Africans, took supper here. Mrs. O had walked six miles. They had not called on account of Measles. A poor family, I suspect. Braiding straw.
Sat. 18th	Cold. Mr. E. finished the flax 22 lbs. Finished Braiding straw.
Sun 19th	Stormy, almost sick. Oh how heart rending to see my partner so stupid[.] my little ones coming on to the stage and neither of us capable of training them up in the way they should go.
Mond 20th	Rainy. Roswell E and William came to our house. R and Stephen [Eastman brothers] spent the night. Mr. E. put rockers onto a chair for me.
Tues 21st	Cold. Washed, Ironed. Mr. Oliver's little Forbes buried today, Measles.
Wed 22nd	Pleasant. Baked Hatchled 22 lb of flax once over. Brother Lee & Sister Betsey are worse of the measles, near a consumption, I fear.
Thurs 23rd	Cloudy. My Babe very uneasy[.] the most I have done is to spin five knots of shoe thread. Small gains indeed.
Fryd 24th	Rainy P.M. sewed some on a hat. Father E. spent the night with us for the first time on account of the high wind and rain.
Sat. 25th	Pleasant. Hulburt done work for us for the present. Colder.
Sund 26th	Pleasant. Not very well but numbers around me are sick.

Mond 27th	Cold. Hulburt took leave. Undertook to finish. Hatchelling. My babes were both so cross I could do nothing but tend them.
Tues 28th	Cold. finished Hatchelling at midnight, very tired indeed.
Wed 29th	Snows. Washed. The measles are still raging about us.
Thurs 30th	Cold. Ironed, mending etc. Mr. Amos Hazen lost a child, measles.
Fryd 31st	Pleasant. Miss Susan Selah buried today of the measles[.]

April 1826

Sat. 1st	Cold. Mrs. Harrington was yesterday blessed with a daughter.
Sund 2nd	Pleasant. headache. Washed this eve on account of my Babe sleeping nights and uneasy days. Read but little. Stupid.
Mond 3rd	Pleasant. Had an agreeable visit from Sister Sophrona. Rode to Mr. Rockwell's on an errand. Mr. E. began to tap the maples.
Tues 4th	Pleasant. Finished my little Henry's hat. Ironed, mending etc.
Wed 5th	Pleasant. Made a cap for my Babe. Saw a fox in pursuit of hens.
Thurs 6th	Cooler, little snow. Spun shoe thread. Mrs. McAllister took [tea] with me.
Fryd 7th	Cloudy. Mr. E sugared off ninety Lbs of sugar. Washed some.
Sat. 8th	Pleasant. A.M., high winds & some rain through the night. Visited Father E's on horseback. Very tired & almost sick. Mrs. Hazen buried today of the measles. Heard of the death of Mr. Chubb.
Sund 9th	Rainy morn, pleasant eve, but a slothful creature indeed.
Mond 10th	Cold. Baked, spun some. David & Sophrona moved to the other house.
Tuesd 11th	Pleasant. Mr. Hulburt, Mr. A Osgood came here this eve to work.
Wed 12th	Cool. I hear nothing but one continual run of ridicule.

Thurs 13th	Pleasant. A pedlar dined with us purchased Essence of wintergreen, transparent soap, thread. Binding shoes. B.E. called. Washed some.
Fryd 14th	Pleasant. Visited by Miss Susan Western, Cynthia McAllister. Mr. Wilkinson supp'd with us. sick of having Hulburt about.
Sat 15th	Pleasant. Visited by Mother Easman & Sophrona. heard of a Mr. Bradely cutting his throat at Potsdam yesterday. Spent the eve with us.
Sun 16th	Rainy. Spent the day in idleness and discontent, unhappy.
Mond 17th	Pleasant, warm. Betsey spent the day with me. Rainy evening.
Tues 18th	Baked. Betsey quite sick. My health is not very good. my joints are weak and sore, I know not the cause of it. Rheumatism with drowsiness[.]
Wed 19th	Pleasant. Finished making sugar. Made vinegar. visited Sophrona.
Thurs 20th	Cold, snow flurries. Prepared for weaving. Do but very little but look after my little Boy, who runs to the barn every change he gets.
Fryd 21st	Snows again. Washed some. Wove little. Very unwell and lame.
Sat. 22nd	Snow. Done little or nothing. Left my Babes with Sophrona and called over to see Mrs. Rockwell. Found her very low, discouraged.
Sund 23rd	Very Pleasant. but my mind is rolling like the tumultuous sea and dare not ask for a place of rest and yet there is not one place of safety and I fear I never shall reach it.
Mond 24th	Cloudy. Had a very large washing today. Baked, etc. Very tired.
Tues 25th	Cloudy. Ironed little. Cleared dooryard some, but almost sick.
Wed 26th	Cloudy. wove little. Visited by S.E. lost my thimble. Mr E. ploughing
Thurs 27th	Cloudy & cool. Visited by Miss L. Newton. Ironed, wove some.
Fryd 28th	Pleasant. made half barrel of soap today. Thanks to my God for his goodness.
Sat. 29th	Showers of rain. Oh that they were of grace and righteousness.

Sund 30th Pleasant. Uncle & Aunt Brooks called. Oh Lord wilt thou assist them to set a better example for their little ones on the Sabbath[.] And may I not for mine and my partner & him for me.

May 1826

Mond 1st Cloudy. Baked. Have the Rheumatism in my joints, & fingers.

Tuesd 2nd Washed, starched and ironed. Mary E. commenced a school yesterday in this district and Betsey in the East one, Hopkinton.

Wed 3rd Warm. Wove some. A Wolf hunt for naught. Mr. E. came home, was very sick through the night. Mr A. Hopkinson a visit to Sister Betsey from Ogdensburg.[73] Mr Wells buried a babe.

Thurs 4th Rainy. Baked gingerbread, pound cake, etc. Mary took tea[.]

Fryd 5th Showers. Scoured and cleaned my house. gathered ground pine.

Sat 6th Showers. Almost sick, done but very little and that to no profit.

Sund 7th Showers. Scarcely able to sit up. read Oliver Hulbard's Sermons.

Mond 8th Pleasant. Washed. Bought and read the Narrative of the three Brothers that were executed at Buffalo for the Murder of John Love[.][74]

Tues 9th Pleasant. Ironed. Wove one yd Diaper. It appears as though I never work.

Wed 10th Pleasant. Mr. E. almost worn out with labor while I do nothing.

Thurs 11th Pleasant. Mrs. Chase blessed with a daughter. Mrs. Rockwell, Mrs. Flower visited me. Called over to Mr R & Mrs. R. out of health.

Fryd 12th Cloudy. Had a raging fire all around us but God preserved.

Sat. 13th Rainy. wove some. Called over to the other house to tea to see Mary.

Sund 14th Some rain. My Babe three months old, weighs 13½ lbs.

Mond 15th Very warm. Washed. Mr. E commenced planting. I have hard cold.

Tues 16th	Very warm. cleared flax seed on a reed. Wove some. Mr. A. Osgood done work here and I rejoice to be alone with my family.
Wed 17th	Rainy. Wove some. Starched, Ironed, plated caps to lend. Black flies thick.
Thurs 18th	The flies and musketoes are almost insufferable. Ironed, sewing. Baked. sowed onions and Lettuce. Miss M. Lewis & Miss B. Newton called[.]
Fryd 19th	Pleasant. Wove some. Sister Mary called this eve from her school.
Sat 20th	Smoaky. Washed & ironed some. Visited by Mary. Making a bonnet.
Sund 21st	Pleasant and warm. Attended meeting. Once more heard Mr. Wilkinson preach from these words, A.M.: So teach us to number our days as to apply our hearts until wisdom; P.M.: For I have learned to be content, etc. Two excellent sermons. Will God be pleased to assist us in wisdom and contentment for a contented mind is a continual feast.
Mond 22nd	Pleasant. Enjoyed my mind better than usual. Cut off the seed end of potatoes for planting, five Bushels[.] God is still kind.
Tuesd 23rd	Pleasant. Weaving. Mr. Flower to work here. God is merciful to us.
Wed 24th	Pleasant. Washed. Wove ¾ of a yard. How charitable is God to me & mine.
Thurs 25th	Pleasant. Worked in the garden some. Wove some, Baked, picked wool.
Fryd 26th	Pleasant. Wove one yard. Ironed, starched. My Babe is a sweet peaceable child and I trust will prove a blessing if trained up in the way she should go. Will God assist us therein.
Sat 27th	Fine, showers. Weaving. Sister M. [Mary] came home to spend the Sabbath.
Sund 28th	Cloudy. I sit with a guilty conscience for not performing my duty to my God, my family. Mr. E gone to Uncle Brook's. Oh God wilt thou hear the prayer of my heart and teach him to set a better example before me, my children, & the world, also quietly.
Mond 29th	Rainy and Cold. Finished the long web of Diaper that has been in the way so long. Thanks to my God for his goodness to me and mine

Tues 30th Pleasant, visited Uncle Brooks. Aunt is comfortable as could be expected[.] She has another little daughter, born last night.

Wed. 31st Pleasant. Spent the day with Mrs. A. Rockwell. almost sick.

June 1826

Thurs 1st Baked. Picked some wool. Mrs. Chase very sick indeed, with the measles. Her life is short unless God pleases to lend her a helping hand.

Fryd 2nd Fine growing season. Picking wool slowly. I think we shall call our sweet Babe Mary Elizabeth. may she be blessed with piety as those were of old time. she is now quiet and agreeable, too good for me.

Sat. 3rd Pleasant. my health is poor or else I am extremely lazy. I think both. Mr. Eastman's health is very poor. Called in the Doctor to see him. Took tea with us. Broke a tooth twice for me. Sister M. came to spend the Sabbath.

Sund 4th Rainy Mr. E took an emetic, I fear to little effect. distressed him much.

Mond 5th Washed some. Baked. Mr. E rather better. How many mercies we enjoy.

Tues 6th Pleasant. Picking wool. Called over to Mr. Rockwell's this eve. Mrs. R blessed with only Son. may he be a blessing to them in their declining years.

Wed 7th Showers. Almost sick. Mrs Sampson's life is not expected, measles.

Thurs 8th Pleasant. Visited Aunt Brooks. Found her in a dangerous condition. despairing of life with without hope in a Saviour. Lord, wilt thou convict and convert her even at the eleventh hour. Took tea at Mr. R.

Fryd 9th Cloudy. Mr. E. gone to Parishville to the Machine Mill etc[.] Aunt better.

Sat. 10th Pleasant. Mr. Converse['s] son died of the measles today, yet we go on to sin[.]

Sund 11th Showery. visited Aunt Brooks. She is, I think, going to her long home.

Mond 12th Pleasant. Washed. How thankful ought I to be for health while others sick. my Babe weights 14½[.]

Tues 13th	Pleasant indeed. Good season so far but sickness still prevails greatly[.]
Wed 14th	Cloudy. Ironing, sewing etc. Maria D [Durfey] spent the P.M. with me. I went with my Babes and spent the night at Uncle Durfey's. God is good.
Thurs 15th	Pleasant. Picked a few [wild] Strawberries. Returned home. Aunt Brook's life is not expected. Oh, God, wilt thou not be a Father to her little children.
Fryd 16th	Pleasant. Sewing. Mr. E gone to the village. Miss L. Newton, T. Bell, M.E. called.
Sat. 17th	Pleasant. Colouring with Copperas. Mrs Sampson is likely to live.
Sund 18th	Pleasant. read Thornton Abbey[.] a very entertaining book indeed.[75]
Mond 19th	Pleasant. Scarcely able to sit up. My Babe unwell. I am not worth much[.]
Tues 20th	Rainy. Baked. Mr. Oliver and James O came to begin their job of slashing eight acres. Left his family sick[.] an unfortunate man.
Wed 21st	Pleasant. spooling. I am so drowsy I can scarcely keep awake to eat or work.
Thurs 22nd	Pleasant. Baked and Washed. Five men to dinner but I am nothing & lazy[.]
Fryd 23rd	Cloudy. Baked again. cleared my house etc. Oh that I could say home.
Sat. 24th	Rainy. sewing all day. Mary E. called home again from her school.
Sund 25th	Showers. Took a walk in one of them, became very wet. Aunt Brooks, I fear, will not live but a few days longer. Oh, my God, wilt thou support her through death's iron gate into the heavenly Jerusalem. Thunder.
Mond 26th	Very Rainy. Sewing. Aunt Brooks little easier this morning.
Tues 27th	Frequent showers. Three Mr. Olivers work here. Mr. E. killed a calf. Visited by Mrs. E. My Babe very sick this evening. she is a blessing far too great for me.
Wed. 28th	Showers in the P.M. Rode over to see Aunt Brooks[.] she was thought to be dying, this morning rather easier, but, alas, she must die. I must give up my dear friend and confidant. She will never converse with me again. Her senses are broken, her ideas are scattering and not a consolating word that she is prepared but I must give her up to a just God. Oh that I might profit by her death. What a tender sympathizing friend shall I lose, but what is my loss compared to that of my

dear Uncles and her dear children. Mr. Brownell and I sat up with her all night. Almost sick myself.

Thurs 29th Returned home. Had eight men to get dinner for and washed.

Fryd 30th Pleasant. Not well. After puking freely, feel better. Received information this morning that Aunt was supposed to be on the very brink of eternity. Father E carried me and my Babe over immediately. But alas, her speech is gone. never no never shall we again hear her pleasant voice. To us she is no more yet her life is not gone. Not one anxious look, not one parting kiss, not even a last Farewell but lies stupidly waiting the Lingering approach of death. If she has the sense of life, she does not make it manifest. So she has lived through the day and night. We have all sat by her expecting to see her breath leave her body and her departing should plunge into Eternity until the morning has arrived and she yet lives.

July 1826

Sat 1st Pleasant. Aunt appears to be rapidly falling into the icy arms of death. At about seven she filled with phlegm and appeared as if to was to strangle her to death. Uncle took a swab and cleared her throat and mouth as fast as it filled, until it ceased. She lived until nine when she died without a struggle or a groan. An awful spectacle of death but after her mouth and eyes were closed, she looked more natural and pleasant. I staid until she was decently laid out in plain Muslin and returned home. Mrs. Flower and Miss Bell spent the P.M. with me. I am not far from insanity. Oh wilt thou be pleased to take my life with my senses and not leave me a living affliction to my family. My little son is gone to Mr. E's.

Sund 2nd Very warm. Attended Funeral. Left my Babe with Mrs. Chase. Mr [Wilkinson] preached from these: Let us live the life of the righteous for the end of that man is peace.

Mond 3rd Pleasant. washed a little, but almost sick. Mr. Oliver finished his job of slashing for us. How thankful ought I to be that my dear husband does not have to work out for his bread.

Tues 4th Cloudy. Visited at Father E's today. Had a tooth drawn by Dr. S. [Sprague][.]

Wed 5th Pleasant. mended some. Visited at Mr. Flower's. Uncle Brooks called.

Thurs 6th Pleasant. Washed. I wish I had any ambition to work. Pleasant. Called over to Mr. Sampson's. Engaged Miss Maryann Heath to spin for me when she is done work for them. Called to Mr. Chases.

Fryd 7th	Pleasant. Ironed, mended clothes, but I fear I have not earned my wages.
Sat 8th	[No entry.]
Sund 9th	Another Sabbath has arriven with no better deeds.
Mond 10th	Pleasant Commenced making small cheeses of three curds. churned, washed Mr. E. commenced Haying for his Father.
Tues 11th	Pleasant. My little Boy very sick all day, high fever.
Wed 12th	Pleasant. Drew in a web of linen. Baked mince pies etc.
Thurs 13th	Cool. Visited by Mrs Dewey. I believe a strange person indeed.
Fryd 14th	Pleasant. Wove a little but have no ambition or strength.
Sat. 15th	Pleasant. Mrs. Rockwell spent the day with me. Mending.
Sund 16th	Showers. Spent most of the A.M. in sleep. How can I sleep on the brink of destruction[.] Oh, God, wilt thou rouse us up to do thy will and to live so like the beast[.]
Mond 17th	Cloudy. Spend my time choring and tending Babes. my little one weighs Sixteen pounds. Uncle Brooks called. Wrote a letter to Mrs. B. Brownall an unfortunate woman.
Tues 18th	Cloudy. Left my children to Father E's. Rode to Hopkinton. ten yards three-fourths of Calico. Mr. Weed looks as though he had not long to live. Spent the P.M. at Mr Covey's. Sister Betsey came home with me and spent the night.
Wed 19th	Pleasant. Sister B returned to her school. Made the skirt to my spencer. Mrs. Sprague's life is not expected.
Thurs 20th	Warm. Wove all day for less than a yard. Rotten fill in.
Fryd 21st	Rainy. Washed some. almost sick, almost discouraged.
Sat 22nd	Cloudy. Picked a few Berries to dry. Baked, largely. Prepared dinner for a Pedlar. Mending, etc. Thunder, lightning.

Sund 23rd Cloudy. Brother Roswell & Lee dined with us. Took a walk in the field which are richly laden with abundance but all this and a thousand other mercies which we are blessed with are nothing to be compared with the poor mendicant that is blessed with sweet Religion. This is the blessing I crave for me and my family[.] without it I cannot be happy.

Mond 24th Pleasant. Visited at Father E's. Work some on my gown. Miss Maryann Heath came to spin for me while I am lazy.

Tues 25th Cloudy, a shower P.M. Visited Sister M's school. Spent the P.M. at C. Rockwell's. My new gown has been wet & soiled.

Wed 26th Baked pies, etc. How vain are all things here below. Pleasant.

Thurs 27th Pleasant. Almost sick. Hired my washing done. Oh, shame Phebe!

Fryd 28th Ironed. Mr. E. came home to live once more. Have cucumbers.

Sat. 29th Pleasant. Prepared dinner for ten men, unexpectedly.

Sund 30th Pleasant. Went as far as Mr. Flower's for meeting. Was none.

Mond 31st Showers. Mr. G. Covey[.] Mr. Phelphs reaping. my web rotten.

August 1826

Tues 1st Cloudy, some rain. Wove a little but mostly [illegible word] Have green corn.

Wed 2nd Very warm. G.C. [G. Covey] J.P. [Jacob Phelps?] at work here today. Discouraged of work.

Thurs 3rd few drops of rain. visited by Miss Sophia R. Mother E. Mr R. [Rockwell] called.

Fryd 4th Pleasant. Miss Mary Ann Heath gone to Mr. R. [Rockwell] two days.

Sat. 5th Cloudy but no rain. Mending all day. Mr. Thomas Lee and wife come in from Cornwall, Vermont. J. Osgood left. Father's.

Sund 6th Cloudy. Great want of rain but none came. Uncle Brooks called over. Mr. E gone to visit his Cousins at Father's. Heard that Grandmother Brooks had set her house on fire and fastened herself in her room probably calculating to burn up.

Mond 7th	Pleasant. Cleaned the house with Mary Ann's help. Visited this P.M. by Mr & Mrs Lee, Father & Mother E. Baked pies
Tuesd 8th	Pleasant. Starched, Ironed, etc. Visited at M. Rockwell's Became acquainted with Mr. Richard, Miss Maria Douglass of Cornwall.
Wed 9th	Pleasant. Almost sick of visiting. Visited at Father E's. Betsey came home with me. Mary Ann, poor girl, has got to go home again. Her Mother is sick and unable to do without her. Took leave of Mr. Lee. He has bought Brother David's house and farm.
Thurs 10th	Pleasant. Washed. Mary Ann gone home. once more alone with my family.
Fryd 11th	Great want of rain, the crops are drying in the field, yet blessed be God we have enough and to spare. Think. O, thanks!
Sat. 12th	Cloudy. Baked. Spun[.] sore eyes[.] Oh how do we live? Stupid.
Sund 13th	Pleasant. Mary spent the day. Mary Ann returned. Wrote a Letter to Father. Heard Mr. Sampson's house was burnt. I have a heavy mind.
Mond 14th	Pleasant. Mr. Austin from Vt. gave me a letter from Brother Isaac [Orvis]. Wrote to Eleazar. Picked fourteen quarts of Blackberries.
Tues 15th	A few drops of rain. Washed. Visited at Uncle D's. Mr. Peck's sawmill raised[.]
Wed 16th	Pleasant. sick today. Received a Letter from Harriet Charter of Castleton. Wrote to Mrs. Taylor. Stephen E. came here today.
Thurs 17th	Pleasant. Not able to do my work today. a number called.
Fryd 18th	Pleasant. My Babe is unwell and so troublesome I cannot do much else but tend her. Visited by Mrs. Covey, D. Dewey.
Sat. 19th	Very Smoaky. Done a few chores. a gentleman most of the night.
Sund 20th	Pleasant, but my mind is uneasy, My peace is disturbed. My companion who ought to be my guide in the path of duty is spending the Sabbath at the Mill Pond while I am left to view the situation of my friend and family. Received a Letter from Mrs. Betsey Brownell. Wrote one in return.

Mond 21st	Pleasant. Washed & Baked. My Babe I think is sick indeed.
Tues 22nd	Great signs of rain but all fail. Vegetation suffers.
Wed 23rd	Cloudy. Can do nothing but my chores and attend my Babe.
Thurs 24th	Cloudy some part of the day and then clears off. My Babe worse.
Fryd 25th	Pleasant. If it were not on account of teeth I should fear of losing my Babe.
Sat. 26th	Cloudy. My Babe is very near the Dysentery. Henry almost sick.
Sund 27th	Pleasant. Sister Betsey called over from her school she has taken.
Mond 28th	A few drops of rain. Wove all one day for three-fourths yd.
Tues 29th	Baked. I find I cannot get along with work so well when I have a hired girl as I can without, although she does chores.
Wed. 30th	A little shower. My Babe has one tooth cut through.
Thurs. 31st	Pleasant. cool nights and warm days. Mr. E cutting his corn.

September 1826

Fryd 1st	Pleasant. Baked. Washed floors, ceilings etc. Disappointed of company. The drought and grasshoppers are destructive to everything in Vermont. Cattle are turned into cornfields to save their lives and many die. grain is very dear.
Sat 2nd	Cloudy a number called. done but little indeed. Unwell.
Sun 3rd	Cloudy, a few drops of rain. A number called. My mind is as uneasy as the boisterous Ocean. I find no rest.
Mon 4th	Cloudy. Wove a little. It looks dismal to see a web always in the loom[.]
Tues 5th	Some rain out in a shower. Washed. Called over to Uncle Durfey's.
Wed 6th	Cloudy. Uncle Brooks came after me to go to his house. Miss Caroline Hayden is very sick at his house. I spend the day, sat up through the night with her. Poor girl I fear she will die. dog killed[.]

Thurs 7th	Pleasant. Baked, washed floors, prepared for company. Disappointed.
Fryd 8th	Pleasant. Mr & Mrs Wilkinson visited us this P.M. Mr & Mrs Flower in the evening, but again disappointed of other company.
Sat 9th	Pleasant again. Baked, scrubbed etc for the same company and none came. I hope they will not send me word again this week.
Sund 10th	Cloudy. I attend no meeting. Called over to Uncle Brook's, found Caroline H. rather better. Mr Hopkins called while I was gone. Mary called. I spent the night alone with my Babes. wrote a lengthy letter Miss Lucinda James, Cornwall [VT].
Mond 11th	Cloudy. Wove all day for one yard. spun ten knots this evening.
Tues 12th	Pleasant. Wove some. Visited by Harriet D. [Durfey] Mary Ann H. [Heath] returned. Spun five knots this evening. My cough is better.
Wed 13th	Cloudy. Mrs Heath died this day. Finished my web. Sewing until 2 o'clock. They have a dance to the other house. My husband is there. Oh that he were at home attending prayers with his family but alas there is no hopes for such things.
Thurs 14th	Cloudy. Washed some. Preparing to attend funeral. My Babe sick.
Fryd 15th	Cold. Attended funeral. My Babe worried so I could not hear much.
Sat 16th	Cold, frost. Spun some My Babe needs great care, hard cold.
Sund 17th	Hard frost. my mind is uneasy the whole time. There is no peace to the wicked, saith my God. Mary Ann H. [Heath] spent the night.
Mond 18th	Cloudy. Gathered weeds for colouring. Baked largely. My poor Babe cries continually unless I have her in my arms which makes it difficult to get along.
Tues 19th	Pleasant. Mr. E broke a leg to one of his pigs. Obliged to kill it. Baked it and mince pies. Preparing all day for his departure.
Wed 20th	Pleasant. General Training at Norfolk. Mr. E. gone. scoured wooden vessels, washed floors, sewed some. Finished knitting one pair of socks [first] this fall. My Babe cries yet very much.
Thurs 21st	Warm. Washed all day as fast as I could at the brook and let my Babe cry only when it was necessary. I should take her.

Fryd 22nd Rainy day, and night. Spun five knots. Churned for first time this fall. Ironed, etc. My cough is better.

Sat 23rd Rainy. Mended all day. Mr [E.] caught a wolf in a trap of Lee's. has half the bounty. Carried the head to Stockholm. Mrs Sprague departed this life about ten o'clock this day.

Sund 24th Pleasant. Read the History of Zoa, who released Rodomond from a pit in her Father's garden, the Banyan in disguise.[76] They fled from the Malays, this beautiful female Indian afterwards became his wife. Read also Lisette and Login who were deeply in love.[77] Login a nobleman, Lisette a peasant daughter, the only child of her widowed Mother[.] at length Lisette by the purest love yielded her innocence to her lover. He then left her under the pretence of the army. instead of which he married a rich widow. Poor Lisette drowned herself in consequence of her lost lover and the mother her daughter.

Mond 25th Pleasant. Washed and Baked. Walked to Uncle D's. Found Aunt D very sick indeed. Returned. Headache.

Tues 26th Rainy. Pain in my head. Done but very little. Scoured.

Wed 27th Cloudy. Walked to Uncle D's. Wove a yd, and half for her. Did chores until one o'clock. Uncle Brook & Caroline H spent the night. Aunt rather better. My Babe is worrisome.

Thurs 28th Rainy. Wove five yards[.] they have now Louise Newton.

Fryd 29th Rainy. Came home almost sick. Spooled a little.

Sat. 30th Baked, washed. Roswell, H.E. spent the night with us.

October 1826

Sund 1st Rainy, Read the History of Rome that mighty empire.[78]

Mond 2nd Pleasant. Mr. Thomas Lee and his family arrived and took possession of his dwelling, a few rods from us. Visited them.

Tuesd 3rd Pleasant. Finished spooling my web of woolen. Mrs. Lee sick, spent the evening with them. Ate a couple of pears.

Wed 4th Warm and pleasant. Baked, washed floors etc. My Babe cross[.]

Thurs 5th Warm. Had a small load of Apples presented us, I fear unwelcome.

Fryd 6th Cloudy. wove last evening and today eleven yards. Hired Mary Ann H [Heath] to attend my Babe for one dollar per week.

Sat. 7th Finished my web. Coloured yellow. Hard showers.

Sund 8th Pleasant. Mr. Stephen Wead buried at Malone in the Masonic order. Finished reading Goldsmith's "Rome, It's rise and downfall." Mr & Mrs Lee spent the evening.

Mond 9th Pleasant. Finished spinning wool, double & twisted yarn etc.

Tues 10th Pleasant. Baked twice. Two travellars spent the night from Vt.

Wed 11th Pleasant. Called over to Mr. Rockwells and to Uncle Durfeys to get a reed. Drew in my web. Wove three yards. Uncle Brooks called.

Thurs 12th Pleasant. Wove eight and half yards. Washed floors.

Fryd 13th Pleasant. Wove seven yds, finished weaving my woollen cloth.

Sat 14th Pleasant. Walked to Uncle Brooks. Worked until I was tired of staying alone. I then called over to Mr. Smith's, took tea, returned home.

Sund 15th Cloudy. Read the Life of Xavier, a pious Christian.[79] Melancholy.

Mond 16th Rainy. Mending. Almost sick and tired out. Very high winds.

Tues 17th Pleasant. Put in a web of twilling and bags. mended some.

Wed 18th Pleasant. Aunt Durfey rode as far as our house but I fear she never will again.

Thurs 19th Rainy. Mr E. sick all night. Come to Parishville to Mill unable [illegible word]

Fryd 20th Pleasant. Gathered all the garden sauce. Mr. E. very sick and sore.

Sat. 21st Rainy. Mr. E. no better. I try everything in my power to retry him and his hard cough. He is almost discouraged. sweating[.]

Sund 22nd Cloudy. Mr E. not so well. Made him a syrup. Uncle B called.

Mond 23rd	Pleasant, but cold. Mr E. much worse, sent for spirits etc. I have as much as I can do to wait upon him, the children and keep potatoes boiled for the Hogs. Churned. I sit up the most of the night. Almost tired out.
Tues 24th	Cold and Cloudy. Mr. E. not so well but insisted upon my leaving him to attend a quilting. I did at Mrs Flowers. I shall not again.
Wed 25th	Cloudy & cold. Mr E better A.M. worse evening. Visited by Miss Denton from England.
Thurs 26th	Stormy. Mr E had a distressed night, burning at the stomach; cold, chills, coughing and puking. Baked pies. very unwell, almost sick self.
Fryd 27th	My dear companion no better. He thinks he never shall be. I mean to [do] everything in my power for him but nothing but the arm of God can save him. I have hope of his recovery[.]
Sat. 28th	Pleasant. Dr. Parker called to visit Mr. E. told him his case was alarming. Left him 2 potions of Jalap, Gum Camphire Coal and Caland salts of tartar[.]
Sund 29th	Cloudy. I fear my dear companion is going to his long home. Oh God wilt thou have compassion on his precious soul.
Mond 30th	Cold. Mother E. came and spent the day with me. Mr & Mrs Flower the evening. Baked. Mr F has lately experienced a hope in God.
Tues 31st	Washed. Pleasant. Mother returned. Mr E no better, raises immense phlegm[.]

November 1826

Wed 1st	Pleasant. A.M. Rainy eve. Sister Mary spent the night. [Mr.] E. no better.
Thurs 2nd	Cold and windy. Mr. E. much worse. Unless he gets immediate help he must die. I am almost tired out. Mary washed.
Fryd 3rd	Pleasant. Mr E some better. My Babe badly burnt.
Sat. 4th	Pleasant. Mr. E appears to be on the gain. Uncle D calls. Father took home my little Boy for a while to favor me.
Sund 5th	Pleasant. some one in all day; Mr. T.S. Abbot[,] Mr & Mrs D.[,] Dr P [Pettibone] called.

Mond 6th	Rainy. Mary Ann Heath worked for me today. Mr. E better.
Tues 7th	Pleasant. Mr. E recovers slowly. I am favoured with health.
Wed 8th	High winds and some rain. I work too hard for my strength.
Thurs 9th	Rainy. Mr E. very weak, yet sat up most of the day. Procured Mehlock gum for plaster. Have to work night and day.
Fryd 10th	Rainy. Mr. E walked out to the door. Oh Lord wilt thou convict us of our manifold Sins and covert our hearts to thee.
Sat 11th	Pleasant. Washed. Uncle Brooks called. Mr. E. much better.
Sund 12th	Cloudy and Cold. Mr. E and myself walked slowly (though presumptuous for him) to meeting on the South Road. Heard a powerful sermon by Elder Culver form these words. "Why, what hath he done" Mr Seymour Flower, Miss Lovina Moon were baptized by immersion. May they never cloud their profession.
Mond 13th	Pleasant. Spent most of the day at Father E's. Brought home our boy.
Tues 14th	Cloudy. My Babe is so worrysome I do nothing but chores.
Wed 15th	Cloudy. The Lord appears to be doing wonders about us. Oh that our hearts might be renewed by divine grace.
Thurs 16th	Almost sick. My children very peevish, almost discouraged.
Fryd 17th	Some snow. Mr. Flower called over on purpose to talk with my dear partner, to have him come out of the miry clay.
Sat. 18th	Pleasant. I long to have the time come when I can see some signs of religion at home, family worships etc. I trust I will.
Sunday 19th	[No entry]
Mond 20th	Stormy. Making Leather Mitten. Spent the eve at Mr. Lee's.
Tues 21st	Some snow. Cut out a new flannel frock for myself. Made M. one.
Wed 22nd	Snow'd. Mr. E attended my Babe today. I washed. An Irishman spent the night. Poor fellow longed for his native country.

Thurs 23rd Cold. Sewing on my gown. Do but little of anythin[g] but tend Babe[.]

Fryd 24th Cold and windy. Spent the P.M. & A.M. with Uncle Durfey.

Sat. 25th Rainy. Mrs. Lee spent the P.M. Almost sick. I fear the Lord will pass us by, and not call us to repentance. God forbid that it should be so.

Sund 26th Read Milton's Paradise Lost. Mr E attended conference this eve. I hope the Lord has seen fit to awaken his mind in some measure. He for the first time attempted family prayer. Oh Lord may he Persevere and never omit it again in life. I thank my God that he has heard the prayer of my heart and thus far answered it. Oh that I was more engaged in his cause.

Mond 27th Mr. Flower called and prayed with us this morning. Agreeable.

Tues 28th Mr. E. appears serious, reads his Bible, prays in his family.

Wed 29th Pleasant for the season. The Lord is doing wonders in this place.

Thurs 30th My mind is like a troubled Sea whose waters cannot rest.

December 1826

Fry 1st No snow yet. Yet my heart is colder than snow or ice. Dear Saviour, wilt thou warm it with they love that I may praise thee.

Sat 2nd I think I may say with propriety as Jacob did surely, "the Lord is in this place." It is none other than the house of God and this is the very gate of heaven, glorious time.

Sund 3rd Stormy. I was in hopes the family altar would never be again neglected in our family. I was obliged to retire on account of a sick headache. When Mr. E. returned from his visit at the other house, he retired without prayer. I lament that he should so soon fall away. Assist me, Oh Lord, to pray for him and myself.

Mond 4th Cold. Washed a little. my Babe is so worrysome that I can do nothing[.]

Tues 5th Some snow. Finished my flannel gown. Making my children's . . .

Wed 6th Pleasant. Uncle Brooks called over about one o'clock morn to have me do some work for his motherless children. My Babe was so unwell I could not. Her neck is badly swollen. I know not the cause. Baked twice with my Babe in my arms. Very inconvenient. Mumps.

Thurs 7th Wet and Lowry. Thanksgiving. Mrs Lee spent the evening with me. Mr E & Lee attended meeting at schoolhouse. I sat up all night to prepare for meeting tomorrow. Finished my Babe's Bonnet.

Fryd 8th Very wet and muddy indeed. Mr E & myself walked and carried my Babe to the other district, attended meeting. Heard eleven give their relations to the Church, viz; Mrs. Huldah Chase, Parker & Daniel Rose, Mrs. Elizabeth Capil [Capel], Henry Capil [Capel], Lorenzo Hoyt, Lucinda Brownell, Betsey Newton, Josepher Brownell, Patience Simonds, Martha Welch. Returned home after sunset. Went to Mr. Lee's and brought home my little boy. I was by this time very tired indeed with a violent headache. It seemed as though I could not sit up when Mrs. Lee came and insisted on my spending the evening at their house with Mr & Mrs Flower. I told her I felt as though I could not go; however, I did. My visit was not agreeable, for it was all twitting and ridiculing the Church to which I belonged. I was accused of having a Baptist heart and a Congregational head by my husband. Another says "Samuel will bring her over to be a Baptist." Another says "what are you going to do with your children? They have not been sprinkled, etc." In the frame of mind I was then in and not being able to sit up, disappointed of an agreeable religious visit, (it being Rainy, tarried late), it seemed as if my heart would burst. I waited for my Babe to awaken as long as I could and left her for her Pa'a to bring home when the rain ceased. As soon as I came into the road I burst into tears and prayers until I reached home, that if I was in an error respecting doctrine, that God would direct me in the right way. When I went from home I felt in my mind if I was alone as to sentiment that Church and all the object of my visiting this evening was thinking possibly sooner or later I might united with my husband in agreement. possibly some light might be thrown in my darkened mind. But alas I am much farther from it than ever. I feel as if I had not a friend in the world, my nearest friend against me. But, oh, my God, may I not judge but may God forgive them for they know not what they do. I do not think they meant to injure my feelings but to make me dislike every order but theirs. But their lack of charity drove me from it more tha[n] my Bible. almost sleepless night.

Sat 9th Cold, began to snow some. Mrs Rockwell called over. Mr E, H.F. attended church meeting. Mr F. [Flower] spent the evening, she he did not know but my feelings had been injured & he was willing to acknowledge.

Sund 10th Snowed fast all day & night. Sister Betsey came this way alone to meeting and insisted upon my going with her. I knew not why. I have since learned that Elder Culver told her that I was going forward in Baptism. Strange report. She & sister Sophrona were immersed and twenty one others. Oh, God, wilt thou keep them in the strait and narrow path until they should arrive at the Bar. Attended conference this eve but the expressions I heard on the way deprived my mind of that enjoyment I could wish.

Mond 11th Snows yet. Took my sewing, called over to Mr Lee's. Uncle Brooks came and brought his motherless children for me to keep a while and make them some clothes. My Babe is so afraid of them I must hold her all the time.

Tues 12th Snows some yet, the children are so noisy it seems as if I should be crazy[.]

Wed 13th Mrs Rockwell visited, Spooled and warped a Blanket. not well.

Thurs 14th Stormy. Made twenty doz of candles, sat up all night. Almost tired out[.]

Fryd 15th My family begin to want to go home. Uncle came back from his visit.

Sat 16th Rainy. Dismissed my little cousins after washing their clothes.

Sund 17th Rainy some. I want to do nothing but read my Bible. I wish we both might be more persevering. Mr. E. gone to conference. My mind is in such a frame that I have neglected writing.

Sund 31st Very stormy, snow very deep. Attended meeting. 24 baptized. Brother David, for one the work is still progressing.

January 1827

Mond 1st Very stormy. Mr. E. killed two Fawns. I read more than I work[.]

Sat 6th Pleasant. attended church meeting at Hopkinton village. staid all night at Father's. [all night] Heard the religious experience of twelve.

Sund 7th Pleasant. Attended meeting, Hopkinton. Saw ten immersed I have enjoyed my mind better than usual. Came home almost sick.

Mond 8th Pleasant. Visited this evening at Mr. C. Rockwells. L. Newton came home [with me].

Tues 9th Cold. Mr. E killed five hogs, the least weighed three hundred and thirty six. My Babe is troublesome, When I have anyone to help me. That it makes it unprofitable. sold one hog to T.L. [Thomas Lee].

Sund 14th Spent the day at home but unfaithful. Visited this eve at Mr. Lee's. Mr E. gone to Conference, the snow very deep.

Mond 15th Cold. washed. Mary Ann Heath visited us again. Visited this eve at Uncle Durfey's. The reformation increases rapidly. The weather is so cold and the snow so deep there is but little done.

Sund 28th Attend no meetings lately. Mr Arnold called, from Vt.

Mond 29th Stormy. Visited the Ladies at the other house. Spent eve.

Tues 30th Cold and stormy. Washed. Visited by Mr & Mrs Lee, Mr & Mrs Arnold Miss L. Eastman. Our conversation too much of the world. Oh, God, wilt thou incline my heart to thee[.]

Wed. 31st Very stormy indeed. H.D. called today. Almost sick.

February 1827

Thurs 1st Cold. Visited at Mr. Rockwell's[.] Mr Culver called a few minutes.

Fryd 2nd Cold. Visited at Brother Es P.M. Uncle Durfey evening. almost tired out.

Sat 3rd Cold. Visited for the last time with our Vermont friends.

Sund 4th Pleasant. Twelve persons Baptized at Sodom. Attended conference at the schoolhouse. Oh, that I was more engaged.

Mond 5th Cold, stormy. Washed. Fourteen Baptized at the South Road.

Tues 6th Pleasant. My dear Mrs. Taylor visited me. Deacon T and Mr. E. attended the Consociation. Had an agreeable visit with my friend.

Wed 7th Cold. Visited at Uncle D with Mrs. T. from Stockholm. Two ordained for the ministry at Parishville. Visited at Mr. Covey's this eve. Oh that God would give them Religion and all their neighbors.

Thurs 8th Cold, almost sick. Visited by Mrs. Chase, Mrs. Lee. Dull & stupid.

Fryd 9th Cold. Endeavoring to weave on a Coverlet. Brother Kelly [Kelley] and Mr. Griffin spent the night with us. Sister Sally unwell.

Sat 10th Still Cold. Baked pies, washed floors. Wove half yard. Mr. Dowe called on us from Vt. Miss Lucy Harris, a cousin of Mr E's, died last of Jan after an illness of four days. She was delivered of a child in about minutes she died. [May] we take warning to Be also ready. How we be so stupid with regard to death.

Sund 11th Very tedious day. Spent the day as usual in a stupid manner.

Mond 12th Stormy. Washed some. Wove ¾ of a yd of coverlet. very cold days indeed.

Tues 13th Snowed all day. Wove some, starched, ironed caps. Mr. Kelly and Brother Lee, Mr Dowe visited us this eve. Heard of the death of Mr Ezra Smith, Newhaven, Vt. occasioned by falling from a beam of a Barn. Death cometh in an hour when we think not. My sweet babe is one year old this day. Oh, Lord, I would give her to thee. Ah that she may seek thee early and that thou would answer, forgive and defer not, but show mercy. Snow very deep.

Wed 14th Pleasant. Many called in and have wove but a trifle.

Thurs 15th Some snow and rain. Wove some. Finished Mary's flannel frock. I have enjoyed myself better than usual, yet not as I could wish.

Fryd 16th Somewhat stormy. wove some. Fried cakes. Visited by Mr. Pettibone, an agreeable minister, a firm Christian and exemplary man.

Sat 17th Very pleasant. Finished Sally's coverlet. Have the sick headache very hard. Sick night. We have no prayers at night.

Sund 18th Rainy. Not able to sit up much. Had no prayers today. read the Scriptures much. Mr. Hulburt spent most of A.M. My mind is more clear this evening than it ever was before respecting doctrine. Infant Baptism has been a dark subject for me to treat upon. It is now all light and clear.

Mond 19th Blustering. Sewing. Finished Mary's Cambrick shirt. Better.

Tues 20th Pleasant. Washed some, starched, ironed. Made a pair of pantalettes for Henry. Petticoat for Mary, etc. Preparing for a ride. Sister Mary, Brother Lee spent the night. I sat up all night.

Wed 21st Some snow and rain. Took our children and started for Fowler. Called at Potsdam, Canton, Russel. The Children sley sick, became wet and Cold. Arrived at Brother Kelly's [Daniel Kelly], found them in health but not religious.

Thurs 22nd	Stormy. Visited this eve at Mr. Comstalk [Comstock] & Earl's. Almost sick[.]
Fryd 23rd	Pleasant. Almost tired out. I like the place better than I expected. It is a very uneven country & that appears natural.
Sat. 24th	Pleasant. Cold. Returned home. Saw Mr. R. Dunshee at Potsdam. my Babe has a very sore mouth. I am not able to sit up.
Sund 25th	Thaws. Obliged to court the pillow today. Very unwell.
Mond 26th	Pleasant. Very unwell. Sewing on great coat. Mending some.
Tues 27th	Rainy. Washed woolen clothes. I fear I shall not be able to do much[.]
Wed 28th	Cold. Washed linen & Baked pies, Cake etc. Received a letter from S[.]

March 1827

Thurs 1st	Deep snow. scoured all day. Made a mat this evening.
Fryd 2nd	Very stormy indeed. Baked. Mr. Smith & Alexander McGary to work for us. Heard there were sixteen persons Baptized by immersion at Hopkinton on Wednesday. Yesterday, Parishville twenty-one.
Sat 3rd	Very cold. again. Visited at Mr. Searl's[.] Our family altar is forsaken entirely. No prayers nor thanks to our God. Oh how can we live so[.]
Sund 4th	Pleasant but Oh how stupid we live - no duties of the Christians - no not even a glimpse of it. Oh God forbid that we should so live. Oh, that we did but make it the business of our lives to serve God and obey his commands. For my part I wish to but I have been in hopes of my friend would accompany me but I have but little hopes. Therefore I must flee to the mountain nor tarry in all the plain. I have long lingered by the cold stream of Babylon with my harp, upon the willows hung but I wish not to tarry any longer, if I must go alone if it is not thy will, Oh God, that my friend should accompany me, Oh God, wilt thou assist me to persevere alone or be thee my Companion, my protector and my guide in the strait and narrow path that leads to joys on high. But my heart bleeds for myself and my companion. Oh God wilt thou not be entreated to call him home to thee, to seek thy face and favor and do all to thy glory. We attended conference this evening. I feel as if I was richly repaid for going, although I said nothing, but my heart was grieved for our unfaithfulness and rejoiced that we were more faithful. I pray God we might be up and doing.

Mond 5th	Very pleasant. visited Mrs. Lee. Returned very unwell indeed.
Tues 6th	High winds Mr. E gone to Town Meeting. Visited by Mrs. Lee and Mrs. Searls. Very sick A.M. I feel better this P.M. Mrs Lee had her looking glass broke yesterday into nine pieces by a chip.
Wed 7th	High wind, rain & snow. Visited by Mother E & Mrs. Rockwell.
Thursd 8th	Pleasant. Washed a little. I do not feel able to work. Read the narrative of James Pearse. Auction held on the goods of Stephen Wead[, Malone]. deceased. Mr. E attended.
Fryd 9th	Pleasant. Washed. Until night, I read considerable but I fear it is of little avail. I fear I am becoming more stupid. Oh God forbid that I should remain so.
Sat. 10th	Cloudy. heard that Aunt Nicholson had lost another child. Oh that God would sanctify this dispensation to their minds for good and to put their whole trust in the Lord. Brother Lee has come to tarry with us. Oh that God would convict his heart and bring him to a knowledge of the truth as it is in Jesus, so to all.
Sund 11th	Very pleasant, but my eyes are drowsy. I fear I shall not be faithful. Will God assist me to be more faithful to him.
Mond 12th	Rainy. Spread out my linen to whiten. Baked, mended etc.
Tues 13th	Very high winds, some snow. Washed, mended. Visited at Mr. Lee's, called over to Mr. Searls this evening. Why was it not my lot to live in want of the necessaries of life instead of this poor family[.]
Wed 14th	Stormy. Mending all day. Oh that I might amend my ways.
Thurs 15th	Pleasant. Mending. Mr. E attends the Wyen today. Mr Covey also[.]
Fryd 16th	Pleasant. Mending. Visited Mrs. Rockwell. almost tired out[.]
Sat. 17th	Pleasant. Mending. Not well today. My little boy has six teeth.
Sund 18th	Rainy. We attend no meeting, no prayer. Oh that we might.
Mond 19th	Washed. Cut straw for Hat. What am I without my God.
Tues 20th	Braded ten yards of straw. visited by L. Newton, a follower of Christ, I trust. Oh God wilt thou enable her to persevere in well doing.

Wed 21st Pleasant. finished a hat for Henry. Baked pies S.E. [Stephen or Sophrona Eastman?] called.

Thurs 22nd Colder. Braided but five yards. Very unwell. Brother R. [Roswell] called. Oh God, wilt enable him to bear with all persecutions and trials for thy sake with cheerfulness.

Fryd 23rd Cold. Braided eleven y'ds. Mr. E. attended meeting this eve. A Scotch missionary. Oh God, may it arouse up their minds.

Sat. 24th Pleasant. Finished Braiding straw, mending etc. I expect that Brother Lee [Eastman] will make it his home with us this season.

Sund 25th Cloudy, some rain. I staid with my little ones while Mr E. Attended Meeting at the Corners. Oh that I had more patience with them. It seems as if they would craze me often.

Mond 26th Smoaky & high winds. Washed. the snow wastes away fast.

Tues 27th High winds. Spooled & warped two webs. Made fifty yards of Cord. Heard there were six Baptized at the Brook. very warm.

Wed 28th Cold, rained, some snow. Mr. Smith commenced hewing timber for our barn. Mary Ann H. [Heath] spent the night with us.

Thurs 29th Pleasant, but Cool. My little boy very sick, teeth trouble him.

Fryd 30th Pleasant. Sewing. Oh that I might ever be on my guard with lye[.]

Sat. 31st Pleasant. Mr. S. gone home sewing[.] Oh how good is my God to me.

April 1827

Sund 1st Beautiful day. I spent most of the day with Mrs. Lee. Read the Christian Economy translated from the original in Greek of an old manuscript found in the land of Palmyra where St. John wrote his Revelations found with scroll of the Scriptures on a shelf. hewn from a rock in a cave. Composed of XI Chapters Mon. II Redemption 3rd Faith 4th. The first illuminations of divine grace. The means of Grace 1st prayers, 2nd Reading the Scriptures, 3rd The Lords Supper. 4th The fruits and marks of the spirit or evidence that the means of grace have proved successful 10th Temptation and persecution 11th. Death and Judgment. Oh that I might attend to it.

Mond 2nd Pleasant. Trying to clear the logs of our house from dust and webs.

Tues 3rd Pleasant. scalded bedsteads etc. My strength is not much.

Wed 4th Rainy. Drawing in a Blanket. Not very well. sold 65 lbs of pork[.]

Thurs 5th Pleasant. Wove some. Oh that I were more faithful.

Fryd 6th Pleasant. Made a little sugar yesterday. My babe not well.

Sat. 7th Pleasant. I intend if the Lord will to attend meeting tomorrow.

Sund 8th Cool. Pleasant. Walked to the four Corners heard Mr. Reynolds preach "Isaiah 33rd. 20th Look upon Zion, the City of our solemnity thine eyes shall see Jerusalem a quiet habitation, a tabernacle that shall not be taken down one of the stakes thereof shall ever be removed. Whither shall any of the cords be broken." Returned, took tea at Mr. Flower's. Almost tired out, I fear I shall not be able to do it again.

Mond 9th Pleasant. A.M. Rainy P.M. Sister Betsey went with me to the South schoolhouse[.] heard Mr. Safford preach "Zecharieh [Zachariah] 4th 7th "and he shall bring forth the headstone there with shoutings crying grace unto it." Mrs Oliver, Mary Ann Heath, Lucinda Allen were immersed. Returned to the house. It rained so. that we had an excellent Conference. Returned home. The wind blew trees down not far form us, but God was our protector.

Tues 10th Pleasant. Almost sick. Baked. Called over to Mr. Lee's.

Wed 11th Pleasant. Boiling sap for vinegar. Betsey returned home.

Thurs 12th Finished sugaring. Stored the tubs. Almost worn out.

Fryd 13th Pleasant. Mrs. Lee visited me. I am almost spiritless today.

Sat. 14th Clouds, very high wind. Saw a Rainbow last evening. My little girl very sick awhile[.] I intend to wean as soon as possible.

Sund 15th	Rainy. Alexander McGaffy spent the night with us.
Mond 16th	Pleasant and cool. Sewed little. Visited by Mrs Searls. Almost sick. My Babe does much better than I expected about weaning, yet it appears hard.
Tues 17th	Pleasant and cold. Washed. My strength is but feeble. It is hard work for me to do a little. I feel as if I never could do my work.
Wed 18th	Cold & pleasant. Mending. Visited Mrs. Lee. Not very well.
Thurs 19th	Pleasant. visited Mrs. Chase. Borrowed a Book of Mrs. D.
Fryd 20th	Pleasant. Unwell. Mending. My Babe wants great attention. Read Washborn's Sermon and may God grant that I may profit thereby, be more faithful in all things than I have been.
Sat. 21st	Pleasant A.M., rainy eve. Visited by Mrs. Remington, H. Durfey.
Sund 22nd	Pleasant. Reading sermons. Mr E attended meeting, very dull one, too. Oh that we might awake out of sleep and Christ would give us light
Mond 23rd	Rainy eve. My children almost sick with a cough[.] H. Hulburt and a stranger, a travellor, spent the night. Going to Oswego.
Tues 24th	Rainy. Finished weaving L.N. Blanket Father E had a Barn raised. Uncle Brooks called, a man of trouble and affliction.
Wed 25th	Rained steady all night and today. mostly snow. Mending. What I have to be thankful to my God that he has provided me with food and clothing & a shelter in the bosom of my Saviour and theirs where we shall be safe from all harm.
Thurs 26th	Cloudy, some snow. Washed, Ironed. My God is yet kind to me. Oh that I might be more faithful to him and those around me.
Fryd 27th	Rainy. Sewing. Enjoyed myself tolerable well but want more grace.
Sat 28th	Rainy. Saw Mr. Martin Delong of Bristol. Informs me my aged Grandparents are upon the brink of the grave. Will god grant them repentance unto life. Received a Letter from Brother Abraham, some dried apples from Mother. Wrote two letters to Father's family. [illegible word] Vilas, a Pedlar put up with us.

Sund 29th Pleasant. Mr. E attended meeting, Lee his traps, the pedlar his rags, I my children. Oh, that we might all attend to our soul's welfare as much as the body. Heard Mrs. Converse sick.

Mond 30th Pleasant. Purchased a pamphlet: The Exposition of the Olive Tree. by Ashbel Parmarlee of Malone.[80] Done but little.

May 1827

Tues 1st Rainy. Scoured the ceilings. Baked. Visited by Delong & Isaac. Sat and wrote until 3 o'clock morning to Mrs C Prime, Uncle Brooks[.]

Wed 2nd Pleasant. Preparing for company. I feel as if I ought to be with the sick.

Thurs 3rd Pleasant. Unexpectedly attended Sister Betsey. Wedding business was transacted more ignorantly. It was not so regular and agreeable as I could wish. God grant that they may live happy, seek God and his righteousness that all things may be added. [Betsey Eastman married Aaron T. Hopkins, from Ogdensburg, NY.]

Fryd 4th Rainy. Disappointed of the company of Brother and Sister Hopkins.

Sat 5th Pleasant. Disappointed again and shall I not be disappointed in the day of retribution and be forever cast off. God forbid I should.

Sund 6th Rainy. Attended meeting at Hopkinton. Babe unwell, left meeting. Had an agreeable visit with Sister B[.] spent the night[.]

Mon. 7th Pleasant. spent the A.M. at Uncle Durfey's returned home. A. H. [Aaron Hopkins] spent the P.M. with us[.] When shall I ever get weaned from the world.

Tues 8th Pleasant. Visited by Mrs. Converse. Almost sick, my Babe very worrysome.

Wed 9th Pleasant. Almost sick. Visited Mrs. Converse. I think she is near the gate of death will God prepare her for that awful change.

Thursd 10th Pleasant. God is visiting our vicinity with sickness.

Fryd 11th Rainy. Spend the evening late at Mr. Lee's which keeps me sick.

Sat. 12th	Rainy. Baked. Uncle Brooks spent the night with us. Mr. Bran [Brand] buried today. Prepare us, Lord, for thy right hand, then come the joyful day. Come death and come celestial band and bear our souls away. May we ever be on the watch.
Sund 13th	Pleasant. Visited Mrs. Converse, I think she can live but a little longer. A child of Mr. Tupper's buried today. Headache.
Mond 14th	Pleasant. Washed. Called over to Mr. Converse. Mrs. C departed this life about three o'clock this morning. The Children are dangerous.
Tues 15th	Cloudy. Very unwell. Not able to attend funeral. The Miss Deweys called, took tea. Mr. Flower very unwell. I fear he is going the way of all the earth. Will God support him through life.
Wed 16th	Pleasant. Mr. Wing died today of a Consumption. Baked[.]
Thurs 17th	Pleasant. Washed again. Mr Lee has fire close by us but God is our preserver and bountiful benefactor. Let us trust him.
Fryd 18th	Pleasant. Ironing. Visited by Mrs. Lee. Saw Raymond V. Wilkinsin from Vermont. Mr. E has a rapid fire through his slash.
Sat 19th	Pleasant. Baked largely. A child of Mr. Stickney's died today.
Sund 20th	Pleasant. Called over to Mr. C. No better. Mr & Mrs. Flower in bed sick.
Mond 21st	Cloudy. Washed, Ironed. Sent for to watch at Mr Cs Staid until about twelve. Came home my little girl thinks she is abused.
Tuesd 22nd	Rainy. Wove two yards towelling. I am very dull and drowsy.
Wed 23rd	Wove about two yards. My God is yet kind to me. his mercy is ever near. Oh that I was more deserving of his goodness & mercy
Thursd 24th	Pleasant. Took my Children and walked to Father E['s] Spent a sleepless night with Sister Betsey, perhaps the last.
Fryd 25th	Pleasant and warm. Called to Uncle D's. Rode home and visited by Mrs Pier. I am almost sick yet God is yet my Preserver.
Sat 26th	Warm. Oh that my heart was as warm with the love of God. Brother Rosewell spent the night with us. God bless him.

Sund 27th Pleasant. Conversed with Brother R. I believe him to be a follower of Jesus. Took his leave. Read sermons Mr. W's[.]

Mond 28th Cloudy, some rain. Baked. Wove some. God is exceeding kind to me. I wish to love him more and serve him better[.] Oh that my heart was always with God. Every [illegible word] bespeaks a God and I desire none of it. For my portion I want my God and to be his.

Tues 29th Pleasant & cool. Wove what I could. Visited by Mrs. Lee. I feel as God had been good to me today. I think much of again uniting again with his professed children. God, direct me.

Wed 30th Cloudy. Not well. Spent the P.M. with Mrs. Lee. altered a frock

Thurs 31st Cloudy, some rain. Almost sick. Sat up all night with Mrs. Lee[.] left both my children with Brother Lee.

June 1827

Fryd 1st Rainy. Spent the day, part of the night with Mrs. Lee. She is blessed with a fine Son. I have not been so fatigued lately as I am now. I can do no more for her at present.

Sat 2nd Pleasant. A child of Mrs. Converse buried today. Spent the A.M. with Mrs. Lee. Visited by Mrs. Harrington. Very tired.

Sund 3rd Very pleasant. I am not so engaged as I could wish. Sick headache. My health fast decays as well as flesh.

Mond 4th Almost sick this morn. Baked. Had an agreeable visit with Sister Betsey, perhaps the last. She has gone to Ogdensburg. Wrote to Mr. Hopkins. Patience S. [Simonds] almost killed.

Tuesd 5th The warmest day we have had this season. Washed. Called over and assisted Mrs. Lee. Twice. she is highly favoured of God.

Wed 6th Warm & pleasant. The light horse train to day. Heard Betsey arrived safe in Ogdensburgh. Began my wool. picked two fleeces.

Thurs 7th Great want of rain. Sewing. I have so much to do I know not what to do first. The things I would not that I do.

Fryd 8th	Pleasant. Made two Bags one towel. Very dull and drowsy. Mr. Stephen E. spent the night with us. Some rain.
Sat. 9th	Pleasant A.M. Rainy P.M. and night. cleaning house all day. Mr. E been to Parishville to Mill. Ill treated by Mr. Brownell.
Sund 10th	Pleasant. P.M. Disagreeable to hear such conversation on the Sabbath - Law, Hunting, Trapping and the like.
Mond 11th	Pleasant. Called over to Mr. Converse, his family are better. Visited by Mary Ann Heath. Sat up with Miss P. Simonds.
Tuesd 12th	Pleasant. Almost sick. Mr. Pomeroy & Covey commenced framing our barn. Brother Stephen took leave of us.
Wed 13th	Very unwell. Mr. P sick. Brother Lee is very sick indeed.
Thurs 14th	Rainy. Baked, fried cakes. Visited by Mrs. E. A house full.
Fryd 15th	Pleasant. Washed. Visited by Mrs. Wright. Our sick better.
Sat. 16th	Pleasant. Washed. Visited at Mr. Lees. Wrote to Betsey.
Sund 17th	Rainy. Very drowsy all day. It seems as if I could not work.
Mond 18th	Pleasant. Washed. Called over to Mr. D's. Saw Mr. Garrett.
Tues 19th	Mr. E. is sued unjustly. Court come on today. Adjourned. A mad dog has done a great deal of mischief. He is killed.
Wed 20th	Rainy. I am almost tired of such a family. Picked a little wool[.]
Thurs 21st	Rainy. Mending. Mr. Austin spent the night with us.
Fryd 22nd	Rainy. Traded four Dollars with pedlar, Bedticking, comb, pin[.]
Sat. 23rd	Rainy. Visited Miss Simonds, she is some better. Mad dogs killed yesterday. Most of the dogs for miles are bitten.
Sund 24th	Pleasant. Mostly Reading the Christian Instructor, containing a summary explanation and defence of the doctrine and duties of the Christian religion by Josiah Hopkins,

Newhaven, Vt.[81] Spent much of the day in tears. Oh, how blind are those that won't see and how deaf are those that won't hear, and to what length will prejudice carry a person. Oh, God, wilt thou visit them with thy spirit, pierce them with thine arrow of conviction and bring them to the truth[.]

Mond 25th Pleasant. Washed. Visited at Uncle Durfey's[.] Picked strawberrys.

Tues 26th Pleasant. Baked three times preparing for company.

Wed 27th Rainy. A.M. Had our barn raised. This P.M. visited by Mrs Covey, Mrs. Rockewell, Mrs. Chase, Miss L. Newton, Miss M.E. [Mary Eastman] wrote to Sister Hopkins. Oh that I could say I was a Christian, that I could give up all this world for Christ.

Thurs 28th Rainy. Almost sick. What an ungrateful creature I am.

Fryd 29th Rainy. Meeting house raised at Hopkinton. Mr. E. gone[.]

Sat. 30th Pleasant. Visited at Father E's. Picked strawberries. Brother Roswell E and Sister M spent the night with us. Very warm[.]

July 1827

Sund 1st Rainy. Mrs. Rose[,] Mr. Wing Baptized today. A number to tea.

Mond 2nd Baked. Almost sick. I do but little for my God or myself.

Tues 3rd Picking wool. Visited by Mrs. Lee & Searles. Oh, that they were righteous Christians. Oh, that I were more prayerful.

Wed 4th Rainy most of the time. Mr. E is boarding his barn.

Thurs 5th Visited by Mrs. Covey. I hived a swarm of bees. one stung me which closes one eye and almost the other. Washed some.

Fryd 6th Starched. Ironed. Prepared for court. Almost sick.

Sat. 7th Pleasant. Baked. Sewing. Melancholy pervades my mind.

Sund 8th Pleasant. My mind is much disturbed. This day much labor done. Ah when will this be done a way. I fear never.

Mon 9th	Very warm. Mr E and his Brother started for Ogdensburg on a Jury. Sister Mary tarrys with me while out of school.
Tuesd 10th	Pleasant. Picked green peas. Oh, that God would guide me.
Wed 11th	A fine Rainy day. Visited by Mother E. Mr. E came home sick.
Thurs 12th	Very warm Mr. E. little better. visited tonight by Searles[.]
Fryd 13th	Pleasant. Lee came home sick. Received a Letter from Sister Hopkins of Ogdensburg. Mr. S. [Searles] brought us shingles for Barn.
Sat 14th	Pleasant. Mr. E rode to Parishville to training. Oh that we were wise.
Sund 15th	Pleasant. Took a walk to view the blessing that God hath bestowed on the labors of my husband which are abundant. Almost sick.
Mond 16th	Pleasant. Washed a large washing but my sins I fear will never be washed aways. Uncle Brooks has married again to Miss M. Cook.
Tues 17th	Pleasant. Mr. E to work for [Mr.] Lee My health is not good this season.
Wed 18th	Cloudy. I feel uneasy, a wish to visit my neighbours more.
Thurs 19th	Pleasant. Visited at Mr. Flower's. Mr. Lee's people displeased.
Fryd 20th	Rainy. Oh, that I were on some desert isle to spend my days away from all strife and contention. Oh God forgive my faults[.]
Sat 21st	Rainy. but showers of grace. I hear but little of grace at present.
Sund 22nd	Pleasant Sabbath, but my tongue does not speak the pleasant language of Canaan as it ought. Oh, how slavish is the fear of mortals[.] Will God assist us to live more to his glory.
Mond 23rd	Pleasant. Mr. E. gone to Parishville for nails. Miss S.L. called.
Tues 24th	Rainy. Two workmen shingling. almost sick myself.
Wed 25th	Rainy. Three workmen. I feel unable to wait upon them.

Thurs 26th Rainy. Sat up but little. Erected another Bed. 4 oz tea.

Fryd 27th Rainy. Mary Ann Heath spent the night. God will be with her.

Sat 28th Pleasant. Our workmen have shingled one side of a barn this week[.]

Sund 29th Pleasant. Alone with my children. Some baptized today, some work at hay. Oh God wilt thou incline them other way.

Mond 30th Pleasant. Baked. Mr. C. finished work here. Mr. Lee and R.E. [Roswell Eastman] to work here and so I am imployed in the service of the world.

Tues 31st Pleasant. my foot appears to be lame, very sore on the ankle.

August 1827

Wed 1st Pleasant. Feel very uneasy. Called over to Mr Chase's Mrs. C[hase] is very unwell. Will God bless her with his presence.

Thursd 2nd Showers nights. God is abundant in mercy and we in sin and unthankfulness. Oh when shall I be more prayerful and my husband attend to religion [that] we may bring up our little ones in the way they should go. God grant it.

Fryd 3rd Shower. Scouring my house, I fear not cleansing the heart.

Sat. 4th Pleasant. Cleaning house. washed some. Discovered a spot like what is called a death mole on my left great toenail. Oh God, if thou hast given this for a token of my death, wilt thou assist me to meet it with a smile, be ready at thy call. May I live as if it were my last and Oh God wilt thou bless me with my reason and speech until my latter ends and may it be to thy glory.

Sund 5th Pleasant. Alone with my children. while my family and others are gone to hear I fear an imposter. God be with them. I feel a wish to visit my friends in Vermont but God's will be done if I never see them again until the judgement. I am favored with more earthly blessings than I deserve. I want to live more to the glory of God and see all those around me laying up their treasures in Heaven instead of earth and then our little ones will learn the way. The preacher Mr E. heard today denies the Trinity.

Mond 6th Pleasant. Not able to wash but little. Sewed some, ironed some.

Tues 7th	Pleasant morn, showery eve. Washed, Mending etc. My foot is better. Enjoyed my mind tolerably well today. God is good.
Wed 8th	Pleasant A.M. Rainy P.M. Not felt able to weave, have been mending all day. How good is my God to me to provide food and clothing for my [me] and my little ones without my labor and yet how few returns of love to him. Oh that I did but speak his praise at every breath.
Thurs 9th	Pleasant. Baked, Ironed, made cheese etc. it seem[s] as if I worked very hard according to my strength but bring but little to bear. God has been very good to me today, I have been comforted.
Fryd 10th	Cloudy. Finished making cheese, Baked pies etc. Almost sick tonight[.] Oh when shall I be at rest from this toilsome world.
Sat. 11th	Cloudy. Hard rain last night with thunder. Not able to do but little today. Called over to Mr R's. Too far for me. Sister M spends the night with us my God is my portion.
Sabb 12th	Pleasant. My Father and Mother & Brother Abraham, Uncle & Aunt Durfey visited me. Oh, the goodness of God in providing friends and means to visit me. Grandmother [Ruth Brooks] is almost gone the way of being and John Hawkins with a Consumption.
Mond 13th	Cloudy. Almost overcome with joy, feel unable to work. We all visited at Father Eastman's P.M. Spent the night at Uncle Durfey's. What a privilige it is to visit with my friends and not be obliged to work for a morsel of bread.
Tuesd 14th	Rainy. All of our relatives spent the P.M. at our house. Uncle Brooks. Durfeys. Mary E etc. Brother Lee very sick.
Wed 15th	Pleasant. our relatives took an affectionate leave of us and proceeded on their journey. Harriet D and myself were almost overcome with sorrow I do not mean to complain, it is weakness.
Thurs 16th	Pleasant. Called over and took tea with Mrs Searls. Mending[.]
Fryd 17th	Pleasant. Mending. I feel as if my stay on earth is short.
Sat 18th	Pleasant. Washed. Maryann spent the night. Oh that I did but consider my latter end, God grant that I may.

Sund 19th	Pleasant. Alone at home, the rest in the wood. Oh that I might see my family brought up different[.] I fear I shall not.
Mond 20th	Pleasant. Mother E visited. A severe pain in my side. In great distress most of the day. My rolls almost spoiled.
Tues 21st	Pleasant. Baked. Spun fifteen knots of wool. Very tired.
Wed 22nd	Pleasant. spun one runn. Ten persons called, took tea. Going to Camp Meeting, Potsdam. Sister M. spent the night.
Thurs 23rd	Rainy. Walked to Mr. Rowley's. Engaged spinning. M. Heath spent the night. Heard of the death of Rev Daniel Barnes[.]
Fryd 24th	Pleasant. Spun ten knots. Gathered weeds for colouring yellow.
Sat. 25th	Pleasant. My uncle yet troubles me much. Mending holders.
Sund 26th	Pleasant. My mind is disturbed much today. headache etc. Four men called to upper. Mary [Ann Heath] spent the day & night.
Mond 27th	Pleasant. Washed. Mr. Delong, Rugg, Isaac dined with us. Heard from Vt. Received a letter from Clarissa. Very lame.
Tues 28th	Pleasant. Been and hired Ziba Rowley to spin for me. Spun ten knots, very dejected. Low spirits. my distant friends are on the brink of the grave. I feel as if I ought to be there, too.
Wed 29th	Pleasant. Spun fifteen knots. Baked. My ankle pains me.
Thurs 30th	Pleasant, cool nights. Spun ten knots, mended some. Lame.
Fryd 31st	Pleasant. Few drops of rain. Ironed, spun ten knots. Yet lame.

September 1827

Sat. 1st	Pleasant. Gathered nearly half a Bushel of Cherries. Sister M spent the night with us. Baked pies washed floors.
Sund 2nd	Pleasant, but I am idle. Oh that I did do more for God and my own soul, prepare for death and eternity.

Mond 3rd	Pleasant. Very lame. Mended some, Baked. How stupid am I[?]
Tues 4th	Pleasant. Visited Mrs. Searles A.M. Visited by Uncle Brooks and his bride, a pleasant agreeable woman. Sewing. Very lame.
Wed 5th	Pleasant. Spent the day at Father E's. But partly, made a cap. Mr. Calvin Bell buried in the Masonic order.
Thurs 6th	Pleasant. Picked a peck of cherries. Visited at Uncle Durfey's.
Fryd 7th	Pleasant. Picked half bushel of Cherries. Visited by Mrs. Searls[.]
Sat. 8th	Pleasant. Baked, made mince pies. Visited by Anna Harrington. Sister M. and Amos Dunshee spent the night.
Sund 9th	Pleasant. A house full of boys and one thing and another. How grievous to have so little of the Sabbath.
Mond 10th	Pleasant. Washed all day at the brook. Very tired indeed.
Tues 11th	Rainy night and day. Visited by Mr & Mrs Lees. & S. A pedlar spent the night with us. Bought a number of wooden bowls, leak sadly as yet. How good is my God.
Wed 12th	Pleasant. Visited by Mrs. Searles & Drake. Coloured yellow.
Thurs 13th	Rainy. Little Mary sick. Baked. Have a number of workmen.
Fryd 14th	Rainy. Wove some. Someone to get victuals for almost all the day[.]
Sat. 15th	Rainy. Finished a web of towelling that has been in the loom a long time. Visited at Mr Lee's. Dressed six squirrels[.]
Sund 16th	Rainy. Oh that my head were waters and mine eyes a fountain of tears that I might weep for my family.
Mond 17th	Pleasant. Washed. Ironed. Attended a Bee of picking wool. Sister M. Spent the night. I have gone beyond my strength.
Tuesd 18th	Pleasant. Done but little of anything. Visited by M. Heath. Not able to sit up this eve, but God is very merciful.

Wed 19th Rainy. Mended little but not able to do but a trifle.

Thurs 20th Rainy. Mr. E. gone to Norfolk to training. Mended.

Fryd 21st Rainy. Mending, rather better. Mr. E brought me tea.

Sat 22nd Rainy. Spun twenty two knots of tow & Linen.

Sund 23rd Rainy. Almost sick again and of so much company on Sabbath and no sign of worship or Christianity.

Mond 24th Pleasant. Washed. Visited by M. Durfey & C. Brooks

Tues 25th Visited A.M. by H. Durfey. We visited school and at Mr. Harringtons after. Very wet and rainy. Tired out.

Wed 26th Rainy. Almost sick. Visited by Mrs. Drake & Searls & Lee[.]

Thurs 27th Cloudy. Mr. Drake moved away. Put in a web of wool.

Fryd 28th Hard frost. Made six beers of harness. Wove three yards[.]

Sat. 29th Pleasant. Wove three yards. It is almost a yard and a half wide and has lamed my side. Have men & boys to work.

Sund 30th Very pleasant. All at work around me. Oh God wilt thou teach them to serve thee better and set a better example before the world, especially our childs. Washed this eve, ironed, mended until one o'clock, To gain time to husk corn tomorrow, if able.

October 1827

Mond 1st Washed, Baked strained honey etc. Almost worn out.

Tues 2nd Bad weather for the farmer but God is pleased to send it for good[.]

Wed 3rd Pleasant. Husked some corn, the squirrels are carrying it off fast.

Thurs 4th Not able to husk the corn, is mourding [moulding] and rotting fast.

Fryd 5th Pleasant but cold. Husked some. Mary Ann Heath visited me. Almost sick.

Sat. 6th	Very wet, muddy season. Wove some. Mr. Covey I hope has done work here for the present. It takes almost all my time to cook.
Sund 7th	Pleasant. Spent most of the day in tears oh how stupid are all men.
Mond 8th	Washed. I often get discouraged about getting my work done.
Tues 9th	Pleasant. Worked hard today. Shed many tears. My husband I think used too harsh expressions. Oh that grace was regent of his heart. Uncle Brook's little Harriet died this eve at twelve. Blessed be God.
Wed 10th	Pleasant. Visited by Sophrona E. mending most of my time.
Thurs 11th	Cloudy. Almost sick. Visited by Mrs. Searls. Harriet B buried today.
Fryd 12th	The weather rather more favorable and how few thanks do I hear to God[.]
Sat. 13th	Cloudy. Took my Children through mud and water over shoes to Uncle Durfey's and left them. Went to the Carding machine which made three miles and brought ten pounds of rolls to Uncle D's. They have been there until matted together. I think it a shame that I have to do in this manner but the Lord will soon take me away.
Sund 14th	Pleasant. Staid to Uncle's until afternoon for my husband to come and help me home with my children but in vain. Came home found them all at work. Oh God how long will thou suffer they Sabbaths to be thus treated. Oh make us look to do better.
Mond 15th	Cold, little snow. Wove out a web. Spooled, warped, beamed another.
Tues 16th	Rainy. Drew in my web. Mending some. Visited at Mr. Lee's. Finished husking corn.
Wed 17th	Rainy. Wove some, Mending, etc. I earn but little yet I have living.
Thurs 18th	Cloudy & Cold. Visited at Mr. C. Rockwells but not able to, sick.
Fryd 19th	More pleasant. Very unable to do anything, but I have a shelter for my little ones, food and clothing. What more can I ask.
Sat. 20th	Cold storm. Able to work a little and that little helps much.

Sund 21st	Rainy & cold. I am twenty-six years old today. perhaps I shall never live to see another year but God grant that I may be ready to go when God shall call. Then, farewell.
Mond 22nd	Cloudy. Rainy visited by Mrs. Root. Mary Ann H. [Heath].
Tuesd 23rd	Rainy. Baked. Afterwards confined to my bed in great distress through the night all is for the best, I trust.
Wed 24th	Cloudy, some rain, snow. Worked very little, weak and sore.
Thurs 25th	Some snow. Done a number light chores. Made fourteen dozen of candles. Sat up untill one o'clock at night. Almost tired out[.]
Fryd 26th	Storm of snow. Mending all day I don't know when my weaving will be done. I hope for the best and let it rest, perhaps too long. Visited at Uncle D's. Bought four bushels of apples, fifty cents per bushel.
Sat. 27th	Rainy. Almost sick. Mended little spun eight knots finished my web.
Sund 28th	Pleasant. most of the day. I spend my Sabbaths mostly alone excepting my children, while the one that ought to guide and instruct me in the path of duty is in the fields as I know not where. Oh God wilt thou pierce his heart with arrows of conviction, bring him humbly at thy feet to plead for mercy daily, Train up his children in the way they should go and all seek that narrow path.
Mond 29th	Rainy. Sewing. Visited this eve by Mr & Mrs. Chase. R.E. spent the night[.]
Tues 30th	Rainy. Wove six yards kersey. Finished weaving linen ticking.
Wed 31st	Pleasant. Done but little, mending some. Almost discouraged. Baked pies.

November 1827

Thursd 1st	Pleasant. Scoured twenty three runs of yarn. Washed some. Hired two girls this P.M. for a day or two. Made two Bedticks.
Fryd 2nd	Smoaky. Had house cleaned, not able to do much myself.
Sat. 3rd	Rainy. Baked, mending etc. Visited by Miss L. Newton. Girls gone[.]

Sund 4th Very Smoaky, dark day indeed. Mr E attended meeting.

Mond 5th Cold, looks likely for snow. Washed. Gathered running pine & [illegible word]

Tues 6th Cold. Trimmed my house. Mending. Mr. E thirty-one years old.

Wed 7th Some snow. Baked. I do not get time to weave, warped one web.

Thurs. 8th Cold. All chores. Erected a new bed for the children. A gentleman from Morristown spent the night with us and thirty-six swine. Lee came in from his hunt south.

Fryd 9th Cloudy. The winter is approaching and death also. Oh God may we be prepared to meet both cheerfully and willingly.

Sat. 10th Cloudy. The Sabbath approaches. Oh, may we spend it to God's glory.

Sund 11th Rainy. Ah, it is not a rain of righteousness, how dull & stupidly do we spend our Sabbaths. Oh that we were alive to God and dead as it were to the world and all its vanities. Uncle Brooks and wife called over. I was bled. Wrote to Sister B.

Mond 12th Colder. Drew in a web of flannel. Almost discouraged about work.

Tuesd 13th Rainy. Harriet D. came to spend a few days with me. Wove but one yard. My web goes hard, do not feel able to weave.

Wed. 14th Colder. Piecing a quilt. Almost sick, scarcely able to visit.

Thursd 15th Some snow. Harriet returned home. Received a pound of tea. Sewing[.]

Fryd 16th Cold. wove two yards, Slow weaving. mending, evenings, all I am Able.

Sat 17th Stormy. Baked. Another week is past and gone and I am spared to my family.

Sund 18th Pleasant. Headache today. Read but little think but little of anything.

Mond 19th Cold and stormy. Washed, Ironed and mended woollen clothes.

Tuesd 20th Stormy. Colouring black. Wove little. I find no time that I ought to weave but that I ought to read more in my Bible.

Wed 21st Very cold, but colder is an heart like mine towards my God.

Thurs 22nd More moderate. Finished colouring. Wove some in the evening.

Fryd 23rd Cloudy. Visited by Mrs. Lee. Wove little but well by any means.

Sat. 24th Few flakes of snow. Baked, cleaned house. Cumbered about many things.

Sabb 25th Cold but pleasant. Headache. Spent the day disagreeably.

Mond 26th Stormy. Washed clothes, yarn & wool of a Cosset sheep. We had thirty-eight pounds of tryed tallow. Almost tired out this eve.

Tues 27th Cloudy. Wove four yards, mended some. I must work off laziness.

Wed 28th More moderate, thaws some, Wove what I could in the daytime and four yards after dark. and finished my web. purchased a new ticking by cash, three Dollars fifty cents of Mr. Harvestson.

Thurs 29th Spooled, warped and put in another web. Most tired out & sick.

Fryd 30th Thaws some. Wove one yard and half, obliged to leave it.

December 1827

Sat. 1st Snow squalls. Washed & Baked. Mr. E. purchased me five pounds of cotton twist, half pound of pepper do [ditto] of spice a thimble, one pound of Ginger. How good is my God to me.

Sabbath 2nd Cloudy. Left alone. Enjoyed myself tolerably well but the things of this world intrude more than I wish they did. When shall I hear and see and know all I desire or wish below. I am at a loss what my duty is to my neighbours. I have some that want the necessaries of life and do but little towards procuring them. Whether they are subjects of charity or not I do not know. Will God direct me.

Mond 3rd A little more snow. Coloured yellow, knitting etc.

Tues 4th Cold. Colouring red, good colour preparing mince for winter[.]

Wed 5th Cold. Finished colouring, had good colour. Not able to do much.

Thursd 6th More moderate. cannot get along with weaving. my web is very tender Killed the last cow I had. Good Beef, sold half.

Fryd 7th	Cloudy. Mending. Mr E spend much time hunting for nothing.
Sat. 8th	Stormy. Finished trying tallow. Visited by Aunt Durfey[.]
Sund 9th	Pleasant. Almost sick and tired out. Read tracts, very good ones.
Mond 10th	Cold. Wove all day for one yard. Poor encouragement to hire spinner[.]
Tues 11th	Stormy. Wove half yard. Mrs. Searles called over a while. Sewing.
Wed 12th	Stormy. Thanksgiving. Worked so hard yesterday, sick today.
Thurs 13th	Thaw some. Had my Loom placed before the fire, wove little.
Fryd 14th	Cold. Wove all day until two o'clock at night for four yards.
Sat. 15th	Very cloudy. Finished my rotten web. Cut out a frock.
Sund 16th	Oh how slothful I am. I read less and pray less than formerly. I hear nothing but hunting stories. Sabbath.
Mond 17th	Stormy. Began a large washing when my little girl scalt both hands, her left the worst burn I ever saw. I do everything I can for her but she suffers greatly. Her arm almost to her elbow to the end of her nails one blister.
Tuesd 18th	Stormy. Sewing. Mr E sold is venison to David E.
Wed 19th	Brother D. [David] started for Montreal. Washed some. My sweet Little Mary is patient as a lamb for me to dress her hand. Her fingers need great care to keep them from growing together and to keep all from getting cold. God is good.
Thursd 20th	Pleasant. Finished washing that I began Monday. I think my girl's hand is doing very well. It is a task to dress it[.]
Fryd 21st	Pleasant. Sewing. Mr. E. purchased a Caldron kettle fourteen $.
Sat. 22nd	Stormy. Finished Mr. E.'s frock, Henry a shirt etc. mended also[.]
Sund 23rd	Pleasant. Idle in the market place. Spooled two coverlets.
Mond 24th	Some snow. Washed. Oh that my sins were all washed aways.

Tuesd 25th	Cold. Mr. Covey finishing the barn. Almost sick of the world, also[.]
Wed 26th	Very cold. Put in a coverlet of six geese. Baked pies retired at one.
Thurs 27th	Cold and stormy. Almost sick, disappointed of a hired girl. Mr. E killed five hogs, two of which weighed 388. Sold one.
Fryd 28th	Snows very fast indeed. Tryed out my lard. washed floors. almost tired out. Lame, faint and discouraged of getting along.
Sat. 29th	Snows yet. Cut and basted a flannel gown for myself. D. [David] came home[.]
Sabbath 30th	The snow is very deep. Oh how stupid are mankind to things of eternity. Oh that I might be more engaged in the cause of God.
Mond 31st	The last day of the year has arriven and Oh that it was the last day of my living in sin, sloth and stupidity. But may I begin with the year to live to God and to the support of his cause, be more attentive to prayer to my Bible and my God. Began a coverlet. Split the great beam in two. I am almost disposed to think it is not right for me to take time to do sewing on my gown.

January 1828

Tuesd 1st	Moderate weather. Wove one yard and quarter. God has been good to me this day. alas may I be more faithful than I have been. Mr. Van Rasselaer Brownell married to Miss Electa Merchant.
Wed 2nd	Thaws fast. Wove one yard most half. Very hard work but God assists.
Thurs 3rd	The snow almost gone. This has been a day of distress of body but God is my preserver and bountiful benefactor. Obliged to hire a girl, Miss Mary Ann Heath, a good girl.
Fryd 4th	The sleighing almost gone. Wove a little but feeble yet weak in faith[.]
Sat. 5th	Some rain, wove some. Cleaned some house. Baked pies, etc. but not well, rejoice at the approaching Sabbath. How sweet are our mercies.
Sabbath 6th	Pleasant. My health is poor today. I stand all the day idle the market place. How can I be so stupid and careless of Eternity.

Mond 7th	Pleasant. Began to make soap, no luck today. Wove but very little.
Tuesd 8th	Frozen. Last night. Made a fire out of doors, boiled all day for nothing. I have more to do than I had before I hired a girl. Almost tired.
Wed 9th	Fine day for the season. Made about two Barrels of soap. Finished[.]
Thurs 10th	Cloudy, cleaned chambers and house. Learning Mary Ann to wash not tractable. Visited by Aunt Durfey. almost tired out. M. Covey.
Fryd 11th	Very fine day. Not able to do but little, wove little on coverlet.
Sat. 12th	Cloudy, dry rainy night. Baked, wove some, fried cakes, etc.
Sund 13th	Rainy. This is the day the Lord hath made. He calls the hours his own.
Mond 14th	Snow and Rain. Washed a large washing. Mending considerable.
Tues 15th	Moderate. Wove but little. Sophrona E. spent the night, mending.
Wed 16th	Pleasant. Almost sick. Wove but little, almost discouraged about work.
Thursd 17th	Thaws. Wove what I could. Mary Ann began my flax. Very good flax[.]
Fryd 18th	Pleasant. Baked pies, prepared for company, disappointed. Not able to weave.
Sat. 19th	Some snow, Colder. Had a fall this eve which injured me some.
Sabbath 20th	Cold. Not able to sit up all day but better than I expected. after a fall.
Mond 21st	Very cold. washed. Cut out pantaloons. Visited by mother E.
Tues 22nd	Very cold. Our house open. Made Henry pantaloons. Not well.
Wed 23rd	Rather more moderate. Wove all I could today. I must get it out[.]
Thurs 24th	Comfortable weather. Wove all the fillen. House full of men this eve.
Fryd 25th	Sewing. Finished my flannel frock. Visited by H. Durfey visited this eve at Father Eastman's Sister Hopkins at home.

Sat. 26th	Rainy. Wove the fringe and coverlets. Visited by Mrs. Searls[.]
Sabb 27th	Snows fast this P.M. How dull and stupid are my thoughts.
Mond 28th	Snows. Not able to wash. Finished Mary's stockings & Lee's socks[.]
Tues 29th	Colder Rain at eve. Washed some. visited at Uncle Durfey's this eve. Wrote a letter to Father Orvis to send by Uncle Brooks.
Wed 30th	Moderate. Cut out two vests, one pair of pantaloons. Almost sick[.]
Thurs 31st	Visited by Mother E, Sister Betsey, Mr Kelly [Kelley] spent the night. The Lord has been pleased to waken this mind to duty.

February 1828

Fryd 1st	Stormy. Visited at Father E Mr E purchased a lb of tea & saw.
Sat. 2nd	Snow is fast going off. Took a coverlet to weave. Almost sick.
Sund 3rd	Snow all gone. Not able to sit up but little today.
Mond 4th	Froze hard again. My health is very poor. Sewed.
Tuesd 5th	helped washed. Undertook to learn Mary Ann to weave Birds Eye but in vain. Wove late this eve myself.
Wed 6th	Warm & pleasant. Wove all the fillin to the Blanket.
Thurs 7th	Finished the Blanket, put in a Coverlet. Rainy day.
Fryd 8th	Cloudy. wove A.M. P.M. visited by the Mrs Rockwells. Mrs Flower, Mrs Lee. High winds with rain. Sick again.
Sat. 9th	Rainy. visited by Susan Lockwood. Wove some, retired early.
Sund 10th	Little Snow. Spent most of my time in bed to bear it.
Mond 11th	Wove all day. Finished the coverlet and fringe. Done too much.
Tues 12th	Colder. Put in a web of 28 yards of Cotton and wool Sheeting[.]

Wed 13th	Warn [warm] and pleasant. Wove seven yards I am anxious to finish.
Thurs 14th	Pleasant. snow gone. plenty of muck. Wove eleven yards.
Fryd 15th	Pleasant as June. Wove ten yards. finished weaving for the present[.]
Sat 16th	Pleasant. Visited by Aunt Durfey & Mrs Covey. Made one sheet and received almost twelve pound of geese feathers of Aunt Durfey. Heard that Grandmother Brooks was dead.
Sund 17th	Pleasant. Mr. E brought home some fish. I refused to cook them which makes him very angry. For my part, I allow it not, neither do I mean to uphold anyone to fish Sabbath day. Spent most of the night in distress and tears. Oh that I could die the death of the righteous. Oh that I could leave this world of tribulation to those that love its charms.
Mond 18th	Pleasant A.M. Rainy P.M. Washed largely quilts & coverlets.
Tues 19th	Cooler. Had a Bedroom partitioned, house cleaned. Lee sued by H.S.
Wed 20th	Rainy. Traded three dollars with a pedlar for cash. Mr E traded about as much at the store on Monday. Sewed some.
Thurs 21st	Rainy. Two Rainbows in the north about eleven A.M.
Fryd 22nd	Little snow last night. Heard from Fowler by Mr Griffin. Baked pies twice. Almost tired out and sick of hiring help.
Sat. 23rd	Very pleasant. finished marking my sheets, made five. settled with my hired girl, her account eleven dollars.
Sund 24th	A few flakes of snow fell. Very stupid are my days.
Mond 25th	Some snow, very rough travelling. Mr Griffin returned. Baked[.]
Tuesd 26th	Likely for a thaw. I find I can keep my house more decent without a hired girl than with one. Making small clothes.
Wed 27th	More snow. Scarce enough for sleighing. Good weather for spinning[.]
Thurs 28th	Thaw and rains so the roads are very bad but God is yet good to me.

Fryd 29th	Rainy. Visited by Mrs. Searls. I know not what to think of this family.

March 1828

Sat. 1st	Heard Sister Hopkins was very sick with an infant daughter.
Sund 2nd	Little snow but very poor sleighing or waggoning. Almost sick.
Mond 3rd	Warm winter indeed. Sister Kelly [Kelley] arrived in town. Her health better.
Tues 4th	Little more snow. Prepared for company. Sewing what I can, made caps.
Wed 5th	Stormy. Visited by Sister Kelly, Father, Mother & Mary E [Eastman] gone to Ogdensburg to visit new baby of Betsey Hopkins.
Thurs 6th	Stormy. Sister K. returned & spent the night. Mr. E. been to Hopkinton. Purchased plaid for a Cloak for M.A. Heath, a Mug, a pair of tumblers and other necessaries of Culver. M.H. returned. Washed, starched, Ironed, Plated caps, etc. Received a Letter from Sally Brooks on Wednesday last, a small cap from Aunt Nicholson by Uncle Brooks. He is not yet well of his hurt he received on his journey.
Fryd 7th	Pleasant. Thaws considerable. M.H. [Mary Ann Heath] returned home. Visited with Mrs Kelly at Mr Lee's, also Mrs. Rockwell, Mrs Prichard of Malone. Heard from Sister B. She has a fever, a cough etc. Mother E has staid to take care of her, Father and M. [Mary Eastman] came home. Mr, Kelly spent the night. Oh that my husband was as engaged in religion as he is.
Sat. 8th	Stormy. visited at Father E's. Little Mary very sick, pukes all her victuals.
Sund 9th	Stormy. Mr Kelly & Lee gone to meeting. My little girl no better.
Mond 10th	Pleasant and warm. Sewing. Mr Kelly & wife returned home to Fowler.
Tues 11th	Pleasant and warm. Sewing. Mr E. gone to Meeting this eve. Bought of A. Squires four reeds which makes ten of my own. alone this eve.
Wed 12th	Pleasant. Was taken in great distress this A.M. obliged to seek aid from a Physician and friends. they spent the night with me.
Thurs 13th	Pleasant. Was bled. Took pills, high fever, palpitations. My neighbours spent the day and night but nothing special.

Fryd 14th Pleasant for the season. Able to sit up most of the day but very low.

Sat. 15th It is pleasant for winter but my mind is melancholy & dejected.

Sund 16th Pleasant. Sat up all day but did not feel able to. Aunt Durfey & Uncle spent the day with me, my friends are very kind to me.

Mond 17th A mild winter. I now do some chores but have a hired girl all the time.

Tues 18th Pleasant. Visited by mother E. Sit up most of the time, inclining to a fever.

Wed 19th Pleasant[.] oh when shall I leave this vale of tears to be here no more?

Thurs 20th Time is yet rollin, am yet spared a space of repentance. Oh my God assist me to improve it. Taken unwell in the night.

Fryd 21st Rainy night, pleasant day, but distressing indeed. About half past ten o'clock was blessed with a daughter, weight 9 lbs.

Sat. 22nd Oh how greatly am I distressed. My burthen is greater than I am able to bear and nature appears sinking under. Oh, God, assist me to bear it with patience all thou hast designed for me. I fear my senses will desert me, forbid it, Lord[.]

Sund 23rd Harriet Durfey visited me. Distressing day. my pain extremely hard. my case is not very promising at this time but God knows what is best for me and may I patiently submit.

[No entries from March 23rd to May 21st]

May 1828

Wed 21st Much rain this season. My Babe two months old today. Mr. Delong, Mr. Isham, Cousin Sally Brooks arrived at Hopkinton.

Thurs 22nd Rainy. Have workmen most of the time. Mr D. [Delong] & I [Isham] called.

Fryd 23rd Pleasant. Visited by S. [Sally] Brooks H. [Harriet] Durfey. Took a fatiguing walk with the little ones over the saw mill. Mr. E washed sheep today[.]

Sat. 24th Cloudy, some rain. Washed, sewed some. A number called today.

Sund 25th	Pleasant. Mr. Stephen E [Eastman] spent the day and night with us. Oh, God, thou knowest how we mispend thy sabbath and how our little ones are growing up without a knowledge of thy mercies. Oh may we do better and those that live with us.
Mond 26th	Washed. Sewed some but nothing done for God. Oh, my children.
Tuesd 27th	Rainy most of the time. My eyes are very poor most of the time.
Wed 28th	Pleasant. Walked to Uncle Durfey's and carried my Babe.
Thurs 29th	Cloudy some rain. My yesterday's walk almost too hard for me.
Fryd 30th	Almost sick. Picking wool. Sally Brooks spent the night with me.
Sat. 31st	Rainy. Making a waist. I get along slowly with work, less with grace. Oh, that I were more faithful to my God.

June 1828

Sabb 1st	Pleasant, rainy. Very drowsy all day. Wrote a letter to Sister Sally Kelly. Mr. E gone to hear Mr. Hickox. Oh that our Sabbath were better employed.
Mond 2nd	Pleasant. Washing. Oh that we would as well cleanse the inward soul from sins as we do our outward flesh from dust.
Tues 3rd	Pleasant. Very warm. Walked to Father E's. Obliged to retire. to bed. It is wrong for me to walk so far on foot. visited with S[.]
Wed 4th	Pleasant. Starched, ironed, finished a frock and cape for my babe[.]
Thursd 5th	Pleasant. How great a blessing is health. Mrs. Angeline T. is near her end. Clarissa McAllister, Miss Chapman.
Fryd 6th	Cloudy. Very unwell, my walk too hard for my constitution.
Sat. 7th	Pleasant. Baked. Gather bushes to trim my house. Brother and Sister Hopkins took tea with us. Father had a raising.
Sund 8th	Rainy. Brother Roswell came home sick from Smithville. He appears consumptive. Very drowsy this spring.

Mond 9th Pleasant. Washed, ironed. My mind is not at ease but like the seas.

Tues 10th Pleasant. Attended a quilting at Uncle Durfeys S.B. almost sick.

Wed 11th Pleasant. Picking wool. My work is always behind others.

Thurs 12th Cloudy, some rain. Visited by Mary Ann H [Heath], E. McAllister, Mr. Hopkins and Ward, a stranger. Backward spring.

Fryd 13th Rainy. Baked. Mr. H & W called on their return to P. [Parishville].

Sat 14th Pleasant, cool. Finished picking my wool. Visited by Mrs. S.

Sund 15th Pleasant. The warmest day we have had this year. Miss Clarissa McAllister died this A.M. at ten o'clock. I hope she is in the arms of Jesus. Mr E gone to meeting. Called over to Mr. R. [Remington] to visit Mary, a sick girl. Borrowed tracts[.]

Mond 16th Pleasant. Washed all day. Sister Mary returned from Ogdensburg Brother Roswell E, Mr. Hopkins, Also. A dumb man has prophesied that it shall rain no more for seven years.

Tues 17th Pleasant. Attended the funeral of Clarissa McAllister. Had the sick headache very hard. Vomited heartily but very sick.

Wed 18th Rainy. Baked. Visited by Mr & Mrs Hopkins. Mother E Etc[.]

Thurs 19th Rainy. Visited all day with our friends. Called over to Mr R.'s [Rockwell's][.]

Fryd 20th Pleasant. Our friends took leave of us this eve.

Sat 21st Very warm. Greased my wool. Called over to Mr Rockwell's. She was yesterday delivered of a son. Oh, stupid am I to wander from my God.

Sabbath 22nd Very warm. Oh, how drowsy are we on the brink of death.

Mond 23rd Washed some. Have workmen chopping a job. Not able to do much.

Tuesd 24th Very warm. Washed a little more. Taken sick in the night at the heat.

Wed 25th Very warm. Our workmen obliged to leave their work on account of the heat. Called over to Mr Rockwell's. Not able to get home with my Babe. The Ladies assisted me home. Sick night but God is good.

Thursd 26th Very warm. Not able to sit up in the A.M. P.M. sat up, cut out a pair of Pantaloons. I know not the cause of ill health.

Fryd 27th Showers. Made Henry's pantaloons. Very feeble but God is good.

Sat. 28th Cloudy. Mending. Number out of health this season, consumptive.

Sabbath 29th Cloudy. Took a walk over our plantation. Crops look well but all this does not create Piety. We are yet stupid and easy

Mond 30th Rainy. Made Mr E a pair of pantaloons. teeth ache, took [illegible word][.]

July 1828

Tues 1st Put in a coverlet for Mrs. Root. My little Boy commenced going to school. Ten men to cook for. Took a Barrel of Park, salt brine, etc Toothache very hard. showry all day. Baked.

Wed 2nd Showery. Not able to do anything but to get dinner for five men. Mr Nichols finished his job of chopping.

Thurs 3rd Rainy. Sewing little. It is suprizing how stupid I am.

Fryd 4th Washed. An old soldier spent the night. Was obliged to wash my coverlet on his account. He had a number of wounds.

Sat 5th Warm. Cleared the chambers, washed floors etc[.] Mr. H [Hopkins][,] Roswell E.[,] M.E. [M. Eastman][,] took tea. Mrs. Baldwin, Mr. Osgood called[.]

Sund 6th Cloudy darkness yet reigns in my hard heart. Oh God forbid[.]

Mond 7th Sewing. Rainy. Mr. Ordway called to get some coverlets wove, but I am not sufficient to do it. letter from Vt.

Tuesd 8th Visited at Uncle Brooks. Aunt's health very poor indeed.

Wed 9th Rainy. Sewing. Not able to do much. Roswell spent the night.

Thursd 10th Pleasant. Washed, Baked. Mr. Laughlin & wife called and left two coverlets to weave. Mr. E. got his foot badly hurt.

Fryd 11th Mr. Harvestson spent last night with us, traded with him five dollars one shilling for Mary Ann Heath. Began weaving.

Sat. 12th	Rainy. Finished a coverlet. Visited by M.H. overpaid 18 shill.
Sund 13th	Cloudy, some rain. Called over to Mr. Rockwell's. Mary very sick.
Mond 14th	Washed. Showers. Mr. E's foot is so that he gets outdoors.
Tuesd 15th	Shower all day. Finished pantaloons for Mr. E. My little Henry has a hard task to go so far in the rain to school.
Wed 16th	Rainy. Made a vest for Henry. put in a coverlet for J.B.
Thursd 17th	Showers. Wove some. My Loom out of square received my rolls. Sat up with Mary Rockwell, I think she will soon leave us.
Fryd 18th	Pleasant morn. Almost sick. carried my rolls away to be spun. Visited by the Mrs. Durfeys. A number sick this season.
Sat. 19th	Showers. Called over to Mr. Rockwell's visited by Mr & Mrs. E. Sophia Remington & Sister Mary spent the night.
Sund 20th	Pleasant. Considerable company but lonely and homesick.
Mond 21st	Cloudy. Mr. E. commenced haying. Mr. McAllister here to work. Mr. Harvestson returned. Paid him four Dollars fifty cents cash.
Tuesd 22nd	Poor hay weather. Engaged to board Mr. Hazelton & son. Baked.
Wed 23rd	Showers. Made Mary a fine shirt. Much thunder & lightning.
Thursd 24th	Showers. Altering my frock, do but little but chores.
Fryd 25th	A very hard shower with much wind. Not able to do but very little. Miss Mary Rockwell died this morn, aged sixteen, an example of piety, a member of Church.
Sat. 26th	Pleasant. Left home in the morning to assist our neighbour, the first time I ever assisted to put a body in a coffin.
Sund 27th	Cloudy. A number called. Our boarder to work all day. Oh how unhappy am I for want of religion and family discipline.
Mond 28th	Pleasant. Wove some. Called over to Uncle Durfey's. 4 lbs of cheese[.]

Tues 29th Tolerable hay weather today but for the most part of the time bad. Visited by Mary Ann H. I am tired of so many men to wait on[.]

Wed 30th Cloudy. Six men again today. Baked, fried cakes, visited Mr. R.

Thurs 31st Almost sick. Sewing some, finished a nightgown for the Babe.

August 1828

Fryd 1st Boarders again[.] all I do is to get change of labor or cash[.]

Sat. 2nd Showers of hail. Sister M spent the night. oh how I am crowded with men[.]

Sund 3rd Pleasant. Our boarders work all day again. My little ones at play. Oh that I had died before they were born.

Mond. 4th Washed. Do a little sewing. My health is very poor, want ambition.

Tuesd 5th Rainy. All are complaining of the weather but it is wrong indeed.

Wed 6th Cloudy. Six men again. Mr. H & Lee finished haying.

Thurs 7th Washed. Mr H. paid one Dollar eighteen cents in cash and took leave.

Fryd 8th Cloudy. wove some. Oh that I could govern my feelings better, I wish Lee would go some where else to live. I cannot live so, it seems.

Sat. 9th Weather cool. Purchased tin pail with cover. Picked black berries for preserves, forty six lbs. Joseph Murray, a Frenchman, spent the night. He says he was taken prisoner by the English. From them he escaped by swimming three leagues, staid four days under a bridge. Was fed by black lad until search was over.

Sabbath 10th Very warm. High winds. My mind is continually fretted by the presence of one I cannot bear, especially on the Sabbath [Brother Lee].

Mond 11th Rained all last night, all of this day. The streams are very high. Baked. Altered a frock for my Babe. Mr. E & Mr A began chopping.

Tuesd 12th Cool morn. Made forty weight of preserves. Washed. Time flies swiftly.

Wed 13th Pleasant. Ironed. Wove on a coverlet the rest of the day, hard work.

Thursd 14th	Rainy. Wove all day for a yard. Almost tired out & discouraged.
Fryd 15th	Showers. the Wheat crop is good for nothing, Rye but little, peas scarcely worth gathering, corn is tolerable good, ours in particular not able to weave. Rode out and visited at Uncle Durfey's.
Sat. 16th	Cloudy. Wove some. Received a Letter from Brother Kelly with the good news that they enjoy their God in prayer together. Oh that I could enjoy this privilege with my family.
Sund 17th	Cloudy. Numbers at work. Oh God is this agreeable to thy will. Uncle E [Elisha] Brooks blessed with another daughter. Thunder showers.
Mond 18th	Rainy. Baked, Washed. The framer is almost discouraged.
Tues 19th	Cool weather. Worked what I could A.M. P.M. left my children with Mrs S., Called over to Uncle Brooks. found Aunt as well as I could expect. My talk too much for me. My babe was afraid and cried.
Wed 20th	Cool yet. wove all day for a little. I am almost sick & my Babe, too.
Thurs 21st	War. Wove until two o'clock at night. Finished the Coverlet[.]
Fryd 22nd	Warmer. Weaving. My Babe unwell, but good natured.
Sat 23rd	Warm. Visited at Mr. Brush, received 21 shill. Cash, one lb of tea. My Babe has almost a Dysentary[.] Mr & Mrs Hopkins called awhile[.]
Sund 24th	Warm. My Babe still worse. I am more wicked. Oh, that I did but Learn wisdom from on high. Teach me, Oh my Father.
Mond 25th	Pleasant. My Babe worrysome. Washed some, Baked, etc.
Tuesd 26th	Very warm. Visited at Uncle Brooks. Washed. Our children with us[.]
Wed 27th	Warm. worked at the Chamber, taking up the floors, cleaning.
Thurs 28th	Pleasant. Doing chores all day and that does not profit.
Fryd 29th	Pleasant. Put in two Coverlets yesterday. very tender indeed.

Sat 30th	Very cool. Mending, etc. One week after another flies away.
Sund 31st	Cloudy, Melancholy days. I want to revisit my friends in Vt.

September 1828

Mond 1st	Rainy most of the day. Washed some, mending, etc.
Tues 2nd	Rained all day steady. The Farmer is again discouraged.
Wedn 3rd	Rainy. I do not earn my board this week. I am dejected.
Thurs 4th	Washing. Visited by M. Heath, A. Rowley. Forty runs of yarn.
Fryd 5th	Some shoers. My little Mary had the misfortune to have her forefinger of the right hand taken off to the first joint by an auger, a loss she can never regain.
Sat. 6th	Cool, but pleasant. Mending all day. Oh that I could revisit my friends in Vt once more before they are gone forever.
Sund 7th	Pleasant. Uncle Samuel Clapp called. Mr. Follit from Vt. received a letter from Brother Isaac. No good news.
Mond 8th	Wove a trifle today, but the warp is very tender indeed.
Tues 9th	Pleasant. Baked. Have workmen. Cut out Mary a frock Mr. [Corea] and another gentleman spent the night. My little Mary gaining.
Wed 10th	Very unwell, kept very still today. What a worthless creature
Thurs 11th	[No entry]
Fryd 12th	Sewing. Sister Mary came to spend a few days with us.
Sat. 13th	Preparing for a visit to Potsdam. Visited by Mrs. Chase. A Mr. Branch spent the night from Pierpoint, formerly from Middlebury.
Sabb 14th	Pleasant. Called over to Uncle Durfeys to see friends from Vt.
Mond 15th	Washed. Almost sick the most of the time. My Babe is as well as she was before she was weaned for ought I know.

Tuesd 16th	Rainy. Baked. Spun some stocking yarn. Gathered weeds for colouring
Wed 17th	Walked to Mr. McAllister's. Engaged Mary Ann H [Heath] to work for me. Baked for General Training. Put on tobbacco soaked in spirits Entirely for Marys finger which heals very fast.
Thurs 18th	Pleasant. Almost sick. Preparing for a short visit too much.
Fryd 19th	Pleasant. Obliged to borrow clothes to wear, A bad practice. Left my children. Rode to Potsdam. Sister B [Betsey] almost sick.
Sat. 20th	Pleasant. Read some but was very lonesome. Mary and I took a walk to the graveyard which was all we visited. Mr. E purchased him a hat. I should be glad to return home tonight.
Sabb 21st	Cloudy. Returned home. found my babe had a sore mouth, tired.
Mond 22nd	My Diary is neglected. Since I have written David has been married to Miss Lorena Baldwin. My Brother Isaac Orvis has visited us this fall.

[No entries from Tuesday September 23rd to Monday December 29th]

December 1828

Mond 29th	Cold. been to Hopkinton purchased Plush for bonnet. traded six dollars.
Tues 30th	All sick today but Mr. E. How we shall go to Vermont I know [not][.]
Wed 31st	Very unwell. Finished a flannel shirt, all I have done this week[.]

January 1829

Thurs 1st	Very cold, snowed some. Mr. Harvestson spent the night with us. Purchased plaid for a cloak, a pair of Leather gloves worsted stockings, Swiss muslin & lace for a cap, Muslin handkerchief worked, Elastics, etc. Paid for a crape frock I purchased last fall. All sick with colds.
Fryd 2nd	Very Cold indeed. Not able to do but little. Made a Handkerchief [.]
Sat. 3rd	Very cold. Washed. Almost sick yet, all of us but getting better.

Sund 4th	Cold yet. Mr. Delong called. My mind is very stupid indeed.
Mond 5th	Washed. Bought three small chairs. Sewed some. Baked mince pies. A. Hazelton spent the night.
Tuesd 6th	Pleasant. Almost sick and all the children with colds and sore Throats[.]
Wed 7th	Very pleasant. Mr E. Butchered the rest of his hogs, four in number. Mr. Stoddard came to making shoes. He too is almost sick. Mr. Freeman Western married to Miss Almira Rowley[.]
Thurd 8th	Colder. Not able to do anything but bound one pair of shoes.
Fryd 9th	Lee & Benjamin came from the woods. a gentleman from Peru [NY] took dinner. Had travelled five hundred miles on foot. Snow[.]
Sat 10th	Very Cold. Done but few chores not able to sit up. Mr S. [Stoddard] returned. Snow[.]
Sund 11th	So cold can do but little. Baked. Almost discouraged.
Mond 12th	Cold. A gentleman called from Prescott, formerly from Massachusetts. Uncle Brooks and Son called and so goes our Sabbaths. Scoured floors washed some, Ironed some this eve. Mr. E been to East Hopkinton after Miss Hawley. Disappointed.
Tuesd 13th	Moderate. Cut out a pair of stays. visited by M Heath. no snow yet[.]
Wed 14th	Pleasant. Have Miss Sarah Holley & Lucinda Delong sewing, making Plaid Cloak, crape frock, Plush Bonnet, Swiss muslin Cap, nightgown, caps, shirts, etc. Preparing for a journey when snows[.]
Thurs 15th	Warmer. Uncle Brook[s] & wife this eve. Mr E been to Potsdam. purchased me a veil, waist, Ribbon, etc, etc. I do little but chores.
	Rained all night last night and day snow almost all gone[.]
Fryd 16th	Thaws yet. Mary A. Heath again. Three hired girls and all of us do little.
Sat. 17th	Thaws. Sewed some. Almost sick. Miss H & D cannot stay any longer[.]

Sund 18th Snows some. The Ladies returned home. We should set out for Vermont tomorrow if we were ready but are far from that.

Mon 19th Snowed last night, snow very damp. Many going to Vermont.

Tuesd 20th Cloudy. Prepared for our journey. Visited at Uncle Durfey's this eve. Sat up all night to be ready to depart. Oh God wilt thou be the protector of our infant Children and keep them as in the hollow of thine hand. May our absence be prospered with health.

Wed. 21st Moderate weather. My Babe ten months old today. Will God watch over her through life. Took leave of my little family, set out for Vermont. Called at Esq. Heaths almost sick and tired out. Called at Roberts. Saw Mr. Squires family & Goulds. Tarried over night with Cousin Betsey Hall. B. Hall and wife spent the eve with us. If I did not wish to see my friends, I should return home.

Thurs 22nd Excellent sleighing. Spent the night at Bankers. Tired out.

Fryd 23rd Pleasant. Travelled among the mountains took tea at Esq. Sykes. Spent the night at Uncle Nicholson's. Aunt's health is poor indeed.

Sat. 24th High winds, stormy morn. Arrived at the Lake. Could not cross until the wind abated. After sundown we braved the troubled deep by the assistance of our heavenly protector we landed in Safety at Hutchins. Went to Vergennes. From there to Father Orvis. Found him very ill but gaining. His life has been despaired of. Very tired.

BRISTOL [VT]

Sund 25th Attended meeting at meeting of Friends. Almost sick. Tired out.

Mond 26th Pleasant. Rode to Vergennes, purchased a pair of Punella Bootees $2, 3$ ribbon. Dined at Hazard's. Took tea at P.V. [Van] Vliets. spent the night at Hazards. Received a few presents for my children.

Tues 27th Stormy. Returned to Father's, from there to Uncle Clapp's, spent the night.

Wed 28th Cold & Stormy. Called to Gen Duntons. Arrived at Grandfather Brooks, found him very low. It looks very lonesome indeed.

Thurs 29th	Pleasant. Washed. Visited at Mrs Miller['s]. Found her very lame.
Fryd 30th	Cold. Visited at Mr. Lee's, Lincoln. Spent the night at Grandfather Hawkins. Excellent visit with a number perhaps for the last [time].
Sat. 31st	Very cold. Returned, called to Mr. Gaige. Mrs. Berry went to Middlebury. Visited the Factory. Called at Olmstead's & store.

February 1829

Sund 1st	Very pleasant. Took leave of Bristol. Arrived at Father's in the eve. Father's health is on the gain. I hope he will yet get well
Mond 2nd	Cold. Almost sick all day. Levi E [Eastman] & Mother [Eastman] spent the eve. disagreeable.
Tues 3rd	Colder. Grandfather Brooks and family spent the night with us. Also Uncle Philander Orvis & family, Delong Etc[.] High spirits.
Wed 4th	Very cold. Took leave of all my friends, perhaps for the last time. Found the ice on the Lake thin and dangerous. Came partly on foot and rode some of the way. Dined at Willsborough Falls. Drove myself the rest of the day. Called at Keyesville [Keeseville], drove sixteen miles to Moors and spent the night. Almost perished. This eve. Many from P'ville here.
Thurs 5th	Cold. Drove all day. Spent the night at John Hall's. Roxanna Brooks almost tired out, left her at her sister's.
Fryd 6th	More moderate. Arrived at home, found them well. Many things broken. many burnt out on the road, unfortunate.
Sat. 7th	Pleasant. Thaws. Very unwell. Visited by Mother E. Dismissed my hired girl. Am not able to do but little.
Sund 8th	Very bad headache, almost sick. My Babe does not know me.
Mond 9th	Pleasant. Visited with J. Hall & wife. Roxanna B [Brooks] at Delong's They & Lucinda D. spent the night with us. Almost tired out.
Tuesd 10th	Stormy. Disappointed of visiting at Catharinesville. Washed some & Baked. My Children very uneasy and noisy.

Wed. 11th Stormy. Visited with Mr & Mrs H. at Mr Taylor's, Stockholm. Mr T. has made good improvement in the study of Divinity. Found Mr Dunshee's family in low circumstances.

Thursd 12th Very cold. Returned home. I think I shall be obliged to leave off visiting and attend to my family concerns.

Fryd 13th Cold. Mr Hall took leave of us. So may in. Most of the time I have, but little time or chance to work or strength.

Sat. 14th Cold, yet washed some, Mended some, etc. What is this work?

Sund 15th Pleasant. Headache. Mr. Hicks had a horse die in the road by our house today, in company with the two Stebbins and wifes, staid to tea. Went on to Potsdam.

Mond 16th Washed all day. My Babe taken sick. Pukes everything.

Tuesd 17th Stormy. Babe very sick. Henry sick indeed. God is yet good.

Wed 18th Pleasant. children very sick. Mrs. & Mrs. Arnold called from Vt.

Thursd 19th Cold. Henry has a very sore mouth indeed. Mr. Stebbins, E.B., dined with us. Baked pies, Bread etc. Almost discouraged.

Fryd 20th Children very sick indeed. L. Moon, D. Dewey called this eve.

Sat. 21st Pleasant & Cold. Washed some. Babe worse. Visited at Uncle Durfey's this eve; they depart for Vermont tomorrow.

Sund 22nd Cold. Babe better. Henry's mouth is very tedious indeed. Visited by Uncle E [Eleazor] and Wife, Mrs. Hawkins. No Sabbath.

Mond 23rd Pleasant, but very cold. Mr. Bachelor & wife, sister Mary called on us. Mrs. Hawkins spent the night. Been almost sick today.

Tuesd 24th Very pleasant. More moderate. Mr. H. took leave. purchased tin to the amount of $2.50. Finished Mary's frock. Lonely.

Wed 25th Very moderate. Visited at Mr. Flower's. Called over to Mr. Rockwell's. Saw Mrs. Parkill. Saw Mr Mrs. Greeno, Mrs. Converse of Madrid from Vt. Lake very poor this season.

Thurs 26th	Very stormy indeed, snow deep & drifted. Preparing quilts. I dreamt last night of seeing my deceased Grandmother looking very pleasant. My aged grandfather will soon follow.
Fryd 27th	Cold. Calculating my quilts. Received Coal for my furnace.
Sat. 28th	Tedious weather, snow deep & drifted. Washed, mended. Dream much of deceased friends and mourning dresses.

March 1829

Sund 1st	Stormy. Read Principle of Friends.[82] I wish I was more wise.
Mond 2nd	Pleasant. Mr & Mrs. Stebbins, Mr & Mrs. Hicks of Burlington. Mrs. H. presented me with a silk handkerchief. Tried tallow. visited[.]
Tuesd 3rd	Rainy. Lucinda sick.
Wed. 4th	Pleasant. Visited with Mr & Mrs F [Flower] at Dr. E. Lucinda very sick.
Thurs 5th	Cold. Washed a little. Babe Very worrysome indeed. Unwell.
Fryd 6th	Pleasant and cold. Can do but very little with my Babe.
Sat. 7th	Pleasant. Visited at Uncle Brooks. Took home a girl by the name of Margaret Duffey an Irish girl. Oh, God, assist me to train her up in the way she should go thus when she is old, she may not depart from it. Aged fifteen.
Sund 8th	Pleasant. Babe some better but refuses to leave my arms.
Mond 9th	Pleasant, thaws some. Took up and cleared chamber floor. Emptied all the straw beds and washed them. Scalt all the bedsteads etc. My Babe cried a great deal today. Took tea at D.E.['s] [David Eastman's]
Tuesd 10th	Pleasant. Sized a short web. Learning Margaret to spool. Have to tend my Babe all the time. L.E. [Lee Eastman] took tea with us.
Wed 11th	Pleasant. My Babe lips swollen greatly, all of a blister mouth.
Thurs 12th	Rainy. Visited by Mrs. Heart [Hart] & Brooks. Mr. Cook dined with us. Uncle & the ladies spent the night with us, agreeable visit.

Fryd 13th	Stormy & cold. C Covey, B. Reeves worked here. Set Margaret to washing a few things, she does that better than I expected. Visit a short time at Davids L., health is poor. Sewed some today.
Sat. 14th	High winds, cold. Margaret braids straw tolerable well. Mr E Sick.
Sund 15th	Pleasant. Headache all day. Mr. Delong dined with us. Mr H came.
Mond 16th	Washed. Mr & Mrs & Miss H. Hazelton visited us. Purchased of Mr Havestson eight yds. of calico for a frock for Lucinda.
Tuesd 17th	Stormy. Drew in a web of Bags. Visited this eve by Mr & Mrs. Blodget.
Wed 18th	Mr. Peck of Malone and Chittendon of Hopkinton here today. Warm[.]
Thurs 19th	Pleasant. Mrs Lee made a saucy call visited at Uncle Durfey.
Fryd 20th	It seems as if my Babe would never get well of her sore mouth.
Sat. 21st	Pleasant. Visited by H.D. [Harriet Durfey], Mrs. Searls. My Babe has a hard time. Sewed some. Eliza Ann Canada [Kennedy] buried today, died of a spotted fever.
Sund 22nd	Pleasant. Children all have hard colds. Henry had a bad fall. When shall I see my family walking in the way of wisdom.
Mond 23rd	Washed. Sewing some, but can do nothing but with a Babe in my arms[.]
Tuesd 24th	Stormy. Visited by Aunt Durfey. A Mr. Swift of Potsdam missing.
Wed 25th	Pleasant. Visited at Father E's, spent the night. My babe yet sick.
Thurs 26th	Stormy. Visited at Uncle D's, returned home almost sick.
Fryd 27th	Pleasant. Almost sick indeed. my Babe's mouth better.
Sat. 28th	Pleasant. Mr. Searls visited. Mr Chipman & Hawley left a number of [spinning] wheels here to be sold but Religion we buy not.
Sund 29th	Pleasant. Fine day for sap and our people are not ready, made no spouts yet. Undertaking to learn Margaret to read.

Mond 30th Washed a great wash. Visited by Mrs. Covey. Very tired indeed. burning spouts. Sick night indeed. Worked too hard today for my constitution.

Tuesd 31st Pleasant. Very unwell. Weaving or trying to learn Margaret.

April 1829

Wed. 1st Cloudy. Almost discouraged trying to learn M. to work.

Thurs 2nd Rainy. Sold Mr Tupper a wheel & reel yesterday, one today.

Fryd 3rd Pleasant. Sold my wheel to Aaron Stearns. Weave very slow.

Sat. 4th Pleasant. Lucinda worrysome, most of the time sick.

Sund 5th Cloudy. Good sap day and sorry to know Mr E is boiling it. Oh when shall I see my family growing up in the fear of God.

Mond 6th Wove all day. Finished my web of bags almost out of patience of ever trying to learn Margaret to weave, very awkward.

Tuesd 7th Cloudy. Making Bags I fear I shall never learn Margaret to sew.

Wed 8th Washed. Visited at Mr N Rockwell's. Our people sugared off.

Thursd 9th Rainy. Mr. E and Humphrey been to the forge to get iron.

Fryd 10th Sewing. Finished Lucinda's frock, cut out Mary's.

Sat. 11th Cool. Lucinda yet worrysome. cleared the dooryard. Tired.

Sund 12th Pleasant. Went to the schoolhouse. No meeting. Tired indeed.

Mond 13th Washed. Visited Lorena. Sewing on my frock. Dull. Sugaring.

Tuesd 14th Cleared and washed the chambers. Almost tired out. Visited Soloda[.]

Wed 15th Pleasant. Visited by Aunt Brooks, heard of their poverty. Why was it not my lot to be pinched with hunger.

Thursd 16th Pleasant. Sewing. Cut out a frock for Margaret. Tried on her.

Fryd 17th Finished Mary's frock. Get along slowly with work.

Sat. 18th Pleasant. A.M., few drops of rain P.M. Finished M's frock. the Small Pox is prevailing through our land at this time.

Sabbath 19th Cloudy. Quarterly meeting today. Mr E, M & S attends.

Mond 20th Cloudy. My left foot to the knee joint is numb and cold.

Tuesd 21st Pleasant. Very sick this morning. Lorena almost sick.

Wed. 22nd Pleasant. Dr. Sprague came and bled me, ordered strong drafts on my foot. I put on pounded horse radish and vinegar. Felt no effects from it, only cold & numb.

Thursd 23rd Cloudy. Made a sun Bonnet for Mary. Arm lame.

Fryd 24th Showery. Finished Margaret's frock & Mary's. Foot yet numb.

Sat. 25th Pleasant. Baked. Mr Abbott's Barn raised. Margaret gone to Mr A's

Sund 26th Pleasant, but very cool weather for the time of the year.

Mond 27th Washed. Cut out a coat for Henry. I know little of business.

Tuesd 28th Rainy. Sewing on a coat. My children all sick, colds.

Wed 29th Pleasant. Sewing. Mr E. removing fence, making garden. Our Clock we bought last week of Samuel Peck runs well.

Thurs 30th Pleasant. Finished the Coat. Visited at Mr Chase's, excellent.

May 1829

Fryd 1st Pleasant. Sowed onions. Visited at Uncle Durfey's. Tired & sick.

Sund 3rd Cloudy. Almost sick and discouraged of ever being good for work.

Mond 4th Cloudy. Washed some. Fixed off the children to school. Was none. Visited by Mrs Newton & Walker Sewed some.

Tues 5th	Want of rain. Almost sick and discouraged with M[argaret].
Wed 6th	Pleasant. Had an agreeable visit with Mrs. Chase.
Thurs 7th	Warm. Visited the shanty. Miss Anna Harrington married to Miss [Mr] John Dustin. My health is poor indeed.
Fryd 8th	Cloudy. Walked this morning to Delongs, spent the day.
Sat. 9th	Cloudy, but no rain. Sewed all day. Finished several garments.
Sund 10th	Rainy. Read the Religious Diary of Garretson.[83]
Mond 11th	Cloudy. Sent off the Children once more to school. Washed, Baked etc. Margaret so saucy I can hardly hear her. Have told her if she did not do better I would not keep her. Traded Pedler.
Tuesd 12th	Wove some but it is too hard work for me to weave Linen.
Wed 13th	Pleasant. Visited at Uncle Brooks. Almost tired out. Uncle brought my Babe home.
Thurs 14th	Disappointed of company. Visited at the Shanty. my Babe beller[s] away[.]
Fryd 15th	Wove two & half yards. My children attend school, Margaret, too.
Sat. 16th	Rainy. Wove three yards. Sick all night, scarcely able to sleep.
Sabb 17th	Pleasant. Read Lorenzo Dows opinion or thoughts.
Mond 18th	Washed. Too much for my health. The ill treatment I receive from Margaret is worse than hard labor, much[.]
Tuesd 19th	Almost tired out. Wove what I was able to, that but little.
Wed 20th	Pleasant. Wove some. Knitting Linen socks for Mr E.
Thurs 21st	Weaving today. Slowly but grace I fear I have none. H & M Durfey visited me. I am fairly worn out with Margaret.
Fryd 22nd	Wove some today. Called over to Mr Heath's for yarn, have none.

Sat. 23rd Dry & windy. Visited by M.H. [Mary Heath], Lorena. My patience exhausted.

Sund 24th Warm & windy. Almost sick. many called that ought be at home.

Mond 25th Washed. Wove some. Mr. Ishaam and Sally Brooks arrived in town today from Bristol. my family well at Vt.

Tuesd 26th Very warm. Baked, prepared for company. Visited by H. Durfey, L Delong, Sally Brooks Isaam [Isham], Aunt Brooks.

Wed 27th Warm day. Disappointed of company. wove and finished.

Thurs 28th Pleasant. Called over to Mr Chases & Converse. Find M[argaret]. tells lies.

Fryd 29th Cut out my brown cloth. Planted some in the garden.

Sat. 30th Visited with all the children at Father Eastman's.

Sund 31st Pleasant. Read Bentley's visit to his friend Clifford wrote to my friends in Chatgua [Chateaugay] & Vt. Mr E very sick.

June 1829

Mon 1st Washed. Making my cloth brown. I think I shall dismiss M[argaret].

Tuesd 2nd Sewing. Visited by Mrs. Rockwell, Mrs. Ford. M.[Margaret] told many lies.

Wed 3rd Rainy. Picking wool, five fleeces. Very cross Babe.

Thursd 4th Pleasant. Margaret lies in such manner Mr E turned her out of doors.

Fryd 5th Pleasant. I am astonished to think that any person can do as Margaret has. I am glad she has left my house.

Sat. 6th Finished my wood ready for the machine. Visited at Mr M Rockwells, borrowed books: Cottage Girl, the Thatcher's wife, affecting instance of Piety.[84] Oh that I might profit by them to the good of my soul.

Sund 7th Very warm. Finished reading the little Books. Oh, that I might live the life of the righteous that my last end may be like theirs that I may die in peace.

Mond 8th	Rainy day. Put in a web of linen. Not able to work hard.
Tuesd 9th	Washed all day quilts & coverlets etc. Mrs. Searls visited me.
Wed 10th	Pleasant. Made soap. Margaret came to tell me I lied once more.
Thursd 11th	Pleasant. Washed. Bees swarmed, one swarm went off.
Fryd 12th	Pleasant. Mr E. Purchased Cotton Cloth 36 yds. Cut out Henry a pair of trousers. Sewed some, get along slow.
Sat. 13th	Baked. Sewing. Mr B to work here How many priviledges I enjoy and how few returns to love do I show for them.
Sabbath 14th	Very little rain. Dull, drowsy. Ah, when shall I awake.
Mond 15th	Rainy. Cut out cloth. Not well, my Babe cross.
Tuesd 16th	Pleasant. Eight men to cook for today. Almost sick.
Wed 17th	Lucinda Delong came to work for me. Mr Covey had a barn raised. A Frenchman stole a rifle. was taken. Very rainy indeed this night.
Thursd 18th	Sewing. My Babe cries almost all the time this week.
Fryd 19th	Washed. Baked etc. Oh that I lived better.
Sat. 20th	Sewing. My days are hastening aways in sin & folly.
Sund 21st	Quite unwell. Read but little. My Bible and my God is neglected almost altogether. Oh shall I not reform. cupboard made[.]
Mond 22nd	Rainy. Washed a little. Almost discouraged to have to hire help.
Tuesd 23rd	Lucinda D. commenced spinning my wool, poor rolls[.]
Wed 24th	Cool weather for June. Spun twenty knots coarse yarn.
Thursd 25th	Washed, sewed some. L.D. almost sick, my weaving not done.

Fryd 26th	Spun little. Visited by Mrs. Perry Mrs Covey, Aunt Durfey, Lorena, Mrs. Chase took tea with us. L.D. gone home.
Sat 27th	Rainy P.M. Finished the coarsest rolls. Visited by Mrs. Stoddard and children. Cold nights, backward times.
Sund 28th	Rainy and cold. Spent the day in idleness. Mrs. Brown . . .
Mond 29th	Rainy. The children were wet to the skin going to school.
Tuesd 30th	Rainy, did not send them. Farmers impatient for the sun to appear on the drooping crops. wove little. David's house raised today. Mr. Harvestson called today.

July 1829

Wed 1st	Rainy. Washed. I am declining slowly to the ground.
Thursd 2nd	Rainy. Harriet D called. We calculated on visiting at Uncle Brooks. Rained so we visited at Davids a/c [on account] my health.
Fryd 3rd	Cloudy. Finished a shirt for L. bought a patent wheel head.
Sat. 4th	Showers. Independence. Lee gone to Potsdam. a Boy lost, six years of age, from Norfolk. Been gone this fifth day, been seen once in Potsdam woods, all search in vain as yet, hundreds in search.
Sab. 5th	Rainy. Scarcely able to sit up[.] I know not what to do. The Boy is found, was pushed into the river on purpose.
Mond 6th	Pleasant. Washed. Mr Harvestson dined with us. Bought one yd of Calico. two sticks of thread. Cut out a cape for myself.
Tuesd 7th	Scoured all I could today, but do not feel able to do anything at all. Read a small book. I am tired of hiring girls.
Wed 8th	Rainy. Spun ten knots. Visited by Aunt Brooks and Mrs. Gibson. Sewing on my cape. Camp Meeting began.
Thursd 9th	Pleasant. Spun six knots. In great distress, abortion followed, in great distress through the day. Mother E [Eastman] spent a part of the day with me. Aunt Brooks the night, as comfortable as I could expect. very weak.

Fryd 10th	Pleasant. Sat up to eat with the family. H. Perry here.
Sat. 11th	Pleasant. Miss Lucinda Allen came to stay a week. My eyes pain me much very weak indeed, body also.
Sabb 12th	Pleasant. Gaining. Aunt Brooks & Mrs. Gould, Aunt Durfey took tea with me. Able to sit up some, very weak.
Mond 13th	Pleasant. Camp Meeting broke up. Began to knit a little in my bed my eyes and head pain me much.
Tuesd 14th	almost crazy with the headache. Mary Redington boarding here. Miss Allen is an excellent housekeeper.
Wed. 15th	Pleasant. Headache, eyes very weak. Sit up half the time.
Thursd 16th	Cloudy. Lorena sent for assistance for nothing again.
Fryd 17th	Cloudy. Rode with Aunt Brooks & Mrs. Hoyt to Uncle Durf[e]ys spent the night agreeably with Harriet. A ride offered[.]
Sat. 18th	Showers. Harriet returned home with me. Traded with a Pedlar for the girls. Miss Allen done work here.
Sab. 19th	Pleasant. Trying with Mr E['s] assistance to do my chores. Very unfit for the task but no one to do it. Wrote a letter to Father, Sally Brooks, Mary Clapp, Betsey Hall to send by Roswell Eastman tomorrow.
Mond 20th	Pleasant. Some better. by being busy all the time I do my work.
Tuesd 21st	Showers. Baked. Spun five knots. Have eight in the family.
Wed 22nd	Cloudy. Spun five knots. Finished a Linen sock since I have been sick. Mrs. Chase visited me. Picked green peas[.]
Thursd 23rd	Showers. Washed some, and floor. Almost tired out tonight.
Fryd 24th	Pleasant. Spun twenty knots after Lucinda done spinning.
Sat. 25th	Pleasant. I am almost sick. To boil a dinner, get tea etc. is all I do.

Sund 26th	Pleasant. Spent the day in idleness. [Sarah] Delong called. Mrs. Hutchins deranged of late. God grant her reason.
Mond 27th	Cloudy. Rainy night. Spun one runn, very tired.
Tuesd 28th	Washed. Spun ten knots, it [is] more than I am able to do.
Wed 29th	Rainy most of the time. Spun ten knots. Baked.
Thursd 30th	Rainy. Spun twenty knots. Called over to David's. Discord is . . .
Fryd 31st	Warm day. Mrs. Chase called A.M. Mrs. Searls visited me. I scoured my blanket yarn. Mr S had an ox die this morning.

August 1829

Sat 1st	Rainy. Dull weather. Toothache. Lucinda D. called. Finished straw.
Sund 2nd	Pleasant. David's wife [Lorena] blessed with a daughter this morn.
Mond 3rd	Baking, Washing. Almost sick and tired out. Lorena's well.
Tuesd 4th	Washed. Rainy night. In the morning I am very feeble.
Wed 5th	Cloudy but God know[s] what is best for us altogether.
Thursd 6th	Cloudy. Received a letter from Brother Abraham[s]. Poor health. a remarkable Hail storm destroyed abundance there [VT] Baked. Visited at Mr. C. Rockwell's. Almost tired out.
Fryd 7th	Warm. Mrs. Lee blessed with a daughter. Carried dinner to the workmen, quite too hard for me. Called over the shanty.
Sat. 8th	Almost sick with the toothache. Have a hard time most of the time.
Sund 9th	Rainy. Delong, G. Covey called. Lucinda returned to spin.
Mond 10th	Washed, baked etc. Get clear down yet sick almost every day.
Tuesd 11th	Wove all day for one yards. I think this linen will not get wove very soon. I wish I liked work better.

Wed 12th	Rainy. Have workmen now all the time. I hope I shall not have a hired girl much longer. Four Frenchmen with their mother staid the night. I have a sore Boil on shoulder.
Thurs 13th	Pleasant A.M. Rainy eve. Lucinda D. took a ride to Potsdam. with G. Covey. Carried dinner again but I shall not any more.
Fryd 14th	Pleasant. Visited at Mr. Coveys. Called over to Uncle's. Tired out.
Sat. 15th	Continue unwell. Visited at Mr. H. [Hart] spent the night at Uncle B[rooks]'s. Called at Mr. Hoits. Her Babe is no better.
Sund 16th	Pleasant. Uncle and Aunt Durfey returned and dined with us.
Mond 17th	Washed, Baked. Stir cream for all the Butter I make.
Tues 18th	Spun sixteen knots. Finished my finest rolls, glad am I.
Wed 19th	Spun one run. Stung on Monday by a Bee on the face. Swollen the worst ever I saw. Lucinda stung on her face which is so painful I cannot do much of anything.
Thursd 20th	Spun thirty-six knots. Mr Smith to work here & Lee's.
Fryd 21st	Spun thirty knots. Sewed some, Ironed. Lucinda sick.
Sat. 22nd	Spun ten knots. Fried cakes, washed some. Unwell yet.
Sund 23rd	Pleasant. Mr E at [original blank space] I am doing no better. What will become of our poor children if brought up in this way?
Mond 24th	Cloudy, warm High winds. Washed a large washing. Baked, scoured twelve runs of yarn and sized it.
Tuesd 25th	Cloudy & Cool. Spun twenty-five knots. Visited by Aunt Durfey. Spooled twenty-seven skeins. Retired at twelve.
Wed 26th	Cloudy. Scoured 16½ runns of yarn. Warped a web. put the most of it in. washed floor. took a Linen web put out roll[.]
Thursd 27th	Cloudy. Not well, hard task to spin. Finished my roll, put in my web but do not feel able to weave.

Fryd 28th Pleasant. Gathered mustard. Wove two yards fine diaper.

Sat. 29th Cloudy. Cleaned the Bedroom, dressed with Cedar. Ironed. Not so well today. I fear I shall never be able to weave much. God knows thanks to him.

Sund 30th Cloudy. Henry can [do] a little in reading. God grant that he may learn & delight to serve his maker in his youth.

Mond 31st Cloudy, warm. Washed & Baked the first pumpkin we have had this year. Also one watermelon.

September 1829

Tues 1st Pleasant & warm. Cut out a vest & pantaloons. Wove three yds fine wide cloth slow weaving. Stray[.]

Wed 2nd Smart shower P.M. Wove six yards very tired indeed.

Thursd 3rd Wove seven yds. Finished my web. Henry sick.

Fryd 4th Warm spooled. Warped a Blanket. Lucinda Sick[.]

Sat. 5th Pleasant. Lucinda sick all night. I find she has the Canker in the stomach & mouth. Gathered Sumach and Red raspberry leaves for medicine for canker.

Sund 6th Pleasant. Visited the springs, found person at work.

Mond 7th Rainy. Making a flannel shirt, fried cakes. Very feeble

Tuesd 8th Rainy & cold. Mending. Lucinda very sick nights[.]

Wed 9th Rainy. making Henry a pair of pantaloons, striped.

Thursd 10th Showery. Scoured some, starching clothes, lace Etc.

Fryd 11th Some rain. David Harkness & Isaac Hallock of Peru spent the night with us. Friends of Orthodoxy.

Sat. 12th Cool visited at Delongs with the Friends. Had a solemn family meeting. Parted in tears, Oh, that I were as good a Christian as Harkness He made me a present of two Epistles from London.

Sabb 13th	almost sick today. my visit too hard for me.
Mond 14th	Baked. Almost gave up my visit to Potsdam. Samuel hired William to go in his room to Norfolk. Rainy. Frost.
Tuesd 15th	Cool. Stephen E spent the night with us. About sick[.]
Wed. 16th	Cloudy. Gathered herbs for colouring, not able to do more.
Thursd 17th	Showers. Aunt Maria visited me helped scour my yarn.
Fryd 18th	Pleasant. coloured a fine yellow, poor red, good black.
Sat. 19th	Cool. Washed all day at the brook it seemed as if I never should do it again. Had my clothes kettle and all to carry.
Sund 20th	Rainy. I think I never shall work again as I have for two days past. Very unwell indeed. Oh my family. Mr. S shot a cow of J. Brownells[.]
Mond 21st	Rainy. Mr Hawkins called from Vt. Baked, washed.
Tuesd 22nd	Lowry. Aunt Brooks and Mrs. Gibson came to spend the week. with us. Put in a blanket, unable to work.
Wed 23rd	Cloudy. Wove some. Received two pounds of tea.
Thursd 24th	Cloudy. Finished my Blanket, put in a web for Maria.
Fryd 25th	Cool Sick today. Visited by Aunt Durfey, Mrs. Covey, Harriet Durfey Lorena. I am unfit to live or to die.
Sat. 26th	Showers. Wove four yards. Visited at Joseph Dufey's.
Sund 27th	Cold. Mrs. G. [Gibson] returned. My visit too hard for me.
Mond 28th	Wove ten yards and did my chores. Wove two yards an hour.
Tuesd 29th	Rainy. Finished the web, weaving is too hard for me.
Wed 30th	Showers. Washed. Visited at Uncle Durfey's. Maria returned.

October 1829

Thursd 1st	Snow storm. Put in a web of Plaid. wove some high slays[.]
Fryd 2nd	Cut out my web. Put in a coarser reed. Corn very poor.
Sat. 3rd	Ironed many clothes. Spun shoe thread, mended etc.
Sun. 4th	Pleasant & cool. Oh, my husband, when will he learn righteousness and leave off work on the Sabbath.
Mond 5th	Pleasant, but cold. Washed. Help pick a load of corn. Ironed. Very tired indeed. Received a barrel of poor apples[.]
Tues 6th	Pleasant. Helped [Mr.] E pick a cart full of corn. Baked, etc. I work as long as I can go and then rest awhile. Tired out.
Wed. 7th	Pleasant. Visited with Aunt D & Harriet. At Uncle B. A Mr. Bigsby found today in the Mill Pond at P'ville. Being in liquor [he] stepped out of the Potash in on Saturday night. Poor mortal is gone forever.
Thursd 8th	Cool & pleasant. Almost sick. Mended some. Husked corn[.] My children almost sick with colds, sore throat.
Fryd 9th	Pleasant. Baked mince Pies. Visited at David's. Mary sick.
Sat. 10th	Cloudy. children very sick, not well myelf. Purchased a washboard. Mr Peck finished D's [David's] house.
Sund 11th	Cool & cloudy. Why stand we idle all the day in market place. What account can we give at the barr of God.
Mond 12th	Showery. A.M. Washed, mended, etc. my children better today.
Tuesd 13th	Pleasant. Wove three yds Uncle B. Children here.
Wed 14th	Pleasant. Wove Five yards my is [original blank space] large indeed. Tired out.
Thursd 15th	Pleasant. Finished my web, put [in] a coverlet called world wonder[.]
Fryd 16th	Pleasant. Do not feel able to weave. Baked, mended some.

Sat. 17th	Pleasant. Beautiful weather for the season. Coloured black.
Sund 18th	Pleasant. But I am dull and stupid am always to be. Mr. Gilbert Covey married this P.M. to Miss Lucinda Delong.
Mond 19th	Rainy. Mended a number of garments. Wove some. Engaged to weave another coverlet for Mrs. Brush; I ought not to.
Tuesd 20th	Washed. Wove what I could. When shall I love my Lord.
Weds 21st	Cold. Twenty-eight years old today, so many years of sin.
Thursd 22nd	Almost sick. Visited by H & M Durfey, yesterday by Saphrona.
Fryd 23rd	Cloudy. Had a pleasant visit from Mrs. Delong.
Sat. 24th	Cold. My side pains me much of late, am discouraged. John Snider spent the night[.] 76 yrs of age. from Qebec [Quebec]
Sund 25th	Pleasant. when shall I see any signs of Religion.
Mond. 26th	Washed. Made each of the girls a frock. last week. Much to do[.]
Tuesd 27th	Pleasant for the season. If my mind was as clear as the weather How happy should be an example worthy of my babes[.]
Wed 28th	Pleasant. Not able to weave but little in a day. very hard.
Thursd 29th	Miss Lucy Gould buried today. Visited at Mr. Rockwell's.
Fryd 30th	Wove all I could today. Baked. I hope to get rid of this Coverlet[.]
Sat. 31st	Finished the coverlet, glad am I. Rainy all day & night.

November 1829

Sund 1st	Rainy. Sick all day. Old Mrs. Lamb died today. 74 yrs.
Mond 2nd	Rainy. Put in a coverlet for Mrs. Brush began it Taber[.]
Tuesd 3rd	Rainy. Wove very little. Roswell spent the night[.] Made bread & candles[.]

Wed 4th	Rainy. All gone to Election. Mended all day, washed this eve.
Thursd 5th	Rainy. Washed, baked. Tired out. I am fit for nothing.
Fryd 6th	Rainy. Visited by M. Durfey. Called over to David's in his new house.
Sat. 7th	Rainy. Made Henry a vest yesterday. Pain in my side all day. Done very little for soul or body. God grant I may.
Sund 8th	Cold, Rainy, Mingled with snow. Winter fast approaching, death also. Oh, may be begin to prepare to meet our God in judgment.
Mond 9th	Pleasant, but cold. A German Dr. Andrew Wyner called. He thinks he can help me. He gave me fever root [triosteum perfoliatum] to cure the inward fever, some drops & gum myrrh, gum Marabed to (take) in spirits three times a day. Cut out a pair of Pantaloons.
Tuesd 10th	Colder. I find my health is declining fast. Sewing a little.
Wed 11th	Rainy. Traded a little with Richardson. Paid him what we owed him before. Baked. Our cloth spoiled entirely.
Thursd 12th	Cold. Lee gone into the woods for a fall hunt, glad am I.
Fryd 13th	More pleasant. Old Dr Wyner took leave. I walked to Uncle Brooks, Purchased cloth, Aunt sick, returned late.
Sat. 14th	Snow. Not able to sit up but very little. Discouraged.
Sund 15th	Pleasant. Very feeble indeed. My work is almost done for this world. Oh God wilt thou assist me to prepare for this last change. Wilt thou have mercy on the tender offspring. Oh, do not visit the iniquity of the Parents on the innocent Children. May we set a better example before them & the world until death.
Mond 16th	Cloudy. Finished Mr E's pantaloons but unable to do more.
Tuesd 17th	Snow & rain. Disappointed of visiting. Cut & made Henry pantaloons[.] Washed a little for the Children. Discouraged.
Wed 18th	Stormy all day. No prospect of my visiting. Tired of home.

Thursd 19th	Stormy. Finished my cap, my weaving will never be done.
Fryd 20th	Stormy. Lee came home. Baked for him. received a visit from Aunt Brooks. Visited at Father E's. Spent the night at Uncle Durfeys with all my children. Sick night[.]
Sat. 21st	Pleasant. The Ladies visited at Uncle's. good visit.
Sund 22nd	Rainy. Returned home tonight. Icy storm.
Mond 23rd	Rainy, high winds. Cut out a coat for Henry. Sick.
Tuesd 24th	Pleasant. Better health, Washed. visited by M.E., M.H.
Wed 25th	Washed, visited by H.D. S.R. assisted H. to warp a cushion.
Thursd 26th	Snow. Visited by Aunt Brooks. Clear down again.
Fryd 27th	Pleasant. Visited by Mrs. Searls. Harriet returned home.
Sat. 28th	Pleasant. Mr. E. plastering the crack of the old house. not able to sit up in the A.M. Miss Harris called for another cushion[.]
Sund 29th	Cloudy, better than yesterday. I feel as if death was advancing slowly. God only knoweth. Oh, that I was ready.
Mond 30th	Cold day. Visited at David's. Mr E raised the hearth. Sewing. hard cold, school commenced today. J. Gibson.

December 1829

Tuesd 1st	Sewing. Not so well today. Cloudy, but no snow.
Wed 2nd	Cloudy. Finished my flannel frock. discouraged almost.
Thursd 3rd	Pleasant. Traded with Harvestson[.] owe him 3.18. washed. Cut out my Bedtick, Children frocks. Old Bachelor [Lee Eastman] at home.
Fryd 4th	Cold & windy. emptied all my coarse feathers into a bed for the children. Sewed some. washed floors etc. many in.

Sat. 5th	Stormy. Sewing. Lee returned to the wood, glad am I.
Sund 6th	Very rainy day & night. Almost sick of work[.]
Mond 7th	Rainy. Cleaning tubs etc. ready for butchering. Mr. E attended court at P'ville. Secured my pickles.
Tuesd 8th	Stormy, Little snow. Scrubbing, Ironed. Tired out again.
Wed. 9th	Cold. Killed six hogs; sold four averaging three hundred apiece. Did what I could and let the rest go undone. House full of men[.]
Thursd 10th	Thaws, Finished trying lard, boiled the mince meat. cleaned the souce [souse] and boiled it. Washed floors. Tired of Lee.
Fryd 11th	Cold indeed. Securing the soap grease. Almost sick.
Sat. 12th	Moderate weather. Cut out with piecing pantaloons for Henry. Received a Bushel of dried applies of D. [David].
Sund 13th	Hard rain. last night. Lee came home sick with cold.
Mond 14th	Colder. Had to get the beds around the fire again.
Tuesd 15th	Sewing on pantaloons. Mr. Farnham called from Vt.
Wed 16th	Pleasant. Aaron Lee started for Vt. Sent two lengthy letters. I am tired of so many men around the fire.
Thursd 17th	Pleasant. Almost sick having Lee to wait upon night and day.
Fryd 18th	Little snow. Made a shirtee. Visited Mrs. Searls. Cut and partly made Lee a shirt, he is better some.
Sat. 19th	Pleasant. Finished the shirt. Baked pies, cakes etc. Worked today when very unable. Hunters all around me.
Sund 20th	Some snow last night. Pleasant mind, dark benighted[.] Washed woolen clothes this eve. Mended some - perhaps wrong.
Mond 21st	Snow squalls. Finished Lucinda a frock. Ironed, mended.

Tuesd 22nd Cold. Washed all day. I am tired of washing for hunters. Uncle Brooks called. Finished a pair of socks.

Wed 23rd Pleasant. Scoured ceilings & floors. Mending Etc. Fried cakes. Called over to Mr Searls. They have moved today farther.

Thurs 24th High winds. Ironed, that is all I have been able to do[.]

Fryd 25th Pleasant. Christmas. Mending. Called over to Mr. Lee's. Malachi at our house lame with a cut on his foot.

Sat. 26th Pleasant. Twisted yarn all day. The old Bachelor is gone tonight[.] Oh that he would but stay away.

Sabb 27th Cloudy, a few drops of rain. Uncle B's girls called. M.L. washed this eve. the children have bad colds.

Mond 28th Pleasant. Wove some. Baked. God is yet kind to me.

Tuesd 29th Rainy. Lucinda very sick today. Mr. Gibson boarding here.

Wed 30th Colder. Wove one yards. H Durfey took tea with me. Hard cough.

Thursd 31st Cloudy. Weaving. I hope my health is better indeed.

January 1830

Fryd 1st New Years Day. Visited by Aunt Brooks. Mr E at turkey shoot, had one to dress. When shall I get done weaving.

Sat. 2nd Cloudy. visited by Mrs. Searls, Mary E. all day. L[ee] to spent the night. Took a short web to weave for Mrs. S.

Sund 3rd Cloudy. Dull and stupid all day. Done some work this eve.

Mond 4th Colder, some snow. Finished a Coverlet. Prepared a web for the Loom. Baked. etc. S. Richards bottomed some chairs this eve. Tired out[.]

Tues 5th Put in a web, wove six yards - five after dark. Mr. A Remington called.

Wed 6th Stormy. Wove six yards. Finished the web. Spooled another for myself.

Thursd 7th	Colder. Mr. Smith took breakfast from Chesterfield. One John Bastian it is supposed shot himself on purpose last Sabbath.
Fryd 8th	Cold. Visited by Mrs. Rockwell, Mrs. Searls, Mr. R. Mr. S. this eve. Many called.
Sat. 9th	Snows little. Coloured Red & black. Uncle D took dinner with us[.]
Sund 10th	Snows little. hard headache. Wove four yards this eve, finished my web.
Mond. 11th	Little more snow. Finished colouring. Prepared a piece of carpeting for the Loom. Baked etc. Sewed some. A very cold day indeed, colder heart. Mrs. Chafy died Sat last.
Tuesd 12th	Very cold. Delong spent most of the day. Settled with him. Made sheet[.]
Wed 13th	Cold yet. Put in and began my carpet, Slow work. Made sheet[.]
Thursd 14th	More moderate. Spent the day at Uncle Durfey's assisted them to move their substance into the new house, for the first time took supper with them in it. Uncle Clapp spent the night from Vermont, heard that my dear father had been thrown from his waggon, broke his collar bone twice, two ribs crushed in his breast bone. I am now able to walk. Uncle intends moving into this county.
Fryd 15th	Moderate. Almost sick. Mrs. Brush called, paid me two dollars. Visited by Mrs. Chase. So many called had not chance to work.
Sat. 16th	Finished weaving. Visited by M Durfey. Almost sick, tired out.
Sund 17th	Frozen hard, but little snow. very glad to spend another sabbath without a loom in sight. God is good to me always.
Mond 18th	Very cold day. Laying our chamber floor double today. Visited by Aunt Brooks Mrs. Gibson came to stay some time[.]
Tuesd 19th	Very cold yet. Can do but little else than common chores.
Wed 20th	Stormy. Washed most of today. Continues to storm.
Thursd 21st	Cold indeed. Washed, cleaned house, Mrs. G is very talkative.
Fryd 22nd	Baked. Not the least thaw yet, continually cold. Almost sick[.]

Sat 23rd	Cold, but thank my god I have enough to eat & drink. and a shelter for my children while many want. visited by Mr & Mrs. Covey[.]
Sab 24th	Clear & cold. Very much out of health today and yet am blessed.
Mond 25th	Stormy. Washed. I can do but little this cold weather.
Tuesd 26th	Very cold yet. Making a nightgown night for the children.
Wed. 27th	Cold extreme. Sewing little but almost sick and tired out.
Thursd 28th	Cold. Baked, Ironed, etc. Grandma'am Gibson has talked me sick. E. had an Ox horn broken off by the fall of a tree[.]
Fryd 29th	Cold is the weather and cold indeed our Love to God and ungrateful.
Sat. 30th	The Coldest day known in the country. Mended little.
Sabb 31st	Pleasant, but cold yet. Scarcely able to sit up. Visited by Uncle Brooks & wife, they took Mrs. Gibson home with them.

February 1830

Mond 1st	Pleasant P.M. Stormy A.M. Washed. Visited at Mr. Rockwell's. Called to see Melissa, her foot is a sight[.] Visited this eve by Mr & Mrs Flower. Mr & Mrs Chase. Excellent visit. very tired.
Tuesd 2nd	Rather more moderate. Made a Vandyke of Blue Calico.
Wed 3rd	Cold. Sewing, Ironing. A time of scarcity at hand, I think[.]
Thursd 4th	Pleasant. Baked twice. Visited by Lorana. Visited at Father E['s] in company with Mr & Mrs Flower & Mr & Mrs Rockwell.
Fryd 5th	Cold. Visited by Mrs. Searles. Lord, wilt thou assist her in time of her distress and poverty. Sold a young creature to Mr. Rider[.]
Sat. 6th	Stormy. Visited by Aunt Durfey. How kind are my friends. rec'd letter, I wrote[.]
Sund 7th	Very unwell. I get tired through the week. Sabbath day is very dull[.]

Mond 8th	More pleasant. Visited by Mother E & Lorena. Mr Smith & Armstrong called for taxes & cow. Henry froze his toe today returning from school.
Tuesd 9th	Stormy. Mr. Hazelton from Lawrence called. Making a cap.
Wed 10th	Pleasant. Visited by Mary Ann Heath. Called over to Mr Searls. Melissa foot better. Visited this eve by Mrs McAllister and Son.
Thursd 11th	Scarcely able to sit up. Sewed a little. my walk yesterday too hard.
Fryd 12th	Preparing for a short journey to the west. Baked fried cakes, etc. Melissa visited at Uncle Durfey's. Received a Letter from Brother Silas Orvis.
Sat. 13th	Pleasant. Aunt Brooks started for Vermont today. Will God bless her.
Sund 14th	Wrote late at night to J.B. Isham, Vt. Mr Ira Farnam died last Tuesday at Hogansburgh in consequence of ardent liquor, a warning to all.
Mond 15th	Very pleasant. Quilted all day for Harriet Durfey. very fine quilt.
Tuesd 16th	Storm some. Visited at Mr. Chases P.M. Flowers eve. Felt the shock of an earthquake about eleven this eve, a sign of last days.
Wed 17th	Pleasant. Visited at Mr. C. Rockwell's. Became acquainted with Mr & Mrs Sperry of Malone. Almost tired of carrying children verily.
Thursd 18th	Pleasant. Washed. Visited at Mr Lee's. Visited this eve by Miss Mary Remington & Lorenda Rockwell. Retired sick, slept but little.
Fryd 19th	Pleasant. Called over and Baked etc. for Uncle Brooks. Visited at Hoits.
Sat. 20th	Pleasant, Thaws fast. Visited at David's. Lucinda sick with a cold.
Sabbath 21st	Pleasant. The snow almost all gone. Many on journey. Not able to sit up.
Mond 22nd	Pleasant. Mrs Gibson come to board with us again. Very feeble, Lucinda, too.
Tuesd 23rd	Beautiful weather. Not able to do but very little yet. Mrs S a son.
Wed 24th	Pleasant. Better today. Washed & Baked. Called over to Searls. snows little.

Thurs 25th	Cloudy. Lucinda very sick indeed. Eastman Bachelor very sick.
Fryd 26th	Pleasant. No prospects of snow. Lucinda no better. Sewed some.
Sat. 27th	Pleasant as June. Made the girls blue capes. Many travelling, gone away.
Sund 28th	The air is cold but beautiful day. Visited the sick at S.A.M. Lee visited

March 1830

Mond 1st	Washed, finished a shirtee. Oh, God, when shall I rejoice in thee?
Tuesd 2nd	Pleasant. Townmeeting. Baked for Mrs. Searls. Visited at Mr Rockwell's. Borrowed tracts, many does much good in hearts.
Wed 3rd	Pleasant. Received a Letter from Sister Clarissa by James Brown of Upper Canada. A Wolf hunt today for nought.
Thursd 4th	Pleasant. Mending. Hard cold. Visited at Mr. Covey's agreeably.
Fryd 5th	Beautiful days. Almost sick. Knitting. Mr Hazelton. & Mr Harvestson dined with us. Bought Calico for the girls bonnets, lace, Lee Broadcloth, for a wedding suit, I suspect. foggy[.]
Sat. 6th	Rainy. Finished a pair of socks and stockings for Mary. Sick.
Sabbath 7th	Rainy. Read a number of tracts. Oh that I might profit by it[.]
Mond 8th	A storm of snow. Not well. Finished a stocking, mending all day.
Tuesd 9th	Stormy yet. Mending. Visited by Mrs. Lee & Lorena Eastman.
Wed 10th	Storm over. Visited by Maria D[elong][.] Sewing on small clothes some[.]
Thursd 11th	Baked. Visited at Uncle D this eve with Uncle & Aunt Clapp & Brooks.
Fryd 12th	Baked, cleaned house. Visited by Uncles C. family, Aunt D. Rainy night.
Sat 13th	Rainy. The snow left us again. Lee has gone to Lawrence.
Sund 14th	Rainy, some snow. Almost sick, sat up but little today.

Mond 15th Very stormy, snow melts fast. Preparing for making soap.

Tues 16th Cold. made some soap, made more Lye. My soap too strong, turned again.

Wed 17th Rainy all day. Not able to do but little today. More called.

Thursd 18th Yet stormy. We have a great deal of rain for March. all right.

Fryd 19th Pleasant. Finished my soap. Washed a great washing. Two friends called by the name of Joel Battey & Stephen F. Stevens from Vermont. Heard from Father's family. Sick.

Sat. 20th Pleasant. Preparing tubs for sugaring. Cleaned two Bedsteads. Thunder & lightning this eve.

Sund 21st Pleasant. Delong called. Wrote a Letter to Father yesterday.

Mond 22nd Pleasant. Cut straw for a hat. Ironed. Visited by Aunt Brooks[.]

Tuesd 23rd Stormy. Mr E very sick and lame. Finished Braiding & sewing a hat for Henry. Made some sugar of the rinsing of Sugar tubs.

Wed 24th Pleasant. Washed all day L & S [Lee and Samuel] make sugar in Co. 97 lbs today[.]

Thursd 25th Pleasant. Finished cleaning Bedsteads. Washing and filling Beds anew boards and logs scalt. tired almost out. A log house is a dirty thing.

Fryd 26th Snow'd all day. Mended ten garments. Sam'l very unable to work[.]

Sat. 27th Cooler. Ironed. Picked wool for quilts. Fried cakes, etc. Thaws little.

Sund 28th Very pleasant. S & L sugar off, 140 lbs of good sugar. I wish they were not disposed to work on the Sabbath. Lee visits at Lawrence.

Mond 29th Pleasant. Pain in my side all night and day, but washed, mended many garments. Samuel very unwell. Hard cough, sap wasting[.]

Tuesd 30th Cloudy. Mended seventeen garments today. I hope I shall be able to get my work done and keep along with it & not always be behind.

Wed 31st	Very little this morn. Baked, mended the rest of the time Mr E yet sick.

April 1830

Thursd 1st	Rainy. Assisted Lorena what time I could get until 12 at night[.]
Fryd 2nd	Pleasant. Went assist L. [Lorena] for the day. Was called upon to spend the day at Mr. Lees [Eastman's] until tired out. She will not get well soon[.]
Sat. 3rd	Pleasant. Almost sick. Visited by Mrs. Searls[.] why was I not as poor.
Sabb 4th	Pleasant. Mrs. Lee [Eastman] Headache very hard. Mr L picked cowslips[.]
Mond 5th	Pleasant. Called over to Mr. R borrowed a kettle. coloured Orange. Quilted p.m. for L. Purchased a paire of side combs, thread, buttons, etc.
Tuesd 6th	Pleasant. Visited by the two Mrs. Rockwell. Scarcely able to do anything.
Wed 7th	Pleasant. Baked, scoured cupboard etc. Put on a small quilt.
Thursd 8th	Very pleasant indeed Worked hard, took cold. So lame I can hardly walk. Visited by H. & M. Durfey, M Eastman L & M Covey, L.E.[,] M..E. & H.D. spent the night. Quilted until two o'clock very little done, P.M.
Fryd 9th	Pleasant. Visited with Sister M. at David's. Finished my quilt at night.
Sat. 10th	Pleasant. Making a valance for my quilt Mr. E. hired a school teacher.
Sabb. 11th	Pleasant. Read heralds etc. Sat up but little. Mrs. Lee not well today[.]
Mond 12th	Pleasant. Sewing. The grass begins to start up afresh, no snow[.]
Tuesd 13th	Pleasant. A small shower. Coloured orange again. Mr. Chase here to work.
Wed 14th	Pleasant. Visited at David's with Mrs. Chase, Rockwell, Simonds. Sat up almost all night to cook for Lee to carry with him.
Thursd 15th	Pleasant. Piecing another quilt. Washed some. Mr. Giltton [Glidden] done working here.
Fryd 16th	Pleasant. Sewed little. In great distress part of the day. Wash little.

Sat. 17th Pleasant. Finished washing, Ironed. Mrs. Searls & Mrs Rockwell called.

Sund 18th Pleasant. Mr A Lee spent the night with us from Vt. Washed the eve.

Mond 19th Pleasant. Washed coverlets, scoured many things. pieced some on quilts.

Tuesd 20th Smoaky & Cloudy Cleaned the door yard. Baked twice. Sewed some[.]

Wed. 21st My cough hard indeed. My health very poor. Sewed. traded some with a pedlar. Sister Hopkins spent the night with us, rested very little.

Thursd 22nd A few drops of rain, high winds. Visited at Davids with Mrs. H. I am not able to sit up, it appears as if my cough would take my life.

Fryd 23rd Cloudy, but no rain. Visited at Mr. Lee's. I think I cannot visit it any more. My health will not allow of it. My cough wrings my very vitals and is wearing me out. Aunt Brooks spent the night with me.

Sat. 24th Cloudy. Mrs. Remington & L called. Have not sat up but little today.

Sund 25th No rain yet. Sat up long enough to write a lengthy letter to Brother.

Mond 26th Baked. Mended some. My work goes on slowly and much undone.

Tuesd 27th Washed some. Sewed some. My cough is a trifle better, hard yet.

Wed. 28th Cooler. Lucinda burnt badly on her hand. There is no peace to me.

Thursd 29th Sew little. Lucinda is less trouble than I should think she could be.

Fryd 30th Cloudy. Visited. My cough is hard indeed, I hope my syrup will effect a cure.

May 1830

Sat. 1st A few drops of rain. Lucinda very sore today. visited by Aunt D. [Durfey].

Sund 2nd Very pleasant. Sat up but little. Mr E brought Mary Reddington home to keep our school and board with us. My health very poor.

Mond. 3rd Pleasant. Finished piecing my quilt. Baked twice. Lorenda R [Remington] called.

Tuesd 4th	Pleasant. Put on a Calico Quilt. Very tired indeed. I fear I cannot work.
Wed 5th	Rainy P.M. Taken very unwell. The neighbours called in, restless night.
Thursd 6th	Pleasant. visited by Aunt & M.D. [Durfey], L.E. [Eastman]. Mrs. R [Remington] quilted for me[.]
Fryd 7th	Pleasant. Mr. P. [Pettibone] dined with us L.E. [Lee Eastman visited]. Quilted myself today until very late.
Sat. 8th	Pleasant. Finished my quilt. Washed some, ironed. Visited by Mrs Lockwood.
Sund 9th	Pleasant. Idle are my thought[s] about a future state.
Mond 10th	Pleasant. A Taylor from Watertown travelling to New Hampshire called. Cut out a coat and vest. Washed, sewed some. Many over[.]
Tues 11th	Pleasant. Finished my two quilts. Washed. My cough better
Wed 12th	Pleasant. Baked. Affa Warner buried today. Sewing.
Thursd 13th	Pleasant. Sewing on small clothes as opportunity presents. Visited by Mrs. L. Covey, M.C., L.E. My cough has left me entirely.
Fryd 14th	Cloudy but no rain. Mending caps and fitting them to wear. Traded two Dollars fifty cents with a Pedlar, Calico, thread[,] combs.
Sat. 15th	Cloudy, frosty morning. Preparing my clothes for sickness.
Sund 16	Cloudy eve. How dull and stupid do we live, how negligent we live as though death would never come.
Mond 17th	Cloudy. Washed, Ironed. Cut and made skirt to a calico frock small[.] There is no rest for me. I find a great deal wants doing every day.
Tues 18th	Rainy night, a mist through the day. Washed all day again. I am tired of washing pigs tracks. Received a letter from Brother Abram[.] his health is very poor indeed. Father gone to New York.
Wed 19th	[No entry]

Thursd 20th	Cold weather for the season. Thunder but little rain. Sewing.
Fryd 21st	Hail storm. Washed, starched, ironed etc. Cut out clothes[.]
Sat. 22nd	Small shower, hail. Finished a calico frock. Mended some. Visited by Aunt Brooks. I taken another hard cold indeed.
Sund 23rd	Cloudy & cold. Sat up but little today. Read Heralds.
Mond 24th	Sewing all day on flannel. No rain yet. Cold indeed for the season.
Tuesd 25th	Cloudy but no rain. Visited by H. Durfey, her health is now poor.
Wed. 26th	Dressed my rooms with pine and cedar. Visited by M. D. [Maria Durfey]. Hired Miss Aluna Ann Hamilton, a good girl. My health is very poor.
Thursd 27th	Pleasant. washed & baked[.] Mr. E. bought the right of using The Columbian Spinner for twenty-five dollars. The Machine will cost fifteen more, to be had at Canton.
Fryd 28th	No rain yet. Picked wool all day. Very tired. Have a good assistant.
Sat. 29th	Great want of rain. Sewed all day. Luna Ann finished picking wool.
Sund 30th	Fine shower A.M. Took a walk to the springs. Very dull indeed.
Mond 31st	Cold, frosty mornings. Sewing what I am able. not well.

June 1830

Tuesd 1st	Hard frost, showers P.M. Court commenced today at Canton[.]
Wed 2nd	Cloudy. Mr. E gone to Canton after his Spinner. Not done.
Thursd 3rd	Mr. E. came home this morn with our rolls, two barrels of salt, Fish, etc. Had scouring done. Have but little for a girl to do now.
Fryd 4th	Pleasant, more like summer. Visited at David's, finished a Cambrick Petticoat. Mr. Delaney died this morning suddenly.
Sat. 5th	Pleasant indeed. Mending. Luna Ann gone home this P.M.

Sund 6th	Rained slowly all day. A. Lee spent the P.M., tired of company[.]
Mond 7th	Rainy. A.M. Lemira Nichols came here to make a coat.
Tuesd 8th	Pleasant. Baked. L. washed. I am tired of doing nothing.
Wed 9th	Pleasant. Lee Eastman married to Miss Harriet Hazelton of Lawrence. God bless them.
Thursd 10th	Showers. Visited by Lee & wife, Sister Mary [Eastman], Wm B. Remington etc. Not able to visit as I could wish how long shall I linger.
Fryd 11th	Pleasant. Miss Nichols finished sewing the coat. Spoiled. Lee moved is things from here. How much it will lighten my cares. None but my own family to do for. Ironed.
Sat. 12th	Pleasant. Piecing quilt[.] we get along very slow indeed.
Sabb. 13th	Pleasant. & warm. Sat up but little today. Stupid & dull.
Mond 14th	Some showers. Prepared a quilt for the frames. L. washed.
Tuesd 15th	Pleasant. Put on and quilted off our quilt. visited by L & F.
Wed 16th	Showers. Had eight men to hoe for us. Baked. L. bound quilt.
Thursd 17th	Pleasant. Mending quilts all day. Get very tired of work.
Fryd 18th	Cool. Prepared another quilt put away my clothing and bedding. perhaps for the last time of my life.
Sat. 19th	Cool. Cloudy quilted and marked half I was able. God knoweth whether I shall ever finish it. Luna gone home. How many privileges I enjoy & yet dull.
Sabb. 20th	Rainy day. That awful day will surely come thence[.]
Mond 21st	Rainy. Quilting what I am able, perhaps my last work.
Tuesd 22nd	Rainy. Quilting. Very unable to work. God grant me one day.

Wed 23rd	Rainy. Finished the quilt, thanks to my God. OH wilt thou grant that I may be submissive to the [thy] will come pain & sickness Life or death, may I not murmur.
Thursd 24th	Pleasant. Sewed some. My mind is like the troubled sea.
Fryd 25th	Showers. When shall I live with only my own family.
Sat. 26th	Showers. Many are in want of the necessaries of Life.
Sund 27th	Hard shower this eve. Visited by Uncle B and wife, very dull[.]
Mond 28ty	Pleasant. Finished quilting a calico quilt for the cradle. Caroline Brooks brought me Rhubarb for pies. My life is yet spared.
Tuesd 29th	Very backward the season will yet prove. Baked pies etc. Time hangs heavily.
Wed 30th	Sewing what I am able, perhaps the last day I am to live.

July 1830

Thursd 1st	Pleasant. Visited by Harriet E., L.C., R. Squire, etc. Could not enjoy myself very well. Oh, that I could live alone one day.
Fryd 2nd	Very warm & pleasant. Arose at one o'clock morn. Oh my God wilt thou assist me to bear with patience what thou hast appointed. Obliged to ask the assistance of our neighbours. Pleasant indeed between the hours of one and two P.M. was blessed with a fine son weighing eight lbs. six oz. My God what a day of distress has this been and how wonderfully hast thou carried me through the trials of this world. But it is nothing to be compared to my Saviour's groans in the Garden of Gethsamane. My pains are yet very hard. My Babe is very poor indeed and screams as if he would died with smarting.
Sat. 3rd	Pleasant. Mr. E. purchased eight yds of Calico for me a frock. Many called today. My pains do not abate in the least. My babe cries.
Sund 4th	Pleasant. Lee & Harriet visited us also Uncle S. Clapp from Stockholm. Aunt C. has been very sick indeed, is better.
Mond 5th	Hard shower. P.M. Visited by Father and Mother E. Gaining slowly.
Tuesd 6th	Cloudy. Have done many things to free me from pain but in vain.

Wed 7th Pleasant. Visited by Mrs. Hamilton. My babe cries a great deal.

Thursd 8th Pleasant. Not so well today, but have no reason to complain[.]

Fryd 9th Visited by Mrs. Covey. Oh that I had strength of body & mind.

Sat. 10th Pleasant. Another week gone and I am yet spared. My babe suffers with pain.

Sund 11th A shower P.M. Mrs. Flanders, Harriet D, Miss Ellethorp called. Very warm.

Mond 12th Very warm. Mary very sick. Rode out to Father E., returned. Mr. E Bough a Patent whell head. I do a few light chores but far from being able.

[No entries between Monday the 12th and Sat the 17th. Sporadic entries afterward.]

Sat. 17th Heavy rain. The water is higher than was ever known in this county. Most of the bridges, mills, etc. all carried off. Immense losses and danger.

Thurs 22nd At Beamans Hollow, New Haven, Vt. fourteen lives lost in the flood. Swept everything in its way. Roads impassable from Burlington to Middlebury. In Peru the damages are unaccountable.

Sat 24th Durst not trust my children to cross the Bridge to school. Walked with them as far as Mr. Rockwell's, tired out. Luna Spinning. I do most of my chores. My Babe has a breach, very bad.

Sund 25th Pleasant. Mr. McAllister was drowned in attempting to ford the west Branch of the St. Regis River.

Mond 26th Pleasant. Washed. Mr. Mc. [McAllister] found a mile below by his son in the midst of floodwood. Buried today. He cumbers the ground no more. May all drunkards take warning of his death.

Sat. 31st Cloudy. Baked. Took all my children with Luna's help and visited at Lee Eastman's with the cart. Too hard for me.

September 1830

Mond 2nd Have done a part of my weaving. Mary Ann Heath spun some. visited by Mary Clapp. Mrs. S. Walked once to P.D.

October 1830

Sunday 3rd	Pleasant. Visited by Mrs. Anna Morrison. My babe sick.
Wed 6th	Pleasant. Lucinda very sick and the Babe. Rode with them and Mrs M. to Uncle D's. Almost sick myself.

The Travel Diaries
September 1–October 4, 1855; October 9–24, 1859

PARISHVILLE
September, 1855

Sat 1st	Brother [Silas] at Ogdensburg.
Sun 2nd	[No entry]
Mon 3rd	on board the "Ontario[.]"
Tues 4th	Oswego. On board the "Mayflower" all night[.]
Wed 5th	sail for Toronto "Highlander" to Whitby. Buggy to Pickering [Ontario][.]
Thurs 6th	Austins to Friends Meeting to Brother Silas[.]
Fryd 7th	from Silas to the lake. Took dinner at Selah Orvis. Tea & spent the night at E.B.O. [Eleazor Orvis][.]
Sat 8th	visited James and Phebe Ann Orvis. Return'd. spent the night at N. Austins [Nathaniel Austin][.]
Sun 9th	Staid overnight with Ira Carpenter. Had an excellent visit.
Mon 10th	Dined at Sylvanus Browns. Called to Rowlands. Took tea at N. Browns. Spent the night at Sister Austin's. Elijah Brooks there.
Tues 11th	Brother and Sister at Brother Silas. Took tea & spent the night[.]
Wed 12th	spent the day at Austin's packing spent the night on board the "Mayflower[.]"
Thurs 13th	Took cars at Toronto to Collingwood. Went on board the "Keystone" in Nottawassa Bay[.]

Fryd 14th	Sail'd through Georgian Bay & Lake Huron. Arrived Manitoulin Isle at eve. Saw nothing of it. Was very sick indeed. Passed the straits of Mackinac.
Sat 15th	Saw some islands. Sailed through Michigan lake arrived at Sheboygan.
Sun 16th	Stage to Fondulac 40 miles coach 7 miles to Oakfield. Isaac spent night[.]
Mon 17th	rainy & cold[.]
Tues 18th	At Isaacs [Orvis][.]
Wed 19th	left Brothers, Sister Yula & Elmira & Anna Diane. John Orvis visited with us at Mr. Warners. Mrs James Cornell[85] spent the night.
Thurs 20th	Mrs. Cornell & son went with us to Brother James Orvis. Brother Isaac & James took tea.
Fryd 21st	Staid all day and night. The Team was lost & could not go to Brothers.
Sat 22nd	Returned to Brothers. Mr. & Mrs. Warner spent the day & night also J & I [James and Isaac]. Brother James & A. Dean accompanied us to Waupon State Prison a large stone building very nice, neat & clean. Return'd through mud and mire. Saw Mr. Parkhill. To Isaacs. Tired & cold.
Sun 23rd	intended to go to Fondulac to church but it has rained. So it is next to an impossibility. Towards night Julia and I visited the graveyard.
Mon 24th	Brother & wife & A.D. visited with us. Tea at Mr. Henry Whites staid to I [Isaac Ovris's].
Tues 25th	took leave of Brother Isaacs family. George took us to Brother James.
Wed 26th	took leave of Brother James family took mail stage to Monterey.
Thurs 27th	arriv'd at Hartland. Left our baggage walked to Merton. Staid to Mr. Warrens.
Fryd 28th	Aunt & Uncle Nicholson visited with us at Stephen Warrens. Spent the night.
Sat 29th	visited at G.M. Skinners Rainy. Visited the graveyard & river. Return'd to Mr. Warrens to spend the night almost tired out.
Sun 30th	attended church service only half the day. Visited Hartland graveyard.

October 1855

Mon 1st visited with friends at Norman Nicholsons. Called at the store etc.

Tues 2nd spent the day until after tea with Aunt and Uncle & they all went with us to S. Warrens on monthly [original blank space] to Brothers[.]

Wed 3rd Mr. E left for the Fair. Visited widow Skinner & Norman Nicholson.

Thurs 4th left for Milwaukee from there to Chicago from Chicago to Gardner[.]

Undated inscription on the back of the travel narrative:

> As the graves of Eleazor Orvis and Emily Orvis lay beneath the spreading Oak and Hickory, his nephew and niece & the grandchildren of Brother Silas, Cynthia daughter of Loren Orvis, here too are the greatgrandchildren of Grandmother Brown all slumbering in the silent yard while the living relatives are far away.

[No further entries until October 1859]

STARKSBORO
October, 1859

Sun Sat 9th Snow two inches deep. Did not attend meeting. Intending to rest as I much needed it. I had a room & a fire by myself for that purpose but soon company came in & now introductions commence. This is Stephen and Lydia Green, ____ Colby, ______ Colby, Orpha Meader, Elizabeth Phillips, etc, etc. Cousins too. They ask when shall I come with a carriage to take thee to our house. Finally stop't at P. Morrison's overnight. Took a ramble to the river with Phebe Maria Morrison after excusing myself from many invitations.

Mon 10th Catherine O'Connell, P.M.M. [Phebe Maria Morrison], took a ride to view the scenery & machinery at a place call'd by some New Boston by others New Jerusalem. Call'd at several places only at the door on account of tobacco, call'd at Mother Grinells until dinner was ready. PM [afternoon] Cousin Joel Orvis came for me to go to his house. High up so we could see far over the lake and steamers upon it. There, too, company had assembled to spend the PM & evening, I overnight.

Tues 11th Very pleasant. Cousin Louis & myself & Hannah Lee took a very high position on Mount Pleasant. Such splendid scenery I never saw before. Such beautiful springs of crystal waters so much of grandeur & sublimity of towering heights. Lengthened space above, beneath & all around. Seemed really enchanting. The eye could not be satisfied with seeing for itself, but oh how I did wish my family could all (and very many others) behold this beautiful scenery. After taking in the view many a long lingering look, we descended to the grave of my mother from there across and up to the place of my birth. A large orchard of trees but now little fruit which my father put out some sixty years since. After viewing sufficiently & excusing ourselves from the most entreating to dine with Mr. Homners family (who had built a nice house in the place) we passed over to Cousin J.O.s then after dinner all went down to Albert Orvis's. Sarah only at home. Call'd at the saw mill of A. O. [Albert Orvis] very nice lumber and a good clapboard mill. Took tea at Uncle Orvis. Company there in plenty. Cousin Joel took me to Bristol. Spent the night with Dr. Hazeltine's family[.] they have a most splendid dwelling.

Wed 12th Made a few calls. Mrs. H. [Hazeltine] & son took me to the burial ground to visit my grandfather and grandmother's grave & the resting place of many acquaintances.[86] From there to Uncle [John] Brooks, took a long ramble alone over the gardens, rocks, hills, and rills. The old rocky cliffs I had so often clamber'd over were the same. The rocky seats so many in number where I once delighted to sit, to read, & sing yet are inviting as ever, as old friends. The old fruit trees yet leaf, but not much fruit. The old thorn trees are full of mellow fruit while an hundred locust trees shade the pathway down to the road planted by my dear old grandfather. Rambled over to the meadow where dear old Uncle was ditching alone. Disappointed of visiting at Mr. Smiths. Aunt gone.

Thurs 13th Cloudy & windy. Pleasant ride to Middlebury. Visited at S. Brooks, attended the Fair saw many friends, spent the night with Miss Cady upstairs.

Fri 14th Rainy. Walked with brother Myron to call on Mrs. Hammonds acquaintances of years gone by. Commenced snowing and raining. Returned to Bristol with Cousin Joshua Orvis, spent the night with John Brooks or Hazeltine.

Sat 15th Cold wind with sleet. Rode 4 in a buggy to the village. Met Cousin Orvis & son to take me to Ferrisburgh. I really suffer'd from the cold. Was very glad to get to Mother's [Lillis Brown] to lodge with her where my dear father had so lately repos'd in his last slumber.

Sun 16th Cold & pleasant. Very glad of quiet & rest. To start again. Mother, myself & the little ones visited Father's resting place & that of the other relatives perhaps for the last time as I must soon leave this to me delightful place.[87]

Mon 17th — Rainy. Assisting Mother & sister Ruth. Took tea at Brother Lorenzo's the dear old homestead newly fitted up.

Tues 18th — Strong cold wind but pleasant. Accompanied by Sister Mary visited Cousin Sarah Hazard. Excellent visit.

Wed 19th — Cold dull weather. Packed clothes ready for our leave.

Thurs 20th — Brother Myron took us to the Cars [railroad cars]. Took boat at Burlington. Strong cold winds. Both Mother and myself were seasick. Brother Stephen K. Smith was in readiness to take us to his home after riding six miles. We were glad to meet with warm kind hearts, warm fire & well prepar'd dinner.

Fri 21st — My 58th birthday. Cold bleak wind with flurries of snow. not well staid within doors. Visited with the family.

Sat 22nd — Pleasant. Mother, Sister, myself & the little ones took a walk over their pleasant little farm –a sugar bush, the only ramble I ever had with Mother or Sister. Concluded to stay until Monday.

Sun 23rd — Very nice day. Attended the Friends meeting. Saw many acquaintances. Address by Samuel Keese prayer by his wife Catharine, returned to dine at 3PM. An excellent discourse from Dr. Moor and lady from Vergennes. Much company to tea & spend the evening. Tired and almost sick.

Mon 24th — left Mr. Smiths at half past two in the morning. Very dark. Took the cars at Plattsburgh. Pass'd many a snowdrift. Arrived in safety at Lawrence Depot. Mr. E [Eastman] in waiting. Raining some took a hard cold dined at Mr. Coolidges. Took tea at Durfeys. Arrived in safety at home.

All well as usual.

Maps

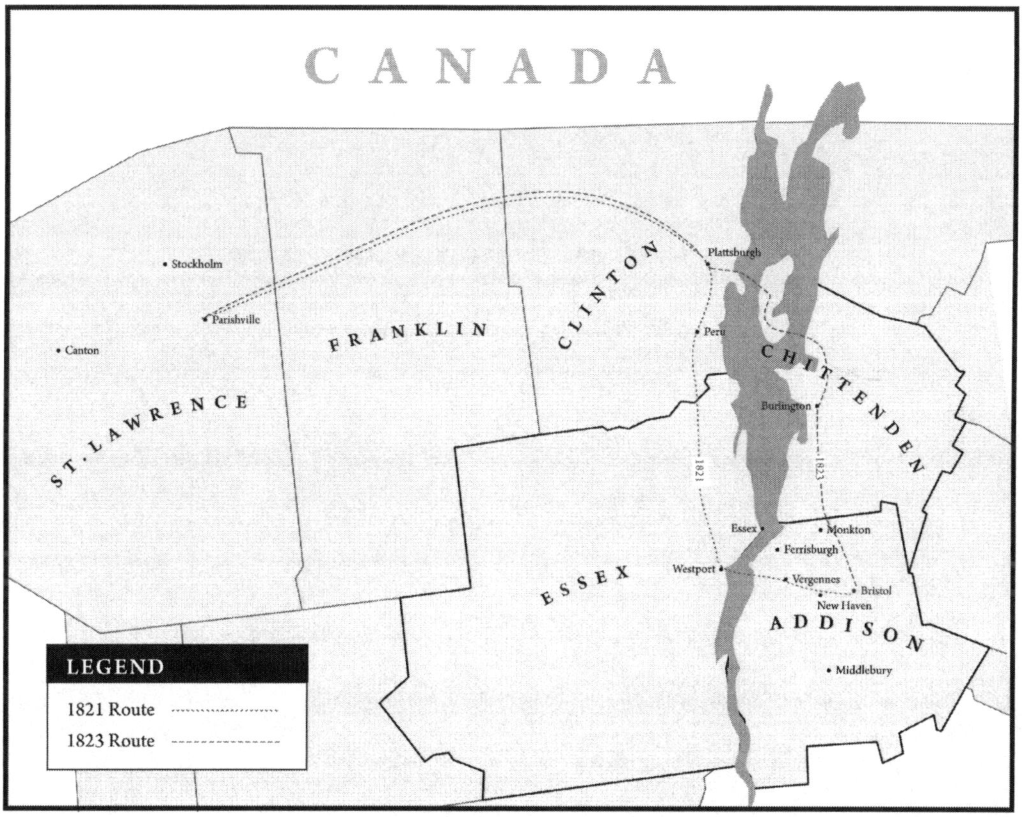

Map 1. Vermont/New York North Country

Map 2. Addison County, Vermont

Map 3. St. Lawrence County, New York

Acknowledgments

Phebe Orvis's story begins with a mystery: How did her manuscript journal survive intact from the time of her death in September of 1868 until it came to light a century later? Where was it? Who preserved it? And why? At this point in time, what we do know is that the nondescript little book went unnoticed and forgotten until the 1960s, when it came to light in Plattsburgh, New York, in a tattered old box of books put up for auction by someone who was not related to the family. At the time, no one knew where it had come from or how it had come to be in Plattsburgh. So, although I would like to imagine that Phebe Orvis's descendants lovingly safeguarded her writings for her sake, it is far more likely that the journal sat neglected on a shelf sandwiched between other abandoned books until someone deemed it flotsam and put it out in a pile of other items to sell.

Serendipity was surely at work when the odd little auction "find" was passed on as a minor curiosity to an amazing historian and independent scholar, Mrs. Mary Smallman. An active octogenarian whose pursuit of the history of the Saint Lawrence County region of Upstate New York spans many decades, Smallman was the Saint Lawrence County historian at the time. She quickly saw potential in the little book, and its author presented Smallman an intriguing puzzle: who was this unknown person that commenced this journal on the first day of July 1820?

Charmed (she would later say obsessed) by the riddle of the unknown author, Smallman followed the first clues, deduced her gender, and then her name, Phebe Orvis Eastman. Over the next few years, Smallman transcribed the journal in longhand, and then laboriously typed the transcription on a manual typewriter. In the process of her transcription work, she established that Orvis had lived the whole of her married life near her (Smallman's) home in Saint Lawrence County. Galvanized by her interest in the modest little journal and her feeling of commonality with this nineteenth-century housewife and mother, Smallman researched and collected what she could of the Saint Lawrence County Orvis/Eastman story.

Moving forward over several decades of research, Smallman uncovered significant details of Orvis's life. The story that slowly unfolded inspired Smallman; she knew that Orvis's journal was a unique lens through which the history of early Upstate New York could be glimpsed. From her perspective as a Saint Lawrence County historian, she was excited by the firsthand details recorded by Orvis. Smallman recognized that Orvis's connection to one of the pioneering families of the area—the Eastmans—meant that she had directly participated in the expansion of the American frontier in the period immediately following the War of 1812. Details in the journal also made it clear that Orvis's writings had the potential to uncover intimate details of the lives of everyday people as they set about building their families, neighborhoods, and communities. As she plumbed the depths of Orvis's writings, Smallman savored the narrative that unfolded and decided to preserve the little book by donating the original manuscript journal to the Saint Lawrence County Historical Association archive after making her typescript copy.[1]

A women's historian before the term gained much traction in academe, Smallman identified and understood the genuine value of a woman outside of the celebrated elite, who are commonly referred to in traditional history narratives. Rather, Smallman recognized that Orvis represented a type of woman closer to an ordinary housewife than someone like Elizabeth Cady Stanton or Abigal Adams. Moreover, Orvis's writings from the early nineteenth century were valuable and rare. This was a time when most trained professional historians had barely begun to esteem the words of women beyond the members of the educated elite. Smallman not only preserved the original manuscript, but also her careful transcript and accompanying research materials for posterity. We owe her a great debt for her efforts.

This book and Orvis's writings would not exist without Smallman's foresight and labors. Further labors on the typed transcripts were done by my administrative assistant, Kelly MacDonald, when she digitalized the diary; additional enlightenment came from the subsequent work of Denise Groll whose enthusiasm and Internet expertise helped to fill in some of the gaps. Finally, the unfailing support of my husband Emile and son Andrew was invaluable as I pursued Phebe Orvis through the landscape of New England and northern New York.

Notes

Introduction

1. For a discussion of diary interpretation, see Bloom, 23–37. All entries have been formatted in the form in which they originally appear in the manuscript journal. In addition, although Phebe Orvis becomes Phebe Eastman after her marriage to Samuel Jr., I continue to refer to her as Orvis to avoid confusion.

2. Ulrich, *A Midwife's Tale*.

3. Bloom, 26.

4. For a discussion of the more emotive diary styles, see Blauvert.

5. Blauvert argues that after marriage most women's journals took on a more resigned tone related to their "narrowed universe, and an eroded sense of self . . . ," 146–183.

6. Orvis, *A History*, 64.

7. Orvis, Journal entry, May 5, 1830.

8. Random notation in the back of the journal: "Feb 16–18, 1842, Eastmans lost three children; sickness in Lee Eastman house."

9. Smallman.

10. Ulrich, Interview.

11. "The past is a foreign country; they do things differently there," Hartley.

12. Ferrisburgh Meeting Minutes.

13. In this unanswered and barely acknowledged ambition, Phebe Orvis had much in common with Hiram Harwood, whose situation bound him to his father's farm and expectations despite a "restive yearning." See Shalhope, 39–46.

14. Orvis, Journal entry, February 5, 1823.

15. Orvis, Journal entry, February 7, 1822.

16. Orvis, Journal entry, July 8, 1821.

17. Orvis, Journal entry, November 27, 1820.

18. A version of this essay titled "Rendered More Ignorant Than Others" was published earlier in the Dublin Seminar Proceedings Journal, *In Our Own words: New England Diaries* (2010).

19. Orvis, Journal entry, January 12, 1823.

20. Orvis, Journal entry April 28, 1822.

21. A version of this essay was published in *Vermont History*. "Religion and Piety in the Journal of Phebe Orvis," *Vermont History* 77, no. 1 (2009): 6–15.

22. Orvis, Journal entry, July 21, 1820.
23. Orvis, Journal entry, August 30, 1830.
24. Orvis, undated entry on back of 1855 travel narrative.

Chapter One

1. Orvis, Journal entry, February 7, 1822.
2. For a discussion of the migration of post-Revolution families, see Opal, 44–68.
3. The same year Vermont gave up its status an independent republic and joined the Union.
4. Orvis, *The History*, 1123.
5. Marriage of Loren Orvis and Elizabeth Brooks, attested to by Amos Eastman, Bristol Town Meeting Records, 1790–1809, 257.
6. For a description of the early settlements and details of Loren Orvis farm, see sections on Lincoln and Starksboro townships in Smith.
7. Potash, 71–79.
8. See Swift, 300.
9. Orvis, Journal entry, September 9, 1822.
10. Albers, 52–63; for a more detailed discussion of Abenaki people, see Calloway.
11. Munsill, 61a.
12. Marriage of Samuel Brooks Jr. and Betsey Rorapaugh, March 16, 1791, recorded in the Bristol Town Records, Volume I.
13. Perkins, 23–24.
14. The lone casualty listed for the 1798 epidemic was Cyprian Eastman. He contracted the disease in while in Montreal on business. He was also an uncle to Samuel Eastman Jr., Phebe Orvis's future husband. See Munsill, 90–93.
15. Munsill, 92.
16. Munsill, 58, 237–239.
17. Munsill, 231.
18. Albers, 126–149.
19. Bristol Town Records.
20. Orvis, Journal entry, July 8th, 1820.
21. See Levy, *Town Born* and Ulrich, *Good Wives*.
22. For a broader discussion of women's work—both rural and urban—and the connections between the development of middleclass sensibility and housework, see Kelly.
23. Despite her move to Waterford, NY, Willard's Middlebury school continued to operate for a few years after her departure and under the supervision of one of her first pupils.
24. Orvis, Journal entry, August 11, 1820.
25. See Opal, 44–68.
26. Smith, 651.
27. Cohn. See also Hill.
28. Farnsworth, 148–150.
29. Smith, 295.
30. For a discussion of Middlebury see Potash, 71–79.
31. Munsill, 187.
32. Seaver, 8.

33. The Durfey and Eastman land purchases in St. Lawrence County were made from Macomb's purchase. There were multiple land exchanges between 1814 and 1817. See Volumes II and III, Saint Lawrence County Land Records.

34. Seaver, 24–26.

Chapter Two

1. For a discussion of liberal courtship and marriage practices of the era, see Gross.
2. Rothman, 23–27.
3. Orvis, Journal entry, July 6, 1820.
4. Orvis, Journal entry, July 7, 1820.
5. Loren Orvis remarried when Phebe was about four years old. He subsequently sold the hill farm in Lincoln and moved to a new place in Ferrisburgh with his new wife.
6. Orvis, Journal entry, July 4, 1820.
7. Thaddeus Dunton was the son of Vermont Militia General Ezekiel Dunton, the war hero (1812).
8. Orvis, Journal entry, July 28, 1820.
9. The importance of practical concerns for couples contemplating marriage remained even as the romantic notion of companionate marriage became more commonly discussed. See Kelly, 127–136.
10. Wages taken from 1821 School Commissioners' Report.
11. The Middlebury National Bank was "robbed" of its funds and the local court assigned the blame to the professional men who were the trustees of the bank, forcing them to make the bank losses good to their depositors.
12. Rotundo, 112–116.
13. Orvis, Journal entry, July 30, 1820.
14. Orvis, Journal entry, September 10, 1820.
15. Orvis, Journal entry, November 4, 1820.
16. Orvis, Journal entry, December 3, 1820.
17. Orvis, Journal entry, January 20, 1821.
18. Orvis, Journal entry, January 10, 1821.
19. Orvis, Journal entry, January 13, 1821.
20. Orvis, Journal entry, January 10, 1821.
21. Orvis, Journal entry, January 21, 1821.
22. Orvis, Journal entry, February 6, 1821.
23. This is clearly a legacy of her education at the Middlebury Seminary as the nature walks and biology were central to Emma Willard's notions on pedagogy.
24. Given the newly energized efforts of the Abolition movement in the period, this comment has radical overtones that suggest real discontent on Orvis's part. Orvis, Journal entry, July 4, 1821.
25. Orvis, Journal entry, April 26, 1821.
26. Orvis, Journal entry, May 7, 1821.
27. Orvis, Journal entry, May 21, 1821.
28. Orvis, Journal entry, June 4, 1821.
29. Orvis, Journal entry, May 29, 1821.
30. Orvis, Journal entry, June 15, 1821.
31. Orvis, Journal entry, January 23, 1822.
32. Orvis, Journal entry, January 18, 1822.

33. Orvis, Journal entry, October 6, 1821.
34. Orvis, Journal entry, July 8, 1821.
35. Orvis, Journal entry, August 13, 1821.
36. Kelly, 115–126.
37. Orvis, Journal entry, September 4, 1821.
38. Orvis, Journal entry, October 7, 1821.
39. Orvis, Journal entry, February 7, 1822.
40. Orvis, Journal entry, March 5, 1822.
41. Orvis, Journal entry, August 22, 1822.
42. Orvis, Journal entry, April 29, 1822.
43. Orvis, Journal entry, November 28, 1822.
44. Orvis, Journal entry, January 1, 1823.
45. Orvis, Journal entry, January 11, 1823.
46. Orvis, Journal entry, January 12, 1823.
47. Orvis, Journal entry, February 5, 1823.

Chapter Three

1. Orvis, Journal entry, November 27, 1820.
2. Kerber, Norton, Main.
3. Pichnarcik, Hendrick.
4. "Mrs. Willard's School."
5. Orvis, Journal entry, July 8, 1820.
6. Orvis, Journal entry, July 8, 1820.
7. Potash, 94.
8. Orvis, Journal entry, October 12, 1820.
9. Orvis, Journal entry, August 2, 1820.
10. Orvis, Journal entry, October 16, 1820.
11. Orvis, Journal entry, September 9, 1820.
12. Rothman, 27–29.
13. Robinson, 388.
14. Orvis, Journal entry, November 27, 1820.
15. Day, 68.
16. Willard.
17. Pichnarcik, Hendrick.
18. "Ladies School."
19. Orvis, Journal entry, December 5, 1820.
20. Orvis, Journal entries, December 17 and 18, 1820.
21. Orvis, Journal entry, January 18, 1821.
22. As I indicated in the Introduction, I believe that Phebe Orvis may have been thinking about becoming a missionary. As a Quaker, she would have been interested in the missionary work abroad, and China was a brand-new frontier for that work.
23. Orvis, Journal entries, December 13, 14, and 21 1820
24. Orvis, Journal entry, November 15, 1820.
25. Orvis, Journal entry, January 10, 1821.
26. Orvis, Journal entries, August 22–24, 1822.

27. Orvis, Journal entry, February 13, 1825.
28. Orvis, Journal entry. September 24, 1826.

Chapter Four

1. Orvis, Journal entry January 29, 1823.
2. Orvis, Journal entry, February 12, 1823.
3. Orvis, Journal entry April 25, 1823.
4. Orvis, Journal entry October 12, 1823.
5. Orvis, Journal entry, January 1, 1822.
6. Phebe Orvis membership record, Friends Meeting Record Book, 49.
7. Smith, 32.
8. Orvis, Journal entry, July 23, 1820.
9. Orvis, Journal entry, November 7, 1820.
10. Orvis, Journal entry, November 21, 1820.
11. Orvis, Journal entry, April 28, 1822.
12. Orvis, Journal entry, April 20, 1823.
13. Orvis, Journal entry, March 6, 1823.
14. Orvis, Journal entry, July 3, 1823.
15. Orvis, Journal entry, May 7, 1824.
16. Orvis, Journal entry, August 21, 1824.
17. Orvis, Journal entry, March 13, 1824.
18. Orvis, Journal entry, December 11, 1825.
19. Orvis, Journal entry, November 26, 1826.
20. Samuel Eastman Jr. exhibits many of the characteristics of the emerging middle class in the antebellum Northeast. He owned his farm outright, served as an officer in the local militia, and eventually joined the local temperance society. He was literate, married an educated woman, and, as this essay demonstrates, joined the ranks of the evangelical Christian movement known as the Second Great Awakening. For a more detailed discussion of the development of the middle class see Blumin.
21. For a general discussion of the Second Great Awakening see Johnson; for a more particular look at Vermont, Potash.
22. Orvis, Journal entry September 9, 1820.
23. See Ryan.
24. See Ryan. See also Welter, 21–41.
25. See Larson. See also Levy.
26. Orvis, Journal entry, December 8, 1826.
27. Orvis, Journal entry, December 10, 1826.
28. Orvis, Journal entry, August 5, 1827.

Chapter Five

1. Orvis, Journal entry, February 12, 1824.
2. Orvis, Journal entry, February 9, 1823.
3. Orvis, Journal entry, February 14, 1823.
4. See Hansen.

5. Orvis, Journal entry, November 12, 1822.
6. Orvis, Journal entry, February 6, 1823.
7. Orvis, Journal entry, December 6, 1827.
8. Orvis, Journal entries, February 25, 26, and 27, 1824.
9. Orvis, Journal entry, December 19, 1822.
10. Orvis, Journal entry, October 23, 1826.
11. Most of the slaughtering activities took place in December and January, since the weather would have made it easier to keep the meat from spoiling before processing could be done.
12. Orvis, Journal entry, April 6, 1823.
13. Orvis, Journal entry, March 11, 1823.
14. Orvis, Journal entry, November 1, 1822.
15. Orvis, Journal entry, March 25, 1830.
16. Orvis, Journal entries, April 2, 1823; April 18, 1823; March 22, 27, and 28, 1826. Hatchelling is the process of combing flax fibers to remove debris and to align the fibers in preparation for spinning.
17. Orvis, Journal. Multiple journal entries. For samples see June 5 and 28, 1823; September 13, 1823; October 14, 1823.
18. Orvis, Journal entry, January 3, 1824.
19. Orvis, Journal entry May 12, 1824.
20. Orvis, Journal entry, August 16, 1823.
21. For a full discussion of the fear of death in childbirth, see Leavitt, 21–28.
22. See Leavitt, 25.
23. Orvis, Journal entry, July 9, 1829
24. For a limited commentary on frequency of live births, pregnancy rates and miscarriages, see Leavitt, 12–16.
25. For a more detailed description of these health problems see Leavitt, 28–30.

Chapter Six

1. For a discussion of the responsibilities of neighborly women, see Ulrich, *Good Wives.*
2. Orvis, Journal entry, July 26, 1828.
3. There are a variety of causes for the illness, including contaminated food or water, infection from a range of viruses, and a number of bacterial causes.
4. Recipe recorded between August 22 and 23, 1820.
5. Orvis, Journal entry, August 22, 1820.
6. For a full discussion of these diseases and treatments, see Swedlund, 46–64.
7. Beebe, entries June 7 and 17; July 3, 1776.
8. Becker.
9. Duffy, *Epidemics*, 16.
10. For a general discussion of the disease and treatments see Fenn.
11. Orvis, Journal entry, May 29, 1823.
12. Orvis, Journal entry, June 1, 1823.
13. Mrs. Elijah Brooks
14. Orvis, Journal entry, May 7, 1824.
15. Munsill, 90–94.
16. Clark.

17. Orvis, Journal entry, September 26, 1825.
18. Orvis, Journal entry, July 20, 1820.
19. Orvis, Journal enrry, December 8, 1820.
20. Orvis, Journal entry, October 19, 1820.
21. Orvis, Journal entry, July 4, 1828. This "old soldier" was probably a veteran of the War of 1812. His suppurating wounds were undoubtedly a persistent health problem.
22. Orvis, Journal entry, February 15, 1830.
23. Orvis, Journal entry, November 16, 1821.
24. Orvis, Journal entry, July 28, 1821.
25. Orvis, Journal entry, November 17, 1822.
26. Orvis, Journal entry, January 7, 1830.
27. Orvis, Journal entry, October 11, 1859.

Conclusion

1. Notation on loose leaf inserted in the journal.
2. Wisconsin became a state in 1848.
3. 1850 Federal Census, 455, l. 38.
4. See Orvis, Travel Narrative, September 14, 1855.
5. See Orvis, Travel Narrative, 1855, ending comment.
6. See Orvis, Journals entries from February 6 to 10, 1821.
7. See Orvis, Travel Narrative, September 4–7, 1855.
8. See Orvis, Travel Narrative, October 12, 1859.
9. Orvis, Journal entry, July 16, 1821.

Journal

1. The first reference may be to the astronomy book by William Frend, *Evening Amusements; or, the Beauty of the Heavens Displayed. In which several striking appearances, to be observed on various evenings in the heavens, during the year 1812*. The second reference may be to *The Twin Sisters: or, Two Girls of Nineteen.*
2. Adolphus Taylor (February 21, 1799–July 9, 1841) and Orra Copeland (dates unknown), daughter of David Copeland, lived in Bristol and was one of Orvis's closest friends.
3. Benjamin Clapp (1759–1825), an uncle of Orvis, lived on the road between Bristol and Monkton. Settled in the area at the same time as Loren Orvis and Samuel Brooks.
4. General Ezekiel Dunton (1768–1824) was a commissioned brigadier-general in the Vermont militia. Served at the Battle of Plattsburgh in 1814. Settled on a farm near the New Haven/Bristol town line with the first wave of Bristol proprietors. Served in multiple municipal offices for the Town of Bristol.
5. Daughter of David Annin and Polly Dunton; granddaughter of Ezekiel Dunton.
6. Mr. Gaige's Inn was the Bristol House, a hotel Abram Gaige opened sometime before 1820.
7. Diaper is a type of cloth, usually utilitarian in nature.
8. Lovina Brooks, wife of John Brooks and Orvis's aunt by marriage. John Brooks and his wife lived on the Bristol flats farm with Orvis and her grandparents.

9. Kersey is a type of woolen cloth.

10. One knot of yarn is equal to eighty yards. Tow yarn is a rough yarn spun from the flax fibers left in the hackling combs. It is usually either woven into a very rough utilitarian cloth or used as candlewicks.

11. A weaving term meaning the density of threads per inch in the laying of the warp.

12. Orvis's news interests ranged widely and although we do not know what newspaper she read, we do know that "the execution of Hull and Hutton" refers to the Baltimore, MD, execution of two men, Perry Hutton and Morris Hull, for the murder of a mail coach driver on the Philadelphia/Baltimore. A local paper must have picked up the story from the *Niles Weekly Register*, Baltimore, MD, July 22, 1820, p1, c1.

13. Diamond Key is a weaving pattern.

14. Another term for dysentery.

15. Freeman's Day, September 5, was a public holiday in Vermont.

16. Jewelry made with human hair, either by a professional hair weaver or by a home crafter such as Orvis, was an expression of the sentimental romanticism of the nineteenth century. Hair jewelry could be a mourning memento or—as in the case of Orvis's ring—a love token.

17. A reed is the part of a loom that determines the number of warp threads per inch in a weave structure.

18. An acrostic is a poem or a riddle where certain letters in each line of the verse form a word. An example of a poem of this type is "An Acrostic" by Edgar Allan Poe.

19. Applying a caustic substance like mustard or onions to raise a blister was thought to "draw out" a fever or a poison in an ill person.

20. Read.

21. Jacob Abbot Cummings (1773–1820) authored *Cummings Geography and Atlas*, a standard textbook published as an introduction to ancient and modern geography.

22. Lucy Burnap became the teacher in charge of the Middlebury Female Seminary after Emma Hart Willard left for Waterford, New York.

23. This was Rev. Josiah Hopkins.

24. Johnson, *Rasselas.*

25. Mr. Eddy's was a Public House kept by the Eddy brothers on the road between Bristol village and the flats. The house was a two story structure built by Robert Dunshee and then sold to John and Amos Eddy for their business.

26. Murray.

27. The commander of the American land forces at the Battle of Plattsburgh and land speculator in the Franklin and Saint Lawrence Counties in the decades after the War of 1812.

28. Ira Smith, probably.

29. The air was smoky because there was a nearby forest fire.

30. It is not clear what the "hard scuffle" was, but it may be that Roswell Eastman was competing with Adolphus Taylor and his brothers for Phebe Orvis's attention.

31. The wages referred to in this entry are more than the $9.92 that school board reported to the Chancellor of Education in Albany earlier, but they do not appear to include board. The $15.00 they were willing to pay Orvis probably represents both wages and the presumed cost of board, which she is not obliged to pay her aunt and uncle Durfey.

32. This may have been a letter to let Orra Copeland know of his intention to resume formal courting of Orvis since the next day they exchanged love tokens.

33. This would have been the "raising" of a neighbor's new house; the whole neighborhood would have contributed labor toward the effort and the frame and roof were probably completed in the one day of labor.

34. This is an odd comment, but it indicates that she is more aware of the need for money than she has been. Perhaps she and Adolphus Taylor had been in discussion about financial aspects of their engagement.

35. Anderson.

36. More.

37. Perhaps to escape her abusive husband?

38. The desire to resettle in Canada was rife among the Brooks and Orvis relatives at this time.

39. Eleazor Orvis and Elizabeth Austin married on January 20, 1825.

40. Vermont Governor Proclamation (1822).

41. Ramsay.

42. Unknown work.

43. Included in the *Christian Spectator*, vol. 1 (Howe and Spaulding, 1818).

44. VanDyke refers to a broad lace or linen collar with long points in the front.

45. Barrows.

46. This could be Mariti, *Travels through Cyprus, Syria, and Palestine* (1792).

47. *The Natural and Artificial Productions of the United States.*

48. Von Goethe.

49. Modern Brooksville.

50. This is the handbook of the Free Masons.

51. Goldsmith, *The Vicar of Wakefield.*

52. The reference to "rolls" is a textile term; these are probably the rolags of prepared wool from the carding mill, which Orvis then spun into finished yarn.

53. Quinsy refers to a variety of ailments associated with the throat, including inflammation or abscesses on the tonsils.

54. The banns of marriage were read publicly for Phebe and Samuel.

55. Orvis may have suspected she was pregnant.

56. This allusion to bleeding and death may have been her disappointment that her menses had begun or that she experienced a miscarriage.

57. Orra Copeland Taylor.

58. Elisha Risdon's wife.

59. Author unknown. There were many biographies of Washington written after his death.

60. A tier is a child's pinafore tied with tapes or cords.

61. The minister who married the Eastmans.

62. Stupid must mean drunk here; training was often accompanied by male drinking activities, as well as drilling.

63. Malan.

64. Steele.

65. Rolls are carded wool rolags ready for spinning.

66. Cox.

67. Possibly Grimshaw, *History of the United States.*

68. Biblical readings included in the King James's Bible.

69. Obookiah.

70. This is a romance novel written by Henry Brooke (1765–70). *The Fool of Quality or, the History of Henry Earl of Moreland*, is mainly a philosophical and religious tract in the guise of a novel.

71. Carrick.

72. A memoir prepared for publication by Daniel Merton in 1819.

73. Hopkinson was courting Betsey Eastman; they later married.

74. A description of the murder of seaman John Love by the Thayer brothers in 1824; they were convicted and hanged in 1825 in the only public hanging in Eerie County, New York.

75. A series of letters on religious subjects written by John Satchel and published in 1811.

76. Cruikshank.

77. Unknown author and publication date.

78. Goldsmith, *History of Rome.*

79. Unknown author and publication date. Francis Xavier was a Catholic missionary celebrated for his success in foreign mission work.

80. A local pamphlet.

81. Hopkins.

82. Fox.

83. Unknown author and publication date.

84. *Cottage Girl, the Thatcher's Wife* reprinted in Owen.

85. Emmeline Orvis Cornell

86. Greenhaven Cemetery along the New Haven Road east of Bristol on Vermont Route 17.

87. Union Cemetery on the south side of Middlebrook Road in Ferrisburgh Center.

Acknowledgments

1. The typescript copy was made on a manual typewriter and utilized carbon paper to make a second copy.

Bibliography

1850 Federal Census, Non-Population Schedules, Agriculture. Parishville, Saint Lawrence County, New York.

Albers, Jan. *Hands on the Land: A History of the Vermont Landscape*. Cambridge, MA: MIT Press, 2000.

Anderson, A. *The Economy of Human Life*. Philadelphia: Jacob Johnson, 1807.

Barrow, John. *Travels in China*. London: A. Strahan, 1804.

Becker, Ann. "Smallpox in Washington's Army: Strategic Implications of the Disease During the American Revolutionary War." *Journal of Military History* 68, no. 2 (April 2004): 381–430.

Beebe, Lewis. "Journal of Dr. Lewis Beebe." *Pennsylvania Magazine of History and Biography* 59, no. 4 (October 1935): 320–361.

Blauvert, Martha Tomhave. *The World of the Heart: Young Women and Emotion, 1780–1830*. Charlottesville: University of Virginia Press, 2007.

Bloom, Lynn Z. " 'I Write for Myself and Strangers': Private Diaries as Public Documents," in *Inscribing the Daily: Critical Essays on Women's Diaries*, ed. Suzanne L. Bunkers and Cynthia A. Huff, 23–37. Amherst: University of Massachusetts Press, 1996.

Blumin, Stuart M. *The Emergence of the Middle Class: Social Experience in the American City, 1760–1900*. Cambridge, UK: Cambridge University Press, 1989.

Bristol Town Records, Vol. I. Town Clerk's Office. Bristol, Vermont.

Brooke, Henry. *The Fool of Quality or, the History of Henry Earl of Moreland*, rev. ed. London: Smith, Elder & Co., 1859.

Calloway, Colin. *The Western Abenakis of Vermont, 1600–1800*. Norman: University of Oklahoma Press, 1990.

Carrick, John Donald. *Life of Sir William Wallace of Elderslie*, 4th ed. Glasgow: Thomas D. Morison, n.d.

Clark, James. *A Treatise on Pulmonary Consumption*. Philadelphia: Carry, Lea & Blanchard, 1835.

Cohn, Arthur B. *Lake Champlain's Sailing Canal Boats: An Illustrated Journey from Burlington Bay to the Hudson River*. Basin Harbor, VT: Lake Champlain Maritime Museum, 2003.

Cox, Robert. *The Life of the Rev. John William Fletcher, Vicar of Madeley*. Philadelphia: George & Byington, 1837.

Cruikshank, Robert. *The Beautiful Indian, or, The Interesting History of Zoa*. London: Hodgson & Co., 1824.

Cummings, Jacob Abbott. *Cummings Geography and Atlas*. N.p., n.p., 1813.

Day, Jeremiah. *1828 Yale Report*. Reprinted in *Curriculum* by Rudolf Frederick. London: Jossey-Bass Publishers, 1978.

Duffy, John. *Epidemics in Colonial America*. Baton Rouge: Louisiana State University Press, 1953.

Fenn, Elizabeth. *Pox Americana: The Great Smallpox Epidemic of 1775–1782*. New York: Hill and Wang, 2001.

Frend, William. *Evening Amusements; or, the Beauty of the Heavens Displayed*. London: J. Mawman, 1818.

Friends Meeting Record Book.

Fox, George. *A Declaration of the Christian Faith and Doctrine, of the Society of Friends.* N.p.: Joseph R. A. Skerrett, 1827.

Goldsmith, Oliver. *The History of Rome*. London: George Cowie & Co., 1825.

———. *The Vicar of Wakefield.* 1766. Reprint. Mineola, NY: Dover Publications, 2004.

Grimshaw, William. *History of the United States.* Philadelphia: Benjamin Warner, 1821.

Gross, Robert. *The Minutemen and their World.* New York: Hill and Wang, 1976.

Hansen, Karen. *A Very Social Time: Crafting Community in Antebellum New England.* Berkeley: University of California Press, 1994.

Hartley, L. P. *The Go-Between*. London: Folio, 1985.

Hendrick, Robert. "Ever-Widening Circle or Mask of Oppression?: Almira Phelps's Role in Nineteenth-Century American Female Education." *History of Education* 24, no. 4 (1995): 293–304.

Hill, Ralph Nading. *Lake Champlain Key to Liberty*. Taftsville, VT: Countrymen's Press, 1977.

Hopkins, Josiah. *The Christian's Instructor*. Middlebury, VT: J. W. Copeland, 1825.

Johnson, Paul. *A Shopkeeper's Millennium: Society and Revivals in Rochester, New York, 1815–1837.* New York: Hill and Wang, 1978.

Johnson, Samuel. *The History of Rasselas, Prince of Abyssinia*. 1759. Reprint. New York: Penguin, 1977.

Kelly, Catherine. *In the New England Fashion: Reshaping Women's Lives in the Nineteenth Century.* Ithaca, NY: Cornell University Press, 1999.

Kerber, Linda. *Women of the Republic: Intellect and Ideology in Revolutionary America*. Chapel Hill: University of North Carolina Press, 1980.

"Ladies School," National Standard (Middlebury, Vermont). February 22, 1820.

Larson, Rebecca. Daughters of Light: Quaker Women Preaching and Prophesying in Colonies and Abroad, 1700–1775. New York: Alfred A. Knopf, 1999.

Leavitt, Judith Walzer. *Brought to Bed: Childbearing in America, 1750–1950*. Oxford, UK: Oxford University Press, 1986.

Levy, Barry. *Quakers and the American Family: British Settlement in the Delaware Valley.* Oxford, UK: Oxford University Press, 1988.

———. *Town Born: The Political Economy of New England from Its Founding to the Revolution*. Philadelphia: University of Pennsylvania Press, 2009.

Main, Gloria L. "An Inquiry into When and Why Women Learned to Write in Colonial New England." *Journal of Social History* 24, no. 3 (spring 1991): 579–89.

Malan, Cesar. *The Watchmaker and His Family*. New York: American Tract Society, 1810.

Mariti, Giovanni. *Travels Through Cyprus, Syria, and Palestine.* Dublin, n.p.: 1792.

Milton, John. *Paradise Lost.* London: T. Spillsbury & Son, 1794.

More, Hannah. *The Shepherd of Salisbury Plain*. Philadelphia: American Sunday School Union, 1825.

"Mrs. Willard's School." *National Standard* (Middlebury, Vermont), August 27, 1817.

Munsill, Harvey. *The Early History of Bristol, Vermont*. Bristol: Bristol Historical Society, 1970.

Murray, John and Judith Sargent. *Records of the Life of the Rev. John Murray*. Boston: Munroe & Francis, 1916.

The Natural and Artificial Productions of the United States. Unknown authors. N.p., n.p., n.d.

Norton, Mary Beth. *Liberty's Daughters: The Revolutionary Experience of American Women.* New York: Cornell University Press, 1996.

Obookiah, Henry. *Memoirs of Henry Obookiah*. Philadelphia: American Sunday School Union, 1830.

Opal, J. M. *Beyond the Farm: National Ambitions in Rural New England*. Philadelphia: University of Pennsylvania Press, 2008.

Orvis, Francis Wayland. *A History of the Orvis Family in America.* Hackensack, NJ: The Orvis Company, 1922.

Orvis, Phebe. Journal, 1821–1859. In the possession of the author.

———. Travel Narrative, 1855. In the possession of the author.

———. Travel Narrative, 1859. In the possession of the author.

Ouellette, Susan M. "Religion and Piety in the Journal of Phebe Orvis," *Vermont History* 77, no. 1 (2009): 6–15.

Owen, John. *The Grace and Duty of Being Spiritually Minded*. London: James Nisbet, 1828.

Parson, Levi. *Memoir of Rev. Levi Parsons, First Missionary to Palestine from the United States*. Hartford: Cooke & Co. and Packard & Butler, 1830.

———. "Rendered More Ignorant Than Others," in *In Our Own Words: New England Diaries, 1600 to the Present,* Vol. I. ed. Peter Benes. Boston: Boston University, 2009.

Perkins, Nathan. *A Narrative of a Tour through the State of Vermont*. Woodstock, VT: Elm Street Press, 1930.

Pichnarick, Lisa. "'On the Threshold of Improvement': Women's Education at the Litchfield Female and Morris Academies." *Connecticut History* 37, no. 2 (1996): 129–158

Potash, R. Jeffrey. *Vermont's Burned Over District*. New York: Carlson Publishing, 1991.

Ramsay, David. *Memoirs of the Life of Martha Laurens Ramsay*. Charleston, SC: Samuel Etheridge, 1812.

Read, Martha. *Monima, A Beggar Girl*. Eaken & Mecu, 1803.

Robinson, Harriet. "Early Factory Labor in New England," in *Fourteenth Annual Report*, Massachusetts Bureau of Statistics of Labor. Boston: Wright and Potter, 1883.

Rothman, Ellen K. *Hands and Heart: A History of Courtship in America*. New York: Basic Books, 1984.

Rotundo, E. Anthony. *American Manhood*. New York: Basic Books, 1993.

Ryan, Mary. *Cradle of the Middle Class: The Family in Oneida County, New York, 1790–1865*. Cambridge, UK: Cambridge University Press, 1981.

Saint Lawrence County Land Records, SLC Courthouse. Canton, New York.

School Commissioners' Report. Saint Lawrence County. Series A0228, Box 2. Parishville. New York State Archives, Albany, New York.

Scott, Freeman. *The Twin Sisters: or, Two Girls of Nineteen*. Philadelphia: MW Trask, 1797.

Seaver, Frederick J. *Historical Sketches of Franklin County and Its Several Towns*. Albany, NY: J. B. Lyon Company, 1915.

Shalhope, Robert. *A Tale of New England: The Diaries of Hiram Harwood, Vermont Farmer, 1810–1837*. Baltimore: Johns Hopkins Press, 2003.

Smallman, Mary. Interviewed by Susan Ouellette. Canton, New York, February 27, 2001.

Smith, H. P. *History of Addison County*. Syracuse, NY: D. Mason & Co., 1886.

Steele, Zadock. The Indian Captive; or, A Narrative of the captivity and sufferings of Zadock Steele. Montpelier, VT: E. P. Walton, 1818.

Swedlund, Alan. *Shadows in the Valley: A Cultural History of Illness, Death, and Loss in New England, 1840–1916*. Amherst: University of Massachusetts Press, 2010.

Swift, Samuel. *History of the Town of Middlebury*. Middlebury, VT: A. H. Copeland, 1859.

Ulrich, Laurel Thatcher. *A Midwife's Tale: The Life of Martha Ballard, Based on Her Diary, 1785–1812*. New York: Knopf, 1990.

———. *Good Wives: Image and Reality in the Lives of Women in Northern New England, 1650–1750*. New York: Vintage Books, 1991.

———. Interview in *A Midwife's Tale*. Blueberry Hill Productions, Laurie Kahn-Leavitt, 2005.

Von Goethe, Johann Wolfgang. *The Sorrows of Young Werter*. Leipzeig, Germany: n.p., 1779.

Welter, Barbara. "The Cult of True Womanhood, 1820–1860," in *Dimity Convictions: The American Woman in the Nineteenth Century*, ed. Barbara Welter, 21–41. Athens: Ohio University Press, 1976.

Willard, Emma. *A Plan for Improving Female Education*. Reprint, Marietta, Georgia: Larlin Corp., 1987.

Index